Strength In Diversity
a reader in physical anthropology

Edited by
Ann Herring and Leslie Chan

Canadian Scholars' Press Inc.   Toronto   1994

Strength in Diversity: A Reader in Physical Anthropology

First published in 1994 by
Canadian Scholars' Press Inc.
180 Bloor Street West, Suite 402
Toronto, Ontario
M5S 2V6

Visit our Web site at **http://www.interlog.com/~cspi/cspi.html**

Canadian Cataloguing in Publication Data

Main entry under title:

Strength in diversity: a reader in physical anthropology

ISBN 1-55130-042-7

1. Physical anthropology. I. Herring, Ann, 1951–
II. Chan, Leslie, 1959–

GN60.S77   1994   573   C94-931729-2

Printed and bound in Canada.

Dedication

To my parents, and Robin, Dora, and
Connor for their care and support.

Leslie K.W. Chan

For Glen, as always.

Ann Herring

Table of Contents

APPLIED PHYSICAL ANTHROPOLOGY

Introduction

Ann Herring and Leslie Chan

The idea for this collection of articles was initially born out of our dissatisfaction with the generic nature of introductory textbooks, which rarely convey the excitement, variety, or contemporary relevance of current research or give students a feel for what it is like to work in a particular field or explore a problem in detail.

Because of this, teachers are often forced to search for high quality supplementary articles to enliven general texts, introduce the latest developments, highlight important research projects, and draw students' attention to current thinking on on-going debates and controversies. With the enthusiastic support of our colleagues, we began to develop this reader as an attempt to begin to fill the gap between general textbooks and detailed case studies for undergraduates enrolled in introductory physical anthropology courses.

Physical anthropology is a particularly diverse subdiscipline of anthropology, encompassing a broad evolutionary and biosocial framework, multiple methodologies, a wide variety of field sites, all covering the panorama of human evolutionary history. How can such diversity be captured? Quite obviously, it can't! and we make no claim to doing so with this reader. What we have tried to do is to reflect some of the gamut of questions, approaches, and passions that consume physical anthropologists in the course of doing research. This volume showcases some of the different ways physical anthropologists investigate the human place in nature and the relationship between culture and biology — be it through theory-building, qualitative observations of non-human primates, statistical analysis of demographic data, chemical analysis of bone, interpretation of fossil evidence, multivariate statistics, archival research, health surveys, anthropometry, or the deconstruction of scientific thought.

We chose to organize this variation along thematic lines, rather than in terms of traditional areal foci, such as demography, primatology, osteology, paleontology, medical anthropology, or human diversity. The questions physical anthropologists ask and the issues they explore cross-cut area boundaries, with the most common underlying concern being to understand the origins and diversity of human bio-social experience. We see this diversity as the fundamental strength of physical anthropology, offering a variety of ways of finding out, learning, and evaluating what we think we know. This is the source of the title of the book, too.

The five sections of this volume offer a variety of approaches used by physical anthropologists to address five themes: (1) theoretical issues (2) sex, mating and reproduction (3) reconstructing past populations (4) health, nutrition and disease in the life cycle, and (5) human diversity and applied physical anthropology.

(1) Theoretical Issues: The authors in this section explore current debates in evolutionary theory and ask questions about the scientific cultures in which physical anthropologists carry out their research. Although physical anthropologists accept human evolution as an established fact and the "Modern Synthesis" as paradigm, there have always been tensions, dissensions, and debates over how the natural world actually works and how best to study it. The articles by Leslie Chan and Shelley Saunders introduce the student to the fundamental tenets of evolutionary theory, but direct their attention to alternative perspectives to its currently accepted formulation within physical anthropology. Saunders focusses on the historical conflict between Darwinian (natural selection) and Lamarckian views (inheritance of acquired characteristics) and examines challenges to the Darwinian model arising out of recent microbiological research on bacteria and viruses. Chan concentrates on efforts within evolutionary biology to redirect evolutionary thinking away from a view of nature dominated by natural selection and adaptation.

Asquith and Burton consider how cultural and intellectual traditions influence the construction and reproduction of knowledge. Asquith discusses cultural differences that underlie the disparate theories and methods of primatologists from Western countries and Japan. Burton traces the search for objective techniques for studying non-human primate social behaviour and makes the case for a return to qualitative methods and holism.

(2) **Sex, Marriage and Reproduction:** One of the characteristic features of the Order Primates, and hominids in particular, is diversity in sexual and reproductive behaviour. Sex, mate selection, and reproduction are also critical components of evolutionary theory. Linda Fedigan and Mary Pavelka consider theories to explain the evolution of menopause, a reproductive phenomenon unique to human females and surprisingly invariant in its cross-cultural expression. Larry Sawchuk and Andrew Irvine examine marriage patterns in the 20th-century urban centre of Gibraltar, illustrating the complexity of the social, economic, political, and historical processes that influence and transform marriage behaviour.

Eric Roth considers marriage and fertility behaviour in a vastly different cultural context than Sawchuk and Irvine, analysing demographic data for Rendille pastoralists in northern Kenya. He addresses a fundamental theoretical debate within physical anthropology that turns on whether population regulation strategies are best explained by the models of cultural ecology (group selection) or evolutionary ecology (individual selection). Mary Jackes shows that information from skeletal remains can be used to reconstruct the fertility behaviour of past populations. She demonstrates how judicious inferences drawn from ethnohistoric accounts and ossuary remains from southern Ontario can offer new pieces in the puzzle of the demise of the Huron in the seventeenth century.

(3) **Reconstructing Past Populations:** Much of the work of physical anthropologists is directed toward developing ideas about how our ancestors lived in the deep and recent past, describing their relationship to their social and biophysical context, and understanding their evolution. This section begins with an article by David Begun in which he addresses the question of how paleontologists attempt to understand through the methods of cladistics the process of transformation in the hominid lineage. He considers several candidates for the position of closest evolutionary relative (sister lineage) to the Great Apes, the African apes and humans, and explores the forces that lead to human origins. Jennifer Thompson is interested in diversity amongst the Australopithecines and shows how a statistical methodology employing the Coefficient of Variation may help to detect the species differences in the Plio-Pleistocene fossil record.

Pamela Willoughby addresses the controversial issue of modern human origins from the perspective of molecular, archaeological, and fossil evidence. She contrasts the "mitochondrial Eve" and "continuity" models and discusses her research on behavioural changes associated with the appearance of modern humans in the Western Rift Valley of Tanzania. Moving closer to the present, Megan Cook's analysis of mummified human remains from the Dakhleh Oasis, Egypt, clearly illustrates the value of a multi-disciplinary project and diverse methodologies for interpreting social and biological change from the 1st to the 5th century A.D. at the town site of Ismant el-Kharab.

(4) **Health, Nutrition and Disease in the Life Cycle:** The growing field of medical anthropology has led physical anthropologists to investigate thoroughly the interaction between culture and human biology, as expressed through population differences in disease and nutrition. The first two articles in this section consider the relationship between diet and health, gender and diet, and changes in health over time. Christine White weighs the relationship between diet and health among the ancient Maya from Lamanai, Belize, probing whether their diet varied according to social status, sex, and age. She provides support for substantial shifts and social differentiation in the Maya diet from the Pre-Classic to the Conquest period, based on evidence from dental pathologies and stable isotope analyses of bone collagen. Bill Leonard and Peter Katzmarzyk draw on their fieldwork among the Evenki reindeer herders of Russia to discuss human nutritional ecology and energetics among living populations. They find that the Evenki's herding lifestyle requires high levels of energy expenditure, which explains their relatively good health and nutritional status compared to other indigenous northern populations of the Americas; Evenki women, however, show greater evidence of obesity than men, signalling potential future health problems.

Nancy Lovell and Ping Lai demonstrate the importance of bringing together historical writings and osteobiographies for reconstructing occupational stresses in past populations. They examine patterns of arthritis and joint modifications from 19th-century Fur Trade Period skeletons from the Seafort Site in Alberta and interpret some to be consistent with the carrying, lifting, and paddling exertions associated with the Hudson's Bay Company's voyageurs. Like Lovell and Lai, Sue Jimenez uses historical sources and indicators of traumatic injuries from 19th-century skeletal remains, but in this case, her study site is an Anglican cemetery in a town in southern Ontario. She finds that traumatic injuries were quite common during this period but show marked gender differences, reflecting the contrasts in their occupational contexts.

Ann Herring examines the impact of a 20th-century virgin soil epidemic, the 1918 influenza pandemic, in several Cree/Métis communities in the central Canadian subarctic. Relying on archival data, mission records, and interviews with elderly individuals, she stresses the importance of exploring the specific socio-ecological conditions of communities to understand why there are substantial differences in mortality from infectious disease epidemics.

(5) Human Diversity and Applied Physical Anthropology: The last section of the volume presents some of the ways in which physical anthropologists act as consultants in policy-making and apply theory and method to contemporary, practical problems. Scott Fairgrieve and Eldon Molto discuss the growing area of forensic anthropology and explain methods for collecting and analysing evidence from crime scenes where human remains have been intentionally cremated.

Hermann Helmuth presents a modest proposal that physical anthropological data on contemporary human variation be applied to the design and engineering of seats and desks in classrooms, such that they actually fit the dimensions of today's students! Patty Stuart-Macadam makes the case that skeletal biologists adopt a more analytical, processural, and problem oriented approach to their research. She argues that signs of anemia in prehistoric populations have relevance for interpreting modern patterns of health and disease and implications not only for the individual, but also for general medical practice, public health issues, and government policy. Joseph So considers the relationship between migration, ethnicity, health, and health care as illustrated by his analysis of the 1990 Ontario Health Survey. From the flaws in the Survey, he advocates that medical anthropologists be full and equal partners in medical teams, involved from the outset in the design of research protocols to assessing the appropriateness of care giving within the cultural context of the culture of the recipient.

While the research presented in this volume has been carried out by physical anthropologists working in Canada, the subjects, methods, and concerns are clearly international in scope. We originally solicited previously published papers to be reworked for the book, but many turned out to be original contributions, written specifically for the collection. To a great extent, this is a reflection of the peer review process each article underwent and a tribute to the willingness of the authors to reconsider their work in light of reviewers' suggestions. We wish to express our deep gratitude to a host of anonymous reviewers in Canada and the United States who took time out of their busy schedules to help the authors and us with the project. Both they and the authors were unusually generous in meeting the ridiculously short deadlines we had to set to ensure that the volume was published within the short span of one year. A vote of thanks goes to the inventors of e-mail and to Edward Glanville, Chair of the Department of Anthropology at McMaster University, for footing the bill for postage and supplies over the course of the project. We wish to thank Damien DeShane for designing the cover.

Finally, this volume would not have been possible without the vision and concern of Jack Wayne at Canadian Scholars' Press Inc. and without the able assistance of Brad Lambertus and Lynda Sydney at CSPI. Brad Lambertus kept us calm in the last phases of production with his sense of humour, ability to solve problems, and willingness to accommodate our sometimes outrageous requests. Of course, any remaining errors are our own.

1

The Enduring Tension
Darwinian and Lamarckian
Models of Inheritance

Shelley R. Saunders

Modern physical anthropology is grounded in two fundamental bodies of knowledge derived from the biological sciences. These are Darwinian contributions to evolutionary theory and Mendelian genetic principles of inheritance. Therefore, students of physical anthropology need to be aware of the conflict that has existed for decades over the proposed mechanisms of evolutionary change. Charles Darwin proposed natural selection as the major mechanism in which heritable variation is produced without purpose but is then selected by environmental stress or change. The theory of the inheritance of acquired characters (mistakenly attributed to Lamarck) says everything that individuals acquire or lose as a result of extended use or disuse is conveyed to subsequent generations. It is a debate between chance and purpose and is therefore, a philosophical debate.

Acquired inheritance can be viewed in two ways, a crossing over of somatically acquired heritable variation to the germ line (Weissman's barrier), in which the heritable variation can be initially randomly produced and selected for within the body of the organism or, directed mutations, in which cells are assumed to "choose" the mutations they will produce. In the 1970s, E.J. Steele proposed a process called somatic selection, which effectively argued for routine crossing of Weissman's barrier. While presumably mechanically possible the ubiquity of this process has not been demonstrated. More recently, bacteriologists have argued for directed mutation in at least, bacterial cells. This paper argues that both

chance and purpose (or direction) are a necessary duality and part of the evolu-
tionary process. The genetic system must be conservative and resistant to change
if it is to maintain constrained development; it is better for genetic information to
allow for somatic flexibility rather than to genetically "fix" all responses to
change. A random component is necessary in evolutaionary change and as such
is part of human adaptation, human culture and the workings of the mind.

INTRODUCTION

Physical anthropology today is the study of human biological development within an evolutionary framework. Physical anthropologists are
interested in the origin of the human species, its similarities to and differences from other species and the causes of biological variation amongst
humans and closely related species. But the development of human culture is equally important as a force that has shaped the species throughout
its evolutionary history. Consequently, physical anthropologists are particularly concerned with the relationships between biology, culture and
ecology or, *biocultural* interactions.

Until the late nineteenth century, and continuing even after into the
twentieth century, physical anthropology dealt with descriptive classifications of racial stereotypes, a rigid typological approach. The development
of modern evolutionary theory completely reversed the basis for research
to the view that all individual organisms and populations are variable,
ensuring the ability of species to adapt to changing environments.

Consequently, students of physical anthropology need to understand
evolutionary theory thoroughly and clearly. While its basic tenets have
become paradigmatic, there has always been a current of discontent, a
tension, over explanations of how things really work in the natural world.
This tension has been more apparent outside of Britain and North
America, partly for historical reasons.

I first became interested in the debate between what have been called
Darwinian and Lamarckian models of evolution while studying human
skeletal variants and their origins. As a physical anthropologist, my task
was to try to determine whether any of these variants or traits had a
genetic basis so that they could be used as genetic markers of population
relationships. If we could find clearly measurable genetic traits on human
skeletons then they could be used to examine biological relationships
from the excavated remains of prehistoric bones. On the other hand, if
traits were produced by physical activity or outside stress placed on the
skeleton then any strong genetic basis would be suspect.

A good example of such a trait is the peroneal tubercle. This is a raised margin of bone found on the lateral surface of the calcaneus or heel bone. Since the tubercle develops between two muscle tendons that supply the foot, it might be thought to be simply a result of intensive muscle activity. But its presence in observed samples does not differ by side or between males and females, nor does the tubercle increase in size with age. It is also found in very young individuals, an observation that questions the role of physical stress in its production.

A number of early twentieth-century researchers argued that traits like the peroneal tubercle were good candidates for the inheritance of acquired characteristics. They would be produced initially by one generation's response to stress but then become entrenched in the hereditary stream of life. This could be called anticipatory evolution, a rejection of the notion that variation is produced without any reference to what is needed, that is so essential to Darwinian natural selection. On the other hand, selectionists argued that traits represent selection for chance variants that just happen to appear in some individuals.

The following discussion describes the historical background to the biological theory of evolution and the initial conflict or tension between Darwinian and Lamarckian approaches that arose to explain its workings. While one side appears to have won out, I examine some recent challenges that have far reaching implications for the overall theory. Finally, I consider the effects of these recent claims on physical anthropologists' attempts to reconstruct human evolution.

DARWIN'S CONTRIBUTIONS

Historians of science have documented the intellectual and philosophical contributions of a number of forerunners to Charles Darwin but it is this man who has been credited with overthrowing many fundamental beliefs about the natural world that were entrenched in nineteenth-century science. In fact, so great has been the twentieth-century attention to his influence on a changing worldview that we refer to his intellectual achievement as the Darwinian Revolution[1]. Mr. Darwin became the hero of modern science because he presented a sufficient mass of factual evidence that evolution, or descent with modification, has occurred, as well as a mechanism, natural selection, for how evolutionary change has taken place. The facts of evolution were summarized in his book, *The Origin of Species by Means of Natural Selection or The Preservation of Favoured Races in the Struggle for Life*. What ideas and information were original to this book

3

that is seen as so important to modern biological science?

The transformation of Darwin's life as a scientist can be traced to the five year voyage he spent aboard the HMS *Beagle* as ship's naturalist. This was a survey ship that was sent out by the British Admiralty to chart the waters around South America. During the voyage, Darwin questioned the concept of the stability of species, created complete and unchanging, and began to favour the view that the world is dynamic or constantly changing. He also rejected the idea that catastrophic earth movements explained the disappearance or extinction of species in favour of a gradualist or uniformitarian model of change. While he did recognize that phenomena such as earthquakes can produce substantial permanent effects on the land surface (he witnessed the consequences of a major earthquake in Chile) he recognized that over long periods of time such events could produce large scale effects such as the building of mountain ranges. This concept of gradualism, while reinforced by Darwin's observations, was essentially adopted from the eminent 19th-century geologist, Charles Lyell, whose uniformitarian theory of geological change said that processes in the past are the same as processes that can be seen going on in the present and therefore that the earth's history has been one of long and gradual change.

The visit of the ship to the Galapagos Islands, towards the end of the voyage, has been seen as crucial in helping to alert Darwin to the concept of geographic speciation. While he had some sense of the great diversity of animals on the islands it was not until after his return to England that he learned that some groups consisted of separate species and others of varieties indicating that species were always forming gradually and were not fixed.

Darwin did not formulate the mechanism of evolution, natural selection, until two years after his return from the voyage. He recorded his developing ideas for natural selection in a series of notebooks over those two years but he is believed to have been greatly influenced by a reading in 1838 of Thomas Malthus' *Essay on the Principle of Population*, which showed that all populations have the tendency to overbreed beyond the availability of the food supply, which results in a constant "struggle for existence". Consequently, Darwin reasoned that organisms who do better in the struggle for existence and who therefore survive to transmit their inherited features to their offspring are those that are best adapted to environmental change.

The next twenty years of Darwin's life were spent investigating geology, taxonomy, botany and other subjects. He examined artificial selection practised by pigeon fanciers and dog breeders claiming that this research helped him to define and refine his ideas on variability and the origins of species. He did not publish *The Origin of Species* (a much larger work had been in progress) until prompted by Alfred Russell Wallace's coincidental discovery of natural selection.

Darwin's theory of evolution has been described as actually a "bundle of theories" (Mayr, 1991). Dissecting out his various contributions following Mayr (1991) allows a clear summary of which of Darwin's ideas were original and which were adopted from or held by other scientific thinkers. It is important to remember though, that it is the combination of these ideas that helps to make Darwin's contribution so unique and important:

(1) *Evolution* The natural world is constantly changing and organisms are transformed over time. This idea was not new, it was promoted by many scholars including Lamarck and the Comte de Buffon in the eighteenth century. But constancy or stasis (the world had not changed since the creation) was still the dominant view in the mid-nineteenth century. It provided a basis for the idea that species arise, change and become extinct.

(2) *Common descent* All organisms are descended from a common ancestry. There is unity in life, not simply because of God's creation, but explainable by natural processes. This idea was one of Darwin's unique gifts to science (Mayr, 1982). Others before him had accepted natural classifications or groupings of organisms without recognizing that they were based on common descent. Darwin also included humans in this scheme (though not overtly in *The Origin*) thereby generating a major uproar amongst religious thinkers and the general populace.

(3) *Diversification of Species* Species multiply by splitting into daughter species or by founding geographically isolated populations that evolve into new species. This horizontal form of evolutionary change is distinct from transformation over time. This idea was also essentially new to Darwin and explains the fantastic amount of organic diversity that he observed.

(4) *Gradualism* Adopted from Lyell and applied to biological organisms, Darwin insisted that evolutionary change was gradual and never sudden. Many other evolutionary

thinkers accepted saltationism, or rapid change, and this concept has been resurrected over recent years (Mayr, 1991).

(5) *Natural Selection*   The mechanism of evolution and recognized by many as Darwin's most important contribution (it forms the focal point for a modern Synthetic Theory of Evolution). The theory of natural selection states that abundant heritable variation must exist. This variation arises without purpose and without reference to the direction of evolution. A few individuals survive owing to well-adapted combinations of characters that they pass on to subsequent generations.

Darwin contributed other important theoretical ideas but those listed above have probably had the greatest impact on the development of a modern theory of biological evolution. He also reversed his position one or more times on some of his ideas so that it sometimes becomes difficult to trace the development of his thought (Ghiselin, 1969; Mayr, 1982; Kohn, 1985).

LAMARCK AND HIS INFLUENCE

Darwin's mechanism of adaptive evolution, natural selection, has traditionally been contrasted with one other adaptive theory, the inheritance of acquired characteristics. This second theory is usually associated with Jean Baptiste de Lamarck, the noted French naturalist and scientific philosopher who lived from 1744 to 1829, even though the idea was not original to him and was just one proposition in an overall set of theories he had developed on natural philosophy. Lamarck, living before Darwin, is sometimes seen as one of Darwin's intellectual precursors, but Darwin denied that Lamarck's ideas ever had much impact on his thinking (Mayr, 1982).

Lamarck developed most of his thoughts on evolution while working at the Natural History Museum in Paris. He contributed a four volume botanical study of the flora of France and spent a great deal of time studying, analysing and writing about the museum's collections of invertebrates. He initially believed in the fixity or immutability of species but later changed his ideas partly because of the influence of his investigation of fossil and recent marine mollusks, which showed slow and gradual change through time. He summarized his thoughts on natural philosophy in his book *Philosophie Zoologique* published in 1809.

There has been some difficulty sorting out Lamarck's theories. They are complex and some contradict each other. In addition, almost immediately after Lamarck's death, interpreters of his work began to disagree over the threads of development of his thought (Mayr, 1982; Jordanova, 1984). We can summarize the most fundamental of his ideas in the following manner.

Lamarck believed in the increasing perfection of organisms as explained by an innate process of increasing complexity of their structure, not because of their adaptedness to the environment. Humans were the end product of this perfection of complexity. He also recognized an almost amazing diversity of organisms that were able to fill all possible space and environments available to them. This principle of plenitude (all possible forms exist and are necessary) was taken from the influence of the 17th-18th-century philosopher, Leibniz.

Lamarck came to a truly evolutionary point of view when he argued that there is a slow or gradual transformation of species into changed forms. He believed in a very great age for the earth and the problem of the extinction of species (which troubled more religiously dogmatic thinkers because God does not allow species to disappear) he explained by the fact that species transform over time into new species. However, he did not come to the concept of the common descent of all living forms. He stated that there was spontaneous generation of lower life forms.

Most important is Lamarck's explanation for the mechanisms of species transformation. First of all, he felt that there was an intrinsic drive to perfection in the living world, initiated by God. Secondly, he felt that organisms could also change by their response to the environment. There would be a change in the environment from which organisms would sense a change in their needs (besoins) to respond to the environment. Consequently, organisms would alter their behaviour to satisfy these needs. This would result in differential use or disuse of certain body parts, which would gradually become altered over time. The idea that an organ could be strengthened by use or weakened by disuse was an old one but Lamarck applied it more rigorously and called it his "First Law". The inheritance of acquired characteristics, again an ancient and widely held idea (Zirkle, 1945) he called his "Second Law". Here he stated that everything that individuals acquire or lose as a result of extended use or disuse is conveyed "by generation to new individuals" (Lamarck, 1914, the English translation of Philosophie Zoologique) descending from their ancestors. He never did state how these things could take place, which would require an explanation of the principles of heredity or how parents pass characteristics to their children, but simply adopted a widely held view in service to his concept of dynamic evolution.

After the publication of Darwin's *Origin of Species* in 1859 many interested observers rediscovered Lamarck's writings but somehow assumed that Lamarckism simply meant the inheritance of acquired characteristics, thus the mistaken but persistent association of this man with an old concept. This new definition of Lamarckism became the counterpoint for those who wished to reject natural selection as the mechanism of evolutionary change. Ironically, Darwin himself was indecisive on the origins of variation and the nature of inheritance. He allowed for a role of the inheritance of acquired characteristics either by use or disuse of organs, the indirect effect of the environment in increasing variability and even the possible direct effect of the environment on changing structures (Bowler, 1989).

Nowadays, natural selection (sometimes called Darwinism but see Mayr (1991) for a discussion of the multiplicity of meanings of that term) and the inheritance of acquired characteristics (usually always called Lamarckism) are contrasted by a series of cartoons portraying the evolution of giraffes. Under natural selection, some ancestral giraffes will carry inherited characteristics that produce slightly longer necks and these giraffes would survive to reproduce in an environment in which having longer necks (stretching to reach leaves, perhaps) contributes to survival. In this case, random variation (variation without purpose) comes first and the environmental impetus later. The inheritance of acquired characteristics would have giraffes stretching their necks to lengthen them during their own lifetime and then passing this "acquired" feature on to subsequent generations. In Lamarck's view this change would take a long time (many generations) but some later Lamarckians would allow direct, single generational changes to produce the effect. In this case, the environmental stimulus comes first and variation responds with what is needed.

AUGUST WEISMANN, THE STRICT SELECTIONIST

The rejection of acquired inheritance was championed by August Weismann, a noted embryologist who argued that only the germ cells contained heritable material. The work of Weismann became the link between Darwin and the later discovery of the basic tenets of genetics, Gregor Mendel's laws of inheritance. In a series of publications between 1882 and 1910, Weismann came to the conclusion that under a theory of natural selection characters must be transmitted from parent to offspring without being affected by changes in the parent's bodies. This was termed "hard inheritance" in contrast to "soft inheritance" or the possibility of single generation effects by the inheritance of acquired characters (Mayr, 1980). Weismann's idea was termed the The Doctrine of the Continuity of the Germ Plasm. It was based on Weismann's and others' observations that the future germ cells in various types of invertebrates are set aside after the first division of the developing embryo and lose their physiological connection with the body cells (Churchill, 1985). While the germ cells contained heritable material, the somatic or body cells performed only a supportive role because of their irreversible conversion into differentiated body structures.

Under modern evolutionary theory, Weismann turned out to be right, but for the wrong reasons. As Ernst Mayr puts it (1980), a separation of the germ plasm from its expression in the phenotype (physical structure of the organism) was correct; but we now know that the crucial separation is between the DNA program of the nucleus of a cell and the proteins in the cytoplasm of the cells whose construction the DNA directs. It has been shown experimentally that all somatic cells are totipotent, carrying all the genetic information required to produce the organism, but acquired modifications cannot be inherited because the path from DNA to proteins is seen as a one-way street. Changes in the DNA may produce new proteins but changes in the proteins cannot impress themselves upon the DNA. This is called the Central Dogma of molecular genetics (see Figure 1).

Nevertheless, since it is true that many organisms sequester their germ cells early in development, Weismann's barrier represents one way in which acquired inheritance can be refuted. But if Weismann's barrier does not exist then perhaps some variants occurring in the body cells of the individuals get into the eggs or sperm. Very recently, Leo Buss, in a book titled *The Evolution of Individuality* (Buss, 1987) has shown that there is a way that acquired inheritance might occur depending on what structural units of the body can become heritable.

In all of the animals that possess notochords and many insects and other evolutionarily primitive animals, the primordial germ cells are sequestered very early in development. For example, in the fruitfly there are 13 cellular divisions of the fertilized egg before the germ \cells are differentiated from the rest of the soma. Up to this point, development is directed by maternal instructions provided by the mother's oval cytoplasm. In contrast, an animal like the hydra, which is a freshwater polyp, has asexual or budding cells called *I cells* that remain multipotent and mitotically active throughout the lifespan of the animal. Therefore, variants that might arise in these multipotent cells could become potentially heritable to the next generation of offspring.

In animals like arthropods or the chordates it is appropriate to view the individual as the unique, genetically homogeneous unit but not so for organisms such as the protists, the fungi or the plants and also for a number of what may be considered primitive animal phyla. Therefore, according to Buss, until molecular genetics demonstrated that DNA replication is independent of the environment, there was no theoretical reason for denying the inheritance of acquired characteristics, at least for certain species, because Weissman's barrier does not exist strictly for them. Buss argues that the plants, colonial invertebrates and fungi may all violate Weismann's doctrine because they display enormous physical plasticity and considerable variation (however, normal mechanisms of genetics produce considerable variability). Is it possible, though, that there are examples amongst these phyla of bodily variants produced in response to environmental changes that then become passed on to subsequent generations because these body cells form part of the substance of the offspring?

Buss, himself, does not necessarily accept acquired inheritance; he wants to change the way in which we think about how selection acts. In fact, he says that no one can seriously expect that the essential elements of the Darwinian notion of evolution will be fundamentally altered. Buss favours an hierarchical view to organismal variation that allows for selection at a multitude of levels. He argues that the history of life is a history of transitions between different units of selection, units such as self-replicating molecules, organelles, cells, individuals and species. Another way of expressing his view is to say that even if the barrier between the soma and the germ cells, Weismann's barrier, is breached, the production of heritable variation would still be random, that is, the transfer of information is not from the environmental agent to the germ cells to tell them to make a change. Rather, somatic cells or cells that might contribute to the formation of offspring (such as budding or grafting in plants) might have randomly produced variants in their nuclei that later prove adaptive.

Thus, there are two ways of thinking about the material possibility of acquired inheritance. One is to say that Weismann's barrier could be breached, thus transferring randomly produced but heritable variants formed in the somatic cells to the germ cells so that they can be expressed in offspring of the next generation. Nevertheless, this way does not really fit the spirit of Lamarckism because the production of variants is still without purpose or non-anticipatory. However, the second way to view a mechanism of acquired inheritance is the occurrence of nonrandom or directed mutations. Under this view, the appropriate variants occur in response to the pressures or "needs" placed upon the organism. The organism thus determines its own fate and in turn directs the evolution of the species. In organisms that sequester their germ cells, directed mutations occurring in body cells would presumably have to be inserted somehow into the eggs or sperm or the directed mutations would have to occur in the germ cells themselves.

In the early days of this century and still today, some observers reject a Darwinian model of evolution because of the chance or accidental aspect of the production of heritable variation and the mechanistic cast that this model seems to have. A number of earlier and recent authors, including literary figures, have taken this approach (Butler, 1879; Shaw, 1921; Koestler, 1971). There was also strong ideological resistance to natural selection. Marxist philosophy considers natural selection to be a reflection of capitalism or the free-enterprise system and counter to all notions of human equality. Lamarckian acquired inheritance attained the level of official political policy in the Soviet Union under the leadership of T.D.Lysenko. This scientific, ideological and political movement lasted from the 1930s to the 1960s. Lysenko claimed that a process of treating wheat to germinate earlier in the spring (something of great value to the Soviet Union with its short growing seasons) could be inherited by future generations of wheat. Mendelian genetics was denounced as "bourgeois" and many scientists who subscribed to its principles were sent into exile. Described by various authors as an ugly, bizarre, nightmarish or scary event in scientific history (Lewontin and Levins, 1976; Mayr, 1982; Dawkins, 1982; Bowler, 1989) Lysenkoism had a great impact on Western science, not the least of which was to prevent most researchers from even exploring the concept of acquired inheritance.

THE SOMATIC SELECTION HYPOTHESIS

A resurgence of interest in the inheritance of acquired characteristics appeared at the end of the 1970s when an Australian immunologist by the name of Ted Steele proposed a modernized version of what was described as a Lamarckian model of evolution. Most importantly, Steele contended that his hypothesis was experimentally testable. In the earlier part of the century many authors had argued that acquired inheritance could be demonstrated based on the close fit between environmental requirements and the strange and marvellous features that could be found on organisms. But none of these claims could be substantiated since it was necessary to prove that the heritable variants were passed immediately from parents to offspring and were nonrandomly produced, a result of organisms' desires or directed needs.

Steele's theory is based on certain properties of the antibody producing immune system. He begins with the fact that, at a few days notice, the individual's immune system is able to produce antibodies that will recognize almost any foreign organism or molecule (antigen) that might infect or be injected into an animal. The mechanism of such antibody production has been debated for a long time. As Medawar (1980) has put it, how can a rabbit not yet born react specifically to a chemical not yet synthesized? The potential diversity of antibodies is really quite staggering; antibodies can recognize an apparently limitless array of foreign antigens, and in turn each antigen can stimulate the production of hundreds of different antibodies.

Most scientists used to explain antibody diversity by invoking the germ line theory, which assumed a huge library of genes coding for all possible antibodies. The library, they thought, would be passed from one generation to the next in the genomes of eggs and sperm. But others, such as Steele, subscribe instead to the somatic mutation and clonal selection theory (Burnet, 1959), the notion that mutational events occurring in the somatic cells of the immune system during an organism's growth produce much of the diversity. The antigens entering an animal during its lifetime would select those somatic mutations that code for the antibodies giving the "best fit" to those particular antigens. This is a type of intraorganismic Darwinian natural selection that does not involve the germ cells. The presence of the antigen would then trigger an expansion of the number of cells (clonal selection) producing the selected antibody; these cells would proliferate and produce numerous antibody-secreting progeny to destroy the offending antigens.

The Lamarckian aspect of Steele's hypothesis comes next. He proposed that cells with somatic gene mutations such as immune cells (although he would like to generalize the process to other kinds of cells in the body) would be picked up by viruses composed of RNA and known to normally live within the body. These RNA viruses, carrying the mutated gene or genes, would then cross the tissue barrier partitioning the gametes in the gonads and infect the ova or the sperm (either in the chromosomes or travelling via extra-chromosomal elements) and synthesize a copy of germline DNA via a method called reverse transcription.

RNA viruses carry a gene coding for the enzyme, reverse transcriptase that catalyses the synthesis of a DNA copy from an RNA template. The discovery of reverse transcriptase (Temin, 1971) partially eroded the Central Dogma of genetics by showing that messenger RNA can be transcribed back into DNA (Figure 1). However, this does not mean that proteins can be reversely translated into RNA (Steele was not claiming this), although such a possibility has been discussed (Cook, 1977).

Figure 1.

Thus, in the first part of his hypothesis, Steele is still relying on randomly produced variation via the Darwinian mechanism of natural selection. The second part of his hypothesis breaks Weismann's barrier by proposing that random somatic mutations can become incorporated into the germ cells via the viral vector. This process could be adaptive, for example, as an antibody response to a new disease. The next generation of animals would benefit directly from the experience of their parents without having to experience the relevant antigens themselves (or relevant environmental stress).

Experimental support for the hypothesis was claimed when immunological tolerance to three different antigens was induced in male mice and transmitted to the first and second generation offspring. The reason for using male mice was to avoid the possibility that the transfer of information could be through the maternal cytoplasm of an ovum rather than the reverse transcription of information into the DNA. Separate attempts to repeat the experiments yielded both positive and negative results. One major defect of all of the experiments is that they were conducted at the phenotypic (bodily) level; none of them directly tested for the mechanism of the hypothesis, the viral vector that supposedly picks up mutated somatic genes and inserts them into germ cells.

The most cogent logical argument that can be mustered against acquired inheritance is its inconsistency. If populations are continually adapting to an ever-changing environment in a purposeful way, but the adaptive changes are also being continually fixed into a heritable program, then there is a basic conflict between heritable constraint and responsiveness or adaptiveness. Critics of Steele recognized this problem, pointing out that acquired inheritance creates genetic chaos and the disruption of genetic consistency if all somatic mutations are incorporated into the germline. Of course, Steele saw this too, and admitted that some sort of "sorting" process must be at work. In fact, his hypothesis as framed is not truly acquired inheritance because it does not argue for directed mutation. It introduces selection both at the beginning of the hypothesis, in the form of clonal selection of somatic mutations, and at the end, when Steele says that Darwinian selection will act on the altered progeny of the first generation. The only Lamarckian aspect of the hypothesis is the soma/germ transfer that allows for a single generation change. As Dawkins (1982) points out, the question is whether the antibody formation was instructive or anticipatory. Is it the environment, in the form of the introduced protein molecules, that directly moulds the antibody molecules in the parent organisms? In fact it is not, because clonal selection of somatic mutations is a random selection process of random mutations.

RECENT POSSIBLE EVIDENCE FOR DIRECTED MUTATION

A few years ago two well-respected biologists suggested that organisms can respond to environmental stress by reorganizing their genomes in a purposeful way (Cairns, et al., 1988; Hall, 1988). Their experiments with bacteria arose out of earlier studies on the existence of random mutation conducted in the 1940s and 50s. In the first of these earlier experiments, Luria and Delbruck (1943) sought to determine whether fluctuations in mutant strains of the bacteria, *Escherichia coli*, to resist bacteriophage T1, a virus that attacks and kills bacteria, were produced as a direct and specific response to the presence of the bacteriophage or were spontaneously produced.

In their test (Luria and Delbruck, 1943), a population of bacteria was divided and each subpopulation was analysed after growth in the presence of the virus. The number of colonies of resistant cells sampled for each subpopulation was expected be more or less the same if the environmental

14

agent *induced* mutations to resistance, because the probability of mutation would be the same in each subpopulation of cells. On the other hand, the number of colonies of resistant cells would fluctuate between none and hundreds per sampled subpopulation, depending upon the number of pre-existing mutants that happened (randomly) to be present before the bacteria in each subpopulation were subjected to the virus. Luria and Delbruck found evidence of fluctuations in the numbers of surviving resistant mutants in various subpopulations of bacteria cultured from a parent population, supporting the hypothesis of random mutation.

Since in the first experiment mutants were not isolated without first exposing the cells to selection, Lederberg and Lederberg (1952) later developed a method of testing bacterial cells' siblings instead of the cells themselves in the presence of virus. They were able to detect the presence of rare pre-existing virus-resistant mutants in a virus-free environment. This constituted final proof that at least some mutant forms of bacteria are occurring spontaneously.

However, Cairns and Hall argued that these earlier experiments had demonstrated the existence of random mutations but did not disprove the existence of nonrandom mutations. The earlier researchers may have overlooked mutations that occur specifically when they are advantageous. Cairns and colleagues looked for mutations occurring under conditions of *nonlethal* selection where the cells might have the opportunity to construct "product-oriented" (1988:142) mutations. They grew certain *Escherichia coli* cells that are deficient in their ability to utilize the sugar lactose (Lac-cells) in the presence of lactose. The results fit both models, that is, some mutations (Lac+) appeared to be occurring randomly prior to selection while others occurred only after selection. They also found that, with the incubation of Lac-cells in the presence of lactose, Lac+ mutants accumulated over time while cells grown in the absence of lactose did not accumulate Lac+ mutants. In his work, Hall (1988) showed that certain double mutants were observed only under selective conditions. A number of similar experiments followed suit with further positive results while some other researchers have reported similar phenomena in yeast (Steele and Jinks-Robertson, 1992).

The Lamarckian interpretation of these results is that the cells can somehow monitor or anticipate the consequences of potential genetic changes for their fitness and then choose to specifically change to what would be most advantageous. These experiments did not test for the explicit mechanism of how such mutations might occur. Cairns and his colleagues suggested that there is some "reversible process of trial and error" (Cairns et al., 1988) in the bacteria that allows for the transfer of information back from protein to DNA. It might be that the cells produce a highly variable set of messenger RNA molecules and then reverse transcribe the ones that make the *best* protein. For this, the cells would need something that "somehow monitors the products of the proteins and determines whether mRNA should go on being translated or should be transcribed into DNA" (1988:145). Reverse transcription has been found in *Escherischia coli* though not in the types of cells used in the experiments cited above. In fact, while the present evidence seems to support the existence of a phenomenon of directed mutation in (at least) bacteria there is no clear explanation of the mechanism of how this takes place.

Critics of the experiments argue that under conditions selective for the appearance of mutants there is enough "normal" non-selective growth to account for the appearance of the apparently selection-induced mutants (Lenski and Mittler, 1993). Respondents point out that there are certain types of mutations that occur under selection that seem to be distinct from those that occur during non-selective growth (Thaler, 1994). For the present, work is being carried out by Cairns and others to try to test for the mechanism that would explain the results that they are getting in their experiments.

CONCLUSIONS

Is the search for the evidence of directed mutation in bacteria really relevant to physical anthropology and the study of complex multicellular organisms like humans? Presumably, if directed mutation occurs in bacteria, it can occur in all kinds of cells including cells that construct multicellular organisms. But then, we would be back to the issue of Weismann's barrier, that is, the need for the directed mutations to somehow cross over from the soma to the germ cells to contribute to the next generation. We would also be back to the issue of genetic chaos; there is some reason why genetic material is somewhat protected from continued alteration (and why there are mechanisms of DNA repair).

While recent research in molecular and microbiology has demonstrated that it is at least possible that the barrier can be breached by viruses bearing reverse transcriptase or by some other means, there must be a reason why germ cells lines are sequestered in the first place. The reason is most probably the need for conservatism. There must be continuity of form from one generation to the next. Organisms must follow some basic

16

structural and developmental patterns in order for their bodies to function during life in a coordinated fashion. Regularities in the development of the individual are equally as important as is the provision of heritable variability to respond to changing conditions.

How do multicellular organisms respond to changing conditions during their lifetimes? Physiologically, they do so by having a range of response to changing conditions and this range of response also varies from species to species. Certain fish can only live within a narrow temperature range but mammals can exist and adjust to a much broader band of temperature and climatic change by regulating their internal body temperatures. Humans moving from sea level to high altitudes experience immediate bodily changes such as panting and rapid heart rates. But over time, the body acclimates by adjusting respiration, expanding the rib cage, increasing haemoglobin levels and so on. Populations living in mountainous areas may pass on some of these characteristics to their offspring but the shift from somatic flexibility to genetic stability only occurs when environmental stresses are constant over long periods of time. Somatic flexibility is adaptive to humans because it allows them to respond to a variety of physical situations (Bateson, 1979).

But there is also behavioural flexibility that allows biological organisms to adjust tremendously to changing conditions, even choosing their environments and anticipating change. I would suggest that behavioural flexibility and complexity in multicellular organisms have evolved hand-in-hand with the need for developmental stability and conservatism. Anthropologists, of course, emphasize the complex development of human culture as an ultimate means of behavioural adjustment that has allowed humans to become quite dominant on this planet. Many of us view human culture and the human mind as very special, unique examples of behavioural flexibility, whose evolution is presumably difficult to explain. Human culture and the workings of the human mind are Lamarckian in character in that they produce novel responses to change that are adopted and incorporated by subsequent generations.

In genetic systems, responsiveness and change are necessary, but the rate of change is limited by the Weismannian barrier between somatic and genetic change and conservatism of the developing embryo. Full and complete inheritance of acquired characteristics does not make sense because without selection, this kind of inheritance would irreversibly eat up somatic flexibility (Bateson, 1979). Natural selection makes sense but, in deference to its critics, has de-emphasized the interactive role between the organism and its environment. "Chance" and "purpose" in evolution are like many other reciprocal concepts in the world, they are a necessary duality. This is no doubt true also for human culture and mind.

The goal of this discussion has been to show, first of all, that the debate between "Darwinian" and "Lamarckian" approaches to evolution has a convoluted history and that words such as these have been used in many different ways, thereby confusing meaning. The basis of the debate is between the concept of natural selection and the concept of the inheritance of acquired characteristics. Natural selection presupposes heritable variation that is undirected, purposeless, random or produced by chance. The external environment does the selecting and consequently, over time, the inherited *form* of the population changes. Inheritance of acquired characteristics presupposes purpose. The biological systems of organisms anticipate change, the selecting is carried out internally, which then produces change in the heritable variation.

A cultural or behavioural system can be viewed in a similar way. Although its mechanism of change is Lamarckian or anticipatory, an element of randomness and some degree of conservatism must also be present. These are broad concepts for physical anthropologists to learn and apply to their research.

ENDNOTE

1   Darwin's contribution of evolutionary ideas, especially the theory of natural selection is matched by the second most momentous event in biological science, Mendel's discovery of the principles of genetics. Darwin did not understand how parents pass hereditary information on to their offspring, believing in a continuous mixing of information from each parent rather than the contribution of individual and autonomous particles of hereditary information (genes) as Mendel showed. While the concept of the individual organism and its separation from the genes it will pass on becomes important later on in this chapter the basic conflict of evolutionary theory is expressed as a conflict between Darwin's and Lamarck's models of evolutionary change. Lamarck's explanation of evolution addresses generational change explicitly, hence the term "acquired inheritance" but it is a model of evolutionary change.

REFERENCES

Bateson G (1979) *Mind and Nature A Necessary Unity*. New York: EP Dutton.

Bowler PJ (1989) *Evolution The History of an Idea*. Berkeley: University of California Press.

Burnet FM (1959) *The Clonal Selection Theory of Acquired Immunity*. London and New York: Cambridge University Press.

Buss LW (1987) *The Evolution of Individuality*. Princeton, New Jersey: Princeton University Press.

Butler S (1879) *Evolution Old and New*. London,England: Harwicke.

Cairns J, Overbaugh J and Miller S (1988) *The origin of mutants*. Nature 335:142-145.

Churchill FB (1985) Weismann's continuity of the germ plasm in historical perspective. *Freiburger Universitats-blatter* 87/88:107-124.

Cook ND (1977) The case for reverse translation. *Journal of Theoretical Biology* 64:113-135.

Dawkins R (1982) *The Extended Phenotype: The Gene as the Unit of Selection*. Oxford, England:Oxford University Press.

Ghiselin MT (1969) *The Triumph of the Darwinian Method*. Berkeley: University of California Press.

Hall BG (1988) Adaptive evolution that requires multiple spontaneous mutations. I. Mutations involving an insertion sequence. *Genetics* 120: 887-897.

Jordanova LJ (1984) *Lamarck*. Oxford, England: Oxford University Press.

Koestler A (1971) *The Case of the Midwife Toad*. London, England:Pan Books Ltd.

Kohn D ed (1985) *The Darwinian Heritage*. Princeton: Princeton University Press.

Lamarck JBPAM (1914) *Zoological Philosophy* Translated by Hugh Elliot. London: reprinted New York, Hafner,1963.

Lederberg J and Lederberg EM (1952) Replica plating and indirect selection of bacterial mutants. *Journal of Bacteriology* 63:399-406.

Lenski RE and Mittler JE (1993) The directed mutation controversy and neo-Darwinism. *Science* 259:188-193.

Lewontin R and Levins R (1976) The problem of Lysenkoism. In: Rose H and S Rose (eds.) *The Radicalization of Science: Ideology of/in the Natural Sciences*. London: Macmillan pp. 32-64.

Luria SE and Delbruck M (1943) Mutations of bacteria from virus sensitivity to virus resistance. *Genetics* 28:491-511.

Mayr E (1980) Prologue: Some thoughts on the history of the evolutionary synthesis. In E Mayr and WB Provine (eds.) *The Evolutionary Synthesis: Perspectives on the Unification of Biology*. Cambridge, Mass.: Harvard University Press.

Mayr E (1982) *The Growth of Biological Thought*. Cambridge, Mass.: The Belknap Press of Harvard University Press.

Mayr E (1991) *One Long Argument Charles Darwin and the Genesis of Modern Evolutionary Thought*. London,England: Allen Lane The Penguin Press.

Medawar PB (1980) Lamarckian approach to immunology. *Trends in Biochemical Science* 5: XV.

Shaw GB (1921) *Back to Methuselah: A Metabiological Pentateuch*. London, England: Constable.

Steele EJ (1981) *Somatic Selection and Adaptive Evolution on the Inheritance of Acquired Characters*. Chicago: The University of Chicago Press. Second Edition.

Steele DF and Jinks-Robertson S (1992) An examination of adaptive reversion in Saccharomyses cerevisiae. *Genetics* 132:9-21.

Temin HM (1971) The protovirus hypothesis: speculations on the significance of RNA-directed DNA synthesis for normal development and for carcinogenesis. *Journal of the National Cancer Institute* 46:3-7.

Thaler DS (1994) The evolution of genetic intelligence. *Science* 264: 224-225.

Zirkle C (1945) The early history of the idea of the inheritance of acquired characters and pangenesis. Trans. *Amer. Phil. Soc. N.S.* 35:91-151.

2

Changing Conceptions of Evolutionary Theory

Leslie K.W. Chan

Evolutionary theory has been undergoing a healthy period of ferment for the last two decades. In particular, the view, central to the synthetic theory of evolution, that natural selection acting on small mutations constitutes much of evolutionary change has been severely challenged. New metaphors and mechanisms of evolutionary processes are being developed and debated. These advances, however, have had little impact on the practice of biological anthropology. In part, this is because alternative views are being formulated by specialists outside anthropology while studying other organisms. However, the primary reason why new ideas are slow to filter into the study of human evolution is that the notion of adaptation through natural selection is so ingrained that its status as the only explanatory framework is rarely questioned. This chapter outlines selected areas of recent conceptual development, including a multi-leveled view of causality, developmental constraint, phylogenetic systematics, and the role of behaviour in evolution. The significance of these ideas for interpretation of human evolution and diversity are discussed.

INTRODUCTION

Among scientists today, the idea that humans evolved from an ape-like ancestor several million years ago is no longer controversial. However, just why and how humans evolve, and why there is so much behavioural and biological diversity within the human species, are still largely matters of debate. In other words, while we accept human evolution as an established fact, its mechanisms and causes in both the recent and deep past are far from clear. The lack of consensus amongst anthropologists regarding the mechanisms of evolutionary change reflects the broader intellectual framework within which theories of human evolution are situated. Uncertainty about the mechanisms of evolutionary change is not unique to anthropology, but is indicative of the state of the entire field of evolutionary biology.

Despite the uncertainty regarding the mechanisms or physical causes of evolutionary change, biological anthropologists are united by a commitment to the belief that the diversity, as well as the unity of humankind, is the result of the evolutionary process. The geneticist Dobzhansky's (1973) aphorism: "nothing in biology makes sense except in the light of evolution" has served as a motto for anthropologists since the formalization in the 1940s of the Neo-Darwinian synthetic theory of evolution, commonly known as the "Modern Synthesis". Indeed, it is from this view of evolution, with its emphasis on natural selection acting on random mutations as the primary mechanism of change, that most recent anthropological ideas concerning human diversity and evolution arose. The "New Physical Anthropology" advocated by Sherwood Washburn in the late 1950s and early 60s was certainly a direct effort to forge an intellectual link between the Modern Synthesis and the practice of biological anthropology. Not surprisingly, therefore, the anthropological literature on human biology is dominated by selectionist explanations of everything from variations in blood groups, protein and enzyme diversity, and disease patterns, to the enlargement of the human brain, the emergence of bipedalism, differences in skin colour and even the shapes of nose and eyes.

For many years the synthetic view of evolution was virtually unchallenged in North America, but recently it has been questioned by biologists from various disciplines. Evolutionary biology is now besieged by exciting efforts to redirect thinking about the processes of evolution. Curiously, these recent developments have had little impact on biological anthropology and on the conceptualization of human evolution and diversity. This lack of recognition has prompted Colin Groves (1989:vii) to write in the preface to his recent book:

> The ferment that has been going on in evolutionary theory for some fifteen years has largely bypassed the anthropological community. Textbooks on human evolution still present

Natural Selection, acting on Mutation, as The Way in which evolution works; anagenesis, the story of human evolution. [sic] Punctuated Equilibria may get a paragraph; but neutral evolution, macromutaions, speciation theory, internal processes, and so on, seem generally not to rate even a mention in most works on human evolution. There are, of course, honourable exceptions, but they are few, often timid, always restricted in scope.

A reading of the recent texts on human evolution and biological anthropology (e.g., Harrison et al., 1988; Klein, 1989; Poirier et al., 1990; Relethford, 1990; Campbell, 1992) certainly attests to Groves' observation. The primary intent of this paper is to convey the growing realization that evolutionary theory is not solely concerned with the search for optimal or best possible mechanisms of adaptation to the physical environment, but is a research program that contains a plurality of views, beliefs and concepts about organic diversity and uniformity. I will highlight what I perceive to be significant developments in evolutionary biology within the last two decades, and consider their possible impact on the present view of human evolution. This paper is not meant to be an exhaustive review of the literature of evolutionary theory; rather, it is a sampling of the literature that reflects the breadth of the research currently being done on the topic, along with discussion of a number of seminal works that describe the essential concepts that are being developed.

I begin by giving an outline of the central tenets of the synthetic theory of evolution, followed by a discussion of the major sources of the present discontent with this orthodox view. I then introduce several ideas that are emerging out of the recent challenge to Neo-Darwinism in the context of a number of recurring and interrelated themes. These themes have the common thrust of questioning the all-pervasiveness of natural selection and adaptation, and replacing them with a plurality of concepts and reasons for how biological structure and behaviour evolve. The themes, briefly outlined and then discussed in greater detail in subsequent sections, are that:

(1)   Causality in evolution operates at a number of distinct though interrelated hierarchical levels such that explanation at one level cannot be reduced to that of a lower level. This view has implications for understanding the relationships between evolution within populations and evolution between species.

(2) Organism and environment are not dichotomous or

opposing elements, but they interact in complex ways so that the distinctions between them are often blurred. Organisms do not simply respond to environmental pressure, but their behaviour plays an active role in deciding their own evolutionary fate.

(3) Developmental processes are crucial links between genotype (the set of genes inherited by an individual) and phenotype (all aspects of the individual's morphology, physiology, behaviour, and ecological relationships). Understanding how phenotypic variations are generated and expressed is a prerequisite to the understanding of evolution.

(4) Biological characteristics of species today are products of interaction between current and historical processes. Evolutionary interpretation of genetic, physiological, morphological, and behavioural patterns must be made in terms of the evolutionary history, or phylogeny, of the species in question.

An underlying concern here is that evolutionary theory is highly dependent on metaphors to make sense of the world. While metaphor often brings novel insights because it allows "understanding and experiencing of one kind of thing in terms of another" (Lakoff and Johnson, 1980:5), it can also lead to a reduced and distorted view of reality when the metaphor is mistaken for the actual phenomenon itself. Just as it is common to think of organism as "machine" and genetic instruction as "program", so too there is a tendency to view "nature red in tooth and claw" as an objective representation of the organic world. "Survival of the fittest", "struggle for existence", "maximization", "cost and benefits" are examples of central concepts of orthodox evolutionary theory but their original status as metaphors is often forgotten. Periodic re-examination of the conceptual tools with which we interpret the world is therefore important.

DARWINISM, NEO-DARWINISM AND ULTRA-DARWINISM

Darwin (1859) stated clearly in *The Origin of Species* that he had two goals: (1) establishing the fact of evolution — namely that organisms have descended with modifications from common ancestors, and (2) that natural selection is the mechanism by which evolutionary changes can be explained.

In proposing natural selection, Darwin departed from his forerunners and provided a thoroughly mechanistic causal explanation for the origin and maintenance of living things. Darwin rejected the long-held western mode of "typological" thinking, which views species as permanent and unchanging, and individual variations as inconsequential, and introduced, instead, the variational view that differences between individuals are the raw material for future change. Darwin arrived at this view by drawing on the analogus process of "artifical" selection, whereby plant or animal breeders can create desired new "varieties" from existing organisms. Darwin reasoned that small differences between individuals, accumulated over a long period of time, eventually result in the formation of distinct species. What remained to be explained was how natural selection could take place without human or divine intervention. Darwin found an answer in the political philosophy of Thomas Malthus and his model replaced the role of the breeder with the "struggle for survival." Of this famous phrase, Darwin (1859) wrote:

> I use this term in a large and *metaphorical* sense including dependence of one being on another, and including (which is more important) not only the life of the individual, but success in leaving progeny....
> A struggle for existence inevitably follows from the high rate at which all organic beings tend to increase. Hence as more individuals are produced than can possibly survive, there must in every case be a struggle for existence, either one individual with another of the same species or with the individuals of distinct species, or with the physical conditions. It is the doctrine of Malthus applied with manifold force to the whole animal and vegetable kingdoms; for in this case there can be no artifical increase of food, and no prudential restraint from marriage. (italics mine)

According to Gould (1989:66-67), the restriction of selection to "struggle" among individual organisms was central to Darwin's new paradigm of nature. As such, all phenomena traditionally ascribed to God's creative power could arise as incidental consequences of nature's only causal process — the struggle among organisms for personal reproductive success. Evolution can only take place when the variations needed to permit change at a given place and time happen to be available. Variation is, therefore, apparently due to chance because it occurs without reference to the needs of the organism in its particular environment. However, selection, the necessitating component of evolution, indirectly shapes lineages of organisms through differential reproduction in more adaptive and survival-inclined directions (Monod, 1970). Hence, features of organisms and their behaviour that appear purposeful need not have been purposefully designed by a Creator. Natural selection could appear as a director of evolution by the combined action of the two stage process of chance variations and selection.

While the operation of natural selection is predicated on the existence of heritable variations amongst organisms, Darwin was unable to explain how such variations arose in the first place, beyond suggesting "a tendency to vary, due to causes of which we are quite ignorant" (Darwin, 1872:146). Without a firm foundation for the material basis of inheritance and variations, natural selection fell into disfavour soon after its introduction (Bowler, 1983). The confirmation that natural selection is, indeed, viable had to await the rediscovery of Mendel's experiment at the turn of the century on the segregation of discrete factors, now call genes, as the basis for the inheritance of differences between individuals.

With the advent of the science of genetics, the origin of variations became identified with the process of mutation and recombination. However, natural selection was not initially or universally accepted by Mendelians such as De Vries (1906), William Bateson (1922), and Goldschmidt (1940) who maintained that the inheritance of large genetic differences between organisms, known as "macromutation", was responsible for the discontinuities between species. Evolution, in their view, takes place rapidly rather than through the gradual accumulation of small differences, the latter being a fundamental presupposition of Darwin himself. In the 1920s and 30s, a group of mathematically oriented biologists, also known as biometricians, began to develop statistical models for predicting the distribution of genetic characters from the parental to the offspring generation. The works of Wright (1931), Fisher (1930), and Haldane (1932), in particular, fostered a view of evolution in terms of the steady shift of an entire population rather than of the production of new forms from macromutations. Accordingly, mutations are regarded as playing "little or no creative role in evolution but that natural selection shapes adaptations out of an infinite supply of very small mutations." (Orr and Coyne, 1992:727). To paraphrase the geneticist Monod, mutation provides the noise, from which natural selection draws out the music!

At the same time that mathematical models of genetic composition of populations were being developed came observational findings by Chetverikoff in the Soviet Union, and others elsewhere, indicating considerable genetic variation in natural populations upon which selection could act (Grene, 1981). All these studies helped establish the concept that it is the population that possesses the variability necessary for evolutionary genetic change through space and time, whereas an individual only acts as the raw material of evolution: populations evolve, not individuals.

The shift from a typological approach to what Ernst Mayr called "population thinking" gave rise to the trend, best exemplified by Dobzhansky's (1937:11) statement in *Genetics and the Origin of Species* that "since evolution is a change in the genetic composition of populations, the mechanisms of evolution constitute problems of population genetics." This emphasis on the genetics of populations helped transform evolutionary thinking into its modern form.

In addition to the rise of population genetics, a number of lines of evidence converged during the 1940s from paleontology, biogeography, and systematics that once again affirmed the status of natural selection as the principal mechanism of evolutionary change. This convergence of lines of evidence was called the "Modern Synthesis", and is usually associated with the work of people like Mayr, Dobzhansky, Simpson, Stebbins, and many others (for an in-depth history and references see Mayr, 1982). The Modern Synthesis is often referred to as Neo-Darwinism, an appropriate name since this is essentially Darwin's own vision of evolution. As Provine (1982:505) points out, "the new Darwinism appeared to differ from the original chiefly by addition of Mendelian heredity, field research, and an overwhelming vote of confidence from biologists."

Mayr (1980:1) summarized succinctly the two major tenets of the synthetic view of evolution:

> The term "evolutionary synthesis" was introduced by Julian Huxley in *Evolution: The Modern Synthesis* (1942) to designate the general acceptance of the two conclusions: gradual evolution can be explained in terms of small genetic changes ("mutation") and recombination, and the ordering of this genetic variation by natural selection; and the observed evolutionary phenomena, particularly macroevolutionary process and speciation, can be explained in a manner that is consistent with the known genetic mechanism.

Thus, Darwin's notion of evolution, based originally on phenotypic change, was redefined in genetic terms as "any change in the frequency of alleles within a gene pool from one generation to the next" (Curtis and Barnes, 1989:974). By extension, evolutionary mechanisms operating at the population level, usually refered to as microevolution, can also be used, by the process of extrapolation, to explain evolution at higher taxonomic levels, that is macroevolution (See Figure 1). Restated, changes on a small scale, given sufficient time, give rise to changes at higher taxonomic levels, such as those of species, genera and family. The principles and mechanisms of population genetics are then seen as both necessary and sufficient to account for all evolution (Charlesworth, 1982; Ayala, 1983; Stebbins and Ayala, 1981). Within this context, when biologists claim to have evidence of evolution, it usually means that they have detected a change in the frequency of genes in a population. As genes are passed on through reproduction, reproductive and associated activities came to be identified as the quintessential components of the evolutionary process. Mayr's classic definition of species in terms of reproductive isolation (see Thompson, this volume, for detail), which has dominated the literature in the last few decades, is predicated on such a concern for genetic transmission. Within this gene-centred perspective, a population can be further reduced to aggregates of gene complexes tending to vary this way or that. A population is easily conceived in terms of its "gene pool", while natural selection, random genetic drift, mutation and gene flow are considered the four primary "forces" that can cause changes in the frequency of genes within populations. Population genetics has successfully provided mathmatical and predictive models for these primary forces, particularly natural selection (Hartl, 1988). This success in turn guarantees the central role of population genetics within the synthesis.

Gould (1983) notes that in the early days of the synthesis, views pertaining to evolution were rather pluralistic, but later "harden" around the adaptationist and genetic core. The decade following the 1940s saw the complete denunciation of Lamarckian inheritance (see Saunders, this volume), typological thinking, and a host of biological theories not compatible with the central tenets of the synthesis (Grene, 1981). While many biologists continue to acknowledge the fact that Neo-Darwinism is not a singular theory but a pluralistic research program with many corollary hypotheses, those who subscribe to Neo-Darwinism tend to equate evolutionary explanations with those based on natural selection (Ho, 1988).

ULTRA-DARWINISM

As population genetics theory came to dominate the Modern Synthesis, both the definition of evolution and of natural selection became more restrictive. Just as changes in the genetic content of a population have become a measure of the degree of evolution, so differential reproductive success between individuals with different genotypes has become

28

an indication of the action of natural selection. In other words, individuals who possess a variant of a gene that accords greater advantage in competition within a particular environment will leave more offspring than those individuals who lack such a gene. Similarly, differential mortality is predicated on genetic differences between individuals. All manner of evolutionary change, in morphology, physiology, and behaviour is assumed to be genetically determined. Thus, natural selection, while appearing to operate at the level of the individual, actually takes place at the genic level. All explanations depending on higher level processes such as "group selection", according to which natural selection favours attributes that help one group compete with another, are rejected. This individual-centred view of evolution is most forcefully stated in one of the most influential evolutionary treatises in recent decades: G.C. Williams's *Adaptation and Natural Selection* (1966). Williams' demolition of the group selectionist thinking appears so decisive, and his demonstration of genic selection so convincing, that evolutionary biologists have largely confined their explanations to the level of the individuals (Williams, 1986; but also see D.S. Wilson, 1989, 1993 for a defence of group selectionism).

Figure 1. The Conceptual Relationship Between Micro- and Macroevolution According to the Modern Synthesis

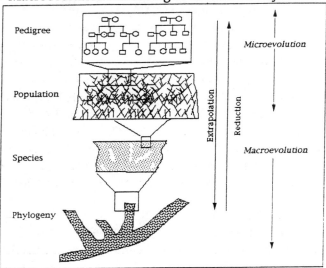

Mechanisms operating at the individual level can be extended to explain origin of higher taxa such as species. The layers on the left represent levels of detail in biological history, from individuals in a family tree, to the species in an evolutionary tree.

The conviction that all evolution occurs by natural selection acting upon individuals competing for personal reproductive success has had important, thought not necessarily a positive, impact on how evolution, and particularly of behaviour, is studied. It has created the common impression that since reproductive success must be measured in terms of the number of genes transmitted to the next generation, any behaviour that maximizes such transmission will be favoured. In addition, Hamilton (1964 a, b) showed mathematically that an organism need not suceed by means of its own reproduction; helping relatives who share enough of one's genes may serve equally well if evolution is measured in the expanded currency of "inclusive fitness". Fitness, in this context, depends not simply on how many offspring one has. An individual can maximize his genetic representation, or fitness, in future generations by ensuring the survival of his relatives since they carry genes in common with him. It follows that the more closely related the individuals, or the more genes they share, the more likely they will be to aid one another because each benefit from the interaction. This notion, known as kin selection, became the cornerstone of modern sociobiology that took shape in the late 1970s. Sociobiology, in turn, became a buttress of ultra-Darwinism (Eldredge and Grene, 1992), the extreme version of Darwinism that reduces the evolution of all social behaviour to differential reproductive success. Sociobiology takes behaviours (such as altruism, or self-sacrificing behaviour) that seem contrary to the key Darwinian belief in fitness maximization, and shows how they are adaptive in the service of individual reproductive success.

In the more extreme form of this reductionist thinking, known as self-ish-gene theorizing, individual organisms are simply regarded as transient vehicles for carrying genes from one generation to the next (Dawkins, 1976, 1982). According to this view, individuals are thought to live in social groups only because group living is benefical to the individuals because it provides greater protection against predators, or greater support during feeding competition with other groups. Social structure, or organization, is then seen as an epiphenomenon, varying this way or that according to the demand ecological factors place on the individuals (see review by Chan, 1992). This principle has been applied to all species that live in groups, from birds to social mammals, and from primates to human foragers (see the papers in Rubenstein and Wrangham, 1986).

Ultra-Darwinism is, therefore, a uni-causal, single level theory of evolutionary causation, with exclusive focus on differential reproduction as the source of all evolutionary explanation, meaning and content (Eldredge and Grene, 1992). As genes are regarded as the ultimate unit of evolution, the study of morphological and behavioural evolution is reduced to a search for genes. In its extreme form, sociobiological study of animal and human behaviour becomes little more than an exercise in "adaptive story-telling" based on hypothetical genes controlling arbitrarily assigned behavioural traits (see Kitcher, 1985 for a critical examination of the assumptions and pitfalls of sociobiology).

CRITIQUES OF ADAPTATIONISM AND ALTERNATIVE VIEWS

Since the 1970s, the main focus of evolutionary theory has begun to swing towards a critique of the central tenets of the modern synthesis and of the restrictiveness of ultra-Darwinism. The challenge to orthodox theory was largely initiated by the theory of Punctuated Equilibrium (the thoery that evolution operates in fits and starts), proposed by Eldredge and Gould (1972), as well as by the growing reaction to human sociobiology. In an influential paper, Gould and Lewontin (1979) criticize what they call the "adaptationist program", or the overzealous use of natural selection and adaptation as the only explanatory principle. They stress the importance of considering chance phenomena such as random genetic drift (fluctuation in gene frequency due to accident) as an alternative explanation for genetic and morphological, as well as behavioural, characters. They point out that biological form can include vestiges of selective forces no longer operating, or incidental products that are the result of developmental processes evolved under selection for other aspects of the phenotype (see explanation below). In particular, Gould and Lewontin fault the adaptationist program because of its two primary assumptions:

(1) that the evolution of complex organisms, including their structure and behaviour, can be understood by the atomization or breaking down of the features into separate traits and then explaining each trait separately.

(2) that the atomized characters are assumed *a priori* to be "optimal solutions" to the evolutionary "problems" posed by the environment.

The first assumption, in fact, rests on the mechanistic notion that the whole is simply the sum of its parts and on the belief that complex organisms can be reduced to their basic components and then reconstituted to form a whole. This approach is the corollary of the Neo-Darwinian extrapolationist strategy of explaining all of evolution in terms of microevolutionary mechanisms. Just as mechanisms at the population level can be extended to explain phenomena at the species level or higher, so explanations at the population level can be reduced to causes at the genetic level.

In addition, Gould and Lewontin (1979) point out that according to the second assumption, similarities between organisms in morphology, behaviour, and even social systems are taken as proof of convergent ecological adaptation to similar selection pressure. The field of study known as behavioural ecology, which has become extremely popular in recent years, rests heavily on the assumption that similar social structures will result when animals, regardless of their evolutionary heritage, are faced with similar ecological conditions. In such a case the goal of research becomes an exercise in demonstrating the way in which the adaptive state has been, or will be, reached (Chan, 1992).

A subtle consequence of this mode of thinking is that the individual organism is treated as a passive entity subjected to external forces. Individuals are driven by genetic predisposition to maximize their reproductive output, and the variants that leave the most offspring in a particular environment will be best represented in subsequent generations. Organisms play little or no role in their own evolutionary fate.

The assumptions underlying the adaptationist program suffer from four major flaws: they ignore the hierarchical nature of biological organization; they deny any active role to individuals in the evolutionary process; they fail to acknowledge the constraints of existing morphology and do not take into account the historical origins and path of the evolutionary characters to be studied.

(1) Importance of the hierarchical concept of biological organization and causality

Since evolution occurs at various hierarchical levels, the reductionist explanation of phenotypic phenomena, which is restricted to events at the genic level, is clearly inadequate (see Figure 2). As an example, the relation of gene and protein molecules may be considered. The information concerning the linear composition of protein molecules is stored in the structured gene. However, once the protein molecule has been assembled from its constituent amino acids, it spontaneously folds to assume its functional three-dimensional conformation. While the physiochemical principles governing the folding are not fully understood, it is clear that the folding instructions are not stored in the DNA sequences. This implies that the information concerning the folding rules represents a higher level of organization than that represented by the lineal amino acid sequence, and that folding rules may be level-specific organizing relationships that cannot be deduced from the DNA molecule. This example, although simplistic, illustrates that when higher level integration and organization are involved, it is misleading to talk of "mapping" or "translation" between levels (Rose, 1981). If a direct mapping between the DNA nucleotide sequence and the three-dimensional structure of protein molecules is questionable, then the one to one mapping between genotype and phenotype are far more problematic (Lewontin, 1992).

Thus, organisms cannot be reduced to a sum of genes, nor societies to a sum of individuals. The latter is not only true for humans, but also for all animal societies. For example, ant colonies exhibit recurring patterns of group behaviour such as foraging and defence that are not apparent at the individual level (Gordon, 1988). Furthermore, research by primatologists reveals that social systems in non-human primates emerge as a consequence of the interaction between individuals for a multiplicity of reasons unrelated to reproduction (Rowell, 1983, 1988). Social traditions arise as a consequence of the social networking between individuals, and the individuals are, in turn, restricted or facilitated by the traditions within which they live (See Burton, this volume). Social tradition, in Burton's view, serves as the repository of social and ecological information pertinent to the maintenence of the group, and tradition therefore constitutes higher level phenomena independent of the individuals comprising the group. Thus, there are level-specific regularities that should be investigated in their own right, and more importantly, these regularities constitute parameters that can determine the behaviour of the constituent parts. In his study of the Rendill, pastoralists of northern Kenya, Roth (this volume) illustrates how an understanding of the complex relationship between social rules, which affect the individuals, and demography, which is measured in group terms, depends on knowing how factors at the group level influence outcomes at the individual level and vice versa.

The strongest objection to reductionist and extrapolationist thinking, therefore, is that there is no direct rule of translation from one level of the biological hierarchy to the next 'down' or 'up' (Eldredge and Grene, 1992). Explanations that may be appropriate at the individual level may not be adequate at the population level. Changes in gene frequency do not always parallel changes in morphology or life histories characteristics, such as longevity and gestation length. Likewise, changes in life history traits or morphology do not necessarily imply changes in genetic components. Molecular biology has also shown that at the genic level, many mutations are neutral; they are neither selected for nor against, and occur at approximately constant rates over the course of evolution (Kimura, 1983). Morphological evolution, on the other hand, occurs at a much more uneven tempo, with long periods of "stasis" or no change, punctuated by relatively rapid bursts of major changes associated with lineage splitting or speciation. (Eldredge and Gould, 1972; Gould and Eldredge, 1993). The prevalance of discontinuous changes at different levels reinforces the recognition that accumulation of selection within populations over time may be entirely inappropriate as an explanation for novel features and diversity (Vrba, 1989).

Figure 2. Causal Relationships Between Levels of the Biological Hierarchy

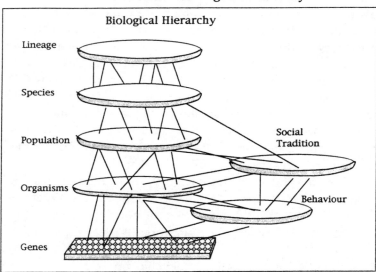

The two-way causal processes, shown as solid line, occur between various levels of the biological hierarchy. Note that new level phenomena, namely behaviour and social tradition, emerged and mediate between lower and higher levels.

(2) Organisms as active agents of evolutionary change

Organisms are neither passive objects driven by genes from within nor simply reactors to environmental pressure from without. In addition, it is overly simplistic to characterize behavioural development as the complex interaction between nature and nurture. As Rose et al. (1984) point out, the organism and environment "interpenetrate" in such a way that there is, in fact, no such thing as organism and independent environment. Lewontin and colleagues maintain the term "environment" does not refer to the external physical world as a whole. "Environment", from the point of view of the organism, means the surroundings as defined by the organism itself. Therefore "there is no environment without an organism" (Rose et al., 1984:273). Similarly, as Groves (1989:33) remarks,

> ...animals do not merely live in an environment and await mutations that may make them better adapted to it: to a surprising extent they select their own niches and their own habitats. It is surely not such an outrageous claim to make that animals, rather than being adapted to an environment because they live in it, may live in an environment because they are adapted to it.

Organisms respond to a "problem" imposed by the environment, but in their response they change the nature of the problem itself. This process referred to as "reciprocal constructivism" by Gray (1988) is a process increasingly recognized by students of behaviour and evolution (see for example Oyama, 1985, 1989; Kitchell, 1990, Bateson, 1988; Hailman, 1982; Lewontin, 1983).

The process of reciprocation between environment, both social and physical, and biology has probably been the most prominent in the course of human evolution, as humans have continously redefined their relationship with the environment. The evolutionary "problems" that confronted our ancestors did not stay the same, and the solutions to them were apt to change. More importantly, however, when evolution is driven by features of the social structure of the evolving species, the process transforms the evolutionary context of the evolving organism. The evolution of language, tool use, complex systems of reciprocity, and of peace making, are not solutions to a set of pre-existing problems facing the human organism. Indeed such "solutions" may, in the course of social evolution, themselves pose new problems that demand further resolution. Thus, behavioural changes set the stage for further evolutionary reciprocation between organisms and their environment, and propel organisms in directions that might not be predictable using purely adaptationist assumptions. There are no pre-defined problems "out there" to which natural selection can fashion stable or invariant solutions (Lewontin, 1983); the organisms and their behavioural repertoire have the final control over the outcomes.

Despite the central importance of human behavioural complexity, the majority of models of how we became humans continue to depict early hominids either at the constant mercy of the harsh tropical African savanna, or embroiled in the incessant struggle for fitness maximization. So bipedalism, a unique evolutionary trait, is often seen as a solution to the various "problems" of "predator avoidance", or "food gathering", or "long distance travelling", or "heat stress" (see the recent review by Jablonski and Chaplin, 1993). Clearly, we need to rethink our entire conceptualization of the interrelations of the human organism and the environment and, in the process, develop a new approach to the entire question of "internal" and "external" causes in evolution.

(3) The importance of developmental constraint

Organisms are not collections of atomized parts, each separate and distinct. Change in one part of the organism may entail correlated change in others, often for structural and developmental reasons unrelated to current adaptation. This phenomenon is true at the genic as well as at the organismal level. Because genes reside on the chromosome, selection for a particular gene often results in the "hitch-hiking" of neighbouring genes that reside on the same chromosome. Thus, the phenotypic effects associated with the hitch-hiked genes are not necessarily those selected for (Lewontin, 1986).

At the phenotypic level, many characters are tightly integrated and are passed on as an integrated suite. Selection of one component of the suite may result in the replication of the entire suite. Thus some components are non-selected though they are also heritable. A case in point is the presence of male nipples, which clearly serve no adaptive purpose. Their presence makes sense because "males and females are not separate entities, shaped independently by natural selection. Rather the two sexes are variants upon a single ground plan, elaborated in late embryology" (Gould, 1987:16). Males nipples are a functionless homologue, character inherited from a common ancestor, maintained because they are a necessary outcome of the developmental sequence that results in female nipples. Developmental biologists thus caution that before we propose an

36

adaptationist hypothesis for a trait, we must first understand how the trait or structure is assembled.

In addition to the tightly integrated nature of some structures, developmentalists also recognize that certain characteristics exhibit long term stability, referred to as "stasis", while some are extremely labile and prone to change. An organism is made up of features of varying antiquity, and some traits appear to evolve relatively independently of the rest of an organism's phenotype. Human morphology embodies many such characteristics; our dental pattern is some 35 million years old, and our tail bone was formed 25 million years ago, while our elbow joint was shaped only 15 million years ago, and our bulbous cranium is a mere 0.10 million years old (Lewin, 1989:78)

The question then becomes why are certain features so resistant to change, and what implications such "stasis" has, especially with regard to the generation of variations and novel features. The answer lies in part in the observation that not all possible morphologies exist for any given body plan (Alberch, 1982, 1990). (There are no flying monkeys, and there are no four-eyed mammals with two heads). So while nature's diversity appears to be boundless, there are, in fact, limits as to what could possibly evolve. Unlike adaptationist thinkers who ask why animals have this or that feature and how it functions in terms of promoting reproductive success, developmental biologists are interested in why one particular form evolves instead of another that might be just as well, or even better, suited to the current environmental problem. This mode of evolutionary questioning has been largely ignored until recently, since evolutionary biologists have traditionally focussed on the issues of change and variation, rather than on stasis and limited possibilities (Wake, 1991; Gould, 1989; see also the various papers in Wake and Roth, 1989).

Developmental biologists interested in constraint or limited possiblity are concerned with rules of internal organization, according to which form precedes function, and with the hypothesis that a set of basic body plans of organisms underlie the diversity of organism observed in nature (e.g., Seilacher, 1990; Alberch, 1990). Primate species are highly diverse in external appearances and in genetic makeup, but they all share the same skeletal structure, albeit in varying proportions. In particular, developmental biologists point out that the development of organisms is an intricately orchestrated and highly conservative process. This process may restrict the amount and direction of variation so that the material available to natural selection is not random, and hence, the channel of evolutionary change is, in part, determined by developmental parameters that limit possible variations. To the extent that variation and evolutionary direction are strongly constrained by internal rules of organization, the role of natural selection as a creative and directing force is simultaneously diminished (see Figure 3).

Figure 3. Relationship Between Ontogeny, Development of the Individual, and Phylogeny

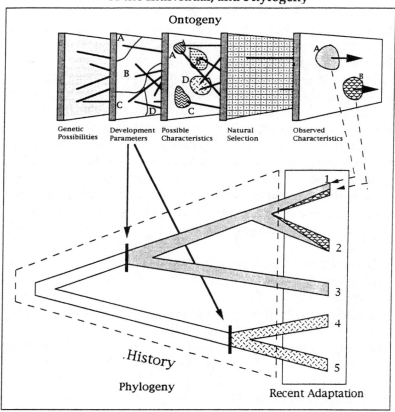

Developmental parameters may be fixed early in a species phylogeny and constrain subsequent diversity. Adaptation, in this context, is seen as recent modification of variations already shaped by development.

Diversity, rather than being generated by chance and necessity, is the result of variations on a common theme. The existence of a theme, or repeating pattern, implies the existence of internal constraint, which in turn allows us to question the scope of possible innovative variation (Muller, 1990). Neo-Darwinians tend to see selection as an opportunist — a "tinkerer," to use the eminent French biologist François Jacob's (1977) term — trying to make the best out of whatever is available. Developmentalists, on the other hand, tend to see the transition between morphological forms as the evolution of the "tolerable" rather than the optimal (Hailman, 1982). But as Wake (1991) points out, the two positions, although defining different methods of analysis, are in fact complementary. Organisms are the embodiment of the past and the present, living in a world of "opportunity within constraint" (Albrech, 1990), being, at the same time, both similar and different from one another. Understanding this paradox is indeed the primary purpose of evolutionary theory. Darwin's great insight was that sameness derives from common descent, while differences arise from modification through selection. The study of evolution is, fundamentally, a study of historical sequence of events, leading to the distribution of novelties and sameness through space and time. Thus, members of the same species share a common evolutionary history distinct from that of other species (Cracraft, 1990). Subsequent evolutionary changes are restricted within the bounds set by the species' history. Understanding of the current adaptation of a species, therefore, calls for an understanding of its evolutionary history, or phylogeny (Brooks and McLennan, 1990).

(4) Evolution as an historical science

Population biologists, although often acknowledging the impact of history, tend to think in ahistorical terms. Most of population genetics, the adaptationist program, and much of behavioural ecology are built on the assumption that the populations under study are in, or are rapidly approaching, equilibrium. That is, the current state of the organism or of the population is the same as it was in the past (Lewontin, 1986). A further assumption is that the current environment is the same as that in which the population evolved. According to this view, to understand the current function of a particular character is to uncover the evolutionary reason why the character evolved.

The assumption that the population is in equilibrium is misleading, however, because as Lewontin (1974) persistently points out, "equilibrium annihilates history". The evolutionary mechanisms that act on any population do so within limits set by the population's history, but this history is obscured if the population is assumed to be in stable equilibrium. Gould and Lewontin (1979) also caution against explanations involving adaptation when the history of a lineage may offer better clues to the current state of affairs. Equally important is the need to distinguish functional explanations from historical or evolutionary questions about origin. For example, there is little doubt that our lungs are highly functional and are, in fact, an important adaptive feature. Yet, it would be senseless to propose an adaptive hypothesis for the number of lungs we have, because the number of lungs is a consequence of the general bilateral symmetry of our bodies and of the developmental mechanisms controlling that symmetry. Bilateral, symmetrical development is a characteristic of the chordate line and there may never have been any variation in its number of lungs. In other word, bilateral symmetrical development sets severe limits on the action of selection. Hence, many features associated with bilateral symmetry remain stable over the course of evolution.

Stearns (1992:94) points out that "the basic design common to a higher taxon shapes the rough boundaries within which the life cycles of all its constituent species evolve." Likewise, many life history traits are invariant at high taxonomic levels (such as Class and Order), and show no variation between populations, while other traits appear fixed at lower taxonomic levels (such as population and species). All birds lay eggs and none give birth to live young; all mammals nurse their young with milk; all primates have an egg supply of approximately 50 years; and most human females experience menopause at a similar age (Fedigan and Pavelka, this volume). On the other hand, many life history traits are highly variable. For example, the degree of parental care varies widely across mammalian species; although most primates give birth to one offspring at a time, intervals between births vary not only between primate species, but also between populations within species. The recognition that certain traits are invariable at high taxonomic levels while others are highly labile serves as an important reminder that historical and developmental constraints are important components of the evolutionary pathway, and so phylogeny must be taken into account when one compares life history parameters across species.

Until recently, adapatationists have largely ignored the role of history or phylogeny, and have overlooked the origin of the traits under study. Without knowledge of the origin of a trait in relation to the organism's phylogeny, it is impossible to ascertain whether the feature first appeared in the species' current environment, or in an ancestor exposed to quite a different environment. Such information might indicate that the trait is "primitive", and shared by a broader set of species belonging to a higher taxonomic level. Consequently, without taking into account phylogeny, it is easy to make the mistake of proposing an adaptationist explanation for a trait when none is needed.

To circumvent this problem, many researchers have adopted phylogenetic methods to try to tease apart the origin of characters from their functional maintenance. One approach consists of establishing genealogical relationships between species first, and then asking if similar traits arose in a common ancestor and have persisted, or if they arose independently due to convergent adaptation. This approach, referred to as the comparative phylogenetic approach, emphasizes the importance of a species' evolutionary history in constraining the features it currently displays and the subsequent directions and rates of evolution open to it (Huey, 1987; Lauder, 1986; Dobson, 1985; Wanntorp, 1983). These features include phenotypic, behavioural, as well as ecological, characteristics. By mapping these features on a well established cladogram, a branching diagram of how species are related to one another, one can estimate when, and how many times, an observed characteristic arose in the group under studied. One can also gain some insight as to what features tend to co-evolve, which features are highly conservative, and which are most labile. This approach emphasizes that adaptionist explanation is only appropriate once the hypothesis that the observed similarities are due to common descent has been rejected (Coddington, 1988). This mode of reasoning in terms of phylogeny, which O'Hara (1988) referred to as "tree thinking", is one of the most important conceptual developments in recent years. Tree thinking is having a substantial impact on the study of ecology and behaviour of a wide range of organisms (see Brooks and McLennan, 1990; McKitrick, 1993; Miles and Dunham, 1993, and references therein), although its effect on the study of human social evolution has not yet fully been explored.

CONCLUSION

Since the triumph of the Modern Synthesis, the concept of natural selection has been accorded *a priori* status. The philosopher of biology, Marjorie Grene (1981), coined the phrase "the axiom of adaptivity" to refer to the belief that most major features of living things are functions of the need to adapt to environmental circumstances, a belief that is so deep-seated that it is scarcely ever mentioned. The popularity of natural selection as an evolutionary explanation also leads to the false impression that adaptations dominate evolutionary change both in frequency and importance. But the real appeal of Darwinism does not lie in its ability to explain organic diversity, but in the set of metaphors it offers. The notions of "struggle for survival", "survival of the fittest", "maximization", reproductive "strategies" are very powerful metaphors and reinforce a utilitarian perception of nature deeply ingrained in capitalist societies. These metaphors also reinforce an ideology that emphasizes competition and strife at the expense of all other human qualities, such as co-operation and mutual care. For decades, the notion of competition has been seen as the central principle in the structuring of ecological communities, so much so that other important phenomena such as mutualism and co-operation have been largely ignored. It now appears that the power of competition in maintaining species relationships has been vastly over emphasized and the empirical support for the phenomenon is highly dubious (Keller, 1988), while mutalism and co-operation are far more common than previously supposed (Margulius and Sagan, 1986; Thompson, 1988; Vandermeer, 1980; Simberloff, 1983). Yet, competitive exclusion continues to dominate discussion of species interaction in non-human primates (Burton and Chan, in press), and subtlely underlie the so-called "Replacement" hypothesis of modern human origins (see Willoughby, this volume). Nevertheless, Mayr (1994:337), the last living founder of the Modern Synthesis, continues to declare that "every property of any living organism has evolved with the assistance of natural selection." Old views tend to die hard.

There have been substantial changes in the field of physical anthropology in the last three decades, beginning with the dismantling of the "man the hunter" model of human evolution in the 1960s, followed by the deconstruction of culturally and politically biassed narratives of human evolution (Wolfe, 1991). At the same time, however, the theoretical framework within which human diversity and uniformity are being interpreted remains substantially unchanged and continues to retain an orthodox, Darwinian core. I hope to have offered some critical reflection on the shortcomings of existing views about evolution and in so doing to challenge the readers to broaden their existing concepts about origins and develop alternative and pluralistic metaphors that better represent nature and our place within it. Evolutionary theory is a powerful and unifying framework for all biology, but it is also a theory that, itself, is continuing to evolve. We risk promoting theory into dogma if we fail to critically question existing views.

ACKNOWLEDGEMENTS

I am thankful to Ann Herring, Shelley Saunders and Emilia Martins for their helpful comments on an earlier version of this chapter. I would like to specially thank Deirdre Breton for her careful reading of my manuscript and for rendering my English readable.

REFERENCES

Alberch, P (1982) Developmental constraints in evolutionary processes. In JT Bonner (ed.): *Development and Evolution*. Berlin: Springer-Verlag, pp. 4-26.

Alberch, P (1990) Natural selection and developmental constraints: External versus internal determinants of order in nature. In J de Rosseau (ed.): *Primate Life History and Evolution*. New York: Wiley-Liss, Inc., pp. 15-35.

Allmon, WD and RM Ross (1990) Specifying causal factors in evolution: the paleontological contribution. In W.D. Allmon and R.M. Ross (eds.): *Causes of Evolution: A Paleontological Perspective*. Chicago: University of Chicago Press, pp. 1-20.

Ayala, F (1983) Microevolution and macroevoltuion. In DS Bendall (ed.): *Evolution From Molecules to Men*. Cambridge: Cambridge University Press, pp. 387-401.

Bateson, P (1988) The active role of behaviour in evolution. In M-W Ho and SW Fox (eds.): *Evolutionary Processes and Metaphors*. New York: John Wiley and Sons Ltd., pp. 191-207.

Bateson, W (1922) Evolutionary faith and modern doubts. *Science* 55: 55-61.

Bowler, P (1983) *The Eclipse of Darwinism*. Baltimore: Johns Hopkins University Press.

Brooks, DR and DA McLennan (1990) *Phylogeny, Ecology, and Behaviour: A Research Program in Comparative Biology*. Chicago: The University of Chicago Press.

Burton, FD and LKW Chan (In Press) Behaviour of mixed species groups of macaques in Kowloon. In J Fa and C Southwick (eds.): *Evolution and Ecology of Macaque Societies*. Oxford: Oxford University Press.

Campbell, BG (1992) *Humankind Emerging*. New York: HarperCollins.

Chan, LKW (1992) Problems with socioecological explanations of primate social diversity. In FD Burton (ed.): *Social Processes and Mental Abilities in Non-Human Primates: Evidences from Longitudinal Field Studies*. Lewiston, New York: The Edwin Mellon Press, pp. 1-30.

Charlesworth, B (1982) Neo-Darwinism — the plain truth. *New Scientist* 94: 133-137.

Coddington, J A (1988) Cladistic tests of adaptational hypothesis. *Cladistics* 4: 3-22.

Cracraft, J (1990) The origin of evolutionary novelties: pattern and process at different hierarchical levels. In MH Nitecki (ed.): *Evolutionary Innovations*. Chicago: University of Chicago Press, 21-46.

Curtis, H and S Barnes (1989) *Biology*. Worth Publishers.

Darwin, C (1859) *The Origin of Species*. London: John Murray.

Darwin, C (1872) *The Expression of the Emotions in Man and Animals*. London: John Murray.

Dawkins, R (1976) *The Selfish Gene*. Oxford: Oxford University Press.

Dawkins, R (1982) *The Extended Phenotype*. Oxford: Freeman.

De Vries (1906) *Species and Varieties: Their Origin by Mutation*. Chicago: Open Court Publishing Co.

Dobson, FS (1985) The use of phylogeny in behaviour and ecology. *Evolution* 39(6): 1384-1388.

Dobzhansky, T (1937) *Genetics and the Origin of Species*. New York: Columbia University Press.

Dobzhansky, T (1973) Nothing in biology makes sense except in the light of evolution. *Amer. Biol. Teacher* 35: 125-129.

Eldredge, N and SJ Gould (1972) Punctuated equilibria: An alternative to phyletic gradualism. In TJM Schopf (ed.): *Models in Paleobiology*. SanFrancisco: Freeman Cooper and Co., pp. 82-115.

Eldredge, N and M Grene (1992) *Interactions: The Biological Context of Social Systems*. New York: Columbia University Press.

Fisher, R (1930) *The Genetical Theory of Natural Selection*. Oxford, Clarendon Press.

Goldschmidt, R (1940) *The Material Basis of Evolution*. New Haven: Yale University Press.

Gordon, DM (1988) Behaviour changes — finding the rules. In M-W Ho and SW Fox (eds.): *Evolutionary Processes and Metaphors*. New York: Wiley, pp. 243-54.

Gould, SJ (1982) Darwinism and the expansion of evolutionary theory. *Science* 216: 380-387.

Gould, SJ (1983) The hardening of the modern synthesis. In M Grene (ed.): *Dimensions of Darwinism*. Cambridge: Cambridge University Press, pp. 71-93.

Gould, SJ (1987) Freudian skip. *Natural History*. 95: 14-21.

Gould, SJ (1989) Punctuated equilibrium in fact and theory. In A Somit and SA Peterson (eds.): *The Dynamics of Evolution: The Punctuated Equilibrium Debate in the Natural and Social Sciences*. Ithaca: Cornell University Press, pp. 54-84.

Gould, SJ (1991) Exaptation: A crucial tool for an evolutionary psychology. *Journal of Social Issues* : 43-65.

Gould, SJ and N Eldredge (1993) Punctuated equilibrium comes of age. *Nature* 366: 223-227.

Gould, SJ and RC Lewontin (1979) The spandrels of San Macro and the Panglossian paradism: A critique of the adaptationist programme. *Proc. Roy. Soc. London, B*. 205: 581-98.

Gray, R (1988) Metaphors and methods: Behavioural ecology, panbiogeography and the evolving synthesis. In M-W Ho and SW Fox (eds.): *Evolutionary Processes and Metaphors*. New York: John Wiley and Sons Ltd., pp. 209-242.

Grene, M (1981) Changing concepts of Darwinian evolution. *The Monist* 64(2): 195-214.

Groves, CP (1989) *A Theory of Human and Primate Evolution.* Oxford: Oxford University Press.

Hailman, J (1982) Evolution and behaviour: an iconoclastic view. In HC Plotkin (ed.): *Learning, Development, and Culture.* Chichester: Wiley, pp. 205-54.

Haldane, JBS (1932) *The Causes of Evolution.* New York: Longmans, Green.

Hamilton, WD (1964a) The genetical evolution of social behaviour, 1. *J. Theor. Biol.* 7: 1-16.

Hamilton, WD (1964b) The genetical evolution of social behaviour, 2. *J. Theor. Biol.* 7: 17-52.

Harrison, GA, JM Tanner, DR Pilbeam and PT Baker (1988) *Human Biology: An Introduction to Human Evolution, Variation, Growth, and Adaptability.* Oxford: Oxford University Press.

Hartl, DL (1988) *A Primer of Population Genetics.* Sunderland: Massachusetts, Sinauer Associates.

Harvey, PH and MD Pagel (1991) *The Comparative Method in Evolutionary Biology.* Oxford: Oxford University Press.

Ho, M-W (1988) On not holding nature still: evolution by process, not by consequence. In M-W Ho and SW Fox (eds.): *Evolutionary Processes and Metaphors.* New York: John Wiley and Sons Ltd., pp. 117-143.

Ho, M-W and SW Fox (1988) Processes and metaphors in evolution. In M-W Ho and SW Fox (eds.): *Evolutionary Processes and Metaphors.* New York: John Wiley and Sons Ltd., pp. 1-16.

Huey, RB (1987) Phylogeny, history, and the comparative method. In ME Feder, AF Bennett, WW Burggren and RB Huey (eds.): *New Directions in Ecological Physiology.* Cambridge: Cambridge University Press, pp. 76-98.

Jablonski, NG (1993) Origin of habitual terrestrial bipedalism in the ancestor of the Hominidae. *J. Human Evolution* 24: 259-280.

Jacob, F (1977) Evolution and tinkering. *Science.* 196: 1161-66.

Johnson, TD and G Gottlieb (1990) Neophenogenesis: A developmental theory of phenotypic evolution. *J. Theor. Biol.* 147: 471-495.

Keller, EF (1988) Demarcating public from private values in evolutionary discourse. *J. Hist. Biol.* 21: 195-211.

Kimura, M (1983) *The Neutral Theory of Molecular Evolution.* Cambridge: Cambridge University Press.

Kitchell, JA (1990) The reciprocal interaction of organism and effective environment: Learning more about "and". In WD Allmon and RM Ross (eds.): *Causes of Evolution: A Paleontological Perspective.* Chicago: University of Chicago Press, pp. 151-172.

Klein, RG (1989) *The Human Career: Human Biological and Cultural Origins.* Chicago: University of Chicago Press.

Lakoff, G and M Johnson (1980) *Metaphors We Live By.* Chicago: University of Chicago Press.

Lauder, G (1986) Homology, analogy, and the evolution of behaviour. In MH Nitecki and JA Kitchell (eds.): *Evolution of Animal Behaviour: Paleontological and Field Approaches.* New York: Oxford University Press, pp. 9-40.

Lewin, R (1989) *Human Evolution*. Cambridge, Massachusetts: Blackwell Scientific Publications.

Lewontin, RC (1974) *The Genetic Basis of Evolutionary Change*. New York: Columbia University Press.

Lewontin, RC (1983) Genes, organisms, and environment. In DS Bendall (ed.): *Evolution From Molecules to Men*. Cambridge: Cambridge University Press, pp. 273-86.

Lewontin, RC (1986) How important is population genetics for an understanding of evolution? *Am. Zool.* 26: 811-820.

Lewontin, RC (1992) *The dream of the human genome*. New York: Rev. Books. May 28: 31-40.

Margulis, L and D Sagan (1986) *Microcomos*. New York: Summit.

Mayr, E (1980) Prologue: some thoughts on the history of the evolutionary synthesis. In E Mayr and W Provine (eds.): *Evolutionary Synthesis*. Cambridge, Massachussetts: Harvard University Press, pp. 1-48.

Mayr, E (1982) *The Growth of Biological Thought: Diversity, Evolution, and Inheritance*. Cambridge, Massachusetts: The Belknap Press.

Mayr, E (1994) Does it pay to acquire high intelligence? *Perspectives in Biology and Medicine*, 37(3): 337-338.

McKitrick, MC (1993) Phylogenetic constraint in evolutionary theory: Has it any explanatory power? *Annu. Rev. Ecol. Syst.* 24: 307-330.

Miles, DB and AE Dunham (1993) Historical perspectives in ecology and evolutionary biology: The use of phylogenetic comparative analyses. *Annu. Rev. Ecol. Syst.* 24: 587-619.

Monod, J (1970) *Chance And Necessity: An Essay on the Natural Philosophy of Modern Biology*. New York: Vintage Books.

Muller, GB (1990) Developmental mechanisms at the origin of morphological novelty: A side-effect hypothesis. In MH Nitecki (ed.): *Evolutionary Innovations*. Chicago: University of Chicago Press, pp. 99-132.

O'Hara, RJ (1988) Homage to Clio, or, toward an historical philosophy for evolutionary biology. *Systematic Zoology* 37: 142-155.

Orr, HA and JA Coyne (1992) The genetics of adaptation: A reassessment. *Am. Nat.* 140: 725-742.

Oyama, S (1985) *The Ontogeny of Information* Cambridge, Cambridge University Press.

Oyama, S (1989) Ontogeny and the central dogma: do we need the concept of genetic programming in order to have an evolutionary perspective. In MR Gunnar and E Thelen (eds.): *Systems and Development*. Hillsdale, New Jersey: Lawrence Erlbaum Associates Publishing, pp. 1-34.

Poirier, FE, WA Stini and KB Wreden (1990) *In Search of Ourselves: An Introduction to Physical Anthropology*. New Jersey: Prentice Hall.

Provine, W (1982) Influence of Darwin's ideas on the study of Evolution. *BioScience* 32: 501-506.

Relethford, J (1990) *The Human Species: An Introduction to Biological Anthropology*. Mountain View, California: Mayfield Publishing Company.

Rose, S (1981) From causations to translation: A dialectical solution to a reductionist enigma. In B Barker and S Rose (eds.): *Towards a Liberatory Biology*. London: Allison, pp. 11-26.

Rose, S, L Kamin, et al. (1984) *Not in Our Genes*. New York, Penguin Books.

Rowell, TE (1988) Beyond the one-male group. *Behaviour* 104: 191-201.

Rowell, TE and DK Olson (1983) Alternative mechanism of social organization in monkeys. *Behaviour* 86: 31-54.

Rubenstein, DI and RW Wrangham, (ed.) (1986) *Ecological Aspects of Social Evolution*. Princeton, New Jersey: Princeton University Press.

Seilacher, A (1990) The sand-dollar syndrome: a polyphyletic constructional breakthrough. In MH Nitecki (ed.): *Evolutionary Innovations*. Chicago: University of Chicago Press, pp. 231-252.

Simberloff, D (1983) Competition theory, hypothesis-testing, and other community ecological buzzwords. *AM. Nat.* 122: 626-635.

Smith, K (1992) Neo-rationalism versus neo-Darwinism: integrating development and evolution. *Biology and Philosophy*. 7: 431-451.

Stearns, SC (1992) *The Evolution of Life Histories*. Oxford: Oxford University Press.

Stebbins, GL and FJ Ayala (1981) Is a new evolutionary synthesis necessary? *Science* 213: 967-971.

Thompson, JN (1988) Variation in interspecific interactions. *Ann. Rev. Ecol. Syst.* 19: 65-87.

Vandermeer, JH (1980) Indirect mutualism: Variations on a theme by Stephen Levine. *Amer. Nat.* 116: 441-8.

Vrba, E (1989) Levels of selection and sorting with special reference to the species level. *Oxford Surv. Evol. Biol.* 6: 111-168.

Wake, DB (1991) Homoplasy: the result of natural selection, or evidence of design limitations? *Am. Nat.* 138(3): 543-567.

Wake, DB and G Roth (1989) *Complex Organismal Functions: Integration and Evolution in Vertebrates*. Chichester: Wiley.

Wanntorp, H-E (1983) Historical constraints in adaptation theory: triats and non-traits. *Oikos* 41: 157-160.

Williams, GC (1966) *Adaptation and Natural Selection: A critique of some current evolutionary thought*. Princeton: Princeton University Press.

Williams, GC (1986) A defence of reductionism in evolutionary biology. In MR Dawkins *Oxford Survey in Evolutionary Biology*. Oxford: Oxford University Press, pp. 1-27.

Wilson, DS (1989) Levels of selection: An alternative to individualism in biology and the social sciences. *Social Networks* 11: 257-272.

Wilson, DS (1993) Group selection. In EF Keller and EA Lloyd (eds.): *Keywords In Evolutionary Biology*. Cambridge, Massachusetts: Harvard University Press.

Wolfe, L (1991) Human evolution and the sexual behaviour of female primates. In JD Loy and CB Peters (eds.): *Understanding Behaviour: What Primate Studies Tell us About Human Behaviour*. New York: Oxford University Press, pp. 121-151.

Wright, S (1930) The genetical theory of natural selection: A review. *J. Hered.* 21: 349-356.

3

The Intellectual History of Field Studies in Primatology
East and West

Pamela J. Asquith

Although nonhuman primates have received special attention since at least Aristotle's time, scientific studies did not get underway, with few exceptions, until the 19th century. Primate studies as a whole encompass medical, comparative psychological, zoological, and anthropological sciences. Study of specifically the naturalistic behaviour of primates, or field primatology, is a relatively young science begun in earnest only about 40 years ago in Europe, America and Japan. The foundations of field studies in Western countries are largely based in zoology and anthropology, which bring both an evolutionary and a structuralist backdrop to theory and method. In Japan, evolutionary explanations have played a less central role than cultural and proximate explanations of primate behaviour. In addition, cultural differences between the traditions resulted in Japanese considering social complexities and intraspecific variation far earlier than their Western colleagues. Both traditions have coalesced to quite a large degree in their goals and orientations since the mid 1980s.

INTRODUCTION

Primatology is the study of the behaviour and evolution of our closest living relatives in the animal kingdom, the apes, monkeys and prosimians. It is a young science begun in earnest only about 40 years ago and its foundations are based in an extraordinarily wide range of disciplines representing both the human and natural sciences. Both the physical characteristics and social lives of these species have been used to test the limits of what might reasonably be speculated about the evolution of our own species. As such, this is a highly self-reflective study, with early descriptions of apes and monkeys based on and reflecting prevailing views about specific human societies and about humans generally. Primate behaviour studies offer insights into how the human observers view themselves through the characteristics they attribute to these closely related species, and through the theories they choose by which to explain the animals' behaviour.

Primatology is also one of the few modern fields of research that was initiated independently in Japan at approximately the same time as in Western countries, with minimal exchange between the cultures during the formative stages. Primatology thus provides a highly visible example of cultural effects on a science. Japanese primate studies were felt by Western researchers to be overly anthropomorphic (attributing human characteristics to animals) and subjective in the first two decades of research. My doctoral research was based on the problem (as it was seen to be) of anthropomorphism in animal behaviour descriptions. I noted at the time that Japanese primatologists appeared unconcerned about avoiding anthropomorphic description in their reports.

It is important to remember that however much nature may reveal to us, our knowledge comes through a filter of the *people* who study and report on it. The kinds of questions, techniques, beliefs, and presuppositions that scientists bring to their study affect what they will see. In the context of this study, Japanese reports of naturalistic primate behaviour were different from Western reports: they were more personal, anthropomorphic, and richly detailed as to individual animal's life histories. I wished to know what, if any, effects a Japanese cultural and intellectual background was having on their studies. I thus went, after completing my doctorate, to do an eighteen-month study of Japanese scientists themselves. As I gradually became able to converse in their own language, rather than the "international language of science" (English), the subtleties of their approach began to unfold. My eighteen-month research project turned into three years. Since that initial study ended, I have returned on numerous occasions and visited Japanese field sites in West Africa to keep up with changes occurring in the discipline. It is from this background, and the perspective it has provided me, that I approach this topic.

Of course, strictly speaking, it is inaccurate to lump the various European and American centres of research under the single term "Western" as if that implies a uniform approach to primatology. Furthermore, although primatology has been moulded largely by borrowings from social science, the different methods and theoretical standpoints of its zoology, ecology, anthropology and psychology practitioners have inevitably given rise to varying and at times conflicting research directions. There are many different and active debates among primate researchers, and not only because they are from diverse disciplinary backgrounds. Added to that are the differences represented by two major traditions in primatology — the Japanese and Western. However, from a broader perspective, differences in such things as underlying assumptions about how to approach animal behaviour studies, and what is the significance and character of the human place in nature, can be discerned between Japan and these Western countries. Pointing out these differences is only useful insofar as it leads to cross-fertilization of ideas and an awareness of the basis on which findings are published.

This chapter will discuss, firstly, early views of nonhuman primates and the background and development of Western and Japanese field studies of primates. It will then examine the intellectual and cultural sources of the different theoretical perspectives of Japanese and Western studies of primates, and how these have developed to the present.

EARLY VIEWS OF PRIMATES IN THE WEST

The taxonomic Order **Primates** includes humans, and our closest living relatives, the apes, monkeys and prosimians. This grouping was first officially recognized by Carolus Linnaeus, in the tenth (1758) edition of the *Systema Naturae*, the first comprehensive classification of all known plants and animals. Since ancient times, however, the nonhuman primates have had a special status because of their humanlike appearance. In western countries, Hanno in the fifth century B.C. and Aristotle in the fourth century B.C. referred to the primates,[1] although it is seldom possible even to identify the animals mentioned in those writings. However, by 130 A.D., Galen made careful dissections of apes and monkeys, recommending their use to gain knowledge of human anatomy (Coxe, 1846). From the second to the early sixteenth century, any acquaintance with primates seems to have perished with its possessors. During the late Middle Ages, primates and other animals were often depicted as religious symbols, though during the sixteenth century, their Christian symbolism faded, and primates were viewed as grotesque and comic caricatures of people (Richard, 1985).

First hand knowledge of apes was introduced to Europe as recently as the seventeenth century. In 1607 Andrew Battell, an English sailor who had been held prisoner for several years by the Portuguese in West Africa, returned to England and provided probably the first eyewitness description of an ape. He recounted having seen two sorts of half-human, half-bestial "monsters", *Engeco* and *Pongo* in local language, which we now recognize to have been a chimpanzee and a gorilla. In 1640 the first live chimpanzee arrived in Europe, a gift to the Prince of Orange in the Netherlands. Nicolas Tulp (1641) published a scientific description of an ape, probably a chimpanzee, from Angola, West Africa. England's first live chimpanzee was shipped from Angola in 1698. He soon died, and was dissected in 1699 by London physician, Edward Tyson, who exclaimed on the similarities between ape and human anatomy.

Some of the earliest known descriptions of monkeys and apes have been recorded in Edward Tyson (1699) and Thomas Henry Huxley (1863). These historical records as well as early twentieth-century descriptions of primates also appear in books by Ada and Robert Yerkes (1929) and Vernon Reynolds (1967). In the early part of this century, most knowledge of primate behaviour was gained through studies of captive apes and monkeys, either kept singly in the home or in groups in private enclosures. An exception to this was the three year field study of the chacma baboon (*Papio ursinus*) carried out by Eugene Marais (1939, 1969) during the Boer War (1899–1902) in the northern Transvaal in South Africa. The work remained in relative obscurity, but it was remarkably prescient of later work: what he sought in the study of baboons was the so-called subliminal soul, or subconscious mentality, of humans that had been masked by what he called the new mentality. Many later primatologists have also sought the bases of human nature in the behaviour of other primates.

Early Western views of primates, then, were based on a mixture of hearsay and observation. The primates were always considered in relation to humans, and the comparison was very often unfavourable to the other primates.

EARLY VIEWS OF PRIMATES IN JAPAN

In Japan, too, there is a long history of interest in nonhuman primates, particularly the Japanese monkey. Unlike Europe or North America, Japan had a primate species at its own front door. The Japanese monkey or macaque (*Macaca fuscata*), sometimes called the Snow Monkey, is native to the Japanese archipelago. Exposure to other primate species, besides the Japanese monkey, was largely through Chinese art, and Japanese artists copied drawings of such species as the gibbon (*Hylobates lar*). Their depictions were realistic, not fanciful as early Western depictions of primates had been, but Japan did not have a scientific tradition and did not carry out scientific studies of primates until this century.

Interactions between humans and the Japanese macaque occurred in both religious and secular life. According to the first written accounts of mythical-historical events of early periods in Japan, the relation between human and monkey extends back more than 1200 years where the monkey appears as a deity. The relationship predates the written record however; the macaque has been hunted for food since preagricultural times (12000 B.C. – 300 B.C.) and its bones ground and powdered for medicinal purposes at least since the sixth century and probably earlier. The monkey has alternated among the roles of a mediator between gods and humans, an animal deity, and a scapegoat for human foibles. In the animistic native religion of Japan known as *Shinto*, the macaque was seen as a messenger communicating between *Shinto* priests and *kami*, spirits of the natural world. When Buddhism was introduced to Japan from China in the sixth century, it did not replace *Shinto*, but was practised alongside the native religion, even mutually incorporating elements of each. The Tendai sect of Buddhism used the Japanese monkey as the model for the well-known Three Wise Monkeys[2] (See no Evil, Hear no Evil, Speak no Evil). Although other animals, such as the fox, were also considered to be messengers between *Shinto* priests and gods, monkeys held a special position among animals as most resembling humans. Their degree of closeness is made clear in the Japanese definition of the monkey as "humans minus three pieces of hair" (Ohnuki-Tierney, 1987). Hair (on the head) in Japanese culture is the essence of the person, as revealed in such customs as offering a tuft of hair of the deceased along with one's prayer at a shrine.

MODERN PRIMATE STUDIES
General Background

Primatology has been described as a discipline best defined by the animal subject rather than the academic speciality of the researcher (Bramblett, 1976). Primate researchers include anthropologists, linguists, neurologists, embryologists, histologists, geneticists, microbiologists, psychiatrists, psychologists, zoologists, taxonomists, ecologists, and even a mathematician.[3] Primatology can be divided broadly into three areas of specialization. One is the use of nonhuman primates for medical research such as the development of drugs, or study, through controlled experiments, of the neurological and physiological bases of behaviour. Overlapping to some extent with neurological studies, comparative psychologists (who compare mental capacities in humans and other animals) investigate social and mental development, such as the effects of early social deprivation on later behavior, physiological processes (e.g., stress), and experiments for cognitive and linguistic abilities in, especially, the Great Apes (chimpanzees, bonobos [or pygmy chimpanzees], gorillas, and orangutans). Thirdly, anthropological research includes morphological (anatomical) and behavioural studies. Morphological studies of nonhuman primates have helped palaeontologists to construct a framework for human evolution. Behavioural studies of primates have contributed to our understanding of the myriad adaptations that have produced both a distinctive (among mammals) primate way of life and our human way of life. Behavioural studies are conducted both in naturalistic surroundings, ("field studies") and in laboratory or restricted surroundings. There are disciplinary differences between these approaches, but both environments have produced complementary data on aspects of primate development and behaviour. Thus, primatology is an amalgam of medical, social and natural sciences. In focussing on field studies, this historical review sets out only one subset of a very wide and dynamic discipline.

Other than the few anatomical dissections of a limited number of animals, more systematic study of nonhuman primates did not get underway until the twentieth century. Belief even among scientists in the savageness and bestiality of apes hampered field studies at the turn of the century. For instance, when the zoologist R.L. Garner (1896) attempted to observe gorillas and chimpanzees, he built a big cage in the forest, for himself, from which to observe the animals. In Western countries before the Second World War, research was overwhelmingly laboratory or experimentally based. Between 1920 and 1940 human engineering projects (design and management of humans for efficient, rational functioning in a scientifically ordered society) came of age and animals, particularly primates, were important in this project. They could be used to construct and test models of human physiology and society and could be subject to laboratory discipline (Haraway, 1978). *Field* studies by both Japanese and Western researchers that sought information on the lives of primates in their natural environment did not flourish until the 1950s. Prior to 1950, such studies had been sporadic and rare, due in part to the upheavals of World War II and the difficulty of travel in the years immediately following it. Prior to World War II too little was known or accessible about wild nonhuman primates, and particularly the Great Apes, to have encouraged much study of them.

Development of Western primate field studies

In America before 1920 there were no scientific studies of the natural behaviour of primates. Concentration had been on studies of anatomy and taxonomy. In 1924 the Yale University Laboratory was set up under American comparative psychologist Robert Mearns Yerkes. He saw the need for field studies to complement the experimental laboratory studies in the psychobiology (study of mental life and behaviour in relation to other biological processes) of primates that were characteristic of comparative psychology at the time. He thus coupled study of animals in their natural environment with comparative psychology. Naturalistic studies of primates began in earnest with Clarence Ray Carpenter (1934), one of Yerkes' assistants, who published a study of howling monkeys (*Alouatta palliata*) in the Panama Canal Zone. Several other studies followed on red spider monkeys (*Ateles geoffroyi*) (Carpenter, 1935), the orangutan (*Pongo pygmaeus*) (Carpenter, 1938) and the gibbon (*Hylobates lar*) (Carpenter, 1940). These were largely studies of factors affecting the coordination and cohesion of the social group, looking at the effects of sex and sex ratios, rank order, and interactions within and between groups. Carpenter had done his Ph.D. research on the sexual behaviour of male pigeons in mated pairs and the effects of removal of their gonads. He then received a National Research Council Fellowship in 1931 to study social behaviour of primates under the direction of Yerkes. For Yerkes, apes were perfect models of human beings and they played a major part in his wish to promote scientific managmement of human society, an idea typical of his generation. Yerkes was interested in the apes in terms of their intelligence and their social-sexual life. It was thus natural that he sent Carpenter to study the dynamics of group life in terms of the controlling vairables of sexual behaviour and dominance. Carpenter likewise viewed sexual activity as the unifying locus of the individual organism and of organic society. He believed that it should be possible to construct a formula for the central grouping tendency of each species. This tendency he considered to be the result of fundamental physiological and psychobiological forces, not

55

of ecological or environmental conditions. This outlook was to change radically in the 1960s under new researchers. Carpenter, however, tied interpretations of the laboratory disciplines of comparative psychology and sexual physiology to evolutionary and ecological field biology (Haraway, 1978).

In 1938, Carpenter trapped over 500 rhesus monkeys (*Macaca mulatta*) near Lucknow, India, and shipped them to Cayo Santiago, a small islet of about 15 hectares off the southeastern coast of Puerto Rico. Just over 400 monkeys survived the trip and they at first organized themselves into six groups containing both sexes and ranging in size from three to 147 animals. By 1940 the remaining 350 monkeys had formed five heterosexual groups ranging from 13–147 animals, with an average of 70 members, and a few unisexual male groups. They ranged freely over the island. The first major study of them was of their sexual behaviour, and Carpenter concluded that intragroup (within the group) dominance by males was strongly correlated with sexual activity, and so presumably with evolutionary advantage. The descendants of the colony have been studied on and off since that time and remain as a field site for primatologists today. The history of the site is recorded in Rawlins and Kessler (1986).

At approximately the same time as field studies began in America, Sir Solly Zuckerman, a South African anatomist, made a detailed behavioural study of a colony of hamadryas baboons (*Papio hamadryas*) at the London Zoo in England. The 1932 book resulting from this study, *The Social Life of Monkeys and Apes*, was considered a milestone in primatology. Unfortunately, it was not recognized at the time that the behaviour displayed by the captive and overcrowded hamadryas baboons was highly aberrant. Although his work attracted considerable attention, including that of Carpenter in America, his conclusion that the main determining factor of social grouping was sexual attraction was incorrect.

During World War Two there was a lull in primate field studies everywhere, but in the 1950s the number of studies increased dramatically. Stuart Altmann (1967) tabulated the cumulative man-months devoted to field studies of primates from 1930 to 1965. He found that since 1955 there was a doubling of actual research activity every five years. The amount of research done from 1962 to 1965 alone was greater than all the research that preceded it. The burgeoning of field sudies has continued: more has been learned about wild primates since 1975 than in the entire history of the field before then (Smuts et al., 1987).

After the war, primate field studies seemed to ignite almost simultaneously in Europe and America. *Primatologia* (subtitled the Handbook of Primatology) was begun in 1956 to publish studies on the morphology of primates. *Bibliotheca Primatologica*, first published in 1962, was devoted to the comparative biology of primates, including behaviour, physiology, taxonomy and morphology. The journal *Folia Primatologica* appeared in 1963, providing a forum for behavioural studies of primates, among others. Articles on primates were published in other journals before these specialist journals appeared, such as in the *Zeitschrift für Tierpsychologie*, begun in the 1940s, which included articles in German, French and English; *Animal Behaviour*, begun in 1953, and *Behaviour*, begun in 1947. Primate scientists attending three major conferences held in 1962 in London, Germany and New York, represented the institutional and teaching nodes from whose lineages most practising Euro-American primatologists have come.[4] In 1964 the International Primatological Society was formed, which included primatologists from Europe, America, Japan and Africa. Since there were no naturally occurring primates in Europe or North America, these researchers were dependent on, especially, African institutions and goodwill to carry out their studies. Uganda, Tanzania, Kenya, Ethiopia and South Africa were the field sources of much early data on primates.

Development of Japanese primate field studies

Although Japanese had already initiated postwar primate field studies in 1948, their work remained largely unknown in the West until after 1958. Thus, this relatively young science was initially developed in quite separate cultural and scientific milieux. Let us now turn to the development of primate field studies in Japan before examining the distinctive cultural and theoretical perspectives of the two traditions that unfolded from the 1960s.

The Japanese macaque inhabits forested areas throughout Japan except for the northernmost island of Hokkaido and islands south of Yakushima off the southern tip of Kyushu. Thus, it is not at all surprising that the first studies of primates by Japanese scientists were made on this local species. However, while this proximity meant that they did not have to mount expensive international expeditions, it proved to be very difficult to follow and to observe the monkeys. Primatology had its beginnings in 1948, at Toimisaki in southeastern Kyushu, when Kinji Imanishi and two of his students, Shunzo Kawamura and Junichiro Itani, started a sociological study of semiwild horses. While there, they spotted a troop of monkeys with mothers and infants, adult males and juveniles, which were crossing a sunny ridge above the ocean. The monkeys made an indelible impression on the small group of researchers as Itani (1961) later described. They soon decided to travel twelve kilometers up the coast to the small island of Koshima where they had heard from local people that there were wild monkeys. On that visit, they could not find the monkeys, but on subsequent visits they had glimpses of the shy animals as they retreated to the forests.

The Primates Research Group was formed at Kyoto University in 1951 by Imanishi and Denzaburo Miyadi. Included in the group were eight young researchers, including Itani and Kawamura. They conducted a series of preliminary surveys of the Japanese macaque habitat throughout the country, from Yakushima in the south, to Shimokita, the northernmost extension of the monkeys' range in Honshu, including the sites that later became synonymous with Japanese primate studies: Takasakiyama, Minoo, Arashiyama, Hieizan, Shodoshima, Boso, Tsugaru and Towada. Research at first was concentrated in Koshima and Takasakiyama.

Despite their efforts, it was four years before they could begin systematic observations of the monkeys. This was because the animals were shy of humans as many groups had been subjected to hunting pressures. Thus, they were only glimpsed as they crossed paths in the forest or fed in the trees. In order to observe the monkeys for longer periods of time, attempts were made at Koshima to provide them with food (a practice known as "provisioning") along their travel routes in the forest. The monkeys accepted the food, and the breakthrough came in 1952 when researchers lured them with sweet potatoes to a sandy beach that was the one open area on Koshima offering an unobstructed view of the monkey group (Figs. 1–3). Finally, troop composition and interactions among all the troop members could be observed. At the same time, the monkeys at Takasakiyama in northeastern Kyushu were provisioned by a priest from the temple at the foot of the mountain. Takasakiyama grew into and is still today a prime site both for tourists coming to view the monkeys at their provisioning site in front of the temple, and for continuing primate behaviour research (Fig. 4). By 1961, more than twenty troops had been provisioned throughout the country (Itani, 1961). Research was conducted on their ecology and social behaviour in a wide variety of habitats, including the sub-tropical south and the subfrigid areas in the Japan Alps and northern Honshu (Fig. 5).

Figure 1. Sandy bay on Koshima Island
(Photos 1–5, and 8 by the author)

Figure 2. Japanese macaques on Koshima

Figure 3. Observing provisioned monkeys on Koshima
(Reproduced with permission of Alan R. Liss, Inc.)

Figure 4. Takasakiyama provisioning site

Figure 5. Japanese macaques ("snow monkeys") in natural hot springs at Jigokudani, Nagano Prefecture in the Japan Alps

After gaining access to various monkey groups, long-term studies based on individual identification of all troop members resulted in pioneering work on dominance rank order (Kawai, 1958a, 1958b; Kawamura, 1958), parental care (Itani, 1959), cultural behaviour (Kawamura, 1959), vocal communication (Itani, 1963), and sexual behaviour (Tokuda, 1961–62).

Early Japanese primate studies were not restricted to the Japanese macaque. From 1955, overseas fieldwork was initiated in South and Southeast Asia, (including India, Malaysia, Singapore, Thailand, Sri Lanka, Nepal and Indonesia), South America (Colombia, Bolivia and Brazil) and East and Central Africa (Ethiopia, Tanzania, Kenya, Uganda, and Zaire). From 1965 the amount of overseas research by Japanese increased sharply. A partial listing of studies in these countries is found in Ikeda (1983). Some of the best known studies by Japanese primatologists have been on the Great Apes, especially the chimpanzee (*Pan troglodytes*) and, more recently, the bonobo (*Pan paniscus*). Originally attempting to find a site at which to conduct long-term studies of gorillas (*Gorilla gorilla*), Imanishi and Itani travelled around equatorial Africa in 1958. Due to unstable political conditions in Central Africa, they changed

61

their focus to study chimpanzees. In 1961 Imanishi organized the Kyoto University Africa Primatological Expedition (KUAPE) to study wild chimpanzees in Tanzania. Studies of chimpanzees in the Mahale Mountains, Tanzania, began in 1965 and continue today (Nishida, 1990). They have become as well known in Japan as the chimpanzee studies at nearby Gombe which were begun in the same year by Jane Goodall.

In 1962 the Primates Research Group became the Laboratory of Physical Anthroplogy and this was divided in 1980 into two laboratories: one focussing on primate behaviour and human ecology studies, and the other on palaeontology and human biology. In 1985, the Center for African Area Studies was created, which houses both primate researchers and anthropologists studying African human populations. Besides these facilities, Kyoto University also runs the Primate Research Institute (PRI), which was built in 1967 in the town of Inuyama, near Nagoya. Additionally, the Koshima Field Laboratory is a small laboratory situated on Kyushu, near Koshima, and is under the management of the Primate Research Institute.

The Japan Monkey Centre (JMC) is a private facility situated beside the Primate Research Institute in Inuyama. Begun in 1956, the JMC has developed an impressive zoo collection of primates, a natural history museum, and research facilities where primatologists also work. The JMC also produces two journals: *Monkey*, a Japanese language popular journal about primates and the Centre's activities, and the international scientific journal *Primates*, begun in 1957, which has been published in English since 1959.

Osaka University researchers also had an early interest in primate studies. Members of the Osaka school are oriented to comparative psychological studies, doing both laboratory and field studies, while Kyoto University members are more oriented to sociological and ecological studies of primates. Today, Japanese primatologists are affiliated with universities and research facilities throughout Japan. It is fair to say, however, that the main thrust of primate studies in Japan was initiated and developed by the Kyoto University researchers under Kinji Imanishi.

Initial contacts between Japanese and Western Primatologists

Despite large geographic, cultural and linguistic distances, the pioneers of Japanese and Western primatology met sporadically. In 1953, Yoshiaki Maeda of Osaka University visited Konrad Lorenz in Austria.

Lorenz was co-founder, with Niko Tinbergen, of modern ethology, or the scientific study of animal behaviour in naturalistic surroundings. Maeda introduced this new science to researchers in Japan. In 1958 Kinji Imanishi visited several European and American centres of primate research, and met such pioneers as Adolph Shultz, Michael Chance, Clarence Ray Carpenter, Sherwood Washburn, and Harry Coolidge (Figs. 6 and 7). In 1961 Imanishi, Itani and a third colleague, Azuma, met Jane Goodall who was beginning her chimpanzee studies at Gombe Stream, Tanzania.

Besides personal contacts, a few lectures were given by Japanese primatologists at international conferences (Imanishi, 1957a; Miyadi, 1959, 1961). Perhaps the most fortuitous occurrence for the future cross-fertilization of primatology was the presence of Jean Frisch, a graduate student at the University of Chicago in the 1950s. He discovered papers, books and the journal *Primates*, which were all published in Japanese about primates. Frisch is a Jesuit priest who was learning Japanese and who intended to teach in Japan. In an article submitted to *American Anthropologist*, Frisch (1959) described the Japan Monkey Centre and outlined what he considered to be original features of Japanese studies. Other articles appeared that described the Japan Monkey Centre (Simonds, 1962) and the Japanese method of study (Imanishi, 1960). A Japanese, Hiroki Mizuhara, participated in the Stanford Primate Year in 1962–63, although he did not contribute to the publication that arose from it. Stuart Altmann had some of the early Japanese papers translated into English and collected in a book, *Japanese Monkeys*, edited by Imanishi and Altmann (1965). C.R. Carpenter had sustained collaboration with Japanese primatologists, making three trips to Japan between 1964 and 1974, even giving advice on how to manage and develop the Takasakiyama colony and contributing to the general development of field methodologies (Carpenter and Nishimura, 1969). Since the third issue, published in 1959, the Japanese journal *Primates* has been published in English although it contained almost exclusively articles written by Japanese primatologists until the 1980s.

Despite these initial contacts, deep-seated differences between the two traditions became apparent during the 1960s based on the way that published reports of behaviour were presented. Let us now turn to the theoretical and cultural perspectives that underly the Western and Japanese traditions in field primatology.

Figure 6. Kinji Imanishi (1902–1992) with Clarence Ray Carpenter (1905–1975) and his son at Carpenter's home in Pennsylvania in 1958. (Courtesy of Junichiro Itani)

Figure 7. Kinji Imanishi and Sherwood Washburn at the University of Chicago in 1958. (Courtesy of Junichiro Itani).

THEORETICAL AND CULTURAL PERSPECTIVES
Disciplinary backgrounds

In the West, After Yerkes' and Carpenter's early work in primatology, people from several fields began to converge on primate studies in the 1950s. Hugh Gilmore (1981: 388-89)[5] has charted this course: Physical anthropologists, psychologists and zoologists initiated field studies. Scientists in each of these disciplines pursued questions that were relevant to their own field. Zoologists had perhaps the easiest entry into primate field research because zoology already had a strong tradition in the naturalistic study of animal behaviour. They were familiar with the new field of ethology. The range of questions they could explore was wider than that of psychologists and anthropologists because they did not restrict their investigations to those aspects of primate behaviour that were relevant to understanding human behaviour.

Psychologists, by and large, tended to treat the field situation as though it were an immensely disorganized and uncontrolled comparative psychology laboratory. They focussed typically on such matters as nonhuman primate problem solving, learning, developmental questions and the proximate (immediate) causes of social cohesion. They attempted, basically, to gain insights into the mental operations of complex organisms (humans, in this case) by studying simpler organisms (the nonhuman primates).

Primatological research conducted by physical anthropologists was, whether anatomical or behavioural, united by a common interest in human evolution. In the 1950s and 1960s the "new physical anthropology", as espoused by Sherwood Washburn, urged study of primates in their natural environment so as to see how the anatomy actually functioned in a behaving animal. This was a radical departure from the traditional static comparison of structural features of primate anatomy. In finding how structures had evolved to *adapt* to living conditions, these could be compared with humans. Once unique features of humans had been identified, anthropologists could propose selective mechanisms that might explain how distinctively human traits had evolved.

The disciplinary background and rationale of Japanese primate studies was somewhat different. The founder of Japanese primatology, Kinji Imanishi, was an ecologist, who had long been interested in the origins of animal societies. His interests began to overlap with those of anthropology after studies of Japanese macaques stimulated his interest in the origin of human society, and of the human family in particular. He reasoned that

65

clues to solving questions regarding the origin of the human family would be provided by two types of research. The first focussed on the social structure of the great apes ("primatological approach") and the second on the social structure of current hunter-gatherers ("anthropological approach") (Nishida, 1990:10). Once it was found that social structure differed significantly among the Great Apes, Japanese primatologists concluded that rather than try to reconstruct what protohominid society was like through direct comparison with ape species, they should aim to make ethological and ecological comparisons between ape and human groups, considering the differences as important as the similarities in understanding the evolution of human society.

Methodologies
(a) Provisioning

Originally, three features were said to characterize Japanese primate research: provisioning, long-term studies and individual identification of the animals. Provisioning, or feeding, drew the group into the open, and allowed clear observation of behaviour and identification of individual animals. However, the merits and drawbacks of provisioning have been, and continue to be, hotly debated by primatologists throughout the world (e.g., Fa and Southwick, 1988). Some scientists maintain that provisioning alters behaviour and population processes so much that studies conducted on food-supplemented groups are not indicative of the animals' natural lives. Yet provisioning has been useful to allow the animals to become habituated to observers so that they can be followed even without the lure of food after a time. Provisioning has saved groups of some primate species from certain extinction in areas of dwindling natural resources. It has also allowed the collection of abundant detailed data on primates that we otherwise would not have, though opponents of provisioning maintain that the data is fundamentally flawed. Leaving aside the debates about the pros and cons of provisioning (a review of provisioning effects can be found in Asquith, 1989), we can examine here what it meant to Japanese and Western primatologists in cultural terms.

Whereas provisioning was part of the Japanese methodology for studying primates initially (they have by no means conducted all studies using provisioning), it was never part of a traditional methodology for Western researchers. Nonetheless, two of the longest studied primate populations in the West are or have been provisioned in the past — the Cayo Santiago rhesus macaque colony, and the Gombe Stream chimpanzees. While Westerners debated effects of provisioning on population processes and behaviour in these and other groups, Japanese talked about their relationship with the monkeys they were feeding, and how it allowed experimentation to be done (such as the famous "peanut test", in which a desirable item of food was thrown between two animals and the dominant animal was expected to retrieve it while the subordinate animal did nothing). By feeding, Japanese said, the researcher positively entered the group and made contact with the monkeys. At the time when most Western researchers advocated strict neutrality with study animals, this was indeed unique.

(b) Social structure and long-term studies

In the West, those studying "structural features" of primate societies also sought evolutionary, or adaptive mechanisms. However, physical anthropologists did not have the zoological background or methodology to carry out field studies. They turned to social anthropology for data collection methods and theoretical orientation. Based on the influential ideas of anthropologist Radcliffe-Brown (1956), primate studies of the 1960s focussed on social structure as an ordered arrangement of individual members. Human social relations were thought to be controlled by norms, rules and patterns that each individual knew. Within a nonhuman primate group, rules and norms were overwhelmingly argued to be relationships of dominance and subordinance, especially among males. Ultimately, the adult male dominance system was viewed as being the stable force that held the society together. With few exceptions, studies tended to be of short duration and if many animals were individually identified, it was the males, who were considered to be the prime players in group social dynamics. Until the ground-breaking work of Thelma Rowell (1967), who noted differences among groups of forest- and savannah-dwelling baboons of the same species, it had also been thought that once you had observed a single group, you knew the "species specific" behaviour for the entire species.

Japanese researchers' idea of long-term observation, on the other hand, contrasted dramatically with most early Western studies that lasted from a few weeks to a few months. Japanese researchers were seeking to understand the so-called species society (Asquith, 1991; Imanishi, 1957b), which included the behaviour and interrelationships of no less than all members of all groups of a species. According to this framework, one began with observation of particular groups, and the study was possible only through individual identification of all the animals. Japanese have kept genealogical records of monkeys extending back to the 1950s for some troops. Perhaps the uniqueness of Japanese primatology is in part reflected by this diachronic or historical approach. They do not observe behaviour only from a synchronic standpoint (i.e., the study of mechanisms of behaviour at a given time), but also from a diachronic one, by studying the life history of individuals and then ultimately the sociological history of the troop in terms of change over time.

An important aim of Japanese studies was to understand what position each individual held in the animal society. More than one primatologist has said that they sought parallel phenomena among primates to what occurs in Japanese society. Within Japanese society, one's identity is to a great extent one's group identity, and since status and social relationships are given much attention, it was natural to look for similar phenomena in the monkey groups. This was one of the first questions to be asked of monkey society — is there anything like rank order?

This may at first appear similar to Western concerns with dominance in primate groups. However, Western researchers looked at male rank order and mating access, whereas Japanese discovered that, in Japanese macaques at least, male rank was only one factor determining social relationships and group composition. Females had a rank order too, and the stable core of the group was made up of lineages of related females, not males. Males emigrated from their natal group on reaching sexual maturity.

(c) The individual and the group

In the West during the 1970s an important theory known as sociobiology was developed that focussed on "individual selection" in which it is felt that the individual acts for its own benefit to maximize its own reproductive advantage ("individual fitness") rather than for the benefit of the group. Thus, for example, an individual lives in a group only because group life is to its advantage. Edward Wilson's (1975) book *Sociobiology* was a landmark in focussing the direction of primate studies towards these ideas of individual fitness, and sociobiology underlies the theoretical orientation of most Western primate studies today.

Early on, Japanese researchers recognized variability or what they called "subcultural" behaviour among different groups of the same species. Likewise, the history of both the individual and the group was considered equally important, while this dual history was almost wholly ignored by Western primatologists in their shorter-term studies. To the Japanese, current variability among groups and change in individuals and groups over time must be ascertained for a complete picture to emerge of the dynamics of a society. Each individual of a species is a member of society and contributes to maintain the species society. Thus, intergroup relations are also important to the whole picture of group life. This differed from a Western view of species specific behaviour being demonstrated by a single group of a species, without considering its relations with other groups, nor with the entire species considered as a whole.

Thus, a major source of difference between the Japanese and Western traditions in primatology up to the early 1980s lay in the significance accorded by Japanese primatologists to both individual variability and to the "group" considered as a society. The latter concept is in strong contrast to the view sometimes expressed by sociobiologists that the social group is simply an aggregation whose form has evolved through environmental and biological pressures on each of its individual members.

The Japanese, then, approached primate studies from a cultural rather than a biological point of view. For Western primatologists with backgrounds in anthropology and zoology, the approach has been to explain behaviour and social structure in evolutionary terms, or in terms of how an individual's reproductive success is maximized. The early Western studies were marked by a rather militaristic, patriarchal approach (Haraway, [1989] has traced the sources of this approach). In Japanese studies, although evolutionary theory provides an important underlying framework, in seeking such things as the evolution of the family, for instance, proximate, nonevolutionary explanations of particular behaviours or forms of social grouping have tended to be more frequent in their reports. Many Japanese primatologists feel that ultimate (evolutionary) explanations are not sufficient to account for the complexities of primate life.

These are, of course, very general characterizations of Western and Japanese primate studies and readers should be aware that there are exceptions in both groups. However, the majority of Western primatologists would not disagree that, ideally, they would like to find an evolutionary explanation for primate behaviour and social organization.

Cognitive abilities and the Cartesian split

Besides differences between the two traditions based on theoretical orientation, basic differences are also evident in assumptions about non-human primate cognitive abilities and their relationship to humans in nature. The Western Judaeo-Christian heritage and Cartesian-based science made any questions about animals' minds illicit until very recently. In fact, until only a decade ago, most Western primatologists were reluctant to infer mental states in animals, and the assumption of mental qualities associated with complex social behaviour in other animal species was thought to be unscientific.

However, for the Japanese, attributing mental states, including motivation, feelings and personality to the primates was taken for granted. Even the possession of a soul is not considered unique to humans. At annual memorial services held by some of the primatology laboratories, both lab and field workers gather to pray for the souls of monkeys or other animals that have been sacrificed to research. Some of the memorial altars are quite grand, as one at Awajishima (Fig. 8), paid for by local villagers, while others are a simple rock erected to the memory of the animals where a ceremony is held annually (Fig. 9). These ceremonies are an opportunity to show both gratitude and contrition for their use of the animals — which should not be taken for granted and which do not exist only for human use.

Figure 8. Monkey Memorial at Awajishima

Figure 9. Monkey Memorial Service at Osaka University
(Courtesy of Masayuki Nakamichi).

In the scientific study of primates, then, Japanese did not restrict assumptions about the existence of certain mental processes to humans. Thus, Japanese have since the beginnings of primatology in the 1950s assumed that these animals have socially complex lives, individuality, are affected by their own and their group's life history and can strategize for future gain. Many of these aspects were not taken up until the 1980s by Western researchers.

CURRENT DIRECTIONS

Research in all areas of primatology has continued to expand, hypotheses have been refined and new theories developed. In naturalistic field studies, primatologists feel that they have barely scratched the surface of the enormous complexities of their study subjects. In addition, there has been a shift during the 1980s away from the traditional concern to relate behaviour of other primate species to human evolution, toward testing of ecological theory across a broad spectrum of species. Thus, former concerns to identify continuities and discontinuities between ourselves and certain primate species have largely been replaced by attempts to identify general ecological principles underlying behavioural and structural variation both within and across primate species.

Alison Richard's (1985) *Primates in Nature* provided one of the first major overviews of this new direction, as did R.I.M. Dunbar's (1988) *Primate Social Systems*. Irven DeVore (1990) gives a brief summary of some of the current socioecological studies.

In the 1970s and 1980s, there has been a trend away from relying almost exclusively on concepts developed in the social sciences, toward grounding primatology within the theories of modern evolutionary biology. In particular, sociobiological theory now underlies many Western studies (see Gray, 1985 for an overview of sociobiological research in primatology). From about the mid 1980s, some Japanese primatologists also began to use sociobiological arguments in their papers. At the same time, more Western researchers have begun to focus on proximate explanations for behaviour, or upon the immediate experiences and motivations of the animals, which were formerly a hallmark of Japanese studies (e.g., Cheney, 1990; Harcourt and de Waal, 1992; Smuts, 1985; Strum, 1987). This is a result of the detailed knowledge we have gained of certain species' behaviour. Japanese and Western primatology have in many ways begun to coalesce and there are several cooperative studies by these two impressive traditions, for example, on chimpanzees (Heltne and Marquardt, 1989, and Nishida, 1990 provide summaries), and on Japanese macaques (Fedigan and Asquith, 1991 provide a summary).

State-of-the-art overviews of the diversity of primate field research can be found in Smuts et al. (1987) and the Introduction in Fedigan (1992). Further studies of the science of primatology itself, including the social, historical and political factors that affected its development, have appeared recently (e.g., Haraway, 1989). This marks a recognition of the powerful influence of culture on science. We have indeed reaped many benefits from study of our closest living relatives. Primatology has not only taught us something about ourselves and our evolution, but about how we do science.

ENDNOTES

1	Hanno, *Periplus*, translated from the Greek by Wilfred H. Schoff (1912); Aristotle, *Historia Animalium*, translated by D'Arcy Wentworth Thompson (1910), Book II.
2	There are, in fact, four Wise Monkeys, the last depicting "Do No Evil".
3	Jeanne Altmann (1974) produced one of the most frequently cited papers in primatology on sampling methods of naturalistic behaviour.
4	See Haraway (1989), chapter 6 "Reinstituting Western Primatology after World War II" and Notes 9–11 (pp. 396–97) for that chapter for a listing of participants at these meetings, their affiliations, and their students.

5　　　Gilmore (1981) appears in a special Jubilee Issue of the *American Journal of Physical Anthropology* published to celebrate the 50th anniversary of the establishment of the Association of Physical Anthroplogy. The issue contains several papers on the history of American physical anthropology to 1980.

REFERENCES

Altmann J (1974) Observational study of behavior: Sampling methods. *Behaviour* 49:227-267.

Altmann SA (ed.) (1967) *Social Communication Among Primates*. Chicago: University of Chicago Press.

Asquith PJ (1989) Provisioning and the study of free-ranging primates: History, effects, and prospects. *Yrbk. of Phys. Anthropology* 32:129-158.

Asquith PJ (1991) Primate research groups in Japan: Orientations and east-west differences. In LM Fedigan and PJ Asquith (eds.): *The Monkeys of Arashiyama. Thirty-five Years of Research in Japan and the West*. New York: SUNY, pp.81-98.

Bramblett CA (1976) *Patterns of Primate Behavior*. California: Mayfield.

Carpenter CR (1934) A field study of the behavior and social relations of howling monkeys (*Alouatta palliata*). *Comp. Psychol. Monogr. 10(2)*:1-168.

Carpenter CR (1935) Behavior of red spider monkeys in Panama. *J. Mammal. 5(16)(3)*:171-180.

Carpenter CR (1938) A survey of wild life conditions in Atjeh, North Sumatra, with special reference to the Orang-utan. *Communications, Nr.12*. Amsterdam.

Carpenter CR (1940) A field study in Siam of the behavior and social relations of the gibbon (*Hylobates lar*). *Comp. Psychol. Monogr. 16(5)*:1-212.

Carpenter CR, and Nishimura A (1969) The Takasakiyama colony of Japanese macaques (*Macaca fuscata*). Proc. 2nd Int. Congr. Primat.: *Social Organization and Ecology. Vol.1*. Basel, Switzerland:Karger, pp.16-30.

Cheney DL (1990) *How Monkeys See the World: Inside the Mind of Another Species*. Chicago: University of Chicago Press.

Coxe JR (1846) *The Writings of Hippocrates and Galen*. Epitomized from the Original Latin Translations. Philadelphia: Lindsay and Blakiston.

DeVore I (1990) Introduction: Current studies on primate socioecology and evolution. *International Journal of Primatol. 11(1)*:1-5.

Dunbar RIM (1988) *Primate Social Systems*. Ithaca: Comstock Publ. Assoc.

Fa JE, and Southwick CH (eds.) (1988) *Ecology and Behavior of Food-Enhanced Primate Groups*. New York: Alan R. Liss, Inc.

Fedigan LM (1992) *Primate Paradigms. Sex Roles and Social Bonds*. Chicago: The University of Chicago Press. 2nd edition.

Fedigan LM, and Asquith PJ (eds.) (1991) *The Monkeys of Arashiyama. Thirty-Five Years of Research in Japan and The West*. New York: SUNY Press.

Frisch JE (1959) Research on primate behavior in Japan. *Amer. Anthropol. 61(4)*: 584-596.

STRENGTH IN DIVERSITY: A READER IN PHYSICAL ANTHROPOLOGY

Garner RL (1896) *Gorillas and Chimpanzees*. London: Osgood.

Gilmore HA (1981) From Radcliffe-Brown to sociobiology: Some aspects of the rise of primatology within Physical Anthropology. *Amer.J.Phys.Anth.* 56:387-392.

Gray JP (1985) *Primate Sociobiology*. New Haven: HRAF Press.

Harcourt AH, and de Waal FBM (eds.) (1992) *Coalitions and Alliances in Humans and Other Animals*. Oxford: Oxford University Press.

Haraway D (1978) Animal sociology and a natural economy of the body politic, Part I: A political physiology of dominance. *Signs, 4*, 1:21-36.

Haraway D (1989) *Primate Visions. Gender, Race and Nature in the World of Modern Science*. New York: Routledge.

Heltne P, and Marquardt LA (eds) (1989) *Understanding Chimpanzees*. Chicago: Chicago Academy of Sciences.

Huxley TH (1863) *Evidence as to Man's Place in Nature*. London: Williams and Norgate.

Ikeda J (1983) Overseas field works, 1956-1981. *Recent Progress of Natural Sciences in Japan*, Vol. 8. Tokyo: Science Council of Japan, pp.127-155.

Imanishi K (1957a) Conservation of Japanese monkeys. *Proc. and Pap. 6th Tech. Meeting. International Union for the Conservation of Nature and Natural Resources*, pp.71-72.

Imanishi K (1957b) Social behaviour in Japanese monkeys (*Macaca fuscata*). *Psychologia Kyoto* 1:47-54.

Imanishi K (1960) Social organization of subhuman primates in their natural habitat. *Curr. Anthrop.* 1(5-6):393-407.

Imanishi K, and Altmann SA (eds.) (1965) *Japanese Monkeys. A Collection of Translations*. Edmonton, Canada: SA Altmann.

Itani J (1959) Paternal care in the wild Japanese monkey, *Macaca fuscata*. *Primates* 2:61-93.

Itani J (1961) The society of Japanese monkeys. *Jap. Quart.* 8:421-30.

Itani J (1963) Vocal communication of the wild Japanese monkey. *Primates* 4(2):11-66.

Kawai M (1958a) On the rank system in a natural group of Japanese monkeys. I: The basic rank and dependent rank. *Primates* 1:111-130. (Japanese with English summary). Also in K Imanishi and SA Altmann (eds.) (1965): *Japanese Monkeys*. Edmonton, Canada: SA Altmann, pp.66-86.

Kawai M (1958b) On the rank system in a natural group of Japanese monkeys:II: In what pattern does the ranking order appear on and near the test box. *Primates* 1:131-148. (Japanese with English summary). Also in K Imanishi and SA Altmann (eds.) (1965) *Japanese Monkeys*. Edmonton, Canada: SA Altmann, pp.87-104.

Kawamura S (1958) Matriarchal social ranks in the Minoo-B troop: A study of the rank system of Japanese monkeys. *Primates* 1:149-156. (Japanese with English summary). Also in K Imanishi and SA Altmann (eds.) (1965) *Japanese Monkeys*. Edmonton, Canada: SA Altmann, pp.105-112.

Kawamura S (1959) The process of sub-cultural propagation among Japanese macaques. *Primates* 2:43-60.

Marais E (1939) *My Friends the Baboons*. London: Blond and Briggs, Ltd.

74

Marais E (1969) *The Soul of the Ape*. London: Anthony Blond, Ltd.

Miyadi D (1959) On some new habits and their propagation in Japanese monkey groups. In HR Hewer and ND Riley (eds.) *Proc. 15th Int. Congr. Zool. Lond*. London: Linnaean Society, pp.860-875.

Miyadi D (1961) Fission of Japanese macaque troops. *Trop. Ecol. 2(1–2):77-83*.

Ohnuki-Tierney E (1987) *The Monkey as Mirror. Symbolic Transformations in Japanese History and Ritual*. Princeton: Princeton University Press.

Nishida T (ed.) (1990) *The Chimpanzees of the Mahale Mountains. Sexual and Life History Strategies*. Tokyo: University of Tokyo Press.

Radcliffe-Brown AR (1956) *Structure and Function in Primitive Society*. Glencoe, Illinois: The Free Press.

Rawlins RG, and Kessler MJ (eds.) (1986) *The Cayo Santiago Macaques. History, Behavior and Biology*. New York: SUNY Press.

Reynolds V (1967) *The Apes. The Gorilla, Chimpanzee, Orangutan and Gibbon — Their History and Their World*. London: Cassell.

Richard AF (1985) *Primates in Nature*. New York: WH Freeman and Company.

Rowell TE (1967) Variability in the social organization of primates. In D Morris (ed.): *Primate Ethology*. London: Weidenfeld and Nicolson, pp.219-235.

Schoff WF (1912) *Hanno, Periplus*. Translated from Greek by Schoff. London.

Simonds P (1962) The Japan Monkey Centre. *Curr. Anthrop. 3(3):303-305*.

Smuts BB (1985) *Sex and Friendship in Baboons*. New York: Aldine.

Smuts BB, Cheney, DL, Seyfarth, RM, Wrangham, RW, and Struhsaker, TT (eds.) (1987) *Primate Societies*. Chicago: University of Chicago Press.

Strum SC (1987) *Almost Human. A Journey into the World of Baboons*. New York: Random House.

Tokuda K (1961-62) A study of the sexual behavior in the Japanese monkey. *Primates 3(2):1-40*.

Tulp N (1641) *Nicolai Tulpii, Amsterlredamensis, Observationum medicarum libri tres*. Amsterdam: Apud, Ludovidum Elzevirium.

Tyson E (1699) *Orang-outang, sive homo sylvestris: Or, the anatomy of a pygmie compared with that of a monkey, an ape and a man*. London: T Bennet and D Brown.

Wilson EO (1975) *Sociobiology. The New Synthesis*.Cambridge, Mass.: Belknap.

Yerkes RM, and Yerkes A (1929) *The Great Apes. A Study of Anthropoid Life*. New Haven: Yale University Press.

Zuckerman, Sir Solly (1932) *The Social Life of Monkeys and Apes*. London: Kegan Paul, Trench, Trubner.

4

In the Footsteps of Anaximander
Qualitative Research in Primates

Frances D. Burton

Methodology is epistemology: the way of studying a phenomenon depends on the view of that phenomenon. In attempting to avoid anthropomorphism — endowing or attributing human form and especially feelings and abilities to animals — we have developed a particular mode of finding out which we term science. In this mode we feel it is appropriate to be 'objective' that is to remove our own feelings, thoughts and biases from influencing how we study. In this paper I (1) trace the search for objective techniques in the study of non-human primates and (2) present a rapprochment to established anthropological methods that provide a return to holism in the study of social behaviour.

INTRODUCTION

My first monkey studies were anatomical and they were conducted on caged cercopithecines at Louis Leakey's Tigoni Primate Resesearch Centre in Kenya. My interest then was in studying structure and function that relate to hominization — the process of becoming human. The focus of this research was on use of the hand. Caged animals seemed eminently suited for such anatomical studies. The whole story of how they use their hand could be coupled with dissections of monkeys contributed to the centre by local farmers who shot them as pests. But watching them raised so many questions about social behaviour, that I knew subsequent studies had to deal with social groups not restricted by cagedness. I wanted a research site where I could actually come to understand something of the way the primates lived.

I had always been interested in monkeys living near humans. Termed popularly "urban monkeys" they are perhaps more appropriately called synanthropic — that is, living with humans. Two classic locations had been British colonies: Gibraltar, at the tip of Spain and Kowloon/New Territories, the mainland part of Hong Kong. A freshly annointed Ph.D., I chose to study the Barbary "Apes" of Gibraltar, expecting those macaques to conform to earlier descriptions of them as well as to generalizations about social groups. Above all, I expected to be able to view them from a perspective compatible with that deriving from studies of caged macaques. This perspective would enable me to be objective and the monkeys to remain remote animals, functions of their biology subscribing to rules already understood. The Gibraltar monkeys lived in small groups where all members could be studied. I was not prepared for the overwhelming reality of the uniqueness of each one.

What was significant was that I now understood the relationship of primate studies to anthropology and why it had its legitimacy within that field rather than zoology; I further understood the pressure to conform to other animal sciences which was, in the early 1970s a prevailing trend, and I began to examine the issue of how we should gain some understanding of the complex behaviour daily demonstrated before me. That is, what methods should be developed consistent with the nature of the organisms that profoundly recognizes their being, but which also takes into account the nature of the observer. What techniques shall we use? How will we establish the appropriate tools — both methods and skills — to enable us to de-code what is basically unintelligible. The choice of appropriate method is actually a complex issue. It depends on the definition of our subjects — the objects of our research of course: stones require different techniques than do plants. But more than this, our choice of method depends on our recognition of our selves as the chooser. The methods chosen reflect very closely how we view our role as decoder and the values, cultural system and particular history in which we are embedded (Stent, 1985).

This essay presents these thoughts beginning with the history of primate studies, I describe the context in which primate studies began, and where I think it has its legitimacy. I then look at the methodology that has overtaken primate studies and propose an acceptance of pluralistic methods consistent with the nature of the subjects under study.

78

PRIMATOLOGY WITHIN ANTHROPOLOGY

Primatology has its rightful place in Anthropology rather than Zoology. Primate studies exist within the discipline of Anthropology because of our interest in hominization, the process of becoming human. Anthropology has a unique interest in humankind because it wants to understand its unique adaptation: the feedback from biology to culture and culture to biology. This idea is basic to Anthropology; arguably, it is this discipline's distinguishing feature. The recognition of a set of rules, values, ways of doing things that mark off one local group from another, was an enormous contribution the young Anthropology presented to the world in the late 19th century. The notion of "culture" arrived at a time when the origin and definition of humankind was hotly debated. Linnaeus had already noted (1750s) that while primates are mammals, humans are primates. Their special place in nature placed the Order, Primates, within the discipline devoted uniquely to the study of humankind — Anthropology. This was a time when departments of Anthropology had only recently been founded, and ethnological studies of humans throughout the world were becoming field excursions rather than reviews of travellers' or missionaries' tales.

The emphasis on being in the field with the subject of enquiry has become a major chord resonating throughout Anthropology. This being on-site within the group, has led to a lively discourse on how we know what we know; how we gather data for subsequent analysis, and how we go about the analysis. These steps in planning are the glasses that clarify or cloud our vision in the field. As participant informants, social/cultural anthropologists came to witness activities from the perspective of the group they had come to study. The flow of daily life became intelligible because the anthropologist was like a member of the group: spoke the language, contributed labour, watched and took part in activities and even rituals. Trained to be able to evaluate what was seen and experienced, the anthropologist could extract from the richness of this personal exposure, could analyse and so contribute to theory.

Development of Primate Studies

Our current attitude towards non-human primates has developed over centuries. The obvious physical relationships, in particular the five-fingered flexible hand, the rounded face, the ability to stand on two legs, were sufficiently reminiscent to have the monkey serve as physical surrogate in anatomy from the ancient Greeks for nearly a thousand years. This resemblance led the ancients to wrestle with the question of the nature of humanity. Where did we come from? Were we beast or not?

To the ancient Egyptians, the baboon was a sacred deity, Toth. With a body like a man's, and a head of an ibis or dog-headed baboon, it was he who was the god of wisdom and of writing — arguably the highest forms of human endeavour, hence primate-ness confers a special nature. What of the beast, the wild animal?

The Sumerian tale of Enkidu and Gilgamesh illustrates the concern for a definition of human nature. Intuiting that the rise of cities had something to do with humanity as the ancients experienced themselves, they told the tale of the wild man, Enkidu, who loses his innocence and is "tamed" after he comes to the major city, Uruk. The story clearly illustrates that the dilemma of who we think we are and how we define ourselves is at the centre of how we regard other beings, and the means we find suitable to study them.

Aristotle voiced the intuited difference between "us" and "them" in his model that placed life forms on a ladder, from most primitive to most complex. The hierarchical formulation is a constant theme. We read it in early evolutionary theory; in structures like churches and nations; and in social organization of non-human primates. The construct has become "natural" and seen as innate wherever it occurs.

> Nature proceeds little by little from things lifeless to animal life in such a way that it is impossible to determine the exact line of demarcation, nor on which side thereof an intermediate form should lie. Thus, next after lifeless things in the upward scale comes the plant, and of plants one will differ from another as to its amount of apparent vitality.... Indeed, as we have just remarked, there is observed in plants a continuous scale of ascent towards the animal.... *Historia animalium*, VIII, 1. transl. DW Thompson, Oxford, 1910. (Clagett, 1955:67)

A prime variable in the distinction between forms was the possession of a soul. To Aristotle, there were several kinds of soul. The simpler forms, like the vegetative soul, motivated lower forms. Only humans had a soul capable of reason: only humanity could leave the realm of opinion to become capable of seeing the light; to rise to the realm of reason. Aristotle, and later the Greek physician Galen (c. 129–200 C.E.), actually dissected monkeys — probably *Macaca sylvanus*. They acknowledged the similarity in form such that the monkey was even used as the basis for human physiology and structure. Aristotle's teachings were incorporated into Church doctrine and therefore indisputable. Yet this morphological relationship did not suggest kinship over time, that is evolutionary connection. Bodies might look similar; the issue of the soul, and indeed the kind of soul made the difference between beings.

For Europeans, the time after the Fall of the Roman Empire (around 476 C.E.) marked a breakdown in communications and access to knowledge. The great libraries of the Ancient World, such as the one in Alexandria, Egypt, were burned, dispersed or off-limits, accessible only to members of the Church. Stories told by travellers were popular, and if the traveller was given to exaggeration, or recounted a story told by someone else who got it from a third party, so much the more interesting. Stories of monstrous human races were recounted far and wide (Friedman, 1981). Some of these races had no heads, but rather, eyes in the centre of the chest; or walked on their hands, or were dog-faced, or had long tails and lived in trees or caves. It is probable that these latter were at least inspired by observations or accounts of non-human primates (Friedman, 1981). Primates had been used earlier in Egypt and India as metaphors for deities; they were now metaphors for unknown humans from distant locations. Distinctions between human and non-human primates blurred with distance and age of account and were accepted in the guise of these monstrous groups at the fringes of the known world (Friedman, 1981).

These two metaphors, the ladder of life and the monstrous races, influenced the attitudes towards non-human primates. Aristotle's *Scala Naturae* was accepted and extended within the dogma of the Church, so that human was superseded by angels and finally, the deity, the Perfect form, the Source or Type. Examples of the Type were always poor tokens of it, and as humans were not God, so too, were those who resembled humans — primates — less than they. Humans had the soul that enabled them to strive to reach Perfection, but primates lacked the wherewithal (soul) to become more Perfect.

When knowing became formalized as Science in the 16th century and the secrets of the universe were explored, trade expanded (Rossabi, 1992) and technological inventions multiplied, the metaphor for the deity shifted to become the Great Clockmaker. Clocks are made with cogs and wheels, sprockets and rachets, and toys as well as other objects move, dance, whistle, in phantasmagoric evidence of creative genius. In similar fashion does the Great Clockmaker make the creatures of the planet. The exuberance that came from creating things that could simulate life forms was expressed in the attribution of machine characteristics to actual life forms. The grinding of their gears is evidence of the celestial movements that were conferred to them by the Creator as Machinist. Humans as creators, as thinking animals aware that they think, were, however, different to other machines. Personal knowledge that "I think" discriminated between human and animal as keenly as had the different levels of soul. The special attributes of soul had indeed become special attributes of mind. Incidently, but most importantly, the French thinkers who contributed so much to this picture, do not distinguish between 'soul' and 'mind': both take the noun "âme". A more technological age had replaced spiritual, unmeasureable soul with materialist, knowable mind. What made mind palpable was speech.

Since the time of Linnaeus (active 1750s), non-human primates were grouped with humans. From time to time, scholars suggested that apes were actually *Homo alalus* (humans minus language), but the general view through the 19th century was that despite the resemblance in form, there was a great barrier dividing us from them. But the image of the ape was growing. Novelists played with the idea of apes more courteous, charming and distinguished than contemporary 'civilized' Englishmen (e.g., Peacock). Attribution of human characteristics to an ape: knowledge, reason, and emotions (but, of course, not speech), was truly fictitious since there was a general lack of knowledge about the social behaviour of non-human primates and their capabilities. The point was to reiterate an old idea that "civilization" is only superficial trappings imposed on a better, unspoiled nature; the ape became the metaphor for pristine goodness.

INTEGRATION ONE

Themes that have so far been presented are threads of the fabric of modern-day primate studies. Knowledge of non-human primates precedes any sort of "scientific" enquiry. Monkeys are deities before they are subjects; they are mythopoeic forms to link 'animal' with 'divine'; they are models for human anatomy before there is primate taxonomy. Attitudes about them blend with romantic, literary or political motive to form statements bearing only coincidental resemblance to the real thing. Yet science as we know it is formed. Its strictures include the absorption of previous attitudes and metaphors. A materialist view divides all of nature along traditional rungs of the ladder, the divisions now based on 'mind' — a subject at the very beginning of definition and research.

The Modern Era Begins

Systematic studies of apes, however, began with psychological experiments, such as the ground-breaking studies of Kohler in the 1920s on caged *Pan troglodytes*. His findings were consistent with the great ladder: even genius chimps would perform at the mental age of very young human children. His studies confirmed the mental distance between chimp and human, and affirmed the need for terminology that reflected that distance. To be avoided was the egregious error of anthropomorphism. Originally intended in a theological sense, anthropomorphism means the attribution of human form to the Deity. After 1830, it was used for attribution of humanness to non-human animals. While a term, anthropopathy, exists to describe attribution of human feelings, thoughts and motivation to the Deity, anthropomorphic has come to cover that extension to animals as well. Anthropomorphism in this sense, was then, and still is considered a violation of the scientific perspective in European-derived, but not oriental behavioural science (Asquith, 1986). In summarizing his life's work, Kuo, himself Chinese, and an iconoclast amongst animal behaviourists, identified the nature of this non-European contrast in mental pursuit: "Both the American animal psychologists and the European ethologists have made two basic assumptions: the uniformity of nature (environment) and the uniformity of behaviour" (1967:14), and this error resides in epistemological limitations, as these researchers are:

> ...unable to free themselves from the bondage of the somewhat primitive and rather unfortunate Hegelian dialectical formulation, thesis and antithesis: mind vs. body, nature vs. nurture, innateness vs. learning, and so on (1967).

Psychology, as the study of mental abilities, was the locus of behavioural studies. Mentality is the quality or nature of mental action, whereas mentation is an attribute of the brain; it is mental action in itself, or the property of having mind. ('His mentality is keen' versus, 'is there mentation in the chimp?'). The distinction was not always followed, but the emphasis was on mentation in itself, extrapolated from the context of the organism. Psychology established norms of research consistent with the goals of science: to experimentally control a situation so that the variables involved could be tested for their contribution to the phenomenon under study. The first field primatologists were trained as psychologists and went into the field to gain perspective on a subject with the explicit intention to come back to the lab to study the phenomenon. In doing this they were adopting the anthropological design established nearly 100 years earlier. Furthermore, they were following the lead of ethologists like Lorenz and especially Tinbergen who had taught that studying subjects where they lived provided understanding of their life ways. In describing the structure of behavioural patterns of groups, the function, recent history and most importantly the evolutionary history of the pattern could be ascertained.

Ethology was the discipline that studied behaviour of animals and it did so with the assumption that behaviour is just another organ (Tinbergen, 1951). That meant that it was subject to the same rules of evolution as any other organ. Behaviour was taxonomically useful since it was species specific.

ANTHROPOLOGICAL PRIMATE STUDIES

This promising start to field studies went into a decline during the Second World War. It was expressly revived by anthropologists in the 1950s as a subject necessary to and legitimate within their domain. The reasoning was that such studies were cogent to an understanding of "man's cultural and social origins" (Hooton, 1954:187). "The New Physical Anthropology" was introduced by S. Washburn in 1951. It was 'new' because it focussed on the mechanism of human evolution, experimentation in studies of adaptation and the inclusion of genetics and population studies. Anthropological primatology was key to understanding human evolution, and its mandate was:

(1) to reconstruct human evolution
(2) as a model for human social processes.

Understanding the process of becoming human required knowing the antecedents, on the assumption that the behaviour of current non-human primates was closer to that of their ancestors and therefore underlay human behaviour, since their ancestors were our ancestors. The fact that each line has been independently seeking its fortunes for millions of years was not taken as relevant. Whether or not non-human primates could be used as models for humans has remained controversial (Tooby and Devore, 1987).

The father of modern primatology, Clarence Ray Carpenter, extended interest in non-human primates two ways: first, he went down the Scale of Nature and studied gibbons and howler monkeys. Secondly, he studied them in the field rather than the lab. Drawing from his training, he clearly wanted to avoid anthropomorphism in the study of non-human primates, and in order to avoid anecdotal reportage, he included statistical testing to ensure that observations were not chance phenomena. Findings from laboratory and field were both to be judged "in the scientific courts of appeal" by the criteria of "relevancy, adequacy, reliability, validity, and significance" (Carpenter, 1950:1008). Ethological notions of species specificity of behaviour went unquestioned: group size, social structure, diet, even interbirth interval were considered to be part and parcel of the species' profile. It would be several decades until these aspects were seen to be variable depending on history, personality and local circumstances. A decade later, methods had not changed substantially. Schaller was asked to compile the results (1965) from a poll of conference participants on how to go about studying non-human primates. A good study, he found, would include:

(1) An ecological survey...
(2) Detailed observations into the social life of a selected group...concentrating on obtaining the species' repertoire of behavior with quantitative data.
(3) ...experimental procedures, either in the field or the laboratory, to elucidate those points not readily clarified by observation alone. (1965:623)

At the same time, ethologist and mentor to the field, Niko Tinbergen (1963) was establishing the logic of how to study animal behaviour. The implications for methodology were inherent. Description is the first step, followed by a search for explanations of the behaviour described (Hinde, 1983). There are four logical types of explanation: (1) immediate causation, (2) development, (3) function, or (4) evolution. Robin Dunbar differentiates their meaning thusly:

> In asking why one monkey grooms another, we might be asking for an explanation in terms of: (1) the motivations or other physiological or behavioural factors that prompted it to groom another individual (a question about proximate causes); (2) the experiences it has had during its lifetime that prompt it to groom in a given way or to groom only certain individuals (a question about ontogeny or development); (3) the purpose being served by its grooming another individual (a question about function); and (4) the sequence of changes in behaviour

that led to the evolution of grooming in that species (a
question about evolutionary history). (1988:3)

The need to establish the level of inquiry had been seen as critically
important to the progress of biology a decade earlier (e.g., G. Williams,
1975). The contrasts between proximate (near; current) and ultimate (evolutionary) causation blurs however; what the animal does in the here and
now is considered to affect its reproductive history, and therefore evolutionary role. Hence proximate causes and evolutionary history are not
neatly distinguished.

The objective of early research had been base-line descriptions of
species, (inventories or *ethograms)* from which, eventually, general behavioural and evolutionary laws could be derived. Objectivity demanded a
vocabulary and a way of doing things; what the researcher was going to
be objective about was not the concern. Carpenter set out some of the
issues involved in the methodology that would satisfy this aim (1965:25).
Observation was the chief instrument — not hypothesis formation.
Observation however, had to be rigorously structured. Bias easily worked
its way into observation, even by mere movement of the observer's head
choosing to look at this, rather than that. Disturbance of the animals
would alter the results. A strict protocol would make observations more
replicable — a criterion of the scientific method. Documentation with
cameras, tape-recorders etc., increased reliability since the captured
images and sounds could be re-examined "forever". Inter-observer consistency was to be achieved, and repeated observations of behaviour were
to be made. Note that a major assumption here is that the behaviour will
repeat: observers can return and see the same behaviour again (same
players, same stimuli, same observers, same context). That is, that behaviour, like clockwork machines of an earlier time, is 'lawful', following patterns according to knowable principles. Non-human primates were to be
studied in order to elucidate history and process of the human condition.
Interest in social evolution encouraged research into the group as social
environment.

But the methodologies employed were not considered sufficiently rigorous. Jeanne Altmann (1974) proposed a set of instructions on how to
properly study primates. A mathematician, she had studied baboons on
the open plains of Amboseli (Altmann and Altmann, 1970). She labelled
the observation of behaviour as currently practised *"ad libitum"* sampling,
which means 'according to desire', suggesting that the vagaries of interest, not rigorous protocol determined when a note would be taken. She

affirmed the quantitative nature of all behavioural studies, grounding the methods in the tradition of positivism. This early 19th-Century philosophy argued that the methods of natural science should and could be extended to social issues and phenomena.

Altmann's critique had a major impact. Subsequent to its publication, all primate studies followed one or another of the several techniques she described. Over the years, however, the distinctions between sampling methods have faded, and most researchers now use some variant of choosing a particular animal as informant (the focus animal), or scanning the entire group on fixed time intervals for whatever is the subject of interest (see e.g., Paterson, 1992b). In addition, it is generally acknowledged that visibility and not methodology determines what can be recorded, so that "opportunistic" rather than "ad libitum" is the more appropriate term. This is not just a casual distinction. 'Opportunistic' contrasts the natural experiment with the lab experiment. The verbiage in which even our methods are couched reflects the need to neutralize language in the pursuit of objectivity — the stated goal of science.

THE SEARCH FOR NEUTRAL LANGUAGE

Couching description in terms that would be used by humans of or about other humans is considered an illegitimate form of discourse. Given the pre-existing determination that non-human primates are 'lower' animals on a scale where humans are the top, utilizing terms appropriate for humans distorts the statement about their 'lower' relatives. Even when primatologists were talking about cultural processes, that is, about the social development of patterns of behaviour unique to a local group, the terminology sought was chosen because it had no human connotations.

"Conformity" was introduced by K.R.L. Hall (Hall, 1968) because he considered it more neutral a term to describe the regulators of primate social behaviour. It is parallel to rules, regulations, laws and custom in human societies. The parallel term 'specia' coined by Imanishi in Japan (Asquith, 1986) did not gain currency in North America and Europe, probably because the term is morphologically and phonetically too close to 'species'. "Dam" and "infant" were introduced to replace mother and baby to avoid seeing within their relationship bonds of attachment parallel to ours. "Love", that is attachment or bonding to the mother, was empirically studied first by Harlow, later by his co-workers and students because such a phenomenon could not be referred to or accepted in the domain of non-human animals without objective proof. It is still

87

illegitimate to speak of 'love' in non-human primates although 'bonding' is acceptable.

Negative anthropomorphism (or speciesism), the non-attribution or withholding of traits to non-human primates when these assuredly exist, has not been as carefully constrained. We need to avoid overzealousness in attempting to be neutral lest we obscure abilities that exist in other animals. The search for a neutral language has been uneven; sexist language has skewed our interpretation of events. A significant example of this came in a discussion of baboon behaviour, where Hall and DeVore (1965) noted that males form *coalitions*, but a few pages later, females *gang-up*. While the term, *alloparental* behaviour, supersedes mother-care or father-care, 'aunting behaviour' — a term coined by Thelma Rowell in the early 1970s — is still used, although 'fostering' is preferred. Clearly, the only language available is our own (Fedigan, 1982); clearly, we cannot reach past the boundaries of our selves and cultures to experience *in the first person* what another person — let alone non-human primate — is feeling. Where the boundary between 'human animal' and 'non-human animal' is not distinct, as for example, in Shintoism or Buddhism, this dilemma is said not to exist (Asquith, 1986). To the European derived individual, however, this is the existentialist dilemma.

PROBLEMS WITH PARADIGMS

The tension represented by 'opportunistic' and 'ad libitum' is that between language and number: a proverbial Abel and Cain. Language is taken to be imperfect but personal; number is valued as pure reason and objective. The cults of number are legion: from Pythagoras to the Kabbala, the mysticism of number is pervasive. So too is the mythology of number, which holds that to code objects and events numerically, and to manipulate them in formulas, removes those objects and events from the plane of emotion, and thereby brings them a step up towards reason. In truth, however, does one feel less for the lab monkey called "R2D2" than if it is called "George"?

Post-modern textual analysis has demonstrated that all writing is 'text'. A scientific document is no less a mental creation than a poem; its use of language, its discourse, no less a function of the writer — gender, age, ethnic identity, etc. — than is polemic. While we understand "science" to be a special activity of mind, bound by rigorous constraints to ensure validity and replicatability, it is nonetheless an activity of mind. What to describe and how to analyse are choices lying within the researcher, and are based on scientific values current in his/her culture, and even his particular moment (Feyerabend, 1975).

The current paradigm in biology and animal behaviour, termed *Sociobiology* to describe the extension of natural selection to processes of societies, paradoxically uses a form of discourse that has heretofore been considered forbidden in discussing animal motivation. Analyses use terms heavily laden with contemporary cultural meaning. Terms like 'deceit', 'machiavellian intelligence', 'kidnapping', or 'altruism' are used to describe non-human behaviour. Protestations are made that terminology is only metaphor, and not to be taken literally. Nevertheless such words bring with them their symbolic impact. Moreover, negative terms are permissible but positive terms are considered anthropomorphic (Fedigan, 1982). Monkeys may 'cheat' or 'sneak' but not love or help. The notion of a society based on mutual assistance is explicitly denied since the society is the locus for competition between individuals striving to promulgate their own genes at the expense of another member — the more so the greater the kin distance.

However, cooperation has been recognized in baboons and chimpanzees (Strum, 1981; Teleki, 1981). Most recently, the reproductive system of callitrichids, for example *Callithrix jacchus*, is apparently based on cooperation, where the single breeding female receives the cooperation of others in the raising of her multiple births (Abbott et al., 1993). In fact, cooperation is undoubtedly at the basis of the origin of multicellular life, as Margulis has amply demonstrated (e.g., Margulis and Sagan, 1986). Currently, arguments are being made that suggest that the nature of non-human primate life depends on 'cultural' processes — whether these are termed 'traditions' (Burton, 1972; 1992), 'culture' (McGrew, 1992) or 'specia' (Asquith, 1986). Reynolds (1986:56) argues that monkeys lack culture because "There is no book to which monkeys can refer for guidance in social situations, nor is there a body of laws that gives clear indications of when behaviour has to be punished." What he neglects here, however, is that it is only when enormous amounts of variation on a situation exist that laws require codification: each member in a small society can know all other members, and all regulations pertaining. And there *are* regulations. Rules of conduct are precisely those described in analyses of social organization.

Social behaviour is the outcome of the network of interactions between members of a group. The actions of the group members are the result of the individual development and personal history of each member. This is the opposite of a mechanistic view, which sees animal behaviour as the outcome of the cogs and wheels turning (Singer, 1994, 1981). Acceptance of the complexity and subtlety of primate social behaviour requires a re-thinking of methodology appropriate to study the beings that generate these societies. Since behaviour accordingly is not mechanically located in the genes, but rather in the capacity for storage, recall, fusion and innovation of memories (Burton, 1992; Seyfarth and Cheney, 1992), it seems appropriate to develop methods that integrate rather than atomize, that recognize context and the individual in the context. Is the social behaviour of non-human primates, then, restricted to quantitative analysis?

Integration Two

There are different ways of looking at things; of finding out why and how they operate as they do. Underlying the different ways (methods) are philosophies that sculpt the methods. The development of social science is a relatively new phenomenon. At its origins was the positivist impetus to develop a science equivalent in robusticity to those sciences that investigate physical reality. The development of statistics in the same period (late 18th early 19th centuries), supported the view that behaviour could also be described and analysed objectively through the conversion of events to numbers. Quantification would make inquiries about social behaviour objective and congenial to scientific inquiry. The early promise of Positivism was not realized. There was recognition that the number of variables that could pertain to a single behavioural event was enormous. In addition, there was increasing awareness of the ineffable — the unknowablity of phenomena. It is clear how much H and how much O must be joined in what ratio for water to be the result. In social behaviour, the factors themselves cannot be identified. Husserl's reaction, termed Phenomenology, argued that because the variables pertaining to events and activities were unidentifiable, quantification was inappropriate for the study of human thought and action.

Scholars in the humanities suggested that *perspective* of observation profoundly affected knowledge of it. The observer or "interpreter" accepts that research actually begins with what one is and already knows. The observer or "interpreter" applies the accumulation of experience and understanding ("Pre-understanding") as s/he engages the problem. There is consequently a loss of "the aura of objective validity" (Stent, 1985). The caution used in carefully focussing the research and choosing the methods of gathering information, are balanced with the sure knowledge that the data gathered is relative to the moment, the location, the question selected and one's self. Hermeneutics, which arose as biblical interpretation, emphasized that looking **at** is not the same as looking **from**, and that to truly understand a phenomenon, the perspective must shift away from the viewer to that of the individual viewed. Hermeneutical analysis means appreciating the context in which "implicit meaning is embedded before one can uncover hidden meanings in any of its parts" (Stent, 1985). This, of course, presumes that the one viewed is sentient—thinks and processes thoughts as well as feels. By the 1970s phenomenology and hermeneutics were being discussed in the context of non-human primates, because field workers in the 60s were presenting data that confirmed the sentience of their subjects.

METHODOLOGIES

Researchers need to establish credibility. They do this on the basis of (1) their background knowledge of the subject matter as revealed in literature review; (2) by clearly focussing the research question; (3) by the methods that they employ, which assure the audience that while the subjects may not be controlled, the subject matter has been. 'Quantitative' and 'qualitative' research techniques are approaches to research questions. Typically, quantitative research is identified with the "scientific method", a series of steps generally listed as:

(1) definition of the research problem: establishing the hypothesis
(2) producing operational definitions
(3) designing research methodology
(4) gathering data
(5) analysing data: testing the hypothesis
(6) acceptance of [go to (7)] or rejection of [go to (1)] the hypothesis
(7) writing the report

Scientific method depends on statistical treatment of data for verification as it assumes that "...events and statistical regularities are fitted into a causal network..." (Pratt, 1989:105). The goals include testing hypotheses and being able to generate predictions on how phenomena operate. The subject material is broken down into constituent parts with which the researcher can deal, that is, which can be controlled, or more importantly, experimentally tested. Statistics supposes that the world is divisible into categorizeable units; that the definition of these categories is isomorphic (the same as; natural) with the phenomenon under study, and that there-fore patterns of association between these categories and populations as defined by the researcher, can be measured. However, the causal network developed from these associations, is "...largely an abstraction" (Pratt, 1989:105).

Clearly, a researcher would wish to have an analytic description that corresponds to the phenomenon under study; *reconstructing* behaviour from statistical inferences may unwittingly, and even undetectably, falsi-fy the picture (Pratt, 1989). Researchers note the enormous variability in performance in experimental tests as a function of time of day, sampling procedure, or ineffables (Tartabini and Simpson, 1986). The inconve-nience of non-human primate *processing* of information produces 'noise' in the system. Behaviour is irrational and less amenable to statistical pro-cedure that is based on fair chance. Primate groups are typically small — below the requisite size to which normal distribution assumptions easily apply. Thelma Rowell, an uncontested doyenne of primate studies, notes in this regard that "... primates never come in large enough numbers to be able to validate an assumption of a normal distribution, the people who study them were forced to recognize individuality... (Rowell, 1991:255). The impact an individual makes on a society has major consequences: if she is the only breeding female, as in some callithrichids, the genetic information of the group is skewed in her direction; if she is an innovator, a new tradition will add to the repertoire of information in the group. Marshall and Rossman (1989:147) address this issue when they state:

> Positivist notions of reliability assume an unchanging uni-verse, where inquiry could, quite logically, be replicated. This assumption of an unchanging social world is in direct contrast to the qualitative/interpretive assumption that the social world is always changing and the concept of replication is itself problematic.

How wise indeed was the Greek philosopher, Anaximander, (born about 610 bce) who noted that we cannot step into the same river twice because the waters are always rushing in upon us.

In a recent paper (1992a), Paterson attempts to model the relationship of genes, behaviour and culture in non-human primates. Genes produce proteins that form structures becoming physiology. Behaviour, however, is not reducible to biochemical process, as biochemcial imperatives can be overcome or ignored in favour of social requirements. In a CBC film on baboons, Strum shows a male who 'sacrifices' a sexual and politically important relationship with a "dominant" female for caring for a "friend's" infant (Strum, 1992). His consternation is evident; his choice considerable; his motivation beyond biochemical explanation. The ineffable nature of an individual, however, derives from its reactions to some situation based on its personal history and the history of its social interactions. Schaller once remarked (Schaller, 1987:xi):

> But to interpret another culture, one which cannot speak and which leaves no artifacts, requires more than skill with vital statistics and glib scientific notions.... (ix)
> If a scientist takes too much vocal pride in objectivity, beware. Observing is subjective: the animal described is only an illusion created out of a personal perspective, based on which questions are raised, which facts written down, which information ignored. ...asking different questions will create a different animal. The conspicuous, easily described behaviour is turned into statistics; the difficult but no less real behaviour tends to be ignored or considered irrelevant. To describe another being takes not merely reason and fact, but also empathy and intuition.

What methodology is amenable to the analysis of so complex a phenomenon? In the past several years, there has been a growth and extension of what are termed 'qualitative' techniques. These are methods of gathering and analysing data that depend on context. Long used in social/cultural anthropology, qualitative techniques rely on observation of a phenomenon within its setting because it is the entire context that lends meaning to that phenomenon. Male care amongst the macaques of Gibraltar and North Africa, for example, is concerned with nurturance of the young. The enactment of this behaviour, however, has meaning only within the context of the local group where the development of the pattern, its expression and its social significance as a tradition is defined (Burton, 1972; Burton and Bick, 1972.)

In qualitative research, the observer strives for context so that the phenomena under investigation are not "adulterated" (Bryman, 1988:58). S/he is more concerned with the 'natural experiment' than a controlled experiment (Bernard, 1988). The researcher avoids imposing his/her own conceptual viewpoint on the social processes under consideration. While research is grounded in theory, the open-ended format of research permits the retention of context and holism. Bryman (1988:61) summarizes the characteristics of qualitative methods as:

(1) seeing through the eyes of the subjects
(2) describing — forming a verbal picture
(3) retaining the context, ensuring holism that is "An undertaking to examine social entitities in their entirety" (p.64)
(4) emphasizing process, e.g., social life is processual
(5) flexibility and lack of structure (but not of rigour) in research design
(6) rejecting a priori theory and concepts, working inductively, from the material to theory.

Malinowski encouraged anthropologists to get down from the veranda to mix with the natives and developed a method called (1) "participant observation" to reflect that knowing a people and their customs can only be achieved by participating in their realities. Reality, or meaning, is constructed from the interpretations of individual members of the society and their interactions: a fear vocalization, for instance, derives its meaning from the context. It may be a reaction to a snake, or it could be deception of some fellow group member (Cheney and Seyfarth, 1991). A monkey mounts another: the meaning depends on who mounts whom (is the mounter, for example, a male? an adult?). Is the behaviour reproductive, or reassurance or dominace?

Some techniques of qualitative methods resemble quantitative methods in their attempt to control the research situation: (2) interviews and (3) questionnaires are two such methods. (4) Content analysis, which is concerned with the meaning or style of doing something, is a technique found in both quantitative and qualitative approaches as well. Other methods in qualitative research follow an open-ended format. These include: (5) the case study, a tight focus on a given individual or situation, (6) proxemics, the analysis of the use of space, by a group and by its members, (7) kinesics, body movements and the meanings of them, (8) historical analysis including documentatation about the society under study, (9) life history, a form of the case study more concerned with tracing the individual over time, (10) unobtrusive measures (inferences drawn from materials related to activity, such as fruit cores beneath a tree denoting that this fruit has been eaten from this tree) (Marshall and Rossman, 1989). The purpose of these methods is to avoid the contrivance, the manipulation, of the experimental situation (Bryman, 1988: Marshall and Rossman, 1989; Harré in Bryman, 1988; Berg, 1989; Bernard, 1988), because, as Rowell (1967) noted, interference with or constraining the subjects, affects them. Rhesus macaque or baboon mothers usually carry their older offspring dorsally. In caged situations, however, Rowell observed that they carried these older offspring ventrally, because cage-door hatches were too low. Consequently, the research result, while having the appearance of verity, of objectivity, even of replicatability, may be far from the actual expression of a behaviour.

Not all of the enumerated methods are appropriate in the study of non-human primates. Clearly, those methods that rely on the special properties of humanness, especially language, cannot be utilized with non-human primates other than Great Apes. These include numbers (2), (3), (1) and to some extent (4) above. Life history (8) has been used in conjunction with (2) and (3) when seeking background and history about non-human primates and their locale. Recently, tests on individuals, such as personality tests, have been successfully extended to the Great Apes, even in the wild (Buirski and Plutchik, 1991). Content analysis (4), however, might have its utility in a study, for example of grooming, where style, duration, frequency, and donation of the grooming are the content assumed to have meaning that can be interpreted. Grooming amongst barbary macaques in Gibraltar, for instance, varied for duration, frequency and style depending on the relationship between the participants: you groom individuals you do not like as well more often, but closer individuals longer. A rough massage type of groom is sought by some whereas others prefer those groomers who will do a gentle hair-part and pick.

The case study (5), is in fact, a primary form of primate study. In primatology, it is called a "focal animal study" (Altmann, 1974; Paterson 1992b) wherein a particular member of the group is followed extensively; is seen (in anthropological terms) as "ego" so that the point of view is shifted to that animal's perspective. Where possible, the animal's life history (9) is included or forms background to a study. Proxemics (6) and kinesics (7) are useful techniques in ascertaining relationships between members, especially of captive groups (e.g., Hornshaw, 1992, 1985). In confined conditions, where ecological variables are limited, the use of space or the individual's own movements reflect directly on the animal's choice of where to locate itself with reference to those constraints. A group knows something about the health and perhaps even self concept of another by how s/he carries her/his head or tail, the speed of the gait and the like. Wherever possible, background history (8) (including here, (2) and (3)) of the particular group should be documented. Since groups change over time, sampling at any given moment will alter the researcher's view of patterns; the greater the time depth, the more the sample of observations can be evaluated. The landscape, after a typhoon, will alter resources and change routes previously taken. Group structure amongst *Alouatta palliata* at Cano Palma in Costa Rica, for example, changed radically when a neighbouring landlord cut down a number of his trees, severely restricting movement through that terrain and grouping patterns. Similarly, in Kowloon amongst the synanthropic hybrid macaques, alterations to the major road through the reserve in the late 1980s brought into visual contact and conflict individuals who had been able to avoid each other by careful navigation through the forests in that crowded area. At the same time, arboreal pathways between parts of the range were temporarily eliminated, altering resource availability, and therefore dietary patterns.

Non-human primates too are subject to their personal and group histories. The absence, for example, of a single animal from a group can significantly alter its behaviour. Demographic factors, and therefore biological factors, change due to such historical vagaries (Dunbar, 1987). The loss of one animal may affect grooming or foraging patterns, dominance interactions or alliances, and impact on individual members of the group.

Qualitative research depends on drawing inferences from observations, as with technique (10), Unobtrusive measures. Plant remains beneath a tree in the rain forest at Cano Palma gave my students and I testimonial to the fact that a group of elusive spider monkeys had been feeding in this location when that nance tree was in fruit. While exact detail of which member by age and sex ate what part of the plant is not available, the evidence at least suggests constituents of the diet. Fecal remains on the tops of peaks in the mountains of Huashan, Guangxi gave two students testimonial to the fact that a group of elusive leaf eating monkeys (*Presbytis francoisi leucocephalus*) had spent time at those remote locations. While exact details of which member by age and sex had been present was not available, the evidence at least suggested the range of the group.

The research questions establish the *protocol* to be followed. The protocol includes not only the methods to be employed, but the sequence (Spradley, 1980) or priorities to be given occurrences, events, phenomena and observations during the "continuous clock" notation. The protocol establishes what daily information must always be gathered: date, weather, observer, duration of observation, contact hours, locations etc. If the special interest is sibling relationships, then during the course of note-taking, any such interaction takes precedence over any other activity occurring. The protocol may require the interposition of interval (or Time Allocation) sampling to ensure equalization of data acquisition on certain activities, individuals or locations. It provides the discipline, for example, to sample every ten minutes on the hour, recording whatever X is doing; or what every visible member is doing; or whatever is going on at X location. These samples can be used to check against observation bias and to ensure that the observer is alert to recording everything required by the research question and protocol.

The logic of Time Allocation is that by sampling representative acts (for example eating, playing), the percentage **times** an activity is done can be substituted for the percentage of **all** time spent in those activities. A constraint on Time Allocation is sampling a "...sufficiently large number of representative acts... " (Bernard, 1988:281). This number is hard to determine. In a primate's life, would that be eating or playing over five years? 10 years? The usual 18 months? In team work, where the members have been trained in a similar fashion, the protocol assigns tasks to each team member so that, e.g., one may record while another dictates; or one may video according to the direction of another; or each will observe the same activity to later attempt to ascertain what really happened. The protocol also provides the researcher's daily cycle.

Returning from the field is time for thought, transcription, reflection and preliminary analysis. To minimize recording bias, a chart that records entries by time against activity, (or individual or location) assists in evaluating whether or not the allocation of Time Samples is skewed. The absence of any tick marks under the category "play" or "juvenile" for samples taken from 10 a.m. to noon, would alert the observer to ask "am I not picking upon everything? or Why is this activity/age group not represented? The daily Log is entered; foci and activities for the following day recorded and the personal Diary written. Ancillary tools such as video, which ensures 'verbatim' recording of events, (although of a limited frame), enhance triangulation. Context is assured, and re-examination of observations can ensure precision. How many animals were really seen? Did the mother nip the infant before or after she heard a squeal? Was that a directed yawn?

"Triangulation" is a term reflecting the complementary use of quantitative and qualitative techniques. Derived from navigational science, (Denzin, 1978 and Rossman and Wilson, 1985), it brings together several sources of data to bear on a single point (Marshall and Rossman, 1989), and refers to the use of more than one method of investigation (Bernard, 1988; Bryman, 1988). In the early 1980s, Bargar and Duncan (1982) demonstrated that research is fundamentally nonlinear, despite the illusion created by the formalization of research in, for example, journal articles where research is presented as logical. At base, research must be intuitive (Bargar and Duncan, 1982) to describe nature itself, which is nonlinear (e.g., Berge et al., 1986).

This combining of research techniques is natural to and productive in primate studies. Recording observations using the technique of the continuous running clock with Time Allocation (Bernard, 1988) sampling at specific intervals, is one such combination. This permits the preservation of the context while superimposing a discipline. The day's field observations are transcribed onto computer where possible, and preselected categories of information (grooming, or feeding, or socialization) are extracted into appropriate databases or spreadsheets for subsequent statistical analysis. That is, material inherently quantifiable will be treated that way: how many times did Popeye groom Fatty? How many thrusts to ejaculation for the [ul]*M. fascicularis*? for the *M. thibetana*? For the hybrids? What part of the Machilus or fig tree is eaten? By whom? When? and at the same time, material that gives the texture and quality of their life is retained. What was Brit's impact on the long-tails' feeding behaviour? Why does Popeye excite a grooming frenzy from all females in Fatty's group irrespective of age?

Integration Three

In this paper I have traced the search for objective techniques in the study of non-human primates. Increasing awareness of the intricacies of non-human primate social existence warrants searching for techniques that satisfy the subject matter. Departure from forms of research that reduce the complex web of interactions to isolated threads has a long history in Anthropology. It is time for a return to qualitative methods and to holism in the study of primate social behaviour.

REFERENCES

Abbott DH, Barrett J, and George LM (1993) Comparative aspects of the social suppression of reproduction in female marmosets and tamarins. In AB Rylands (ed.): *Marmosets and Tamarins: Sytematics, Behaviour, and Ecology.* Oxford: Oxford University Press. pp. 152-162.

Altmann SA Altmann J (1970) *Baboon Ecology. African Field Research.* Basel: S. Karger.

Altmann J (1974) Observational learning: Sampling methods. *Behaviour* 49:227-267.

Asquith PJ (1986) Anthropomorphism and the Japanese and western traditions in primatology. In JG Else and PC Lee (eds.): *Primate Ontogeny, Cognition and Social Behaviour*. Selected Proceedings of the Tenth Congress of the International Primatological Society. Nairobi. Vol. 3. pp. 61-71.

Bargar RR, and Duncan JK (1982) Cultivating creative endeavour in doctoral research. *J. of Higher Educat*. 53(1):1-31.

Bernard HR (1988) *Research Methods in Cultural Anthropology*. London: Sage

Berg B (1989) *Qualitative Research Methods for the Social Sciences*. Alyn and Bacon: Boston.

Berge P, Pomeau Y, and Vidal C (1986) *Order Within Chaos: Towards a Deterministic Approach to Turbulence*. New York: Wiley.

Bryman A (1988) Quantity and Quality in Social Research. *Contemp. Soc. Res. Series:18*. Unwin Hyman: London.

Buirski P, and Plutchik R (1991) Measurement of deviant behavior in a Gombe chimpanzee: Relation to later behavior. *Primates* 32(2):207-211.

Burnett J, Lord Monboddo (1967) *Of the Origin and Progress of Language*. Menston, English Scholars Press. *English Linguistics, 1500-1800; A collection of Facsimile Reprints, no.48*.

Burton FD (1972) The Integration of biology and behavior in the socialization of Macaca sylvana of Gibraltar. In F Poirier (ed.): *Primate Socialization*. New York: Random House. pp. 29-62.

Burton FD (1977) Ethology and the development of sex and gender identity in non-human primates. *Acta Biotheoretica* 26(1):1-18.

Burton FD (1990) Handspan. In T Corrigan and S Hoppe (eds). *Animals and Women. Vol II. And a Deer's Ear, Eagle's Song and Bear's Grace*. San Francisco, Cleis Publications.

Burton FD (1992) The social group as information unit: Cognitive behaviour, social process. In F.D.Burton (ed)., *Social Processes and Mental Abilities in Non-human Primates*. Lewiston, New York: Mellen, pp. 31-60.

Burton FD, and Bick MJ (1972) A drift in time can define a deme: the Implications of tradition drift in primate societies for hominid evolution. *J. Hum. Evol*. 1:53-59.

Carpenter CR (1950) General plans and methodology for field studies of the naturalistic behavior of animals. *New York Acad. Sci. Annals* 51:1006-1008.

Carpenter CR (1965) The howlers at Barro, Colorado Island. In I De Voie (ed.): *Primate Behavior*. New York: Holt, Rinehart, Winston.

Cheney DL, and Seyfarth RM (1991) Truth and deception in animal communication. In CA Ristau (ed). *Cognitive Ethology: The Minds of Other Animals*. New York: Lawrence Erlbaum Assoc., pp. 243-254.

Clagett M (1955) *Greek Science in Antiquity*. New York: Collier.

Denzin NK (1978) *The Research Act: A Theoretical Introduction to Sociological Methods*, 2nd ed. New York: McGraw Hill.

Dunbar RIM (1987) Demography and reproduction. In BB Smuts, DL Cheney, RM Seyfarth, RW Wrangham and TT Strushaker (eds.): *Primate Societies*. University of Chicago Press: Chicago, pp. 240-249.

Dunbar RIM (1988) *Primate Social Systems*. Ithaca, New York: Comstock Publishing.

Fedigan L (1982) *Primate Paradigms: Sex Roles and Social Bonds*. Eden Press: Montreal.

Feyerabend P (1975) *Against Method. Outline of an Anarchistic Theory of Knowledge*. Verso: London.

Friedman JB (1981) *The Monstrous Races in Medieval Art and Thought*. Cambridge, MA: Harvard Univ. Pres.

Hall KRL (1968) Social learning in monkeys. In PC Jay (ed.): *Primates: Studies in Adaptation and Variability*. New York: Holt, Rinehart, Winston, pp. 383-397.

Hall KRL, and De Vore I (1965) Baboon social behavior. In DeVore I (ed). *Primate Behavior*. New York: Holt, Rinehart, Winston, pp. 53-110.

Hinde R (1983) A conceptual framework. In Hinde, R. [ed]. *Primate Social Relationships:An Integrated Approach*. Sinauer, Sunderland: MA., pp. 1-7.

Hooton E (1954) The importance of primate studies in anthropology. *Hum. Biol* 26(3):179-188.

Hornshaw S (1985) Proximity behaviour in a captive group of lion-tailed macaques (Macaca silenus). In Heltne, PG [ed]., *The Lion-Tailed Macaques: Status and Conservation*. New York: Alan R. Liss, pp. 269-292.

Hornshaw S (1992) Social behaviour in bounded space: Epistemological issues in producing the texts and textuality of primate behaviour. In FD Burton (ed.): *Social Processes and Mental Abilities in Non-human Primates*. Lewiston, New York: Mellen, pp. 109-128.

Kohler W (1925) *The Mentality of the Apes*. London: Routledge and Kegan Paul. Reprint ed. New York: Liveright [1976].

Kummer H (1971) Kummer H (1971) *Primate Societies. Group Techniques of Ecological Adaptation*. Chicago: Aldine.

Kuo Zing-yang (1967) *The Dynamics of Behavior Development*. New York: Random House.

Margulis L, and Sagan D (1986) *Microcosmos: Four Billion Years of Evolution from our Microbial Ancestors*. New York: Summit Books.

Marshall C, and Rossman GB (1989) *Designing Qualitative Research*. London: Sage.

McGrew WC (1992) *Chimpanzee Material Culture: Implications for Human Evolution*. Cambridge: Cambridge Univ. Press.

Paterson JD (1992a) An alternative view: Behaviour as a multi-causal strategy for survival. In FD Burton (ed.): *Social Processes and Mental Abilities in Non-human Primates*. Lewiston, New York: Mellen, pp. 129-182.

Paterson JD (1992b) *Primate Behavior: An Exercise Workbook*. Illinois: Waveland Press.

Peacock TL (1896) *Melincourt: or Sir Oran Haut-ton*. Macmillan: London.

Plato, The Dialogues of Plato. Vol. I. *The Republic. Book VII*. pp. 773-800. Transl. B. Jowett. New York: Random House [1937].

Pratt G (1989) Quantative techniques and humanistic-historical materialist perspectives. In A Kobayashi and S Mackenzie (eds.): *Remaking Human Geography*. Boston: Unwin Hyman, pp. 101-115.

Reynolds, V (1986) Primate social thinking. In JG Else and PC Lee (eds.): *Primate*

Ontogeny, Cognition and Social Behaviour: The Argument from Animals to Man. Cambridge: Cambridge University Press, pp. 53-60.

Rossabi, M (1992) *Voyage from Xanadu: Rabban Sauma and the First Journey from China to the West.* Tokyo: Kodansha Int.

Rossman GB, and Wilson BL (1985) Numbers and words: Combining quantitative and qualitative methods in a single large-scale evaluation study. *Eval. Rev.* 9(5):627-643.

Rowell TE (1967) Variability in the social organization of primates. In D Morris (ed). *Primate Ethology.* Chicago: Aldine. pp. 219-235.

Rowell TE (1991) What can we say about social structure? In *The Development and Integration of Behaviour.* P Bateson (ed.) Cambridge: Cambridge University Press. pp. 255-270.

Schaller G (1987) Foreword. In S Strum *Almost Human.* New York: Random House. pp. ix-xiii.

Schaller GB (1965) Appendix: Field procedures. In I DeVore (ed.) *Primate Behavior: Field Studies of Monkeys and Apes.* New York: Holt, Rinehart and Winston, pp. 623-629.

Seyfarth RM, and Cheney DL (1992) Meaning and mind in monkeys. *Sci. Amer.* Dec. pp. 122-128.

Singer P (ed.) (1994) *The Expanding Circle: Ethics and Sociobiology.* Oxford: Clarendon Press.

Singer P (1994) *The Great Ape Project: Equality Beyond Humanity.* New York: St. Martin's Press.

Spradley JP (1980) *Participant Observation.* New York: Holt, Rinehart, Winston.

Stent G (1985) Hermenutics and the analysis of complex biological systems. In D Depew and BH Weber (eds.): *Evolution at a Crossroad: The New Biology and The New Philosophy of Science.* Cambridge: MIT Press. pp. 209-226.

Strum S (1981) Processes and products of change: baboon predatory behavior at Gilgil, Kenya. In RSO Harding and G Teleki (eds.): *Omnivorous Primates: Gathering and Hunting in Human Evolution.* New York: Columbia Univ. Press, pp. 255-302.

Strum S (1992) The Pumphouse Gang. *The Nature of Things,* CBC Productions, Toronto. 60 mins.

Tartabini A, and Simpson MJA (1986) The use of confidence intervals in arguments from individual cases: Maternal rejection and infant social behaviour in small groups of rhesus monkeys. In JG Else and PC Lee (eds.): *Primate Ontogeny, Cognition and Social Behaviour. Selected Proceedings of the Tenth Congress of the International Primatological Society.* Nairobi. Vol. 3.

Teleki G (1981) The Omnivorous diet and eclectic feeding habits of chimpanzees in Gombe National Park, Tanzania. In RSO Harding and G Teleki (eds.): *Omnivorous Primates: Gathering and Hunting in Human Evolution.* New York: Columbia Univ. Press, pp. 303-343.

Thomas EM (1993) *The Hidden Life of Dogs.* Boston: Houghton Mifflin Co.

Tinbergen N (1951) *The Study of Instinct.* NY: Oxford Univ. Press.

Tinbergen N (1963) On aims and methods of ethology. *Z. Tierpsychol.* 20:410-33.

Tooby J, and DeVore I (1987) The reconstruction of hominid behavioral evolution through strategic modeling. In W Kinzey (ed.): *The Evolution of Human*

Behavior: Primate Models. NY: SUNY Press. pp. 183-237.

Washburn SL (1951) *The New Physical Anthropology*. Trans. of the New York Acad. of Sci.13:298-304.

Williams GC (1975) *Sex and Evolution*. Princeton: Princeton Univ. Press.

5

The Physical Anthropology of Menopause

Linda Marie Fedigan and Mary S.M. Pavelka

Menopause is fundamentally distinct from the reproductive senescence that has been described for other primate females. Three characteristics make it unique to the human female: it is universal, it occurs halfway through the maximum lifespan of the species, and, as a form of reproductive senescence it is highly age-specific, occurring at approximately age 50 in all known populations. Menopause is not a recent historical phenomenon or simply an artifact of modernization. As a species universal showing little variation across contemporary populations, it must be understood in evolutionary terms. Supporters of the "grandmother hypothesis" explain menopause as an adaptive feature in itself, whereas others see menopause as a by-product of increased lifespan in Homo sapiens.

INTRODUCTION

In recent years, menopause has been increasingly examined from clinical, social, and biological perspectives. Physical anthropologists have an approach to menopause that is at once unique and diverse, as it incorporates primatological, historical, cross-cultural, and evolutionary data. While many physical anthropologists are interested in menopause, it is clear that they do not share one interpretation with which all agree, and it is common to find confident yet contradictory statements in the literature. For example, menopause has been described on the one hand as an illness, but on the other hand simply as a developmental process. It is also sometimes described as a unique human characteristic, and at other times as one shared by the other primates; as a recent historical phenomenon, and as a distant evolutionary one; as a primary adaptation, and as a secondary by-product. In this paper, we will argue that menopause is a developmental process unique to humans (i.e., not shared by the other primates), that goes back in time at least to the origins of our species, *Homo sapiens*, and that resulted secondarily from the selection for a longer and longer lifespan during the course of human evolution.

In this paper, we provide an overview of the menopause literature in physical anthropology in order to give introductory students a common base of knowledge on this topic. We will be stressing three characteristics of menopause that make it a unique phenomenon in the life history of the human female: its universality (virtually every woman who survives into her sixth decade will experience menopause); its age-specificity (an average age of 50 years has been widely reported for menopause in many different populations); and its relative timing in the overall life course (menopause occurs approximately half way through the maximum lifespan of the species). Four major questions are addressed:

First, what is menopause? To answer this question, we begin by defining the phenomenon as well as a variety of relevant terms, including climacteric, premenopause, perimenopause, postmenopause, reproductive senescence, lifespan and life expectancy. Next, the physiological basis of menopause is briefly described.

Second, is menopause a uniquely human phenomenon, or is it shared by species of alloprimates (i.e., nonhuman primate species)? A number of physiological studies of captive primates have searched for the existence of menopause in Old World monkeys and apes. We examine this evidence and also the meagre reports from field studies, and we attempt to distinguish between menopause as it occurs in the human female, and the general reproductive senescence that has been described for a variety of other primate species.

Third, is menopause a recent historical phenomenon and hence an artifact of modernization? Historical references to the age at menopause, and cross-cultural evidence for menopause in recent traditional societies are discussed. We also clarify the relationship between menopause and the maximum lifespan of our species, versus the relationship between menopause and the average life expectancy of different human populations.

Fourth, how can menopause be understood in terms of human

evolution? In this final section of the paper, we briefly review the evolutionary explanations that have been offered.

WHAT IS MENOPAUSE?
Definitions

In the strictly scientific sense of the term, *menopause* refers to the permanent cessation of menstruation and menstrual cycles that occurs in women who are usually around the age of 50. In common usage, the word menopause has come to refer more generally to an entire stage of menstrual irregularity and fertility decline leading eventually to the complete cessation of reproductive capacity. In fact, the final cessation of menstrual bleeding is but one notable landmark (see Lock, 1982 and Gosden, 1985) in the transition from reproductive to postreproductive life, a transition that may take five years to complete. This transition period is technically referred to as the *perimenopause*, but is also sometimes called the *climacteric*. In this paper, the three terms, menopause, perimenopause, and climacteric, will be used interchangeably to refer to the lengthy period of transition from the reproductive to the postreproductive phases of the life span. The term *premenopause* is used to refer to a period of reduced fertility that precedes any other signs that the "change of life" is beginning. And *postmenopause* is the time following the transition phase, when reproductive function has ceased.

The menopause that occurs in human females is but one specific case of reproductive senescence, a case that differs from reproductive decline in the other primates in several important ways (see below). *Reproductive senescence* refers to the decline in the reproductive system that is one aspect of overall degenerative aging processes in vertebrates. Reproductive decline may include gonadal changes, loss of secondary sexual characteristics, cessation of ovarian cycles, a fall in sperm production, a decrease in fertilizing power, hatchability, litter size, and viability of offspring (Comfort, 1979).

Since much of our discussion will revolve around the relationship of menopause to the entire life course of the female, a very brief introduction to life history theory and a few definitions of relevant terms are in order (Hill, 1993 provides a very readable recent review of life history theory and evolutionary anthropology). Life history theory is an approach in evolutionary biology and ecology that focusses on how the ontogeny, fecundity and mortality of the organism affects the demography of the population or species. Some of the principal life history traits relevant to primates are: gestation length, age at sexual maturity, age at first birth, number and sex ratio of offspring, interbirth interval, survival of offspring, life expectancy, and lifespan. All organisms pass through stages in a life cycle, but there is an enormous diversity in how these stages are played out. A "life history" or set of "life history patterns" refers to the timing, age-specificity, and nature of the stages in an individual's life cycle. The study of life history "strategies" or "tactics" is closely related to the study of reproductive success, and is concerned with understanding why certain life history patterns have been selected, and how they might affect the individual's reproductive fitness.

Terms of particular importance in our analysis of menopause are life expectancy and lifespan. *Life expectancy* at birth refers to the *average* age to which members of a cohort can expect to live; the members of a cohort being those born into a specified population at a given time. It is important not to confuse life *expectancy* with *lifespan*. *Maximum lifespan* refers to the age by which all members of a cohort will have died — it is the maximum recorded age for any individual in the cohort. Although values are constantly being revised, the average life expectancy at birth of women in Canada is currently set at 80.6 years (Dumas, 1992), whereas the maximum lifespan for our species is estimated to be somewhere between 100 and 115 years (Hayflick, 1987). From historical records, we know that life expectancy values have been increasing in the past 2,000 years. However, maximum lifespan, as a species characteristic, is generally believed to have remained constant over the evolutionary history of our species.

The distinction between the two terms is important because life expectancy is highly influenced by environmental variables, whereas maximum lifespan reflects the innate biological capacity of the organism to maintain life. Thus lifespan generally is assumed to be a fixed, species-specific characteristic. In the context of menopause, it is important to recognize that although modern medicine has increased the proportion of people who survive to advanced age, (and thus the proportion of postmenopausal women in the population), it is unlikely that the maximum lifespan has yet been affected by medical techniques. It will be difficult, if not impossible to achieve an overall decrease in a process as complex and innately determined as the species-specific rate of aging.

All women in industrialized countries who live to the average life expectancy of 80.6 years, and experience menopause at age 50, will spend 30.6 years, or 38% of their lifetimes, in a postreproductive state. If they should live to the maximum lifespan of the species, they will spend more than 50% of their lives in a postmenopausal state. Since menopause occurs around the age of 50 and the maximum lifespan is 100–115 years, the characteristic human pattern is for female reproductive function to cease less than halfway through the lifespan. As such, menopause is distinct from the decline of other biological systems (e.g., the circulatory system); the latter do not decline until the individual has reached an advanced age.

The Physiological Basis of Menopause

The decline of female reproductive ability is in large part the result of the depletion of egg cells (ova or oocytes) for fertilization. The human female is born with a fixed number of potential ova (approximately one million), and no new ova are produced after birth. The vast majority of these egg cells degenerate between birth and menopause, with only about 400 being ovulated during the reproductive years, and 50% of the oocytes being depleted before puberty.

The monthly cyclic changes in the ovary and the uterus, collectively termed the menstrual cycle, are regulated and controlled by endocrine events of the hypothalamus, the pituitary, and the ovaries themselves. With the depletion of egg cells in the ovaries, comes a cessation of ovulation and a failure of the ovaries to respond to pituitary hormones. Since the ovaries are normally responsible for secretion of estrogen, levels of estrogen drop significantly as the ovaries become increasingly inactive (see Ellison, 1990 for a recent review of ovarian function). The menstrual cycle, including monthly periods of menstrual bleeding, ceases secondarily as a result of the great reduction in estrogen and progesterone. Estrogen is necessary for the regular building up of the lining of the uterus in preparation for implantation, and progesterone for the subsequent shedding of this lining if implantation does not occur. Although the uterus, like most organs, does experience some intrinsic aging changes (Gosden, 1985; Naeye, 1983), inadequate estrogen stimulation in the postmenopausal woman is largely responsible for the marked atrophy of the uterus (Gibbons et al., 1979).

During the fertile years between menarche and menopause, estrogens are secreted primarily by the ovaries, but may also be produced by the adrenal glands and by conversion of androgens to estrogens in fat cells. Most women will experience the negative effects of declining estrogen levels to some extent, but the amount of estrogen obtained from these extraovarian sources will vary greatly from one woman to the next. For many women the adrenal secretions and conversion of androgens to estrogens will be sufficient to minimize or prevent altogether some of the secondary effects of menopause (Anderson, 1983). The possible negative effects of declining estrogen levels include the vasomotor symptom complex (the "hot flash"), atrophy of the reproductive organs and tissues, osteoporosis, and possibly increased risk of arteriosclerosis (Harmon and Talbert, 1985).

IS MENOPAUSE A UNIQUELY HUMAN PHENOMENON?
Reproductive Senescence in the Other Primates

Traditionally, it has been assumed that human menopause is unique in the animal kingdom (Finn, 1976). Many have argued that its unique occurrence in humans is due to the harshness of life in the wild for animals, where few individuals are thought to achieve old age at all (e.g., Washburn, 1981; Dolhinow, 1984; cf. Prothero and Jurgens, 1987, Russell, 1987). However, with increased interest in aging and menopause in humans has come the desire to find a nonhuman primate model suitable for laboratory research on aging, and for testing various clinical aspects of the climacteric. Perhaps not surprisingly, the search for menopause in laboratory primates, such as the rhesus monkey and the chimpanzee, has yielded some reports of the existence of a previously undetected reproductive decline in the females of these species, and arguments that a medical model (and even an evolutionary model) for the study of the human climacteric have been found. These reports have generated a great deal of excitement and they have been widely cited in secondary sources. A few reports of evidence for menopausal and postmenopausal monkeys and apes also have begun to come in from the field (Waser, 1978; Hrdy, 1981; Nishida et al., 1990). The findings from these studies will be briefly reviewed.

Physiological Studies of Laboratory Macaques

Hodgen et al. (1977) are widely cited as having provided the best evidence that rhesus monkeys do experience a true menopause. These researchers reported the circulating levels of pituitary and ovarian hormones as well as the pattern of vaginal bleeding in 17 laboratory rhesus monkeys who were at least 22 years of age. These monkeys became available to Hodgen et al. because of recent poor reproductive performance and generalized debilities associated with old age. Female rhesus of 22 years and older are indeed aged, since 30 years is the maximum lifespan for this species (Tigges et al., 1988; Van Wagenen, 1972). In other words, the animals in this sample would likely be very close to the end of their lives, comparable to women aged 75 years and older in industrialized societies. Nonetheless, Hodgen et al. reported that 12 of the 17 monkeys continued to cycle, although eight of them exhibited irregular cycling. Five of the 17 monkeys lacked any sign of menses during the 15 month study, and four of them showed low levels of estrogen.

Hodgen et al. (1977) concluded that their results supported the earlier evidence of Van Wagenen (1970, 1972). Van Wagenen described the reproductive performance of approximately 70 captive rhesus monkeys over a period of 34 years. In particular, two females who lived to 30 years were described. These two ceased to menstruate at ages 27 and 28 years (these values are the equivalent of ages 90 and 93 in a human life course of 100 years). Based on these data, Van Wagenen concluded that 30-year-old females are postmenopausal, and that the climacteric for rhesus monkeys lies between 25 and 30 years of age.

Graham et al. (1979) examined the reproductive history and histology of 17 pigtail macaques in order to evaluate the nature and extent of reproductive senescence in another species of macaque. Analyses showed that there were follicles present in both young and old females, although they were more abundant in young females. Evidence of recent ovulation was found in all but one of the 20+ year olds. This one exceptional female showed all the hormonal and morphological characteristics of menopause. This led the authors to conclude that their study confirmed Hodgen et al.'s findings of a menopausal syndrome in macaques. However, note that in all three of these lab studies of macaques a larger proportion of the sample continued to cycle into very old age than those who did not. Those females who do exhibit reproductive decline, do so at a very advanced age, near the end of the lifespan.

Physiological Studies of Laboratory Chimpanzees

Graham (1979) also analysed reproductive decline in ten aging common chimpanzees. The subjects were known or estimated to be between 35 and 48 years of age, 50 years being the maximum lifespan for the chimpanzee. His analysis showed no clear evidence of menopause in the chimpanzee. "Most of the animals were cycling regularly until death, and all had experienced at least one menstrual cycle within one year of death" (Graham, 1979:291). There was however, a trend toward increased cycle length and reduced likelihood of conception in these old females. The animals in this study were very old and in a state of advanced biological senescence as described by the author ("wrinkling of the skin, joint stiffness, muscle atrophy,... atherosclerosis" 1979: 293), and in spite of this they continued to ovulate and cycle until death, although they did apparently experience a reduction in fertility.

Gould et al. (1981) published an analysis of reproductive senescence in two common chimpanzees (*Pan troglodytes*) and one bonobo (*Pan paniscus*, formerly referred to as the pygmy chimpanzee). The two common chimpanzees were aged 50 and 48 and the pygmy chimpanzee was of unknown age, although estimated to be very old. The two common chimpanzees continued to exhibit menstrual cycles, although with increased cycle length, but the pygmy chimpanzee showed no evidence of menstrual cycling within one year of her death, and her hormonal levels were consistent with menopause.

Interpretation of Physiological Studies of Laboratory Primates

For both common chimpanzees and macaque species, studies show that there are normally enough oocytes to last to the end of the maximum lifespan, and that females will continue to cycle until they die. In the two cases where oocyte depletion is known to have occurred (the one pygmy chimpanzee in the Gould et al. study and the one pigtail macaque in the Graham et al. study), physiological changes similar to human menopause occurred. But we would argue that rather than demonstrating similarity between the menopause of human females and the reproductive senescence of other primates, these studies may in fact be highlighting the critical differences: universal, middle-aged reproductive cessation versus idiosyncratic, old-aged reproductive decline.

It is important to explain why several researchers have argued for the existence of menopause in monkeys and apes on the basis of these laboratory studies, when our own review of the same literature leads us to conclude that menopause is unique to humans. One answer is that we are examining menopause not from a clinical point of view, but from the physical anthropologist's perspective of ontogeny, life history and evolution. It is indeed possible to create a biomedical model for menopause by removing the ovaries of a female monkey or ape, or by examining enough aged females to find the one or two who have experienced oocyte depletion, such as has been done in these studies. The research just described is focussed on the endocrinology of the event, whereas we are concerned with menopause as a life history trait, in which the ubiquity, age-specificity, and timing of the phenomenon vis-à-vis the life course are the essential defining criteria. In these samples of females that have lived way past average life expectancy, a minority have been reported to cease to reproduce. This is a highly variable phenomenon that occurs near the end of the lifespan, and is not distinct from general physical decline due to old age.

Comparative Life Histories of Monkeys, Apes and Humans

Figures 1 and 2 summarize what is presently known about stages of the life cycle, and life histories in macaques, chimpanzees, and humans. The macaque data are taken from Fedigan (1991) and Fedigan et al. (1986), the chimpanzee data from Nishida et al. (1990), and the human data from a variety of sources (primarily Statistics Canada). Figure 1 shows the stages of the life cycle in the three types of primates. Japanese macaques have a gestation period of 6 months, common chimpanzees of 8.5 months and humans of 9.5 months. Macaques and humans wean their babies around the age of one year (this stage is highly variable in humans), whereas chimpanzees continue to suckle their infants until the age of four years. Social maturity ("adulthood") is reached at the age of 5 years in Japanese macaques, 15 years in common chimpanzees and approximately 18 years (again this is highly variable) in humans. The maximum lifespan for Japanese macaques is 32 years, 50 years for chimpanzees and 115 years for humans.

Figure 2 focusses on reproductive life histories and aging in the three types of primates. Japanese macaque females usually give birth for the first time at five years of age, and they have an average life expectancy of 14 years. The oldest females known to have given birth were 25 years old, which represents very old age for these monkeys, but a very few females lived past this to the age of 32 years. Common chimpanzee females first give birth at age 15 and the oldest female known to have given birth was 48 years. The maximum life span is 50 years; thus chimpanzee females spend 4% or less of their lives in a post-reproductive stage. Life expectancy values for free-ranging chimpanzees are not available due to female emigration. Contemporary Canadian women first give birth at the average age of 25 (Romaniuc, 1984), but the mean age at first birth in non-industrialized societies such as the Dobe !King is 18.8 years (Howell, 1979), a value much closer to the 15 years reported for chimpanzees. The average life expectancy at birth for Canadian women is 80.6 years. Human females universally experience menopause at age 50, and their maximum lifespan is 115 years. Thus, the human female may spend as much as half of her maximum lifespan in a post-reproductive stage.

111

Figure 1. Stages of the Life Cycle in Three Primate Species

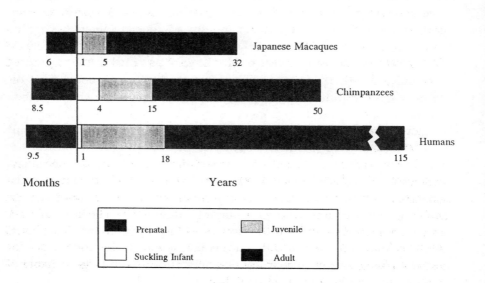

Figure 2. Female Life Histories in Three Primate Species

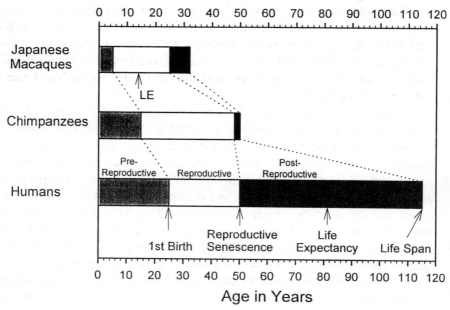

These data show that both chimpanzee and human females cease to reproduce around the same chronological age of 50; however, reproductive senescence occurs at the *end* of the maximum lifespan in chimpanzees, versus the *middle* of the maximum life span in humans. One could argue that a primary development in the evolution of the human female life history pattern must have been the addition of a significant new stage in the life cycle — the post-reproductive phase (see below, "How did menopause evolve?").

Field Reports and Behavioural Studies of Female Reproductive Aging

In her report on aging and reproductive performance in rhesus macaques, Small (1984) noted that there is considerable debate over the existence of true menopause in other primate species. She pointed out that although a few females in captivity are reported to have experienced menstrual irregularities and fertility decline as they age, the total number of females known to have ceased to cycle is very small. She argued that the most striking aspect of macaque reproduction is the large number of females that continue to cycle until death.

Surprisingly few field observations are as yet available to advance our conclusions beyond those of Small. In 1981, Hrdy hypothesized that a lengthy post-reproductive period evolved in female primates in order to maximize the parental investment given to grandchildren and last-born offspring (the "grandmother hypothesis"). She referred to Waser's (1978) study of post-reproductive survival and behaviour in one free-ranging female mangabey. However, no longitudinal studies of sufficient sample size were available to test her hypothesis.

Recently, Harley (1990) published an analysis of age and reproductive performance in captive female langurs that were studied over a ten-year period. She found that these females did indeed experience a fertility decline as they aged, but that they did not exhibit true menopause, that is, cessation of menstrual cycles. She argued that the decline in fertility was idiosyncratic, and in all but one possible case, was caused not by a cessation of ovarian cycles, but by a variety of other reproductive problems, including failure to conceive, failure to carry pregnancies to term, and loss of newborns. Harley argued that her findings do not support Hrdy's hypothesis that there is a post-reproductive period in langurs.

Another recently reported longitudinal study of female reproductive performance came to the opposite conclusion. In their 1990 book

113

summarizing 25 years of work on free-ranging chimpanzees at Mahale, Nishida et al. argued that female chimpanzees experience a post-reproductive life and that some show menopause. Their best evidence for this argument is that five of 11 elderly females ceased to mate and ceased to show estrous swellings in the last one to three years before their deaths. We could infer that this lack of estrous swellings means they had ceased to cycle. However, one to three years is well within the limits of a normal interbirth interval for chimpanzees (6 years at the Mahale site), and females do not mate or show estrous swellings during most of the interbirth interval. Thus it is also possible that these females simply died part way between the birth of one infant and conception of the next. We should also note that six of the 11 elderly females *continued* to cycle until death, or to the end of the study. As with the laboratory findings described earlier, in this study of free-ranging chimpanzees, a larger proportion of the sample continued to cycle than not.

Longitudinal field studies of other free-ranging primates, such as those by Altmann et al. (1988) on baboons, have not documented menopause or lengthy post-reproductive periods, although Strum and Western (1982) did document a decline in fertility in older female baboons.

Summary: The Differences between Menopause in Humans and Reproductive Senescence in Other Primates

We would argue from the evidence available for monkeys and apes that menopause in humans is a unique form of reproductive senescence in several respects; an argument summarized by the following sentence: "All women cease to experience menstrual cycles approximately halfway through the maximum lifespan for humans." The particular points of importance in this summary statement are as follows:

(1) "All women..." Menopause is not a labile or facultative trait — it occurs around the age of 50 in all women across all cultures, and has for over 2,000 years of history. It is less variable than the age at menarche (first menses, see below), and appears to be under strict biological control. By contrast, in the other primates, age at last reproduction is highly individually variable.

(2) "...cease to experience menstrual cycles..." Menopause is not merely a degeneration of reproductive capacity as indicated by declining fertility, irregularity of cycles, or

changes in hormonal levels, such as has been reported for some aged female primates. In humans, menopause is the cessation of menstruation and ovulation — that is, a complete shut down of the female reproductive system. This is a phenomenon that has not been documented in any but a few highly decrepit macaques and chimpanzees close to their death or to maximum lifespan.

(3) "...approximately halfway through maximum lifespan..." Menopause occurs midway through the life course — well before other systems of the body senesce (Snowden et al., 1989) — leading Bowden and Williams (1984) to suggest that menopause should be viewed as a maturational phase rather than a deteriorative aspect of aging. In the nonhuman primates, the decline of the reproductive system is not distinct from the decline of other organs and systems in aging animals. Reproductive senescence in the nonhuman primates is characteristic of extreme old age. Menopause in women is characteristic of middle age.

IS MENOPAUSE A RECENT HISTORICAL PHENOMENON?
Basic Questions

We now turn to a consideration of menopause from a demographic perspective, addressing some historical and cross-cultural issues. For example, at what age did menopause occur in distant historical times? Has there been a recent trend for the age at menopause to decrease, as is the case with menarche (first menses)? What variables have been shown to affect individual age at menopause? Does menopause exist in traditional, non-industrialized societies where the increased life expectancy associated with modernization is absent? Finally, we ask the question: if mean life expectancy of greater than 50 years has only been achieved since the advent of modern, industrialized societies, does it follow that menopause and a post-reproductive life for human females is a relatively recent phenomenon?

The Age of Menopause

Is menopause at approximately 50 years of age a fixed point in all human populations, or does the age at menopause vary historically and cross-culturally? References to postmenopausal women date back to biblical times (Low, 1983; Gosden, 1985). Postmenopausal women may have been more uncommon until recent times, but they did exist. References to the climacteric period of a woman's life can also be found in classical and medieval sources. The first textbook of gynecology, published in England early in the 15th century, demonstrated a surprising understanding of menopause. The actual term menopause was introduced in 1821 in France by Gardanne (Wilbush, 1988). But reviews of medieval sources agree that menopausal women are described and that 50 is the most frequently cited age of menopause (Post, 1971; Amundsen and Diers, 1973). Records from classical Greece and Rome show an age range of 40–50 years (Amundsen and Diers, 1970), with the majority of authors citing 50 years.

There has been a significant decline in the age at menarche (first menses) over the past 100 years (Tanner, 1962; Diers, 1974; Laslett, 1971). This has led researchers to speculate that a similar change in the age at menopause may have occurred in recent times. However, a number of reports confirm that from the 1850s to the present, the age at menopause has remained constant at approximately 50 years (Burch and Gunz, 1967; McKinlay and McKinlay, 1973; Burch and Rowell, 1963). Available evidence indicates that there is no relationship between the age at menarche and the age at menopause (e.g., Treolar, 1974; McKinlay et al., 1972; Jaszmann et al., 1969).

A number of factors that may influence an individual's age at menopause have been investigated (for reviews of this material, see McKinlay et al., 1972; Gray, 1976; Flint, 1976). Suggested factors include: marital status, parity (number of infants born), heredity, altitude, nutrition, and socioeconomic status. Serious methodological problems plague much of this work (McKinlay et al., 1972) and results are inconsistent. However, Brambilla and McKinlay (1989) used an approach that avoided the problems associated with the prior research and they found that when confounding variables are controlled, age at menopause varied with smoking, education and income, but not with marital status, parity, height, weight, or use of oral contraceptives.

Racial and ethnic differences in the age at menopause have also been explored. Goodman et al. (1978) examined the age at menopause among Caucasian, Japanese, Chinese, and part-Hawaiian women. One of the clear findings of their study was the consistency of age at menopause across different groups. Gray (1976) also reported striking consistency of the age at menopause among populations of Caucasians, including British, American Swiss, Finnish, and white South African women. Frere (1971) found the mean age at menopause for South African Bantu women to be 50.7 years, compared with 51.4 years for white women. MacMahon and Worcester (1966) compared black and white American women and found the difference in the ages at menopause to be non-significant. See Table 1 for a sample of published age at menopause values.

Also of interest are ethnographic data on cross-cultural variation in age at menopause, although these data are scarce. The Human Relations Area Files reflect the paucity of ethnographic data on the climacteric. Seldom the direct focus of ethnographic studies, references *in passing* to menopause do occur in cross-cultural literature. For example, it is often noted that changes follow the end of a woman's reproductive career, in particular sex role reversal (e.g., Biesele and Howell, 1981; Amoss, 1981; Sinclair, 1985; Quain, 1948; Levy, 1967; Mead, 1950). Among the !Kung San, Coast Salish, Fijians, Amerindians, and the Balinese, postmenopausal women are described as being released from many restrictions that are associated with menstruation and/or child-bearing. Most of what is available on menopause in the cross-cultural literature concerns women's social experience of menopause, there are few quantitative data available on the age at menopause. When age at menopause is mentioned, it is most commonly cited as age 50.

Life Expectancy and the Proportion of Postmenopausal Women in the Population

As noted earlier, it is reasonable to assume that the maximum lifespan of approximately 100–115 years has changed little over the history of our species, *Homo sapiens*. There has, however, been great variation in the frequency with which people have actually lived out this lifespan (Amoss and Harrell, 1981). Weiss (1981) hypothesized that Neolithic hunters had an average life expectancy at birth of only 19–25 years, and Westerners of the classical and medieval periods only 22–29 years. It is only with industrialization of the past century that life expectancies at birth of over 70 years have been attained. Even in pre-industrial societies of today, life expectancy at birth is usually less than 50 years. Some have interpreted this to mean that women in pre-industrial societies never live long enough to experience menopause, and therefore the climacteric is only a recent phenomenon associated with modernization. However, an increase in mean life expectancy results in an increase in the *size* of the post-reproductive population, rather than the sudden appearance of individuals of that age group. The simple example shown in Table 2 will demonstrate this point. Based on data from 94 completed lives, Howell (1979) reported that life expectancy at birth of a !Kung population was only 34.57 years, well below the 50-year value for menopause. Still 38 of these individuals (40%)

117

lived to be 50 years and older, 23 lived to be 65 years and older, and two lived to be over 85 years. This makes it clear that even with average life expectancy at birth of much less than 50 years, many individuals in the population will live beyond the age of menopause. To reiterate, in industrialized nations the proportion of women living to and beyond their menopausal years has increased, but there have probably always been some *Homo sapiens* women who lived long enough to experience menopause.

Table 1. Sample of Published Age at Menopause Values (Pavelka and Fedigan, 1991)

Population	Mean	SD	Data Source
Caucasians in Hawaii	50.06	4.37	Goodman et al., 1978
Japanese in Hawaii	49.76	3.32	Goodman et al., 1978
Chinese	50.29	3.50	Goodman et al., 1978
Hawaiians	49.20	3.45	Goodman et al., 1978
South African Whites	51.44	0.24	Frere, 1971
South African Bantu	50.70	0.22	Frere, 1971
Netherlands	51.40	3.80	Jaszmann et al., 1969
United States	49.00	3.01	Treolar, 1974

Table 2. Ages at Death in the Dobe' !Kung (Howell, 1979)

	Age at Death	Number of People	Percentage of Population
	<50 years	31	33%
	>50 years	38	40%
	>65 years	23	25%
	>85 years	2	2%
Mean =	34.5 years	—	—
Total =	—	94	100%

HOW DID MENOPAUSE EVOLVE?

Having countered the argument that menopause is only a recent historical artifact of modern societies, we now turn to explanations with an evolutionary time frame. Animals generally reproduce until the end of their lifespan; thus an obvious question is why would natural selection favour the cessation of reproduction in human females only halfway through the maximum lifespan of the species? All other things being equal, longer-lived individuals contribute more offspring to future generations, and thus experience greater reproductive success. Investigations of lifetime reproductive success have shown this to be true for a variety of species (see Clutton-Brock, 1988). Any gene that extends the reproductive phase of life by postponing the onset of reproductive senescence has a selective advantage. Thus, there is a general tendency for natural selection to prolong the reproductive life of the individuals of any species. As discussed earlier, the evidence suggests that this is true for the nonhuman primates, who are able to reproduce until very close to the end of their lifespan. Across the primate order there is a progressive increase in longevity from the prosimians through to the apes, and in all the species except *Homo sapiens*, the female egg supply and reproductive phase last for the same amount of time as the lifespan. Remember that the reproductive senescence observed in nonhuman primates is not a phenomenon distinct from the overall senescence of the organism.

The evolution of menopause in humans requires a different explanation than does the reproductive senescence of other primate females. However, an adaptive explanation for menopause faces the challenge of formulating plausible arguments as to how organisms that cease reproducing in mid-lifespan can be biologically successful (Mayer, 1982). Explanations for the evolution of menopause fall into two broad categories: those that see menopause as an adaptive feature in and of itself (direct selection), and those that see menopause as the by-product of some other adaptive feature (nonselection or epiphenomenon). Chisolm (1993) has recently reviewed the debate between the "adaptationists" and the "mechanists" in explaining the reproductive profile of humans.

Within the adaptationist framework, some discussions of the evolution of menopause imply the existence of a "gene for menopause" — that is, the appearance of, and selection for a new gene that shuts down the otherwise functioning reproductive system. However, this conceptualization is inconsistent with what is known about the physiological basis of menopause. It assumes that without a "shut down" order, the reproductive system would continue to function. In fact, the reproductive system of women has an inherent end point in that the egg supply (upon which the entire system depends) is limited. No external "shut down" device is necessary, as it exists intrinsically. In other primates, and other mammals, the egg supply of the females is sufficient to maintain reproductive function to very near the end of the maximum lifespan of the species. Why is the egg supply of the human female limited to approximately 50 years? An adaptive explanation for humans must explain why natural selection did not favour a larger egg supply, or a supply that degenerates more slowly.

According to Lancaster and King (1985), all "direct selection" explanations are versions of a parental investment perspective. This perspective, sometimes called the "grandmother hypothesis", suggests that menopause represents a further step in the general primate trend toward quality over quantity in offspring production. Females who cease to reproduce halfway through the maximum lifespan, it is argued by direct selectionists, have greater overall reproductive success than do those that continue to reproduce. There is an advantage at this stage in the lifespan to focussing one's energy on ensuring the survival of currently existing offspring and other close relatives, rather than on production of further offspring. Postmenopausal females may enhance their fitness by acting as grandmothers, or surrogate caretakers for their children's offspring.

One problem with the grandmother hypothesis as an explanation for menopause is that it is not necessarily specific to human evolution. Versions of it have been used to explain the gradual reproductive decline of elderly female mammals. By itself, the grandmother hypothesis does not explain why menopause (that is, the cessation of reproductive function halfway through the lifespan) would have been uniquely selected for in human females. A second problem with the grandmother hypothesis is that it may explain the adaptive value of menopause in populations today without explaining the origins of the trait — why it arose in the first place. A recent study of the Ache hunter-gatherers of South America failed to find empirical support for the grandmother hypothesis (Hill and Hurtado, 1991, but see Rogers, 1993).

Often the selectionist argument is contrasted with a nonselectionist explanation wherein menopause is seen to be an epiphenomenon (side effect, or by-product) of some other development in human evolution. Most commonly, it is thought to be a by-product of the increase in maximum lifespan over the course of human evolution (see Weiss, 1981; Jones,

1975; Washburn, 1981). The maximum lifespan of *Homo sapiens* is twice that of our closest great ape relatives. As the maximum lifespan increased over the course of human evolution, why did the reproductive systems of females not increase in like measure? We know of no other system that entirely ceases to function mid-way through the lifespan, well before the other systems of the body are failing. One of the most popular explanations for senescence is Williams' pleiotropy theory (1957), which suggests that features having high adaptive value early in the life course will be selected for even if they result in reduced fitness later in the life course. Senescence of a system is thus a trade-off with the high adaptive value of that system earlier in life. Applying Williams' pleiotropy theory to menopause, one could argue that the human female system of egg production and storage is highly adaptive early in life, but the trade-off is that there are inherent limits in the system (degeneration of the egg supply), which will express themselves later in life.

The human female egg supply may be inherently unable to sustain itself to keep pace with the increased longevity of our species, and this may be understood as a pleiotropic effect. Possibly, a 50-year supply of healthy eggs is a limit inherent in the basic structure of all mammalian female reproduction. Very few mammals have ever been observed to reproduce much past 50 years.

Graham (1979, 1986) showed that chimpanzees continue to have menstrual cycles until approximately 50 years of age, and noted that chimpanzee females and women experience a cessation of reproductive function at about the same absolute age. The chimpanzee is the closest living relative of *Homo sapiens*, and is believed to be the best living model of early human evolution (e.g., Foley, 1989; Ghiglieri, 1989; Zihlman, 1978a,b, 1981). It seems reasonable to suggest that the 50-year egg supply of modern chimpanzees and modern humans is also characteristic of the common ancestor of these two lineages. Fifty-year-old chimpanzee females, however, are at the maximum recorded lifespan, whereas 50-year-old women are less than halfway through the maximum recorded lifespan for *Homo sapiens*. This supports our conclusion that over the course of human evolution there must have been selection for increased longevity, but because of the inherent limits on egg supplies, female reproductive function could not keep pace.

CONCLUSION

In this paper we have attempted to review the information and the controversies concerning menopause from a variety of perspectives relevant to physical anthropology. Menopause has been defined and described from a life history perspective that includes both the physiological and the demographic perspective. Relevant primatological, historical, cross-cultural, and evolutionary approaches have been presented.

If menopause is unique to human females and universal to females of our species, then an evolutionary approach to understanding it is in order. Relatively few attempts have been made to explain the evolution of menopause, despite the fact that its existence is particularly challenging to reconcile with natural selection. How can organisms that stop reproducing be successfully reproduced? The "grandmother hypothesis" suggests that menopause is an adaptive response to selection pressure that favours women who cease to reproduce, and instead invest their energy in the survival of existing offspring and their children. Nonselectionist explanations for the evolution of menopause treat the climacteric as a by-product of increased lifespan and as a pleiotropic effect. We favour the later explanation, and from our examination of the data, we argue that menopause is a process unique to humans, that goes back in time at least to the origins of our species, and that resulted secondarily from the selection for a longer and longer lifespan during the course of human evolution.

ACKNOWLEDGEMENTS

We thank the editors, Ann Herring and Leslie Chan, for inviting us to write this chapter, and John Addicott, Leslie Chan, Usher Fleising, Alison Jolly, Kim Hill, Nancy Lovell, Toshisada Nishida, Emoke Szathmary, an anonymous reviewer, and many others for suggestions that improved the ideas presented in this manuscript. LMF's research is supported by an operating grant (#A7723) from the Natural Sciences and Engineering Research Council of Canada.

REFERENCES

Altmann, J Hausfater G, and Altmann S (1988) Determinants of reproductive success in savannah baboons, *Papio cynocephalus*. In TH Clutton-Brock (ed.): *Reproductive Success: Studies of Individual Variation in Contrasting Breeding Systems*. Chicago: Chicago Univ. Press, pp. 403-418.

Amoss PT and Harrell S (1981) Coast Salish elders, In PT Amoss and S Harrell (eds.): *Other Ways of Growing Old*. Stanford: Stanford Univ. Press, pp. 227-247.

Amoss PT and Harrell S (1981) An anthropological perspective on aging. In PT

Amoss and S Harrell (Eds.): *Other Ways of Growing Old*. Stanford: Stanford Univ. Press, pp. 1-24.

Amundsen DW and Diers CJ (1970) The age of menopause in classical Greece and Rome. *Hum Biol*. 41:125-132.

Amundsen DW and Diers CJ (1973) The age of menarche in medieval Europe. *Hum. Biol. 45*: 363-9.

Anderson M (1983) *The Menopause*. London: Faber and Faber Ltd.

Biesele M and Howell N (1981) The old people give you life: Aging among !Kung hunter-gatherers. In PT Amoss and S Harrell (eds.): *Other Ways of Growing Old*. Stanford: Stanford Univ. Press, pp. 77-98.

Bowden DM And Williams (1984) Aging. In AG Hendricks (ed.): *Advances in Veterinary Science and Comparative Medicine*, volume 28. Orlando: Academic Press, pp. 305-341.

Brambilla DJ and McKinlay SM (1989) A prospective study of factors affecting age at menopause. *J. Clin Epidemiol. 42*:1031-1039.

Burch PRJ and Rowell NR (1963) Menarche and menopause. *Lancet* 2:784-785.

Burch PRJ and Gunz FW (1967) The distribution of the menopausal age in New Zealand: An Exploratory Study. *N. Z. Med. J.* 66:6-10.

Chisolm JS (1993) Death, hope and sex. Life history theory and the development of reproductive strategies. *Curr. Anth.* 34:1-24.

Clutton-Brock TH (ed.) (1988) *Reproductive Success: Studies of Individual Variation in Contrasting Breeding Systems*. Chicago: Univ. of Chicago Press.

Comfort A (1979) *The Biology of Senescence*, Third Edition, New York: Elsevier.

Diers CJ (1974) Historical trends in the age of menarche and menopause. *Psychol. Rep. 34*:931-7.

Dolhinow P (1984) The primates: Age, behavior, and evolution. In DI Kertzer and J Keith (eds.): *Age and Anthropological Theory*. London: Cornell Univ. Press, pp. 65-81.

Dumas J (1992) *Report on the Demographic Situation in Canada 1992*. Ottawa: Statistics Canada.

Ellison PT (1990) Human ovarian function and reproductive ecology: New hypotheses. *Am Anthropol. 92*: 933-952.

Fedigan L (1991) Life span and reproduction in Japanese macaque females. In LM Fedigan and PJ Asquith (eds.): *The Monkeys of Arashiyama: Thirty-five Years of Research in Japan and the West*. Albany: State University of New York Press, pp. 140-154.

Fedigan LM , Fedigan L, Gouzoules S, Gouzoules H and Koyama N (1986) Lifetime reproductive success in female Japanese macaques. *Folia Primatol.* (Basel) 47: 143-157.

Finn CA (1976) Investigations into reproductive aging in experiemental animals. In RJ Beard (ed.): *The Menopause: A Guide to Current Research and Practice*. Baltimore: Univ. Park Press, pp. 1-23.

Flint M (1976) Cross-cultural factors that affect age of menopause. In PA van Keep, RB Greenblatt, and M Albeaux-Fernet (eds.): *Consensus on Menopause Research: A Summary of International Opinion*. Baltimore: Univ. Park Press, pp. 73-83.

Foley RA (1989) The evolution of hominid social behavior. In V Standen and RA

Foley (eds.) *Comparative Socioecology*. Oxford: Blackwell Scientific Publications, pp. 473-494.

Frere G (1971) Mean age at menopause and menarche in South Africa. *S.AFr. J. Med. Sci. 36*: 21-24.

Ghiglieri MP (1989) Hominoid sociobiology and hominid social evolution. In PG Heltne and LA Marquard (eds.) *Understanding Chimpanzees*. Cambridge: Harvard Univ. Press, pp. 370-379.

Gibbons WB, Buttram VC, Besch PK, and Smith RG (1979) Estrogen binding proteins in human postmenopausal uterus. *Am. J. Obstet. Gynecol. 135*: 799-803.

Goodman MJ. Grove JS, and Gilbert FG Jr (1978) Age at menopause in relation to reproductive history in Japanese, Caucasian, Chinese and Hawaiian women living in Hawaii. *J. Gerontol. 33*:668-694.

Gosden RG (1985) *Biology of Menopause. The Cause and Consequence of Ovarian Ageing*. London: Academic Press.

Gould KG, Flint M, and Graham CE (1981) Chimpanzee reproductive senescence: A possible model for evolution of the menopause. *Maturitas 3*: 157-166.

Graham CE (1979) Reproductive function in aged female chimpanzees. *Am. J. Phys. Anthr. 50*: 291-300.

Graham CE (1986) Endocrinology of reproductive senescence. In WR Dukelow and J Erwin (eds.): *Comparative Primate Biology*, Volume 3: *Reproduction and Development*. New York: Alan R. Liss, Inc. pp. 93-99.

Graham CE, Kling OR, and Steiner RA (1979) Reproductive senescence in female nonhuman primates. In DJ Bowden (ed.): *Aging in Nonhuman Primates*. New York: Van Nostrand Reinhold, pp. 183-209.

Gray RH (1976) The menopause — epidemiological and demographic considerations. In RJ Beard (ed.): *The Menopause: A Guide to Current Research and Practice*. Baltimore: Univ. Park Press, pp. 25-40.

Harley D (1990) Aging and reproductive performance in langur monkeys (*Presbytis entellus*) *Am. J. Phys. Anthr.* 83: 253-261.

Harmon SM and Talbert GB (1985) Reproductive aging. In CE Finch and EL Schneider (eds.): *Handbook of the Biology of Aging*, 2nd Edition. New York: Van Nostrand Reinhold, pp. 457-510.

Hayflick L (1987) Origins of longevity. In HR Warner, RN Butler, RL Sprott, and EL Schneider (eds.): *Modern Biological Theories of Aging*, Volume 31, *Aging Series*. New York: Raven Press, pp. 21-34.

Hill K (1993) Life history theory and evolutionary anthropology. *Evol. Anth.* 2:78-88.

Hill K and Hurtado AM (1991) The evolution of reproductive senescence and menopause in human females. *Human Nature* 2:315-350.

Hodgen GD, Goodman AL, O'Connor A, and Johnson DK (1977) Menopause in rhesus monkeys: Model for study of disorders in the human climacteric. *Am. J. Obstet. Gynecol.* 127: 581-584.

Howell N (1979) *The Demography of the Dobe !Kung*. New York: Academic Press.

Hrdy SB (1981) "Nepotists" and "altruists": The behavior of old females among macaques and langur monkeys. In PT Amoss and S Harrell (eds.): *Other Ways of Growing Old: Anthropological Perspectives*. Stanford: Stanford Univ.

Press, pp. 59-96.

Jaszmann L, Van Lith ND, and Zaat JCA (1969) The age at menopause in the Netherlands: The statistical analysis of a survey. *Int. J. Fertl.* 14: 106-117.

Jones ED (1975) The post-reproductive phase in mammals. In PA van Keep and C Lauritzen (eds.): *Frontiers of Hormone Research*, Volume 3: *Estrogens in the Post-Menopause*. Basel: S. Karger, pp. 1-19.

Lancaster JB and King BJ (1985) An evolutionary perspective on menopause. In JK Brown and V Kerns (eds.): *In Her Prime: A New View of Middle-Aged Women*. South Hadley, Mass: Bergin and Garvey, pp. 13-20.

Laslett P (1971) Age at menarche in Europe since the eighteenth century. *J. Interdisciplinary History* 2: 221-236.

Levy J (1967) The older American Indian. In E Youmans (ed.): *The Older Rural Americans*. Lexington: Univ. of Kentucky Press, pp. 231-238.

Lock M (1982) Models and practice in medicine: menopause as syndrome or life transition? *Cult. Med Psychiatry* 6: 261-280.

Low MD (1983) The perimenopausal woman in literature. In JH Buchsbaum (ed.): *The Menopause*. New York: Springer-Verlag, pp. 205-213.

MacMahon B and Worcester J (1966) *Age at menopause: 1960-62*, U.S. Vital and Health Statistics. Series 11, No. 13.

McKinlay SM and McKinlay, JB (1973) Selected studies of the menopause. *J. Biosoc. Sci* 5(4): 533-555.

McKinlay SM, Jefferys M, and Thompson B (1972) An investigation of the age at menopause. *J. Biosoc. Sci.* 4: 161-173.

Mayer PJ (1982) Evolutionary advantage of the menopause. *Hum. Ecol.* 10(4): 477-494.

Mead M (1950) *Male and Female. A Study of the Sexes in a Changing World*. London: Gollaucz.

Naeye RL (1983) Maternal age, obstetric complications, and the outcome of pregnancy. *Obstet. Gynecol.* 60: 210-216.

Nishida T, Takasaki H, and Takahata Y (1990) Demography and reproductive profiles. In T Nishida (ed.): *The Chimpanzees of the Mahale Mountains: Sexual and Life History Strategies*. Tokyo: Univ. of Tokyo Press, pp. 63-97.

Pavelka MSM and Fedigan LM (1991) Menopause: A comparative life history perspective. *Yearbook of Physical Anthropology.* 34:13-38.

Post JB (1971) Ages at menarche and menopause: Some mediaeval authorities. *Pop. Studies* 25: 83-87.

Prothero J and Jurgens KD (1987) Scaling of maximal lifespan in mammals: A review. In AD Woodhead and KH Thompson (eds.): *Evolution of Longevity in Animals: A Comparative Approach*. New York: Plenum Press, pp. 49-74.

Quain B (1948) *Fijian Village*. Chicago: Univ. of Chicago Press.

Rogers AR (1993) Why menopause? *Evol. Ecol.* 7:406-420.

Romaniuc A (1984) *Fertility in Canada: From Baby Boom to Baby Bust*. Ottawa: Stats Canada.

Russell RL (1987) Evidence for and against the theory of developmentally programmed aging. In HR Warner, RN Butler, RL Sprott, and EL Schneider (eds): *Modern Biological Theories on Aging*, Volume 31, *Aging Series*. New

York: Raven Press, pp. 35-61.

Sinclair KP (1985) Koro and Kuia: Aging and gender among the Maori of New Zealand. In DA Counts and DR Counts (eds.) *Aging and Its Transformations: Moving Toward Death in Pacific Societies*. Lanham, Md.: Univ. Press of America, pp. 27-46.

Small MF (1984) Aging and reproductive success in female Macaca mulatta. In MF Small (ed.) *Female Primates: Studies by Women Primatologists*. New York: Alan R. Liss, Inc. pp. 249-259.

Snowdon DA, Kane RL, Beeson WL, Burke GL, Sprafka JM, Potter J, Iso H, Jacobs DR, and Phillips RL (1989) Is early natural menopause a biologic marker of health and aging? *Am. J. Public Health 79*: 709-714.

Strum SC and Western JD (1982) Variations in fecundity with age and environment in olive baboons (*Papio anubis*). *Am. J. Primatol. 3*: 61-76.

Tanner JM (1962) *Growth at Adolescence*, 2nd Edition. Oxford: Alden Press.

Tigges, J, Gordon TP, McClure HM Hall EC, and Peters A (1988) Survival rate and lifespan of rhesus monkeys at the Yerkes Regional Primate Research Center. *Am. J. Primatol. 15*: 263-273.

Treolar AE (1974) Menarche, menopause, and intervening fecundity. *Hum. Biol. 46*: 89-107.

Van Wagenen G (1970) Menopause in a subhuman primate. *Anat. Rec. 166*: 392.

Van Wagenen G (1972) Vital statistics from a breeding colony: reproduction and pregnancy outcome in Macaca mulatta. *J. Med. Primatol. 1*: 3-28.

Waser PM (1978) Postreproductive survival and behavior in a free-ranging female mangabey. *Folia primatol. 29*:142-160.

Washburn SL (1981) Longevity in primates. In JL McGaugh and SB Kiesler (eds.): *Aging: Biology and Behavior*. New York: Academic Press, pp. 11-29.

Weiss KM (1981) Evolutionary perspectives on human aging. In PT Amoss and S Harrell (eds.): *Other Ways of Growing Old: Anthropological Perspectives*. Stanford: Stanford Univ. Press, pp. 25-58.

Wilbush J (1988) Climacteric disorders — historical perspectives. In JW Studd and MI Whitehead (eds.): *The Menopause*. London: Blackwell Scientific Publications, pp. 1-14.

Williams GC (1957) Pleiotropy, natural selection, and the evolution of senescence. *Evolution 11*: 398-411.

Zihlman, AL (1978a) Women in evolution, part II: subsistence and social organization among early hominids. *Signs 4*: 4-20.

Zihlman AL (1978b) Motherhood in transition from ape to human. In WB Miller and LF Newman (eds.): *The First Child and Family Formation*. Chapel Hill: Caroline Population Center, pp. 35-50.

Zihlman AL (1981) Women as shapers of human adaptation. In F Dahlberg (ed.): *Woman the Gatherer*. New Haven: Yale Univ. Press, pp. 75-120.

6

Choosing a Mate
Lessons from Old Colonial Gibraltar

Lawrence A. Sawchuk and Andrew C. Irvine

Using a case study approach, contemporary mate choice is explored in a small urban community located at the tip of the Iberian peninsula. Mate choice as reflected in the age difference between spouses is examined over periods of stability and radical change. Profound differences are seen in the marriage patterns of the middle class during the period of sudden and dramatic economic and political isolation. The increasing role of women in the labour force is seen as a major determinant of changing marriage strategies among the Gibraltarians. The biological implications of the historic marriage structure of the Roman Catholic community is also explored.

INTRODUCTION

A dynamic interplay of factors operates in choosing a mate in human populations (see e.g., Davis-Brown et al. 1987; Epstein and Guttman, 1984; Schoen and Woolredge, 1989). To illustrate the complexity of the process of finding an appropriate marriage partner, this study focusses on the civilian population of Gibraltar, a small highly urbanized community that experienced massive socio-political change in the 1960s. This chapter shows how this transformation further induced a radical shift in marriage patterns.

As Gibraltar possesses no natural resources, links to external sources of revenue have always been essential to the livelihood of Gibraltarians and to the economy of the Town. As a consequence, this dependency greatly increased the realm of social interaction and widened the pool of potential mates beyond the confines of the Rock. This interaction, primarily with Spain to which it is attached by a small isthmus, was severed in the later part of the 1960s in what has been called "the fifteenth siege of Gibraltar" (Jackson 1987). Following a series of constitutional reforms that began in the 1950s, Spain, in an effort to restate its sovereignty over Gibraltar, which it lost to the British in 1704, initiated a series of actions designed to cripple the economy and the political will of Gibraltarians. Restriction on the issuing of frontier passes into Spain represented the first in a series of political and economic actions initiated by the Spanish authorities. These actions had serious economic consequences because a substantial portion of Gibraltar's labour force resided in nearby Spain.

In 1967 a referendum was held in order to give Gibraltarians a choice of either to secede from Britain or to join Spain. The voice of Gibraltarians was heard loud and clear when the ballots of the referendum were counted and ninety-six percent of the eligible voters chose to remain under British protection. On May 6, 1969, the Spanish government closed the frontier to all except Spanish workers and to a few people with special passes. Tourists, a mainstay of the Gibraltar economy, were prevented from coming into Gibraltar by foot. On June 9, Spanish workers, whose numbers had shrunk from 12,000 to 4,666, were deprived of their work permits, thereby curtailing their employment in Gibraltar. The Spanish frontier gates were finally closed on June 22, 1969. Once again, Gibraltar was under siege and would remain so until Feb. 5, 1985.

During the siege, Gibraltar's economy suffered a decline in tourism, an increase in the cost of food and building materials, and a critical shortage in the labour market. Inflation, low wages and labour shortage led to several years of industrial unrest. When the border re-opened in 1985, Gibraltarians had undergone a remarkable transformation the scope of which is only now becoming apparent. The modern-day siege of Gibraltar provides a backdrop for examining the effects of major sociopolitical changes on marital behaviour.

GIBRALTAR AND THE CASE-STUDY APPROACH

The civilian population of Gibraltar can be seen as an effective analytical unit as it captures a broad range of meaningful social and biological interaction that occurs on a daily level. Framed by time and space, community based studies allow physical anthropologists to focus on how primary social and economic factors affect the population's structure and composition and, hence, its biological makeup. As Emery and McQuillan (1988) have pointed out, case studies elucidate local variation in mortality, fertility and natality, the major demographic features of historical populations. Despite the value and need for micro-level investigations, there is a conspicuous paucity of such studies. The reasons for this are varied and complex. Part of the answer may lie in the formidable problems of collecting data on a population over time. Furthermore, it is often difficult to delineate the boundaries of the study community owing to its open and fluid nature. This renders population comparisons next to impossible. Finally, a key factor of population growth is migration. Identification of the 'permanent' versus the 'transient' segments of the community is often problematic.

Application of the case study approach is greatly facilitated in Gibraltar by virtue of a number of unusual features (Sawchuk, 1993). First, the residents of Gibraltar are clearly and easily identified owing to the fact that they were civilians living within the strict confines of a fortress. Second, the comparatively small number of inhabitants and excellent registration system permit the investigator to readily identify individuals over time. Vital information on Gibraltar's inhabitants is available from a variety of sources; parish and synagogue registers, nominal census rolls and finally, government registers of births, deaths and marriages. Gibraltar is also sufficiently heterogeneous in its makeup to allow for the assessment of local variation at the community level as the result of religious affiliation, ethnicity, socio-economic status and so forth. Finally and perhaps most importantly, members of the Gibraltar community are willing and cooperative informants. Without the spirit of cooperation, any study based solely on statistics alone will ring hollow and lack a true anthropological insight.

USING HISTORICAL RECORDS TO RECONSTRUCT MARRIAGE PREFERENCES

The empirical analysis for this study is based on marriage records drawn from the civil registers located at the Supreme Court, Gibraltar. Each marriage record contains the date of marriage, age at time of marriage for both bride and groom, religion, occupation and whether previously married. To eliminate any confounding effects of remarriage, only first unions were examined.

This paper focusses upon one religious group in Gibraltar, the Roman

129

Catholics, who make up approximately 96% of the Gibraltar population. Notwithstanding the occurrence of occasional inter-faith unions that were strongly frowned upon by the clergy, the Roman Catholic community has had a separate sphere of interaction, tradition and attitudes to marriage compared to its Hebrew and Protestant counterparts in Gibraltar.

To understand how differences in wealth might have affected matrimonial behaviour, Roman Catholic unions are examined in terms of their socioeconomic class. This is done to explore the question of whether the cultural construct of social class acts as a mechanism of population subdivision in terms of one's decisions about choosing a spouse. We also examine marital patterns in Gibraltar both pre- and post-1969 and consider the implications of socio-political change and its role in the choice of a marriage partner. We have characterized these two periods as the 'Traditional Period' and 'Crisis Period' respectively.

To assess the effect of age on mate choice, the concepts of *age homogamy* and *age heterogamy* are employed. Homogamy and heterogamy denote respectively the similarity or dissimilarity of the characteristics of couples respectively, without specifically referring to which characteristics are being examined (Davis-Brown et al., 1987; Schoen and Woolredge, 1989).

Following the methodology of Atkinson and Glass (1985), a marriage between a couple whose ages were within five years of each other was deemed homogamous. If the husband was 5 years or more older than his wife the marriage was defined as *male heterogamous*. Similarly, if the wife was five years older than her husband the marriage was considered to be *female heterogamous*.

Since the choice of a spouse can be greatly influenced by one's social and economic standing within a community, the study also examined the effects of social class on marriage patterns both before and after the siege. The socio-economic status of a union was derived from the husband's occupation at the time of marriage (following the protocol outlined in the Registrar General's Report, 1938). While this definition is gender biassed, it is important to note that few women were actively engaged in jobs outside the home prior to the siege. Marital unions were classified into three broad socio-economic categories (SES): Upper or Class I (which included professional occupations); Middle or Class II (which included clerical and skilled labour); and Lower or Class III (partly skilled and unskilled occupations).

Many locals reluctantly confess that a social hierarchy still exists in

Gibraltar, a relic from old colonial times. Class boundaries continue to operate in the contemporary marriage pool. Gibraltar's social stratification is a consequence of a combination of factors. Class consciousness is fostered by large gaps in wealth, linguistic and educational differences as well as personal perceptions of occupational status (Sawchuk, 1992).

Marriages for each socio-economic group can thus be represented in a simple two-by-three box or matrix with each cell in the box representing the three marital types and the two temporal periods. Tables 1 through 3 provide the number of marriages observed in each category, as well as the percentage of each of the total marriages.

In order to evaluate whether the pattern of marriage was influenced by the temporal period or merely the result of chance the chi-square statistic was computed. Chi-square is a statistical measure of how far a sample distribution deviates from an expected distribution. The expected distribution in this case is determined by the law of independent association, that is if two events are independent, the probability of their occuring together can be computed as the product of their separate probabilities. In general, if the observed chi square statistic falls above the .05 level the observed pattern can be attributed to chance association. However, if the chi statistic has a computed probability of occuring less than 5 in, say, 100 trials (i.e., .05) one can assume that the two variables are not independent of each other but they are signficantly associated. In summary, the research strategy employed here is primarily directed at finding patterns of associations or changes in these associations and then to try to account for them.

RESULTS

Table 1 presents information on the 2322 marriages, according to socio-economic status, during the 'Traditional Period' (pre-1969) prior to the seige. The results indicate that marriage type is not independent of social class as the probability of having a chi-square value of 17.83 is only .00134. In other words, the chance of finding such a chi-square deviation was approximately one in a thousand — a very unlikely event. An examination of the column percentages reveals that high socio-economic couples were more likely to engage in unions where the male was at least five years older. In contrast, low socio-economic males were more likely to marry 'older' females. In essence, each socio-economic group had its own marriage preference according to age.

During the siege or 'Crisis Period', the pattern of marriage preference

Table 1. Marital Homogamy by Socio-Economic Status
During the 'Traditional Period'

Homogamy	High SES	Middle SES	Low SES
N	152	767	665
%	62.6	69.3	68.3
Husband Older			
N	85	302	250
%	35.0	27.3	25.7
Wife Older			
N	6	37	58
%	2.5	3.3	6.0
Chi-square=17.825		df=4	p=.00134

changed, as shown in Table 2. Homogamous marriages account for 74.6 percent of unions during this period, as opposed to 68.2 percent in the previous 'Traditional Period'. Nonetheless, differences in mate preference persisted between the three social classes (Chi-square = 11.9928 with a probability of .017). The traditional pattern of high socio-economic unions with 'younger' women and a preference for 'older' women among low socio-economic marriages remained. However, there was a significant change in the pattern of mate choice among middle class couples. Table 3 uses data from Roman Catholic marriages to show that marriage homogamy increased at the expense of both forms of age heterogamy after 1967. During the 'Crisis Period', 76.1 percent of all marriages were between couples 5 years apart, an increase of nearly 7 percent from the preceding period. The question that remains to be addressed is why such a shift in matrimonial behaviour occurred.

Table 2. Marital Homogamy by Socio-Economic
Status during 'Crisis Period'.

Homogamy	High SES	Middle SES	Low SES
N	77	572	160
%	68.8	76.1	72.4
Husband Older			
N	33	166	49
%	29.5	22.1	22.2
Wife Older			
N	2	14	12
%	1.8	1.9	5.4
Chi-square=11.99	df=4	p=.01741	

Table 3. Marital Homogamy among Middle-Class Roman
Catholics during the Traditional and Crisis Periods

Homogamy	Traditional Period	Crisis Period
N	767	572
%	69.3	76.1
Husband Older		
N	302	166
%	27.3	22.1
Wife Older		
N	37	14
%	3.3	1.9
Chi-square=11.25378	df=2	p=.00360

DISCUSSION

All communities have unique histories and it is only through an appreciation of a population's history that we can come to terms with its structure and composition. Gibraltar is no exception, as illustrated by the powerful influence that historical events had on spousal choice.

Pre-siege Gibraltar and the Traditional Marriage System

From the perspective of the local Gibraltarian male, Spain represented a vast pool of potential marriage partners not only because of geographic proximity but also due to a common thread of language, religion, and history. Neighbouring Spain was virtually an extension of the Gibraltarian's social and mental map. With a strong English pound and the relatively weak Spanish peseta, groups of young Gibraltarians would frequent Spanish restaurants and bars, attend bullfights and dances, and engage in other evening pleasures. Within easy walking distance, even the less well-off Gibraltarian could cross the border and enjoy the social offerings of Spain.

On the whole, women in Gibraltar, prior to 1969, remained at home until marriage and thereafter fulfilled the roles of wife, mother and homemaker. Such was the traditional way of life in Gibraltar. Given the expense and the lack of local post-secondary schools, young females were seldom encouraged to pursue secondary schooling and professional careers. As Stewart observed, "only rarely was a girl sent off to school in England, for her parents, however rich and aspiring they might be, would be preoccupied about their virtue" (1967:201). Interviews conducted with many Gibraltarian families revealed that during this time retention of their daughter's 'virtue' and at the same time 'getting her off the shelf' as quickly as possible took precedence over any career development.

Societies, like that of Gibraltar during the 'Traditional Period', that hold less egalitarian views of gender equality tend to have a greater frequency of age heterogamous marriages (Atkinson and Glass, 1985). Some researchers, moreover, suggest that in societies in which males are the main economic providers the greatest age differences will exist between spouses (Bergstrom and Bagnoli, 1993). This theory predicts that men delay marriage in order to increase their economic potential, therefore increasing their chances of attracting a more "desirable" mate. According to this model, women in such societies gain nothing by postponing marriage and in fact become less desirable as they age.

As the analysis of marriage preferences in Table 1 shows, the distinct and rigid class structure in Gibraltar plays a central role in defining the age of a spouse in the 'Traditional Period'. High SES men in Gibraltar were more likely to engage in 'husband older' heterogamous marriages, a trend that fits well with the model presented above. Low SES men are more likely to participate in age heterogamous marriages but of the 'wife older' type. This could be the result of the combined effects of men whose earning potential is not increased significantly by waiting and who end up, by the model's prediction, marrying older women who did not marry higher status individuals.

The 15th Siege of Gibraltar and Changing Matrimonial Behaviour

Under siege, the marriage pattern that existed for at least several generations underwent rapid transformation following a series of changes in the demographic, social and economic structure of Gibraltar. The chronicling of these events provides some insight into why matrimonial behaviour changed.

As a result of the Spanish blockade, Gibraltar was cut off from a source of plentiful and cheap labour as well as an inexpensive source of fresh food from Spain. The overland route for the large and lucrative European tourist trade was also severed. Gibraltarians were braced for hard times and the depletion of the labour market had to be resolved. To meet the crisis in the labour market, many local men held down two jobs or assumed long working hours. Women volunteered to work without pay; such was the public spiritedness of Gibraltarians under a state of siege.

Without the Spanish labour force, the number of men available to work fell short of demand. For the first time in Gibraltar's history, a significant number of local women entered the labour force in positions with the government, city council and private industry. Prior to the blockade, only a small number of unmarried women worked outside the home and they, for the most part, held down positions as typists and stenographers. Prior to the frontier closure, there was a reluctance of women and girls to enter paid employment (Marsh, 1967: 10).

While the blockade created a critical shortage in the labour market, other factors also contributed to create an increase in the number and types of employment opportunities now available for women. One factor was that the educational system in the post WW II period greatly improved and, accordingly, the young women were now better trained to seize newfound employment opportunities. Improved wages for women also contributed to the attractiveness of full-time employment. Another contributing factor was the growing social acceptance of women, their peers and their families, to enter full time employment outside the home. This growing acceptance of female employment was also stimulated by the increasing public solidarity in Gibraltar that prevailed during the early years of the frontier closure. In the small and closed community, word of mouth quickly spread the news that not only were positions open, but that employers were openly encouraging women to apply for positions. As women were successful in their pursuit of employment they, in turn, encouraged more and more women to seek employment.

Day-to-day contact with members of the opposite sex was a new experience for many young Gibraltarians who had attended separate schools since their teens. Once in the workplace, the number of linkages and possible networks available to the young Gibraltarians, particularly women, increased dramatically. This newfound social interaction was particularly evident among the middle class. No longer isolated in the home, women were free to join new peer groups. With more financial independence, women could participate more fully in group activities, precipitating a change towards gender equality.

The pattern typical of the 'Traditional Period' remained among the rich where males could afford to continue their preference for 'younger' women. Among the low socio-economic males there still existed the marked occurrence of female heterogamous unions. The new employment opportunities affected primarily the middle class as the poor were not able to avail themselves of them. While increased female participation in the labour force for the rich may have occurred, this was probably not a critical factor in selection of a mate for the wealthy.

The biological ramifications of the shift in matrimonial behaviour are far from clear and cannot be tested with the marriage record data at hand. However, it is reasonable to speculate that the most important change was that women from Spain were no longer readily available as potential mates and, consequently, there was a cessation of gene flow from Spain. However, the change in marriage selection was not necessarily distributed equally across the social classes. Like other populations, social class acted as a powerful force limiting the size of the pool of potential mates. It is also apparent that within each group there were distinct age preferences and this too could restrict the size of the mate pool. Yet, the only statistically significant trend in spousal selection occurred among middle class Gibraltarians. Since middle class men could no longer secure a Spanish bride, locally born women became necessarily more desirable. Not only did middle class males marry local brides more often but as a result of employment opportunities for women, it was possible to marry earlier. Marriages at younger ages generally translate into earlier first births. A shift of births into the younger age intervals usually lowers the risk of congenital anomalies or birth complications associated with older women bearing children. The reduction in gene flow from Spain through brides, in the short term, meant a temporary reduction in genetic diversity. From the perspective of the long term, the implications are much more difficult to determine. One point is clear, however, that the psychological mindset of the young Gibraltarians changed markedly and the Spanish country-side no longer represents a catchment area for potential mates.

MATE CHOICE AND GOVERNMENT LEGISLATION

Up to this point, we have explored how social class and age affect mate choice. These factors can be seen as internalized features of a society. There are situations, however, where external factors can play a profound role in mate choice. To illustrate this point, let us return to the Gibraltar example.

In the early eighteenth century, thousands of immigrants from the Mediterranean region and north-western Europe gravitated to Gibraltar seeking quick fortune, employment, or refuge. The colonial administration was quick to recognize the heterogeneous nature of the civilian population and assisted in the creation of separate facilities for the running of local affairs in education, regulating and policing its members, and providing health care for the sick and aged. As a result, throughout the nineteenth century the size of the civilian population of Gibraltar rose steadily, causing a number of problems in the garrison town. There was a lack of sufficient and affordable housing. Severe overcrowding and poor sanitation resulted in the ever present threat of a major epidemic. The increasing foreign-born segment of the civilian population challenged the security of the fortress. Owing to Gibraltar's limited territorial size, these problems were greatly exacerbated. Thus, the colonial administration took radical steps to check the unbridled demographic growth of the civilian population. One such step was entitled the Alien Orders in Council (1873). The government legislation not only effectively curtailed immigration. Marriage between a Gibraltarian female to a foreign-born male, following the Alien Order, resulted in the exclusion of the right to residency to the native born woman and subsequent offspring of such a union. This provides an example of the legislative arm of the colonial authorities dictating the mate choice of its civilian inhabitants. The legislation allowed native males to seek mates from outside the confines of the fortress while such opportunities were denied native born females. In biological terms, the legal actions of the government allowed gene flow to occur through females into the population while inhibiting the introduction of new genetic material through foreign-born males. To a foreign-born female, one of the attractions of securing a Gibraltarian male was economic, providing the opportunity to hold a British passport and for an increase in social status.

CONCLUSION

This study set forth to elucidate the complex nature of one aspect of human social behaviour, that of marriage. Marriage patterns are the product of a number of levels of societal relationships, each of which is inexorably linked. These levels range from large scale macro-level factors, as illustrated in Gibraltar, through political legislation of immigration, to other more micro-level factors including the interconnections between the community, the household and the individual. Each level influences preferences for a certain kind of mate. Among Gibraltarians, social class played a profound role in the selection of a spouse. Socioeconomic status influenced where one lived, whom one interacted with, what school one attended, who one's family felt was appropriate to date, all of which are part of the marriage process. Such cultural systems however are dynamic phenomena. Until the border closure in 1969, the pattern of marriage in Gibraltar was stable and conformed to traditional marriage pattern. With the state of siege, new conditions were created that recent generations of Gibraltarians had never experienced. The ripple effect of large scale political change was felt by every Gibraltarian, the result of which led to a new social and economic structure. The ramifications of such change altered marital behaviour and ultimately the structure and composition of the population of Gibraltar.

ACKNOWLEDGEMENTS

The authors wish to thank the many Gibraltarians who assisted us in our research. We are also grateful for the editorial assistance of Monica Dase and Stacie Burke. This research was supported in part by Social Sciences and Humanities Research Council (SSHRC) of Canada.

REFERENCES

Atkinson MA and Glass BL (1985) Marital age heterogamy and homogamy, 1900 to 1980. *Journal of Marriage and the Family*. 33:685-696.

Bergstrom TC and Bagnoli M (1993) Courtship as a waiting game. *Journal of Political Economy*. 101:185-202.

Davis-Brown K, Salamon S, and Surra CA (1987) Economic and social factors in mate selection: An ethnographic analysis of an agricultural community. *Journal of Marriage and the Family*. 49:41-55.

Emery G. and K. McQuillan (1988) A case study approach to Ontario mortality history: The example of Ingersoll, 1881-1972. *Canadian Studies in Population*. 15:135-158.

Epstein E and Guttman R (1984) Mate selection in man: Evidence, theory and outcome. *Social Biology*. 31:243-278.

Government of Gibraltar (1873) *The Alien Orders in Council, Gibraltar*. Gibraltar: Garrison Printing Press.

Jackson WGF (1987) *The Rock of the Gibraltarians: A History of Gibraltar*. Grendon: Gibraltar Books Ltd.

Marsh AI (1967) *Gibraltar Pay Structure Review*. Gibraltar: Gibraltar Library Printing Press.

Registrar General's Decennial Supplement. (1938) England and Wales 1931. Part IIa. *Occupational Mortality*. London: H.M. Stationary Office. pp. 189-210.

Sawchuk LA (1992) Historical intervention, tradition and change: A study of the age at marriage in Gibraltar, 1909-1983. *Journal of Family History*. 17:69-94.

Sawchuk, LA (1993) Societal and ecological determinants of urban health: A case study of pre-reproductive mortality in 19th-century Gibraltar. *Soc. Sci. Med*. 36:875-892.

Schoen R and Woolredge J (1989) Marriage choice in North Carolina and Virginia, 1969-71 and 1979-81. *Journal of Marriage and the Family*. 52:844-865.

Stewart JD (1967) *Gibraltar, The Keystone*. London: Murray

7

Population Regulation in an East African Pastoral Society
Cultural or Evolutionary Ecology?

Eric Abella Roth

Within anthropology today two major paradigms, cultural ecology and behavioural ecology, feature directly opposing views concerning population regulation. Cultural ecologists assume that all traditional populations practised population regulation and stress cooperative group selection behaviour as the mechanism for such behaviour. In contrast, evolutionary ecology's emphasis on individual-level natural selection dismisses population regulation as "a myth". An excellent test case for these opposing viewpoints is represented by Rendille pastoralists who have long been cited as a traditional population regulating their fertility and population growth. Until now, lack of viable demographic data negated direct tests of these claims. This paper analyses Rendille demographic data to provide such a test. In doing so it utilizes both cultural and evolutionary ecological methodology to evaluate group and individual demographic strategies.

INTRODUCTION

A major topic in anthropology today concerns the application of behavioural ecological models originally constructed for animal populations (Krebs and Davies, 1991) to human cultures. Defined as, "the evolutionary ecology of human behaviour" (Cronk, 1991:25), this revolutionary perspective encompasses wide-ranging anthropological concerns including paleontology, food acquisition, social complexity, kinship and child care (cf. Smith and Winterhalder, 1992a). Human evolutionary ecology assumes that cultural patterns are the product of Darwinian natural selection with its inherent mechanism of differential fertility and/or mortality. In this paradigm adaptiveness of a particular cultural trait is ascertained by maximizing effects on an individual's Darwinian fitness, measured via *Lifetime Reproductive Success* (LRS), i.e., the combined effects of differential fertility and mortality.

Evolutionary ecology's focus on individual reproductive success stands in direct opposition to earlier anthropological models of *group selection*, specifically those in which populations collectively dampen their reproductive success for the good of the group. These models arose from Julian Steward's (1955:37) formulation of *cultural ecology*, defined as the study of "the adaptive processes through which a historically derived culture is modified in a particular environment". As outlined by Smith (1984:58-60) a subsequent school of "ecological anthropologists" equated cultural adaptation with the concept of ecosystem equilibrium or *homeostasis*, and stressed the "regulating or homeostatic function of cultural practices" (Vayda and Rappaport, 1968:495). One movement within this school focussed on *population regulation*, that is adjustments in vital rates to keep population size within environmental limits (Bates and Lees, 1979:274). Today this subject exemplifies many of the differences between cultural and evolutionary ecology's theoretical perspectives and methodological approaches.

Table 1 summarizes many of these differences, specific to the concept of population regulation. These differences can be exemplified in the analysis and reanalysis of !Kung birthspacing patterns. As originally documented by the Canadian cultural ecologist Richard Lee (1977, 1979), the maintenance of long, four-year periods between births for this nomadic foraging population of Botswana and Namibia was explained through examination of ecological parameters. Lee considered the actual work involved in raising children in a hunting-gathering society like the !Kung's to be the function of three variables: weight of children, distance travelled and frequency of birth. Quantifying each variable, he demonstrated that longer birth intervals translate into less weight, represented by !Kung children at different ages, carried over identical time periods. Long birth intervals also translate into lower fertility levels and slow population growth, which Lee (1977:337) deemed adaptive on an individual and population level. Specifically referring to the latter, Lee (1977:337) states:

> Long birth spacing alone is not sufficient to keep the population in long-term balance with resources, but the modest amount of excess fertility of the Bushman is readily absorbed by infant mortality, occasional infanticide, and by outmigration.

Table 1. Major Differences Between Cultural and Evolutionary Ecology Paradigms

Variable	Cultural Ecology	Evolutionary Ecology
Currency	Energy Capture	Reproductive Success
Unit of Analysis	Population	Individual
Major Relationship	Group: Resources	Individual: Individual
Goals	Homeostasis	Maximize Reproductive Success
Mechanism	Group Selection	Natural Selection

Birth spacing may seem like a biological, rather than cultural, phenomenon. However, cultural patterns adopted by the !Kung, including a year-long post-partum taboo and breastfeeding on demand for up to four years, are necessary to maintain the long interbirth interval. Lee's analysis also exemplifies a common aspect of cultural ecological models, neo-functionalism, characterized by behaviours yielding an unintended benefit, thereby establishing a causal relationship (see Smith 1991:6). Thus while !Kung men explain the disadvantages of high fertility in the saying, "A woman who gives birth like an animal to one offspring after another has a permanent backache" (Lee, 1977:332), the unintended benefit to the group is lowered fertility levels, resulting in population-resource homeostasis.

Blurton-Jones and Sibley (1978) reanalysed the same material from an evolutionary ecology perspective. They hypothesized that !Kung demography and foraging patterns were the end products of natural selection. Specifically, they proposed that !Kung long birth spacing combined with female food gathering only every third day represented a bio-cultural adaptation to maximize a woman's reproductive success. To test this assumption they developed a computer simulation model incorporating varying birth spacing and foraging frequencies with the resultant weights of food and children carried by !Kung mothers. Their results, termed the "backload model" since weight carried was the most important factor, indicated that combining shorter interbirth intervals with more frequent foraging would not increase the reproductive success of !Kung woman, but rather would place them at a greater risk of injury and/or mortality. Blurton-Jones (1987) later compared this model with actual !Kung mortality data collected by the Canadian demographer Nancy Howell (1979). Both the model's prediction and the empirical data's actual mortality distribution converged on an "optimal birth space", that is one that maximizes reproductive success through the highest level of child survival to age ten, of approximately four years. From this close fit Blurton-Jones concluded that !Kung long interbirth intervals represent an individual, rather than a group, environmental adaptation.

To summarize, these analyses of the same data illustrate the differences in theory and methodological approach between proponents of cultural and evolutionary ecology as shown in Table 1. The former stress group selection, often acting through neo-functionalism, with the goal of population-resource homeostasis. To this group it is evident that, "... we know that people in all cultures and epochs have regulated fertility" (Nardi, 1981:31). In contrast, evolutionary ecology's view equating adaptation with high values of individual reproductive success arising from natural selection relegates population regulation to the realm of myth (cf. Bates and Lees, 1979). Unfortunately vindication of these opposing perspectives remains hindered by a dearth of data. As one test of the validity of these paradigms this paper analyses demographic data for Rendille pastoralists of northern Kenya, a population long cited by various anthropologists (cf. Douglas, 1966; Spencer, 1973; Sato, 1980, Kreager, 1982; Harris and Ross, 1987) as regulating their population growth through elaborate cultural practices.

THE STUDY POPULATION

The traditional Rendille subsistence base featured nomadic mixed-species pastoralism, with Rendille herding camels, goats and sheep throughout the Kaisut Desert in what is today Marsabit District, northern Kenya (Fratkin, 1991) (see Figures 1 and 2). Rendille were thought to dampen their fertility in relation to a low carrying capacity and scarce resources. In particular, it was hypothesized that Rendille regulated their population in accordance with their slow-growing camel herds, which constitute their major source of food, transportation, wealth and status.

144

Figure 1. Ethnic groups in study locale (Courtesy of E. Fratkin, Department of Anthropology, Pennsylvania State University)

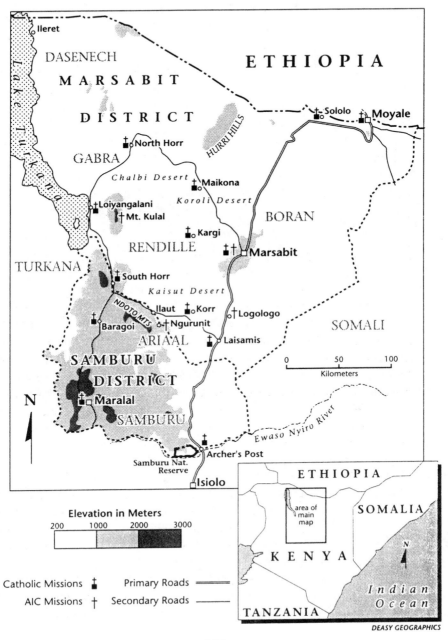

Figure 2. Rendille with livestock (Courtesy of E. Fratkin,
Department of Anthropology, Pennsylvania State University)

Rendille view their camel herds as fixed assets that take years to build. As such they are reluctant to divide them among their children. The society therefore features primogeniture, with the eldest son inheriting all the family livestock. In addition, unlike many Sub-Saharan African populations, polygyny is discouraged among the Rendille, as sons from multiple marriages could dispute inheritance rights. To eliminate potential conflict Rendille have practised infanticide upon children whose inheritance rights may be unclear; making them one of the few societies that practise male, rather than female, infanticide. While monogamy and infanticide can slow population growth, the greatest single factor determining Rendille demographic structure is their elaborate age-set system.

The Rendille age-set system features the formation of new male age-sets every fourteen (lunar) years. Membership in the system begins when a youth is circumcised, marking the transition from a boy to a warrior. Eleven years later warriors marry; immediately attaining the status of elder. These changes represent more than life-cycle transitions. Each is associated with particular economic and social roles. A boy stays close to his father's large patrilineal, patrilocal village, called a *gob*. In contrast, warriors move away from the *gob* to tend livestock in remote animal camps termed *fora*. To complete the cycle, upon marriage the new elder

146

moves back to the *gob*, and establishes a new household. Age-set systems in East African pastoral society serve multiple purposes. They ensure a large labour pool for livestock duties, encourage solidarity among warriors who share age-set membership, and provide an agreed-upon means for the transference of property, i.e. livestock, necessary to establish a new household (for more about East African age-sets see Baxter and Almagor, 1978).

An essential Rendille age-set formation rule is that a son should belong to the age-set three removed from his father's. A first-born son therefore could be over forty years of age before marriage. Since births outside marriage are discouraged due to possible inheritance conflicts this rule delays and dampens male reproduction. Yet the most important features of the age-set system are the cultural concepts of *teeria* and *sepaade*. The former is embedded in the cyclical nature of the Rendille age-set system, which features the repetition of age-set names over time. Every three age-sets forms an age-line, linking grandfather to father to son, as illustrated in Figure 3. One cyclically repeating line, termed *teeria*, and synonymous with "first-born", assumes an elevated status in Rendille society. All daughters of *teeria* men are termed *sepaade*, and are forbidden to marry until all their brothers wed. Thus, a first-born *sepaade* woman could also be above forty years of age before marriage. Since the female reproductive period spans the ages 15–49, such women would greatly sacrifice their reproductive potential.

Figure 3. Rendille Concept of Age-lines, Showing Three Age-lines, A, B, and C Linking Fathers, Sons and Grandsons (After Beaman, 1981: 393)

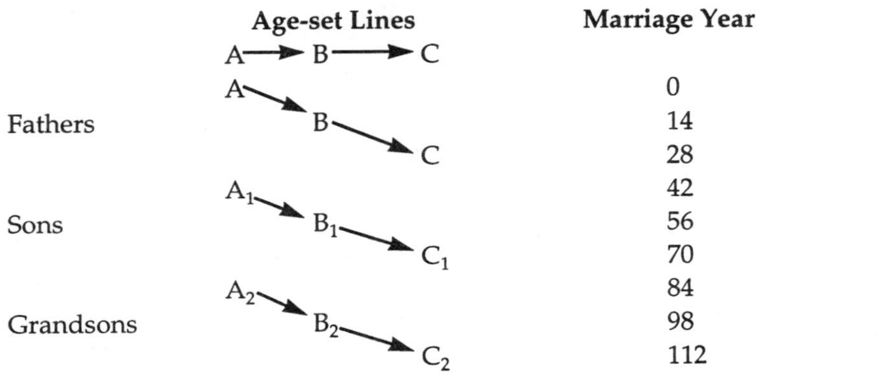

Age-set Lines	Marriage Year
A→ B→ C	
A	0
Fathers B	14
C	28
A₁	42
Sons B₁	56
C₁	70
A₂	84
Grandsons B₂	98
C₂	112

The *sepaade* tradition appears to exemplify group selection, with these women sacrificing their reproductive success to maintain a rough equilibrium with the growth of their camel herds (cf. Sato, 1980). However, as is often the case, this claim of population regulation remained untested due to lack of reliable demographic data.

I had the opportunity to gather such data in 1987 and 1990 when I conducted demographic surveys of Rendille villages in the population centre of Korr, Marsabit District, northern Kenya (see Figure 1). As a result of recurrent drought in the 1970s and 1980s (cf. Fratkin and Roth, 1990; Roth and Fratkin, 1991) the majority of Rendille now live sedentary lives clustered around former famine food distribution centres. The initial surveys, done in conjunction with UNESCO's Integrated Project on Arid Lands, were conducted under the impression that sedentism would result in higher Rendille fertility and population growth rates, as commonly recorded for other populations making the transition from nomadism to sedentism (cf. Roth, 1985). Only after analysing the data from these surveys did I realize that the Rendille age-set system was still functioning and apparently limiting population growth under sedentary conditions.

Table 2. Historic dates in Rendille age-set formation

Rendille Age-Set	Samburu Equivalent[1]	Circumcision Year	Marriage Year
D'fgudo	Il-Merisho	1909–1910	1920
Irbaalis*	Il-Kiliako	1923	1934
Libaale	Il-Mekuri	1937	1948+
Irband'if	Il-Kimaniki	1951	1962
D'fgudo*	Il-Kichili	1965	1976
Irbaangudo	Il-Kororo	1979	1990

* *teeria* - high status age-set, fathers of *sepaade* women
+ Irregularity based on Grum (1977:81; cited in Beaman, 1981:394)

[1] Rendille increasingly use the age-set terminology of their southern pastoral neighbours, the Samburu. The equivalents are therefore included here.
Sources: Spencer, 1973:33, Grum, 1977:79,81,109; Sobania, 1988:135; Beaman, 1981:394; Schlee, 1989:76.

Subsequent fieldwork concentrated on linking vital events, e.g. birth, marriage, deaths, to the Rendille age-set system. Each year within all age-sets is named after a day of the week. Such "day-years", termed *teeba*, are repeated twice in the fourteen-year age-set span. Previous research by cultural anthropologists (Beaman, 1981; Sobania, 1988) used oral histories to fit day names to the Western calendar as shown in Table 2. While Rendille do not know their age in a Western sense, elders drawn from each village readily provided information concerning age-set membership, parity order, birth sequence and survival history for all households within their village. Adult females, excluded from the Rendille age-set system, were enumerated by information pertaining to their fathers' age-set membership and their own birth order. Given such information, age-specific estimates of fertility and mortality were derived by fitting these events to the Rendille historic calendar. Special care was taken to elicit possible exceptions to the prescribed age-set sequence of circumcision, initiation, marriage and first birth. These included early and/or late marriage, births to infrequent, but always present, polygynous marriages, and unusual age-set membership, i.e. not the culturally specified three from one's father. Drawing upon information provided by male informants in a group format, I was able to completely enumerate fourteen large villages, encompassing over four hundred households (Roth, 1993, In Press).

RESULTS

Utilizing standard "female-dominant" demographic techniques in which fertility and population growth are calculated only through female lines, a comparison of *sepaade* and *non-sepaade* women found that *sepaade* possessed significantly lower average number of births over the course of their reproductive span (Roth, 1993). The *sepaade* level of 3.69 was only 61% of their *non-sepaade* counterparts' measure of 6.04. This large fertility differential is due to the significantly higher mean age at marriage of *sepaade* ($\bar{x}$ = 30.2 years), a full eight years above that of the *non-sepaade* ($\bar{x}$ = 22.2) in the sample. Combining fertility patterns with offspring mortality data permitted calculation of annual growth rates for both groups. The resulting measure of +2.9% for the *non-sepaade* sample means that they would require only 24.3 years to double in size. In contrast, the *sepaade* rate of +0.3%, indicates that over a quarter of a millennium would be required for population doubling.

These results favour cultural ecology's concept of group selection, with *sepaade* collectively dampening their reproduction relative to *non-sepaade.* However, in a 1991 pilot study (Roth, 1993) fifty Rendille, evenly divided by sex, denied that the intended primary function of the *sepaade* tradition was population regulation. Instead informants unanimously argued that it was a response to periods of inter-tribal warfare. During these times warriors would go on livestock raids, leaving their own herds unattended. *Sepaade* women then assumed the role of male warriors, living in *fora* and performing traditional male livestock duties, e.g. herding, watering, digging wells, etc. Evidence for these claims is represented by *sepaade* today spending long periods in *fora* camps, as well as the tradition of circumcising *sepaade* one year after the similar ceremony for their brothers' age-set.

Survey respondents also stressed *sepaade's* negative aspects, noting that due to their lower fertility levels *sepaade* frequently failed to produce surviving male heirs to inherit the family herds. Armed with this information, subsequent analysis (Roth, 1993) revealed that fear of such "disinheritance" led men who took *sepaade* as first wives to enter into subsequent, polygynous marriages far more frequently than those who married *non-sepaade*. This raised the possibility of Rendille men utilizing the *sepaade* tradition to increase their reproductive success by first marrying a *sepaade* woman and then taking a younger second wife. In this strategy a man could have offspring by his *sepaade* wife, plus reap the fruits of her considerable labour and knowledge of livestock. These last benefits could be utilized to support offspring from a second marriage, thereby offsetting the lower expected fertility of the *sepaade* first wife. Thus while *sepaade* dampen their reproductive success, a man marrying a *sepaade* could have reproductive levels high, or higher, than his counterparts with a *non-sepaade* wife.

To test this model Lifetime Reproductive Success (LRS) was measured for Rendille males, following Borgerhoff Mulder's (1987) methodology that incorporates both fertility and mortality to yield a Darwinian perspective on reproductive success. This is as follows for males:

L = lifespan
M = proportion of lifespan spent married
W = mean number of reproductive wives per married year
O = number of surviving offspring per wife-year

In this methodology, Lifetime Reproductive Success (LRS) is simply the product of these four measures (LRS = L x M x W x O).

For the present analysis calculations of LRS are confined to men of one specific Rendille age-set, *Il-Kimaniki*, whose members married in 1962. Selection of this group was due to two features. First, with twenty-eight years of marriage first wives had completed their reproductive period by the time of the 1990 survey. Secondly, the survey sample revealed approximately equal numbers of men marrying *sepaade* (n = 22) as *non-sepaade* (n = 24) women, highlighting male mate choice in this particular age-set.

Table 3 presents the components and final measure of LRS for *Il-Kimaniki* men who married *non-sepaade* first wives in comparison with those who wed *sepaade*. As can be seen, lifespan (L) and proportion of lifespan spent married (M) measures are almost identical. As expected, men marrying *sepaade* first wives featured higher polygyny levels, denoted by a higher mean number of wives per married year (W). This is the most important single component of LRS, negating the lower number of surviving offspring per wife-year (O) from marriage to a *sepaade*. The overall result is a higher LRS for men marrying *sepaade* first wives.

Table 3. Calculation of Male Lifetime Reproductive Success (LRS), for Males who Marry *Non-Sepaade* vs. *Sepaade* First Wives

Variable	Non-Sepaad		Sepaade	
	Mean	S.D.	Mean	S.D.
(L) Life Span	63.63	5.50	62.45	6.77
(M) Proportion of Life-span Married	0.45	0.04	0.44	0.07
(W) Mean Number of Reproductive Wives per Married Year	1.13	0.54	1.39	0.67
(0) Number of Surviving Offspring per Wife-Year	0.18	0.07	0.16	0.08
LRS Lifetime Reproductive Success	5.00	1.50	5.18	2.13

DISCUSSION AND SUMMARY

Demographic data for Rendille pastoralists of northern Kenya permitted a test of two conflicting anthropological paradigms. Standard female-dominant demographic analysis favoured cultural ecology's emphasis on group selection, with *sepaade* women featuring significantly lower fertility and population growth measures than *non-sepaade*. In contrast, calculation of Lifetime Reproductive Success for Rendille males revealed *Il-Kimaniki* age-set men who married *sepaade* first wives featured higher LRS rates than did men marrying *non-sepaade*. These contradictory results mirror the distinction made by Low et al. (1992:11) concerning units of analysis between demographers and evolutionary ecologists, "Biologists tend to look at individual lifetimes and how they vary; classical demographers look at groups". Yet which position most accurately depicts Rendille demography?

The answer is both. As the historical demographer E.A. Wrigley (1978:36) observed, while the benefit of fertility strategies "is usually analyzed in terms of the group, it is clear that it must influence individual behaviour if it is to operate at all". On the group level *sepaade* effectively dampen population growth on a cyclical basis, supporting the group selection position of cultural ecology. Simultaneously, evolutionary ecology's emphasis on the individual focusses attention on the individual costs and benefits of the *sepaade* tradition within the larger context of Rendille society. To begin this examination consider how fathers are affected by the tradition. In the patrilineal Rendille culture, a father socially denotes his reproductive success only through his sons. These offspring, and in turn their male offspring, are the only children whose labour and economic support he can count upon in old age. In contrast, his daughters, *sepaade* or otherwise, marry outside his clan and their children will belong to their husbands' lineage. As for husbands, *Il-Kimaniki* men marrying *sepaade* women featured higher LRS than their counterparts who married *non-sepaade* first wives. Overall, reduced reproductive success, which may benefit the entire group's demands on environmental resources, is borne by only one specific, culturally specified, segment of Rendille society, the *sepaade*.

In conclusion, both cultural and evolutionary ecological paradigms proved valuable in examining and understanding the role of the *sepaade* tradition in Rendille population regulation. This finding suggests that rather than representing an either-or dichotomy the two paradigms can be effectively utilized in conjunction to analyse the effects of bio-social behaviour on human demography.

ACKNOWLEDGEMENTS

I wish to express my gratitude to the Office of the President, Republic of Kenya for their support and approval of this research project. Likewise, I am grateful for the financial support provided by the Canadian International Development Agency, the United Nations Educational, Scientific and Cultural Organization, The National Geographic Society, the Social Sciences and Humanities Research Council of Canada, and the University of Victoria. As always, I am thankful for the knowledge, kindness and careful reading of the text by my friend and colleague, Dr. Elliot Fratkin, Department of Anthropology, Pennsylvania State University. Above all, I am indebted to the Rendille people, particularly Mr. Larion and Ms. Anna-Marie Aliaro, who put up with me.

REFERENCES

Bates, D and S Lees (1979) The myth of population regulation. In N Chagnon and W Irons (eds.): *Evolutionary Biology and Human Social Behaviour*. North Sciute, MA.: Duxbury. pp. 273-289.

Baxter, P and U Almagor (1978) *Age, Generation, and Time*. New York: St. Martin's Press.

Beaman, A (1981) *The Rendille Age-Set System in Ethnographic Context: Adaptation and Integration in a Nomadic Society*. Ph.D. Dissertation, Boston University.

Blurton-Jones, N (1987) Bushman birth spacing: A test for optimal interbirth intervals. *Ethol. and Sociobio.* 8:183-203.

Blurton-Jones, N and R Sibley (1978) Testing adaptiveness of   culturally determined behaviour: Do bushman women maximize their reproductive success by spacing births widely and foraging seldom? In N Blurton-Jones and V Reynolds (eds.): *Human Behaviour and Adaptation*. London:Taylor and Francis. pp. 135-158.

Borgerhoff-Mulder, M (1987) On cultural and biological success: Kipsigis evidence. *Amer. Anthrop.* 89: 619-634.

Cronk, L (1991) Human behavioral ecology. *Ann. Rev. Anthrop.* 20:25-53.

Douglas, M (1966) Population control in primitive groups. *Br. J. Soc.* 17:263-273.

Fratkin, E (1991) *Surviving Drought and Development: Ariaal Rendille Pastoralists of Northern Kenya*. Boulder: Westview Press.

Fratkin, E and E Roth (1990) Drought and economic differentiation among Ariaal pastoralists of northern Kenya. *Hum. Ecol.* 18:385-402.

Harris, M and E Ross (1987) *Death, Sex and Fertility: Population Regulation in Preindustrial and Developing Countries*. New York: Academic Press.

Howell, N (1979) *Demography of the Dobe !Kung*. New York: Academic Press.

Kreager, P (1982) Demography in situ. *Pop. Dev. Rev.* 8:237-266.

Krebs, J and N Davies (1991) *Behavioral Ecology: An Evolutionary Approach*. 3rd Edition. Oxford: Blackwell.

Lee, R (1977) Population growth and the beginnings of sedentary life among the !Kung Bushmen. In B. Spooner (ed.): *Population Growth: Anthropological*

Implications. Cambridge: MIT Press. pp. 328-342.

Lee, R (1979) *The !Kung San: Men, Women and Work in a Foraging Society*. Cambridge: Cambridge University Press.

Low, B, A Clarke and K Lockridge (1992) Toward an ecological demography. *Pop. Dev. Rev.* 18:1-32.

Nardi, B (1981) Modes of explanation in anthropological population theory: Biological determinism vs. self-regulation in studies of population growth in Third World countries. *Amer. Anthrop.* 83:28-56.

Roth, E (1985) A note on the demographic concomitants of sedentism. *Amer. Anthrop.* 87:380-382.

Roth, E (1993) A reexamination of Rendille population regulation. *Amer. Anthrop.* 95:597-612.

Roth, E. (In Press) Pastoral demographic regimes: two East African examples. In E Fratkin, K Galvin and E Roth (eds.): *East African Pastoral Systems: Frontiers in Theory and Method*. Boulder: Lynne Rienner.

Roth, E and E Fratkin (1991) Composition of household herds and Rendille settlement patterns. *Nom. Peop.* 28:83-92.

Sato, S (1980) Pastoral Movements and the Subsistence Unit of the Rendille of Northern Kenya. *Senrie Ethnological Series* 6:1-78.

Schlee, G (1989) *Identities on the Move*. Manchester: Manchester University Press.

Smith, E (1984) Anthropology, evolutionary ecology and the explanatory limits of the ecosystem concept. In E Moran (ed.): *The Ecosystem Concept in Anthropology*. Boulder: Westview. pp. 51-86.

Smith, E (1991) *Inujjuamiut Foraging Strategies*. Chicago: Aldine du Gruyer.

Smith, E and B Winterhalder (1992a) *Evolutionary Ecology and Human Behaviour*. New York: Aldine du Gruyer.

Smith, E and B Winterhalder (1992b) Natural selection and decision making: some fundamental principles. In E Smith and B Winterhalder (eds.): *Evolutionary Ecology and Human Behaviour*. New York: Aldine du Gruyer. pp. 25-60.

Sobania, N (1988) Pastoral migration and colonial policy: A case study from Northern Kenya. In D Johnson and D Anderson (eds.): *The Ecology of Survival*. London: Lester Crook. pp. 219-239.

Spencer, P (1973) *Nomads in Alliance: Symbiosis and Growth Among the Rendille and Samburu of Kenya*. London: Oxford University Press.

Steward, J (1955) *Theory of Culture Change*. Urbana: University of Illinois Press.

Vayda, A and R Rappapport (1968) Ecology, cultural and non-cultural. In J. Clifton (ed.): *Introduction to Cultural Anthropology*. Boston: Houghton-Mifflin. pp. 477-497.

Wrigley, EA (1978) Fertility strategy for the individual and group. In C Tilly (ed.): *Historical Studies of Changing Fertility*. Princeton: Princeton University Press. pp. 135-154.

8

Birth Rates and Bones

Mary Jackes

Skeletal biologists attempt to reconstruct populations using the techniques of palaeodemography. While the emphasis has been on mortality, a consideration of fertility may provide useful information on past societies. The cultural and biological determinants of fertility in modern and historical societies provide the context for an examination of Huron fertility in the seventeenth century based on ethnohistorical sources. The value of palaeodemographic estimators of fertility, derived from childhood ages-at-death, is tested using data from three Ontario ossuaries dating from 1500 AD to 1636 AD. The estimators provide credible fertility rates, changing through time. Interpretation of the data in terms of mortality would not accord with information derived from ethnohistory of the Huron.

Anthropologists who work with skeletons think more about death than about birth. Nevertheless, there are reasons why it is worthwhile for anthropologists to turn from death to birth:

(1) The reconstruction of populations and their mortality rates based on the study of skeletons (palaeodemography) has been strongly criticized in the last decade or so and there have been several suggestions that fertility can be more accurately estimated from the study of skeletons than can mortality.

(2) Fertility is a very important aspect of demographic reconstruction: fertility can be regarded as basic to the age

structure of a human population and, because it is sensitive to a variety of factors, it may tell us a great deal about
a population.

All human populations have biological constraints. These are simple
with regard to mortality. There is a "shape" to mortality, a curve that
describes the general pattern of human death. It is well-established that
there is a certain minimum rate of death in the period around the time of
birth, because of congenital defects. Male mortality before 12 months of
age is higher than female mortality and thus the sex ratio, which is in
favour of males at birth, comes closer to 1:1. The sex ratio stays about
even, with female deaths in childbirth matched by deaths in young males
because of accidents or violence. Cultural practices may alter this near
equality: female infanticide in the past in China and the continuing bias
in favour of males in southern Asia causes female mortality rates to be
very high in early childhood. But there are also instances of populations
in which daughters are favoured, including the Huron who inhabited
parts of Ontario up until 1649 (Tooker, 1964:122). In later adult life the sex
ratio is in favour of females.

After the first year or two of an individual's life, it becomes less likely
that death will occur, although children aged 1–4 are very susceptible to
infectious diseases and to famine. Older children (of around 10–15 years)
generally have the lowest probability of death. Death becomes increasingly probable as one reaches maturity and, as people get older, they become
more susceptible to infection and to degenerative diseases. In fact, the
human organism has a time-limit on it. The great majority of people will
die before 100 years of age. In spite of claims of great age in the Caucasus
area, it seems that the oldest attested individual was 113 years (an
American woman who died in 1928; Garson, 1991).

We can assume that, in general, human mortality has had the same
"shape" throughout history and that slight modifications in the general
shape of the curve will arise only under very particular conditions (war,
or certain diseases that may increase the death rates of young adults:
tuberculosis is the major disease in this category). Although it is often
considered that there must have been variations in mortality levels in the
distant past, attempts to demonstrate alterations in mortality at periods of
great change in human history, such as the transition from hunting and
gathering to agriculture, have not been convincing (Jackes, 1993).

In this chapter we will consider two questions: (a) can fertility be a
sensitive indicator of certain population characteristics; and (b) can fertili-

ty be accurately estimated from the age at death distribution of a cemetery?

The age structure of a population has a great influence on its levels of fertility and mortality. In a population with many elderly people, the overall birth rate would be low in comparison with the death rate; in a population with many young adults, the overall birth rate will be high. In the past, such age distribution variants in a population were determined by fertility. Fertility is primary in determining the age structure of the population. If each adult woman has 2.1–2.5 children (depending on levels of medical care), then the human population would remain stationary because two children surviving to reproductive age constitute "replacement-level fertility". Under this circumstance, there would be an almost equal number of individuals at each age. The "population pyramid" with many young and fewer elderly individuals, would become a "population rectangle". In the past, however, any variations would probably have been around a level of slight increase.

A rise or fall in fertility may have been the determining factor in the age distribution of a population in the past. The twentieth-century increase in world population is a result of reduced mortality, brought about by mass vaccination programmes, the availability of antibiotics, and improvements in water supplies. But even in the twentieth century, the fertility rate is an important factor in mortality levels: since the probability of death is highest among infants, reduction in infant mortality reduces the overall rate of mortality.

There is a very complicated relationship between infant mortality and fertility. The death of an infant increases the probability that the bereaved mother will become pregnant sooner. But a decline in fertility has a tendency to reduce the level of infant mortality. The very fact that women have fewer children means that those children are more likely to survive. When the interval between the birth of two children is short, the older child is at risk of death from poor nutrition and the younger sibling is more likely to be premature and of low birth weight.

Modern fertility reductions in developed countries result from an interplay of medical, social and economic factors. But there is reason to doubt that all countries of the developing world today will immediately follow the path taken by the developed countries in the past (Trussel et al., 1989), and we can take it for granted that, if there has been family limitation in the past, it was not based on the same criteria that have altered family life in developed countries so drastically within the last century.

Van de Walle (1992) has pointed out the extraordinary difference between a society in which every marriage potentially results in 15 children or fewer, as "fate" decides, versus a society in which most marriages involve a conscious choice to limit the number of children, on the grounds that limitation is both possible and desirable. It is very difficult for most people in the developed world to realize that even questions about the ideal number of children are irrelevant and unanswerable for societies within the "natural fertility" regime. It is clear, however, that when we try to determine fertility rates for past populations, we should not expect people to have been "numerate" with regard to ideal family size. This is true now even in African populations in which birth spacing by sexual abstinence is a well-established practice.

NATURAL FERTILITY

Natural fertility is the term used for rates of fertility achieved in groups that do not practise any method of birth control. The North American Hutterites are generally used as an example of ferility without contraception, and therefore an indicator of uncontrolled fertility. A better example of natural fertility may be provided by Old Order Mennonites who migrated from Manitoba to Mexico in the 1920s (Felt et al., 1990). The women marry at about 20 years of age and have an average of 9.5 children. Only 3% of women are childless. The first child is born after 18 months of marriage and subsequent births follow every 25 months or so until the woman reaches age 40–41.

MEASUREMENT OF FERTILITY

When a modern census is taken, we get a reasonably accurate idea of how many live births have occurred each year, relative to the number of women in the reproductive years (usually considered to be 15 to 44 years of age). A number of demographic statistics are published by governments so that we know what the various fertility rates are. When we have a group of skeletons we can, theoretically, arrive at very good estimates of the same fertility rates. The estimates are not based on examination of innominates because there is no foolproof method of determining fertility directly from female pelves: palaeodemographers have to use the age at death distributions as the basis for studies of past populations that had no adequate registers of births and deaths.

This is done by the use of the life table, a relatively simple set of columns of arithmetic that makes it possible to determine from the numbers of dead in each age group how many people were alive in each age group.

The *total fertility rate*, the completed family size of the average woman at the end of her reproductive period, can be estimated from the life table column that gives figures on the age distribution of the living population. The estimation is relatively accurate except when a population is increasing rapidly.

The *crude birth rate* (CBR) is the number of live births per 1,000 people per year. Anthropologists have used this statistic for skeletal samples because it is very simple: it can be estimated from 1/mean age at death.

PROBLEMS IN PALAEODEMOGRAPHY

Problems occur with both sorts of demographic statistics when they are applied to skeletal samples, whether based on women of reproductive age, or a group of 1,000 people. You have to be sure that the collection of skeletons from the cemetery includes every single person who died in a given area over a certain length of time and you have to be sure that you know their ages accurately to within a few years. In fact, the buried bones of the very old and the very young do not preserve as well as the bones of active and healthy young adults. Added to this, cultural practices often give a different burial to very young babies than to older children or adults. And it is very unlikely that we can give very accurate ages at death to every single skeleton in a cemetery.

A CBR of 50 would be extremely high, yet this is the sort of birth rate that samples of archaeological skeletons often give. This may often be the result of the methods of estimating adult ages that we use: these commonly give adult ages that are too young (Figure 5 gives an example of this), and the result may be that the mean age of death is around 20 years: $(1/20)*1000 = 50$).

The crude birth rate and the *crude death rate* (CDR) are equal when a population is stationary, that is, when the population is neither decreasing nor increasing. When the population is increasing the birth rate is higher than the death rate. In order to understand why this happens, we can examine Figure 1. Figure 1 is based on the work of Coale and Demeny (1983), who used 326 reliable sets of mortality data from all over the world to provide us with models of human demographic statistics. We use their "West" family of tables because these represent general human mortality, rather than very specific patterns. Figure 1 employs the West 1 tables, illustrating the highest level of mortality with a CDR (and

CBR, when the population is stationary) of 50 or so. We use this high level of mortality because it illustrates what we know of archaeological mortality (Jackes, 1992) and of early mortality in Europe from historical sources (Loschky and Childers, 1993). We plot the age distribution of the West 1 model living population at seven different levels of fertility, beginning with fertility so low that the population is declining by 1%. When the rate of natural increase (r) is 0, then the population is stationary. As the birth rate rises above the death rate, the population increases (here from 1% to 5%). Figure 1 shows that an increasing population has a greater number of young people. As the distribution of ages in the increasing population changes, the mean age at death of the population as a whole falls.[1]

Figure 1. The Age Distribution of Living Populations Based on West 1 Model Data from Coale and Demeny (1983:55, 105).

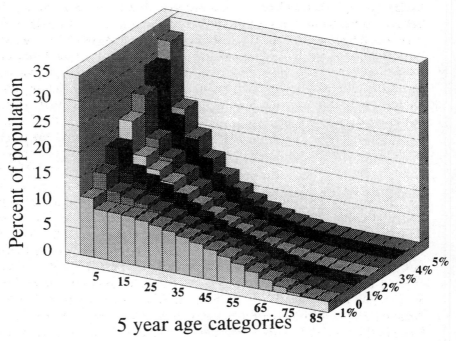

West 1 data (males and females combined) shows how the percentage of children in a population increases when the birth rate is greater than the death rate.

Variations in the mortality or fertility of different groups, in different times, places, and economies, can only be demonstrated if we have a good method of comparison that allows us to avoid the difficulties presented by infant underrepresentation. But, to repeat, this is not the only problem that may confront skeletal biologists. All anthropologists, and especially skeletal biologists, may be dealing with very incomplete data. The data could be inadequate: (1) because the ages of adults and children may not be accurately known; or (2) because a very short time period within a small community may provide unrepresentative figures; or (3) because not everyone living in the community within that time period is represented in the figures, or some combination of all three. For these reasons, which apply to both skeletal and living samples, methods may have to be devised that paint a broad picture rather than a close view accurate in every detail.

One possible method of comparison of the age structures of archaeological groups is based on the assumption that there is a relationship between juvenile and adult mortality, and that age-at-death data within very broad age categories will carry some information about the age structure, and hence, the fertility rate of the population. Since infant mortality rates (that is, the rate of death in the first 12 months of life) are variable and difficult to assess accurately (whether working from skeletons, documentary evidence or interviews), we should not try to estimate overall mortality from infant mortality. But it **is** useful to compare the levels of mortality after one year of age between different groups and reasonably accurate estimates of age-at-death can generally be made for the skeleton of an individual under 25 years. Figures 2 and 3 demonstrate the relationship between the age at death distribution and fertility. In Figure 2 we plot the average probability of dying from age 5 to age 19 against the figures that show whether a population is declining (by .5% or 1%), is stationary (0) or is increasing (by .5% to 5%). The data used come from the West model tables 1 and 5. It is clear that, as a population increases, as the birth rate exceeds the death rate, the dead will include a greater number of people aged 5 to 19. Figure 3 gives a demonstration of the great difference in the age at death distribution between a population that is in decline (-1%) and a population that is rapidly increasing (5%). The importance of the level of fertility to the ages of skeletons found in a cemetery is very clear.

Variations in fertility are, however, based on an extremely complex series of factors and we have to look at some of these factors before we can decide whether we can make reasonable estimates of past fertility.

Figure 2. Deaths in Childhood From 5 to 19 Years.

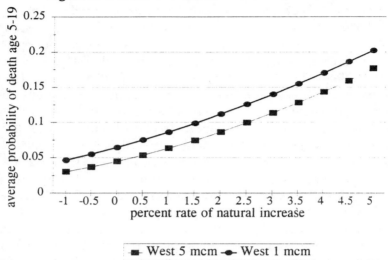

As the rate at which a population increases changes, the average probability of death for individuals aged 5 to 19 increases, based on Coale and Demeny (1983) West 1 and West 5 tables of mortality.

Figure 3. The Age Distribution of Deaths From 5 to 90 Years.

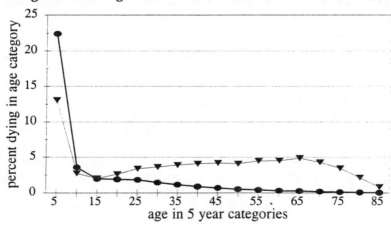

At the same level of mortality (West 1), the age pattern of mortality is altered. Here deaths in populations declining by 1% and increasing by 5% are compared.

DETERMINANTS OF FERTILITY

Demographers have emphasized the importance of what have been called the proximate determinants of fertility (Bongaarts and Potter, 1983). The four determinants identified as of primary importance are: (1) the rate of non-marriage, (2) contraception, (3) lactational amenorrhoea/sexual abstinence, and (4) abortion. Four less important factors are: (1) frequency of intercourse, (2) intrauterine mortality, (3) natural sterility, and (4) involuntary sterility caused by sexually transmitted diseases.

More recently Reinis (1992) has said that it is essential to consider also what is called "stopping behaviour". This means that at a certain point before she reaches menopause, a woman may decide "enough is enough", or social convention may decree that a woman who is a grandmother should not have more children, as, for example, in West Africa. Under some kinship systems, confusion of ages between generations may be undesirable. Such a system would enforce sexual abstinence on women in middle-age.

All people understand the relationship between coitus and conception. It was at one time considered that Australian Aborigines were ignorant of this relationship, a measure of the low esteem in which native Australians were held by 19th-century Englishmen. In truth, Aborigines must have been quite aware of the facts of life, otherwise the control of female sexuality would hardly have been such a key element of social organization. The major error with regard to conception among populations without access to accurate knowledge of reproduction was that the period of menstruation was the time of greatest fertility. This error, and the sequestration of women around the time of menstruation as "unclean", would serve to increase coitus during the most fertile period of the female cycle, the several days around the time of ovulation.

Even under fertility regimes that might be regarded as "natural", that is non-contracepting, there may be practices that limit the size of families. *Coitus interruptus* is accepted as a method of fertility limitation in the Koran, and crude drugs derived from plants probably acted as contraceptives or abortifacients in many regions in the past (Riddle and Estes, 1992). The word "condom" had already entered the written English language by 1700, referring to dried sheep's gut. While condoms may have been used primarily to avoid infection, it can hardly be doubted that contraceptive practices were current during periods demographers describe as times of "natural fertility".

Even under a "natural fertility" regime, variations in fertility rates may be quite broad. Bongaarts and Potter (1983) have suggested, based on American Hutterites, that 15.3 children is the mean family size. But the Hutterites may well be models of exceptional, not general, human fertility. Nutrition is of great importance and the Hutterites may simply be too well-nourished with too much animal fat and protein in their diet to serve as models for pre-industrial humanity.

The role of nutrition in fertility

The age of menarche (the age of first menstruation) is partly controlled by nutritional levels (Danker-Hopfe, 1986). The length of the period of adolescent sub-fecundity may also depend on nutrition, since there is evidence that the age of fertility is controlled by the fat level. The amenorrhea (non-menstruation) and anovulatory (non-fertile) cycling of adolescents suffering from anorexia nervosa has led to a clear understanding of the importance to fertility of weight gain in young females. Amenorrhoea may occur with as little as a 10% reduction in weight. The importance of fat is underlined by the consideration that female athletes, with a high body weight based on muscle, rather than fat, may become amenorrheic. Peak fertility in females occurs when about one-third of body weight consists of fat (Frisch, 1988). While there have been criticisms of the details of Frisch's work (see Ellison, 1990), there is no doubt that a certain level of fat is needed to allow ovulation every 28 days and to support 9 months of pregnancy and several months of lactation. The amount of subcutaneous fat also has an influence upon the age of menopause (Kirchengast, 1993).

The effect of nutrition on fertility and lactation has been demonstrated by the records of past famines: in eighteenth-century Iceland; South Asia in the nineteenth and twentieth centuries; Sudan in recent years; Japan in the last century; and the war time experiences of women in Holland and Russia. The Dutch experience (Hart, 1993) showed that previously well-nourished mothers could bear healthy children during famine. The major effect was the great reduction in conceptions during the period of greatest distress. This is true of all recorded famines: female fecundability is reduced; protein deficiency can affect male fertility; male mortality in famines is high and occurs before the peak of female mortality; famine brings with it diarrhoea and increases susceptibility to diseases like measles; lactation may be prolonged; and there may be migration and spousal separation. Many factors function together to reduce fertility.

Although famines show the effect of sudden and extreme nutritional stress, chronic undernutrition may have more general effects on fertility.

Well-nourished mothers produce infants at term with good birth weights who grow up to produce healthy children themselves, since maternal body size and composition is more important than diet during lactation. Furthermore, the transferral of immunity to nursing infants is most effective in well-nourished mothers so that infant mortality from infection is more likely when the mother herself is ill-nourished. Despite some controversy on the topic, Huffman et al., (1987) show that less milk with a lower fat content is produced by thin than by fat women: this results in intense and constant suckling by infants, which has the effect of reducing fertility. A low level of dietary fat increases the length of menstrual cycles, further reducing overall fertility, and there may be increased intrauterine mortality (fetal loss) with the resultant lowering of overall fertility.

We must not assume, however, that food alone will determine fertility levels. Pennington (1992) has shown that low !Kung Bushman fertility did not alter with a transition to sedentary life.

Cultural determinants of fertility

Whether contraceptive practices and/or abortion are available obviously effects fertility. Even in the absence of effective contraception or abortion there have been practices that function in a similar manner. Infanticide rates of 43.6% among the Yanomama (Early and Peters, 1990); the high infant mortality recorded as caused by "overlaying" in the crowded beds of the poor in eighteenth-century London; the astounding death rates among babies sent away to wet nurseries on the outskirts of cities in France and Russia; all attest to lack of contraception, and paradoxically, such practices serve only to increase the likelihood that the mother will conceive again.

The reason for making this statement is that most evidence shows that prolonged breastfeeding reduces fertility. Although some argue against this proposition (e.g., Fitzgerald, 1992), and post-partum taboos or pressure towards sexual abstinence during breast feeding are relevant (Trussel et al., 1989), lactational infecundity does seem a major factor in increasing birth intervals. Figure 4 gives a clear demonstration that the waiting time to a second or later pregnancy increases as the period of lactation lengthens. As the length of time a mother breastfeeds increases, so does the length of time before the mother again becomes pregnant. Ovarian function is suppressed by the hormone prolactin and prolactin levels are directly related to the intensity and frequency of suckling by an infant: it is clear that questions of maternal nutrition, type and extent of supplemental feeding, and provision of an infant with objects to suck on, will make a difference here. But the data presented by Goldman et al. (1987), and reworked here as Figure 4, give us data with strong predictive value. If we have information on cultural norms for nursing, we have a basis for estimating the number of children the average woman in that culture will bear.

Figure 4. Time of Waiting for Conception of Second and Subsequent Children in Months.

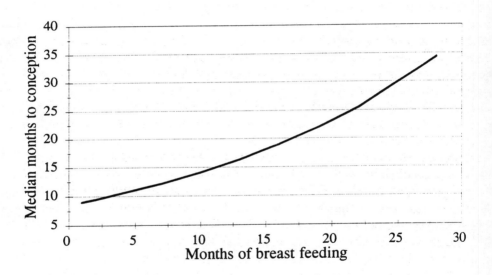

Exponential curve based on months of breastfeeding ($r = .9081$; se = .08). Data from Goldman et al., 1987:138.

The social-cultural norms of human groups have a great influence on rates of fertility. All human societies have social controls on sexual intercourse. Since copulation can result in pregnancy and pregnancy has a high likelihood of adding another member to a group, a new member who must be fitted in to the complex web of biological, social, religious and economic relationships that govern the interaction of human beings and facilitate physical survival, no human society permits unregulated intercourse. The regulations partly determine fertility patterns.

The northwestern European pattern of marriage has been described by Hajnal (1982) and shown to have reduced levels of fertility by half the potential maximum. In the area of Europe west of an imaginary line drawn from Trieste to St. Petersburg in the period up to the industrial revolution: (1) mean age of women at first marriage was 23 years or older (men over 26); (2) the couple was in charge of their own household (with the male, although not much older than the wife, as the head); (3) young people were employed outside their homes as servants before marriage; (4) at least 10% of women never married.

In conjunction with religious influence, the requirement of economic self-sufficiency before marriage (Secombe, 1990), led to slower population growth than in southern or eastern Europe. The extreme example here is Ireland where celibacy rates and the average age of marriage were both very high, especially because marriage was delayed until one son could inherit the family land.

Fertility reduction can, however, result from other, very different scenarios. Just as Ireland has been of interest to anthropologists and demographers for its delayed marriage and celibacy, so there are a number of studies of Jamaica as a system involving delayed marriage without celibacy (e.g., Wright, 1988). A woman in Jamaica is likely to be involved in three types of relationships: visiting unions, common-law unions and marriage. At all ages, visiting unions are most common and marriage is the least common form of relationship. This system reduces fertility quite markedly even though the great majority of girls enter unions as adolescents. The "time lost" through changing partners means that even women who have had 5 or more partners have an average of only 2.63 children, although it might be expected that a women would desire a child within each union.

Another form of fertility reduction that has been widely discussed is polygyny, which is the marriage of one man to many women. We would expect high fertility under this regime because women marry young and they remarry quickly in the case of divorce or widowhood. But fertility reduction will occur because the husband's older age is important in reducing the fertility of his junior wives and because polygynous wives may be poorly nourished. The West African pattern (Caldwell et al., 1992) of early female marriage, delayed and polygynous marriage by men and long periods of sexual abstinence by women (during pregnancy: three years post-partum, unless the baby died, in which case one year; upon becoming a grandmother) served as an efficient fertility check and the breakdown of this system has contributed to the high fertility of late twentieth-century Africa.

Even within populations in which there might seem to be no reins on fertility, it is unlikely that fertility will reach its maximum. India has not been characterized by high fertility in spite of having had virtually universal nuptiality. In Uttar Pradesh, a province in north central India, the average age of female marriage is still under 9 years and the average age of consummated marriage is 14 years (Basu, 1993). Yet, the first birth is delayed until the woman is nearly 19, and in the past the first live birth did not occur until the woman was an average of 21 years old. This long first birth interval occurs because Uttar Pradesh has exogamous villages and patrilocal marriage. The young wife is isolated and of low status in her new home and she is very likely to return to her parents for months at a time until she becomes pregnant (Basu, 1993).

Long periods of breast feeding are the norm in south Asia and long term post-partum sexual abstinence may be enforced. In fact, women may return to their parents for up to a year after the births of their first one or two children (Chaudhry, 1990). While divorce has a very low rate, widowhood occurred in the past at a very early age. In the 1930s women were commonly widowed in their late twenties and Hinduism traditionally forbids remarriage.

A TEST CASE FOR FERTILITY ESTIMATES IN PALAEODEMOGRAPHY

It is quite obvious that human fertility is the result of a complex interplay of physiological, environmental and economic/cultural factors. How can we hope to estimate fertility for past populations based only on skeletal collections? There is one case that provides us with an almost unique opportunity for testing whether this is possible. The Huron who lived in southern Ontario in the sixteenth and seventeenth centuries provide us with an opportunity to test the value of palaeodemography based on skeletal collections. The reasons for this are: (1) burial in ossuaries and (2) detailed reports by French missionaries.

Ossuaries, as found in Ontario, are large communal burial pits that have been filled with the disarticulated and mingled bones of the dead (Jackes, 1994). On the basis of the French accounts, it is believed that the Ontario ossuaries contain the bones of almost all the dead from a limited number of communities within a limited period of time. They therefore should provide information that is much more biologically meaningful than that from most archaeological sites for which we have no such assurance that the dead represent a biological population from a certain time span.

We will consider the ethnohistorical accounts in conjuction with information from Ossossané Ossuary, which is believed to be the site of the burial witnessed by the French Jesuits in 1636 (Kidd, 1953). Here we have an unprecedented opportunity to test the validity of information derived from skeletons, since the French wrote extensive descriptions of Huron life.

THE HURON

Our knowledge of the Huron is based on French descriptions of a period of change, after the introduction of European trade and diseases had probably caused alterations to the way of life, particularly to the patterns of trading, hunting and warfare. By 1580, European trade goods were not uncommon in southern Ontario, and within a short time all the Huron had settled in Simcoe County, probably to take advantage of proximity to a major trading route. Yet Trigger (1986:163, 220) argues that the basics of Huron life would have been maintained in the face of these changes. We will be discussing the period up to 1636, when traditional life still prevailed. By 1649, Huron life in Ontario had come to an abrupt and tragic end and there is no possibility of understanding the Huron past based on modern Huron people living under comparable conditions.

The Huron group we will be examining had probably been settled in Huronia for at least 200 years. They were members of the Attignawantan Nation, the people among whom the French Jesuits lived almost exclusively until 1640. The records of the Jesuit Fathers, the *Jesuit Relations*, upon which we will base our study, are therefore most accurately viewed as a description of life around Ossossané, the largest town of the Attignawantan or Bear Nation. At Ossossané lived the man who was not only the chief of the Bear Nation, but of the whole Huron Confederacy. In the town there were 1500 to 2000 people living in more than 40 longhouses and the town was fortified and surrounded by small satellite villages, probably eight.

Nutrition

A very large proportion of the Huron diet consisted of maize. Heidenreich (1971:163) estimated that 65% of the calories in the Huron diet would have been derived from corn and Schwarcz et al. (1985:201) have calculated a 52% corn contribution to the diet based on stable isotope data. Beans, squash and gathered foods were also important, but Schwarcz et al. (1985) find no evidence that beans were a major source of protein. Fish caught in the autumn and meat from hunting must have rounded out the diet. However, ethnohistorical evidence suggests that fish and especially meat were not important components of the diet. Their major contribution was to feasts. Dogs were eaten but they cannot have provided much fat; probably less than 1% of their body weight consisted of fat. The dogs survived on scraps around the Huron villages and these were not rich pickings (Heidenreich, 1971:148).

It is clear that the Huron diet was low in fat. Animal fat would have been available only in late October when hundreds of men hunted white-tailed deer that had fattened on autumn acorns. However, considering the number of men involved, the time taken, and the distances travelled, the yield from deer hunting was very low. Vegetable oils were available: although oil was not extracted from corn, sunflowers were grown for seeds. However, sunflower oil was used chiefly to dress the hair, and vegetable or fish liver oil and animal fat (deer or bear) were smeared on the skin. Though oil and fat were poured on corn, this normally occurred only on ceremonial occasions (Tooker, 1964:69).

Work

During the 1620s and 1630s the Huron were working extremely hard. European iron axes must have helped the men to clear more land and the women must have worked harder to produce surplus corn meal to trade for furs. Beavers became extinct in Huronia around 1630 and so the trade with the French could be maintained only by the women tilling, planting, harvesting, and pounding the corn meal to trade for beaver pelts and to store against crop failure. The women's horticultural work must have taken all the spring and summer. The spring often required replanting if late frosts occurred, and was also the time for collecting and carrying firewood. The women and children might spend their summers in cabins near the fields weeding and protecting the crops. The women also made pottery, collected hemp and made twine for nets, made reed mats and baskets and prepared skins.

Men fished in the autumn and hunted in October and March (fasting for a week to ensure success in hunting). The men went far to the south and east on hunting trips, possibly involving 300 to 500 men for over a month.

Determinants of fertility

It is immediately clear that the age at menarche among the Huron might have been quite late. Young girls helped with the hard agricultural work and their diet is unlikely to have allowed them rapid adolescent fat development. Nevertheless, corn does provide a good deal of food energy for the amount of effort expended (corn provides more fat and starch+sugar than other grains). Furthermore, there is evidence for an Amerindian adaptation favouring the maximization of body fat in the context of a low fat diet (see e.g., Beizer, 1990).

Sexual activity apparently began at quite an early age. The French priests found this difficult to accept, but we should not interpret the Jesuits' statements to mean that Hurons were complete libertarians. Embracing in public was not permitted and it seems likely that the Huron, whether unmarried or married, tended to have sexual intercourse outside the village in private (Trigger, 1987:440 n.29) except during certain curing ceremonies (Tooker, 1964:106). Since the Huron lived in longhouses in which two families shared a number of central hearths, and the sleeping arrangements involved all family members huddling together by the fire within an area about 14 X 11 feet (Heidenreich, 1971:117–118), it is indeed very likely that the Huron insistence upon self restraint extended to intercourse within the village. Many men were absent from the village for long periods from March to December, and much of the winter was taken up with elaborate feasts and ceremonies. The snowy woods of January and February in northern Ontario cannot be conducive to dalliance, so the frequency of intercourse was probably low.

Sexual abstinence was required before prisoners were tortured and before games of lacrosse between villages. Sexual abstinence was required of lactating females. The premarital sex may have seemed entirely free to the Jesuits, but the adolescents must have chosen their partners from those in marriagable kinship categories. The eight Huron clans were exogamous and people could not marry within three degrees of consanguinity on both maternal and paternal sides. For this reason the initial relationships, whether visiting unions or common-law unions, would have to be with marriageable partners because any of the relationships could lead to marriage upon pregnancy. With the permission of the girl's father a necessary precondition, the pregnant girl more or less chose whom she wished to say was father of the child. It appears that marriages could occur before a pregnancy but, without children, divorce and rapid remarriage was common.

Fertility after the first child

Once a child was born marriages became very stable and adultery was uncommon. If there was a death, marriage to a dead brother's widow or a deceased wife's sister was normal. Remarriage required a wait of one year (Trigger, 1987:52).

Lactation commonly lasted for 2 to 3 years (Tooker, 1964:123), although supplements of prechewed meat might be given. Weaning or the feeding of a child whose mother had died was based on a thin soup of cornmeal boiled in water. Supplemented breastfeeding for such a long period would mean that ovulation was suppressed to some extent, but wide spaces between births was ensured by a post-partum taboo that lasted for the whole period of nursing, the child sleeping between the parents (Tooker, 1964:123).

Marital separation was very common, although the expeditions of the men out of the village were planned so that not all men were away at once, leaving the village unprotected (Tooker, 1964:49).

The Arendahronon Nation originally dominated trade with the French from 1611 on when the Huron began to oust the Algonkian middlemen. Later the Attignawantan Nation with its capital at Ossossané probably took over. Each year in the 1620s a trading expedition was sent to the St. Lawrence, taking a month for travel each way. By 1633 the trading party consisted of 500 men.

Trading corn for the furs, meat and dried fish of the Algonkians to the north was important to the Huron diet, but autumn fishing and winter hunts were crucial. Beginning in 1636, when the autumn fishing was disrupted by epidemics, lack of fish contributed to the crisis. The Huron had already overhunted the local deer and were forced to go on long hunting trips in October and November to find the acorn-fattened deer far to the east and south. Again in March, the Huron set out to hunt when the deer, facing late winter starvation, congregated in clearings searching for food.

Warfare was another cause for marital separation. Every spring and summer 500 or 600 young men went to raid Iroquois territory. They might be away from six to eight weeks, return when their cornmeal ran out and then go out again (Tooker, 1964:29-30).

Altogether, it is hardly surprising that the French said "the women... are far from being fruitful with long suckling and not cohabiting with their husbands all that time" (Charlevoix, 1761:2:80). To this they could have added the hard physical labour and restricted diet of the women and the fact that many of the men were away from home for large parts of the year.

Health of the Attignawantan Nation

The French considered the Huron to be healthy in comparison with the inhabitants of northern France in the first half of the seventeenth century, but we have minimal basis for assessing even the most fundamental factors, such as infant mortality. French Canadian infant mortality rates, perhaps around 183 per 1000 live births in the late seventeenth century (Nault et al., 1990), were low for Europeans of that period. While we have no idea of the proportion of Huron infants dying before age 1, Ontario ossuaries must be assumed to have an underrepresentation of infants among the dead since credible levels of infant mortality (approaching 180 out of each 1000 live born babies dead by 12 months of age) are not reached at any site in historic Huronia. Nevertheless, one of the chief causes of childhood illness and mortality (bad drinking water) can be excluded from consideration since the French stated that the Huron only drank water that had been used to boil corn. Furthermore, long suckling and wide birth spacing must have reduced infant mortality.

The hygiene in the crowded, smokey and lice- and flea-infested longhouses did not impress the French (though they cannot have been models of hygiene themselves). Hands were not washed but wiped on hair or on dogs' coats. Children urinated in the longhouses, although the French commented on the "decency and modesty" of the adults (Heidenreich, 1971:148), and dogs were given free range. The longhouses must have been ideal situations for the transmission of respiratory infections, lungs and eyes irritated by the smoke of the hearths, sweat lodges and tobacco. Huron sinus cavities exhibit marked bone changes indicative of constant infections, and middle ear disease certainly affected the children (Varney, 1994). Pulmonary TB must have been common in Huron villages (Pfeiffer, 1984) increasing young adult mortality. Low level infection deriving from the very high rates of dental pathology beginning in early childhood, with many teeth lost to caries and abscessing, must have been universal. Although it is considered that the most serious diseases among the Huron were introduced from Europe, not only tuberculosis but syphilis was already present (Larocque, 1991), lowering fertility.

Periodic crop failure occurred, leading no doubt to diarrhoea and increased mortality levels among children under five (there were droughts in 1628 and 1635). But even in good years the diet may have been quite marginal. Vitamin C may have been deficient during part of the year, and dependence on maize may have reduced iron and zinc levels, since these minerals are not easily absorbed in a high-fibre diet. A maize-based diet may lead to pellagra as a result of niacin deficiency. Mild pellagra symptoms include emotional instability, hallucinations, diarrhoea and a rash on any part of the body exposed to sunlight. Beans or meat and fish must be consumed in quantity to compensate for the absence of niacin in corn. Furthermore, corn should be cooked in water that has had lime added to it in order to increase the relative amounts of essential amino acids. Heidenreich (1971:165) has suggested that the calcium carbonate in the water in Huronia might have increased the slightly deficient calcium in the Huron diet; it might also have made the water sufficiently alkaline to avoid pellagra. But the greater dependence on corn and the reduction in hunting and gathering because of increased emphasis on trade with the French, and the concentration of population within historic Huronia, might well have tipped the balance, leading to some of the unexplained illness recorded by the French.

From 1634, the French began to record a series of bad years with illness of an indeterminate nature starting in the summers, culminating in an outbreak of smallpox in 1639. Estimates of mortality by the end of 1639–40 indicate a drop in the Huron population from about 30,000 in the early 1620s to about 10,000 in the early 1640s (Trigger, 1986:233). Is the fall in population to be attributed only to increased mortality, or does Ossossané give evidence of falling birth rates in the period up to 1636, when there is no record of severe epidemics?

Analysis of Huron demography up to the early summer of 1636

The method used in this analysis of Huron fertility from skeletal data ignores children under 5 years of age because of the documented burial of Huron infants outside the ossuaries (see e.g., Saunders and Spence, 1986). All adults are grouped into a single category because our present techniques of adult age estimation, together with preservational bias, tend to place too high a proportion of the population within the reproductive years. This is illustrated in Figure 5, which compares the age at death distributions for the site of Uxbridge from skeletal data and model life table data. The method is therefore a substitute for the more usual fertility statistics because those statistics depend on good estimates of the number of children dying before 12 months of age and of the number of women of reproductive age (Jackes, 1988).

Figure 5. Comparison of Age at Death Distributions for
Uxbridge Ossuary and Coale and Demeny West Model
Table Level 4 mortality r = .005.

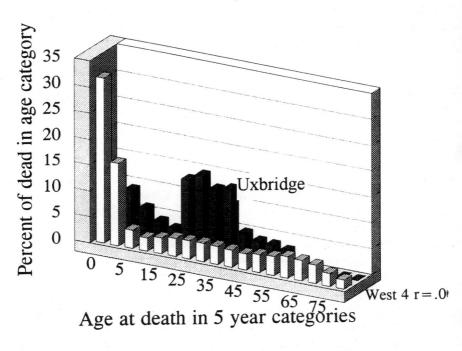

The two distributions have equivalent mean childhood mortality and similar
juvenile adult ratios. Archaeological samples commonly show
increased young adult deaths, which may result from age assessment
techniques.

We need first to establish some idea of Huron demographic parameters before contact with the French. For this we will use Uxbridge, a completely excavated and systematically analysed Huron ossuary (Pfeiffer, 1986). Ossuaries, by definition, are secondary burials, so that an ossuary contains large numbers of disarticulated skeletons, buried after the flesh has decomposed or been removed. For this reason it is very difficult to arrive at a completely accurate count of the number of individuals buried. Bones are mixed and broken, and many will also have suffered postmortem damage. On the basis of mandibles, Pfeiffer (1986) has determined that the minimum number of individuals (MNI) at Uxbridge is 457, with 312 adults of 18 years and over and 145 sub-adults under about 18 years of age. The method of subadult age estimation used was Ubelaker's reworking (1989) of the Schour and Massler dental eruption schedule.

Based on Pfeiffer's age-at-death distribution, we determine values for two "estimators" (see Jackes, 1992 for discussion). These estimators are:

(1) the juvenile adult ratio (JA) proposed by the French palaeodemographers Masset and Bocquet-Appel (e.g., Bocquet, 1979), which is calculated on the basis of the ratio of children 5 to 14 years old to adults 20 years and over;

(2) the mean childhood mortality (mcm: Jackes, 1986), which is the average probability of death between age 5 and age 19 using the probability of death values calculated in a life table.

Figure 6. The Ratio of Juveniles to Adults Among the Dead (West 1, Males and Females Combined)

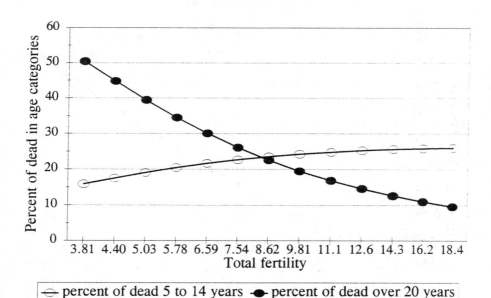

The mortality level is constant but, as the level of fertility changes, the West 1 model data demonstrates that the number of 5 to 14 year-old children increases relative to adults over 20.

Figure 6 shows how the proportions of adults and sub-adults among the dead change as the total fertility of a population changes. The total fertility is calculated here from the combined male and female age distribution of the living, provided by Coale and Demeny (1983) for West model table 1. Figure 7 shows the relationship between total fertility and the average probablity of death between ages 5 and 19 based on West 1. It is clear that the relationship between the estimators and fertility is so close that fertility can be predicted from the estimators. As demonstrated in Figures 1 to 3, if mortality levels are held at about the same level, but fertility levels increase or decrease, then the age structure of the population changes, thereby altering the age distribution of the dead.

Figure 7. The Mean Probability of Childhood Death (aged 5 to 19) Increases as the Fertility Rate Increases, although the Mortality Level (West 1) is Kept Constant.

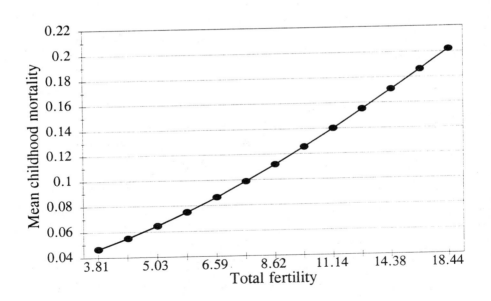

Thus, it is possible to use these two estimators to get an idea of fertility based on the age distribution of the dead. We will use model data as the source of fertility figures, so the only question is to determine the best set of data to use for the analysis. There are many levels of West mortality tables, and there are also a number of model tables published by the United Nations. Here we will use West model tables 1 and 5 because they encompass the levels of mortality exhibited by the Ontario ossuaries and give data on non-stationary populations. We could predict fertility from model table data by regression analysis, but, as in Figure 8, we can simply plot mean childhood mortality, juvenile adult ratio of the dead and total fertility on the one graph and from that get an idea of the fertility levels in archaeological populations. The relationship of the juvenile adult ratio and mean childhood mortality in archaeological samples has been established in a number of analyses which have also shown that the method can give us information about whether the samples are biased or from non-stationary populations (e.g., Jackes, 1993). The total fertility figures are calculated from Coale and Demeny (1983) population data for West 1 and West 5, as (the number of male and female children under 12 months divided by the number of females aged 15 to 44) multiplied by 30, which represents the 30 years between 15 and 44. We exclude the data for populations increasing at more than about 3.5% per annum as irrelevant to the present research.

Uxbridge, which we are using as an exemplar of pre-contact Huron demography, would fall a little way off the line in Figure 8 that expresses the relationship of the juvenile adult ratio (JA) and mean childhood mortality (mcm). This indicates that the Uxbridge Ossuary may represent a population that was not stationary. It is important to know whether the Uxbridge population was non-stationary, and to determine this we can test whether the calculation of the life table with an adjustment for an increasing population will bring the point closer to the line (Jackes, 1986). In fact, calculating the life table for r = .005 (r = the rate of natural increase, here 0.5% per year) allows the Uxbridge estimators to accord with model data. A valid adjustment to the Uxbridge sample might also be the addition of more adults since the French clearly stated that people who died by drowning, freezing or violence were excluded from ossuary burial (Tooker, 1964:132). The point will be lowered slightly on the line by such an addition, meaning that the fertility estimates that we will make will be the maximum, not the minimum estimates.

Using information based on model life tables (Coale and Demeny, 1983) with equivalent values for JA and mcm, we can estimate that total fertility was less than 5. That is, a Huron woman living around 1500 AD who survived to age 45, would most likely have had 4 live born children.

**Figure 8. Trend Line Derived from Decreasing, Stationary and
Increasing Model Populations (West 1 and 5) Shows the
Relationship Between Childhood Mortality, the Ratio of
Juvenile to Adult Deaths and Total Fertility in Huron Ossuaries.**

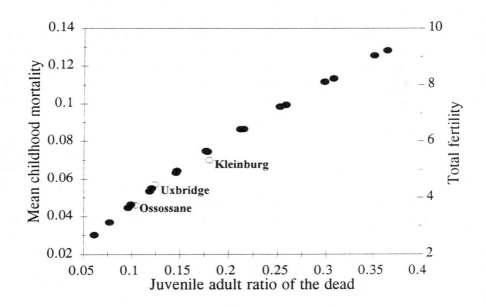

Kleinburg (adjusted for 1% population increase) and Uxbridge and Ossossané
(adjusted for .5% population increase) Ossuaries are plotted to allow an
estimation of fertility levels.

It is not a simple matter to establish the demographic parameters for
later Huron sites. Kleinburg, dated at around 1580-1600 AD, should provide good information on the Huron at the very beginning of contact,
direct or indirect, with Europeans. Ossossané, probably dated to 1636 (in
fact, to the seventh Monday after Easter that year; Kidd, 1953), should tell
us about the period just before the most devastating epidemics and
famines recorded by the Jesuits, and before the introduction of firearms to
the Mohawks intensified the wars with the Iroquois.

Despite the possibility that Huron ossuaries provide the best data
available to palaeodemographers (Jackes, 1986; Sutton, 1988), age estimation for skeletons from ossuaries is particularly problematic because the

ages must be based on isolated bones. Ages based on different skeletal elements, even different methods for the same skeletal elements, may give inconsistent results (e.g., Sullivan, 1990; Jimenez and Melbye, 1987).

It is absolutely essential that the minimum number of individuals (MNI) be reliable: reduction in the MNI will bias the results of our analyses very strongly, increasing the estimator values. Since underrepresentation of adults is known to be a factor because adults who died violently were excluded from ossuary burial, maximum estimates must be used. The best estimates available at present are as follows: (1) 617 people were buried at Kleinburg and around one third of these died before age 15 (Pfeiffer, 1986); (2) 681 individuals were buried at Ossossané and just over 20% of these died before age 15 (Katzenberg and White, 1979; Saunders and Melbye, 1990).

Larocque's (1991) age estimates for Kleinburg and Ossossané will be used for comparison with Uxbridge since the same technique of observing children's tooth development was employed by Larocque as by Pfeiffer (1986).[2] The data plotted on Figure 8 strongly suggest that the Huron population continued to increase until about 1600 AD, perhaps flowering under the impetus of early trade with Europeans, perhaps responding to the passing of a wave of tuberculosis that had affected the Huron the previous century (Jackes, 1988:64). The best estimate for Kleinburg is that the people living there had a total fertility rate of five, and that the population was increasing by slightly under 1% per annum.

During the period just before the recorded epidemics and wars of 1639–1649 the increase appears to have slowed. While the Ossossané population was not stationary, and certainly not declining, the average number of live born offspring seems to have been quite low, at about three. In the face of the epidemics, famines and warfare that were to strike the people within a few months, the fertility rate could not sustain the population.

CONCLUSION

The French stated that long periods of lactation and sexual abstinence were practised by the Huron. Sexual activity for 30 years without contraception, combined with up to three years of nursing per child, might well be expected to lead to birth intervals of four years.[3] Assuming 30 years of unrestricted sexual activity, the maximum Huron total fertility rate would be seven, meaning that the average Huron woman must have had fewer than seven children. The Kleinburg data are in accord with this and illustrate Huron life under ideal conditions. The Uxbridge Ossuary, which is earlier in time, is likely to have had a lower total fertility rate as a result of the high incidence of tuberculosis (Pfeiffer, 1984). Increased population density, intensification of trade, and probable worsening of the diet in the sixteenth century, led to reduced fertility rates and a decline that could not be reversed in the face of epidemics and warfare.

Huron ossuaries provide some of the best palaeodemographic evidence available, and when analysed in detail they may well give us a clear understanding of the decline of the Huron. In the interim, the interpretation of estimators in terms of fertility, rather than mortality, makes good sense. While the estimators cannot be used for the extreme cases in which the population was undergoing rapid decline leading to immediate extinction (Jackes, 1988), the method seems generally applicable. The Huron buried at Kleinburg lived about 50 years earlier than those buried at Ossossané: before the disruptions caused by the intensification of trade with the French, and in a rich agricultural area with a longer growing season. It makes good sense to interpret Ossossané as exhibiting lower fertility, not lower mortality, than Kleinburg.

In sum, we can indeed estimate fertility from past populations based only on skeletal collections, and the results of our analyses accord with known history. We have shown that the age at death distribution for a population known only from skeletons can be used in very specific ways to arrive at a clear idea of fertility. We are able to test the validity of this approach because seventeenth-century Ontario offers us the almost unique combination of (1) reasonably detailed and accurate written records with (2) the burial of almost all the dead of a community over a short period of time in an ossuary. It is important to note that fairly accurate ages at death are required only for the sub-adults, so that we can avoid the problems of age assessment of adult skeletons. The age assessment methods for sub-adults used in the studies cited here are all based on well-established techniques of observing the eruption of children's teeth (recently shown to be generally accurate: Liversidge, 1994). The method of determining fertility that has been used here is straight forward. It involves no more than plotting the average number of children an average woman would bear between the ages of 15 and 44 in a model population equivalent in its level of childhood mortality to the Huron of sixteenth- and early seventeenth-century Ontario.

The fertility estimates allow us to conclude that there was pressure on the Huron population even before the worst of the recorded devastating epidemics, famines and wars that marked the final years of the existence of the Huron Confederacy in Ontario. If we were to interpret the estimators derived from juvenile mortality as indicating overall death rates, we would have to conclude that mortality was falling and that the population was increasing. Unfortunately for the Huron, nothing could have been further from the truth. As history makes clear, the few starving survivors of the Huron who had buried their dead in the Ossossané Ossuary in May 1636, were forced to abandon their country only thirteen years later.

ENDNOTES

1   The value 1/mean age at death now does not accurately estimate the death rate. Since any natural increase in populations requires that births must outnumber deaths in a population, 1/the mean age of death can logically no longer estimate both the CDR and the CBR. For this reason, it has been claimed that 1/mean age of death accurately estimates the CBR in archaeological populations (e.g., Sattenspiel and Harpending, 1983), rather than the CDR. However, estimates of the CBR derived from 1/mean age of death in increasing populations are too high (Jackes, 1992). Furthermore, we cannot rely on the CBR whenever there is any possibility that infants were buried differently than older children and adults or when adult ages might have been estimated inaccurately.

2   Larocque's data are smoothed by redistributing the sub-adults over the possible age ranges for each stage of the tooth eruption sequence, using probabilities under the normal curve. The percentage of the dead falling within each five year age category is the basis for determining the number of Kleinburg and Ossossané sub-adults dying between 5 and 15 years of age, the figures required to determine the JA and the mcm. As with Uxbridge, we use adjusted figures for Kleinburg (r = .01) and for Ossossané (r = .005), because the relationship of the mcm and JA values suggests that the two samples did not come from stationary populations.

3   Figure 4 suggests that a mother would not become pregnant again for almost 40 months after giving birth, if she breastfed her child for 30 months or more.

REFERENCES

Basu AM (1993) Cultural influences on the timing of first births in India. *Population Studies* 47:85-95.

Beizer RA (1990) Prevalence of abnormal glucose tolerance in six Solomon Islands Populations. AJPA 81(4):471-482.

Bocquet J-P (1979) Une approche de la fécondité des populations inhumées. *Bull. et Mem. de la Soc. d'Anthrop. de Paris* 6:261-268.

Bongaarts J, and Potter RG (1983) *Fertility, Biology and Behavior: An Analysis of the*

Proximate Determinants. NY: Academic Press.

Caldwell JC, Caldwell P, and Orubuloye IO (1992) Family and sexual networking in sub-Saharan Africa. *Population Studies* 46:385-410.

Charlevoix PFX (1761) *Journal of a Voyage to North America.* London: R. and J. Dodsley.

Chaudhry M (1990) Role of the social and cultural factors in human fertility in India. *Population and Environment* 12(2):117-137.

Coale AJ, and Demeny P (1983) *Regional Model Life Tables and Stable Populations* (2nd ed.). New York: Academic Press.

Danker-Hopfe H (1986) Menarcheal age in Europe. *Yearbook of Physical Anthropology* 29:81-112.

Early JD, and Peters FJ (1990) *The Population Dynamics of the Mucajai Yanomama.* Sandiego: Academic Press.

Ellison PT (1990) Human ovarian function and reproductive ecology: New hypotheses. *American Anthropologist* 92(4):933-952.

Felt JC, Ridley JC, Allen G, and Redekop C (1990) High fertility of Old Colony Mennonites in Mexico. *Human Biology* 62(5):689-700.

Fitzgerald MH (1992) Is lactation nature's contraceptive? Data from Samoa. *Social Biology* 39:55-64.

Frisch RE (1988) Fatness and fertility. *Scientific American* 258(3):88-95.

Garson LK (1991) The centenarian question: Old-age mortality in the Soviet Union 1897-1970. *Population Studies* 45:265-278.

Goldman N, Westoff CF, and Paul LE (1987) Variations in natural fertility: The effect of lactation and other determinants. *Population Studies* 41:127-146.

Hajnal J (1982) Two kinds of pre-industrial household formation system. *Population and Development Review* 8(3):449-494.

Hart N (1993) Famine, maternal nutrition and infant mortality: A re-examination of the Dutch Hunger Winter. *Population Studies* 47:27-46.

Heidenreich C (1971) *Huronia: A History and Geography of the Huron Indians 1600-1650.* Toronto: McClelland and Stewart.

Huffman SL, Ford K, Allen HA, and Streble P (1987) Nutrition and fertility in Bangladesh: Breastfeeding and post-partum amenorrhoea. *Population Studies* 41:447-462.

Jackes MK (1986) The mortality of Ontario archaeological populations. *Canadian Journal of Anthropology/Canadian Review of Physical Anthropology* 5(2):33-48.

Jackes MK (1988) *The Osteology of the Grimsby Site.* Department of Anthropology, University of Alberta, Edmonton.

Jackes MK (1992) Paleodemography: Problems and techniques. In SR Saunders and MA Katzenberg (eds.) *Skeletal Biology of Past Peoples: Research Methods.* New York: Wiley-Liss, pp. 189-224.

Jackes MK (1993) On paradox and osteology. *Current Anthropology* 34(4):434-439.

Jackes MK (1994) Complexity in seventeenth century southern Ontario burial practices. In D Meyer and P Dawson (eds.) *Debating Complexity: Proceeding of the 26th Annual Chacmool Conference,* November 1993. Archaeological Association, University of Calgary.

Jimenez S, and Melbye FJ (1987) Ossossané revisited. Paper Presented at the 15th Annual Meeting of the Canadian Association for Physical Anthropology.

Katzenburg MA, and White R (1979) A paleodemographic analysis of the *os coxae* from Ossossané ossuary. *Canadian Journal of Anthropology/Canadian Review of Physical Anthropology* 1(1):10-28.

Kidd KE (1953) The excavation and historical identification of a Huron ossuary. *American Antiquity* 18:359-379.

Kirchengast S (1993) Anthropological aspects of the age at menopause. *Homo* 44:263-277.

Larocque R (1991) Une étude ethnohistorique et paléoanthropologique des epidémies en Huronie. University of Montreal, Ph.D. Thesis.

Liversidge, HM (1994) Accuracy of age estimation from developing teeth of a population of known age. *International Journal of Osteoarchaeology* 4:37-45.

Loschky D and Childers BD (1993) Early English mortality. *Journal of Interdisciplinary History* XXIV:85-97.

Nault F, Desjardins B, and Legare J (1990) Effects of reproductive behaviour on infant mortality of French-Canadians during the seventeenth and eighteenth centuries. *Population Studies* 44:273-285.

Pennington R (1992) Did food increase fertility? Evaluation of !Kung and Herero history. *Human Biology* 64(4):497-521.

Pfeiffer S (1984) Paleopathology in an Iroquoian ossuary with special reference to tuberculosis. *AJPA* 65:181-189.

Pfeiffer S (1986) Morbidity and mortality in the Uxbridge Ossuary. *Canadian Journal of Anthropology/Canadian Review of Physical Anthropology* 5(2):15-31.

Reinis KI (1992) The impact of the proximate determinants of fertility. *Population Studies* 46:309-326.

Riddle JM, and Estes JW (1992) Oral contraceptives in ancient and medieval times. *American Scientist* 80:226-233.

Sattenspiel L, and Harpending H (1983) Stable populations and skeletal age. *American Antiquity* 48:489-498.

Saunders SR, and Melbye FJ (1990) Subadult mortality and skeletal indicators of health in Late Woodland Ontario Iroquois. *Canadian Journal of Archaeology* 14:61-74.

Saunders SR, and Spence MW (1986) Dental and skeletal age determinations of Ontario Iroquois infant burials. *Ontario Archaeology* 46:45-54.

Schwarcz HP, Melbye J, Katzenberg MA, and Knyf M (1985) Stable isotopes in human skeletons of southern Ontario: reconstructing paleodiet. *Journal of Archaeological Science* 12:187-206.

Secombe W (1990) The western European marriage pattern in historical perspective. *Journal of Historical Sociology* 3(1):50-74.

Sullivan NC (1990) On a darkling plain: A study of the demographic crisis of the Huron Indians. University of Toronto Ph.D. Thesis.

Sutton RE (1988) Paleodemography and late Iroquoian ossuary samples. *Ontario Archaeology* 48:42-50.

Tooker E (1964) *An Ethnography of the Huron Indians 1615-1649.* Huronia Historical Development Council, Ste-Marie Among the Hurons.

Trigger BG (1986) *Natives and Newcomers.* Kingston and Montreal: McGill-Queen's University Press.

Trigger BG (1987) *The Children of Aataentsic.* Kingston and Montreal: McGill-

Queen's University Press.

Trussell J, van de Walle E, and van de Walle F (1989) Norms and behaviour in Burkinabe fertility. *Population Studies* 43:429-454.

Ubelaker DH (1989) *Human Skeletal Remains. Excavation, Analysis, Interpretation.* Washington: Taraxacum.

Van de Walle E (1992) Fertility transition, conscious choice, and numeracy. *Demography* 29(4):487-502.

Varney TL (1994) Middle ear disease in an Ontario prehistoric ossuary population. Paper presented at the meeting of the Palaeopathology Association, Denver, Colorado.

Wright RE (1988) Fertility, partners and female labour supply in Jamaica. *Genus* 44:205-223.

9

Sisters and Ancestors
Looking for Human Origins in Miocene Europe

David R. Begun

Ancestors are difficult to identify with certainty in the fossil record because of its fragmentary nature, particularly with regard to evidence of the processes of evolution. However, relations among well known forms are easier to disentangle. Once revealed, relations among forms provide clues as to the anatomy of the ancestors of these forms. In this chapter I consider several candidates for the position of sister lineage, or closest evolutionary relative, to the African apes and humans. Once the closest relative of this group is identified, it is possible to focus in on the anatomy of the ancestor of the African apes and humans. Though we have no fossil evidence of this ancestor, it is likely that many of the attributes shared between the African apes and humans and its closest relative were also present in the common ancestors of both. Once this ancestral form is reconstructed, it should be possible to deduce patterns of relationship within the African apes and humans, based on the patterns of morphological divergence from this ancestral form. Patterns of relationship within the African apes and humans is a central theme in paleoanthropology today, and involves a resolution to the chimp-human-gorilla trichotomy. In most research on this subject, this boils down to one question with three mutually exclusive answers: Are chimps most closely related to gorillas, humans, or both? Here I will argue that chimps are closest to humans, and that this conclusion has specific implications for reconstructing the first human, and for understanding the processes that contributed to human origins.

INTRODUCTION

Paleoanthropology is often envisioned as the quest for an understanding of our ancestors and of our place within the diversity of life. Most of us have a good sense of what an ancestor is. But the issue of our place among our fellow organisms is somewhat more difficult to comprehend. Much of the paleoanthropological literature is devoted in one way or another to the analysis of human ancestors, or to establishing the ancestral status of known fossil forms. Ancestors are our evolutionary antecedents, directly related to us by descent. Unique ancestors are organisms from which species evolved directly, whereas common ancestors link species via a form from which they diverged. Common ancestors inform us about relations among forms, because, by definition, we share a last common ancestor with the forms to which we are most closely related. This may sound circular, but upon reflection it is not. This is because the data necessary to establish ancestry are different from those needed to establish closeness of relationship (see below). In other words, if we could somehow establish from which ancestral forms modern forms are descended, we would know how modern forms are related to one another. Conversely, if we could establish to which living form another living group, say, humans, for example, is most closely related, we could deduce the nature of our common ancestor. Looking for ancestors or looking for relationships are really two means toward the same end. However, the nature of the data bearing on evolutionary relations is easier to understand than that which could be used to identify ancestors.

TAXONOMIC BACKGROUND

In this chapter a number of formal and informal taxonomic categories will be used, and some of these need to be defined before we can proceed to the data. By chimps or chimpanzee I mean the common chimp, *Pan troglodytes*, and not the bonobo or pygmy chimp, *Pan paniscus*, the relations of which are unclear at present. By humans, I refer to everything more closely related to us than to any other living form. This is not so much a definition of human as it is an operational concept. We can leave aside the question of the *definition* of human for the musings of philosophers and others, such as paleoanthropologists, for example, who worry about calling Neanderthals and other pre-modern forms "humans" because these fossil forms have not left in their wake clear-cut indications of symbolic behaviour we can understand. The operational concept of human used in this chapter is based on the approach to systematics (the science of naming biological units of analysis) known formally as Phylogenetic Systematics (Hennig, 1966), or more colloquially as cladistics (e.g., Brooks and McLennan, 1991; Wiley, et al., 1990; Tattersall, et al., 1988). Here, human is the name given to the group that includes all forms more closely related to us than to any other form, which in cladistic terminology is known as a monophyletic clade (a clade is essentially the same thing as a lineage). Strictly speaking, in a cladistic classification all taxa (named biological units, i.e., species, genera, families, kingdoms, etc.) must be monophyletic, though not all relations among taxa have to be named taxa.

Two examples serve to illustrate the concept of monophyly. The taxon Reptilia (a class) is a useful, well known and well understood category. It is not monophyletic, however, and does not accurately represent relations among forms, so it is rejected by cladists. Reptiles include turtles and tortoises, lizards and snakes, sphenodons (a lizard-like form), crocodiles, and, among fossil forms, dinosaurs, icthyosaurs, mosasaurs, plesiosaurs, pterosaurs and mammal-like reptiles. Though these are all descended from a single common ancestral taxon, two other forms not included in the Reptilia are also descended from that same ancestor. Because the Reptilia does not include either of these (birds, class Aves, and mammals, class Mammalia), it is paraphyletic (Carroll, 1988). Paraphyletic clades exclude forms to which some of their members are in fact more closely related than they are to some included forms. Reptiles in general are apparently more closely related to birds and mammals than to turtles, which appear to be the most primitive of all reptiles. Since Reptilia excludes birds and mammals, it is not monophyletic. Birds and mammals are traditionally excluded from Reptilia because they are remarkably specialized creatures, with numerous fundamental physiological and anatomical differences from reptiles, most of which are related either to their ability to fly or to their energy intensive lifestyles. So, that means that reptiles are defined basically by a set of primitive characters, including scales instead of fur or feathers on the outside, and cold-bloodedness (with a few exceptions), a simpler skull and dentition, and other anatomical and physiological characters on the inside. And, this is a basic attribute of paraphyletic taxa. They exclude forms that are specialized, even if these forms are close relatives of included forms, because they are defined by sets of primitive characters, many of which are not retained in the more specialized descendants of common ancestors. Birds and mammals independently diverged from something indistinguishable from the reptile that gave rise to all reptiles except turtles. To classify them apart is to overstate their evolutionary differences from reptiles, which may be desirable to some, but is not the goal of evolutionary biology. Though the reptiles as a paraphyletic clade have some heuristic usefulness, it is misleading in an evolutionary sense and should be avoided in a classification based on evolutionary relations.

Pongidae (a family) is also a well understood, heavily utilized and equally misleading term, from an evolutionary perspective. Pongids include orangs, the Asian great ape, and the African apes (the chimpanzee, bonobo and gorilla). Yet, most paleoanthropologists and molecular systematists (molecular systematics is the science of classification based on evolutionary relations as deduced from the study of biomolecules, usually proteins, DNA and RNA or various types, and chromosomes) believe that African apes are more closely related to humans than they are to orang-utans (Huxley, 1863; Andrews and Cronin, 1982; Pilbeam, 1982; Sarich and Wilson, 1967; Goodman, 1963, 1973; Groves, 1986; Tattersall, et al., 1988). So, to exclude humans from this group is like excluding birds from reptiles; its a paraphyletic group based on primitive characters (thick coats of hair, large faces, large canine teeth, small brains, long arms, quadrupedalism, opposable big toes, arboreality, simpler lifestyles, etc.), all of which characterized our ancestors. Like proto-birds and proto-mammals and their relationship to reptiles, humans evolved from something indistinguishable from the set of primitive characteristics used to define the pongids, so they cannot be used to exclude us from this group. However, humans cannot be included in the Pongidae because humans form the basis of the typological definition of the Hominidae, which has priority over the Pongidae, since it was named first. The Hominidae was named by in 1825 (its formal designation is Hominidae Gray, 1825), while the Pongidae was named in 1913 (Pongidae Elliot, 1913). The simplest solution, and the one adopted here, and by an increasing number of paleoanthropologists (Groves, 1986; Tattersall, et al., 1988; Begun, 1992a,b; Andrews, 1992; Dean and Delson, 1992), is to call all great apes and humans hominids, and to drop the Pongidae altogether. This means that Hominidae is not available for the group with which it is most often associated, modern humans and our fossil relatives. So, to designate that group, humans is used here instead. Orangs are further separated, at the subfamily level as before, within the pongines, and African apes and humans united in the hominines. Further subdivisions are possible but not required. They are based on currently controversial theories of relationship (see below) which are not yet firmly enough established to merit formal taxonomic designation. The currently available names (hominina, hominini, panina, panini, etc) also tend to get confusing, and will not be used here. The formally designated taxa used in this chapter are classified as follows (see text for discussion):

Hominoidea
        Hylobatidae
                Hylobates (gibbons and siamangs)
        Hominidae
                Griphopithecinae
                        Griphopithecus
                        Kenyapithecus
                Ponginae
                        Pongo
                        Sivapithecus
                Homininae
                        Dryopithecus
                        Ouranopithecus
                        Gorilla
                        Pan
                        Australopithecus
                        Homo
        Hominidae *incertae sedis* (of uncertain status)
                Oreopithecus
                Lufengpithecus
                Gigantopithecus

HISTORICAL AND THEORETICAL BACKGROUND

Most paleoanthropologists, ever since Darwin in fact, assume that the last common ancestor of humans and our closest living relative lived in Africa. The earliest direct ancestors of humans are widely thought to have come from Africa as well. In fact, all the early (pre-1 million years ago) human fossil material comes exclusively from Africa, and our closest living relatives also live there today. So, a great deal of time, energy and resources have been spent looking for actual fossil ancestors of humans in Africa. Success has been considerable concerning the discovery of fossil vestiges of our lineage. However, the last common ancestor of ourselves and our closest living relative, and also the first identifiably different organism to depart from this ancestor in our direction, remains complete-ly unknown. The latter is no surprise, for there is a basic difficulty in identifying specific taxa as directly ancestral to subsequent taxa. As illus-trated in Figure 1, detecting an *actual* ancestor is methodologically diffi-cult because you usually can not know if fossil form, such as A, is literally ancestral to B or if they share an unknown common ancestor with attrib-utes of both. To establish an ancestor descendant relationship between two known forms you need information about the process of transforma-tion. What caused morphology to change? What caused behaviour to change? You need a process linking two forms. This usually takes the form of adaptational hypothesis of selection, like, bipedalism evolved to free the hands for tool use. But adaptational hypotheses are notoriously difficult to test. How can we demonstrate that bipedalism evolved for a specified purpose? And if we can not, how can we be sure that one form evolved directly from an other, as opposed to both evolving from a third? Compounding the difficulty in this case is the fact that the fossil record of hominoids is sparse at the appropriate time. So, finding an ancestor of humans has proven very difficult.

Figure 1. A Phylogeny Depicting an Ancestral-descendant Relationship on the Left and a Cladogram Depicting a Sister Group Relationship on the Right.

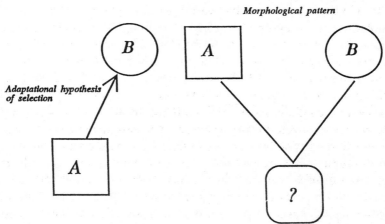

The conclusion that B evolved from A, on the left, depends on the reliability of the adapta-tional hypothesis explaining the transformation from A to B. Given that these hypotheses are often speculative and always difficult to test, the sister group relationship on the right is more reliable. While it is possible that A evolved from B, it is more likely that both evolved from an unknown common ancestor. See text for discussion.

If direct ancestors are difficult or even impossible to identify with confidence, what about common ancestors? Looking for common ancestors is an attractive alternative because they can be inferred from patterns of evolutionary relationship, as opposed to deduced from inferred processes of evolutionary change. Organisms that are most closely related by definition have a common ancestor they share with no other organism. By establishing relationships among forms, the ancestors of these forms can be reconstructed, without ever being recovered from the fossil record. Since the fossil record of primates is estimated to contain fewer than 10% of all primate species that have ever lived (Martin, 1990, 1993), looking for a fossil ancestor may well be an exercise in futility. However, the traits found only in most closely related forms in most cases come from their last common ancestor. These most closely related forms are known in cladistic terminology as sister taxa. Sisters inform us about their ancestors, from which they have inherited the characters unique to them as a group. Establishing sister relationships, which is the key to this type of analysis, allows us to reconstruct their ancestors. This type of analysis is complicated, but is nevertheless more straight-forward than identifying specific ancestors, and more amenable to the generation of testable hypotheses. This type of analysis is basically a pattern recognition problem rather than a process description problem. Patterns of morphology are relatively easily detectable in the fossil record, and testable with new fossils. On the other hand, the processes of morphological transformation are not so easily recognized or tested. So, though not without its own difficulties, its generally easier to find sisters than ancestors. It is probably also statistically more likely. You can only have one ancestor, and, as noted above, it is unlikely to be preserved in the fossil record. Furthermore, this ancestor must have undergone some transformation to produce a descendant, so, it will be difficult to find and possibly impossible to recognize, even if it is preserved. You can have many descendants, however, and each of these is a sister taxon to the others that have evolved from the same common ancestor. Once you have a basis for interpreting sister relationships, you can reconstruct their ancestors. You can reconstruct their ancestral morphology (Figure 2). You can also reconstruct their behaviour, based in part on their own functional anatomy, but also based on behavioural traits shared among descendants. And, you can even test adaptational hypotheses. Hypotheses of selection resulting in the origin of a taxon should account primarily for the presence of traits unique to that taxon. An adaptational hypothesis accounting for the origin of taxon D in Figure 2 should evoke selection for increases in the frequencies of 11, 12, and 13, but not 1–10, even if still present in D.

Figure 2. A Cladogram Representing the Methodology for Reconstructing Ancestral Forms.

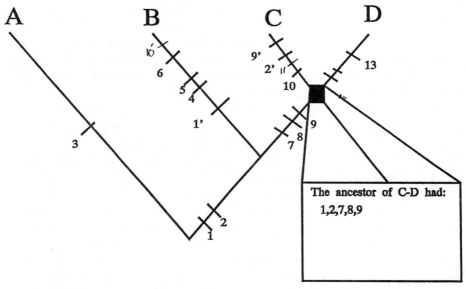

Numbers represent traits and their points of origin consistent with their distribution in the taxa under analysis. Numbers with apostrophes represent parallelisms. What this all means is that the common ancestor of A-D, represented by the apex at the bottom, had only primitive traits. Derived traits arise during the evolution of this group at the points indicated. A first branch yields the ancestors on A on the one hand, and B-D on the other, i.e., A branches off first, and is defined by trait 3. The B-D clade is defined by traits 1 and 2. A is the sister to B-D and is no more closely related to B than to D. The B clade branches off next, evolving its own set of unique characters (4-6), including two parallelisms. B lost trait 1 and "re-evolved" 1', found independently in some ancestral form, and it also evolved 10' independently from its occurrence in C. The C-D clade is defined by traits 7-9, and C by traits 10-11, and the parallelisms 2', 9' and 10', while D is unique in possessing traits 12 and 13. The determination of parallelism depends on the observation that more characters support this arrangement than any other. A smaller number of characters argue against this arrangement (for example, B and C share trait 10', which could be used to argue that they are most closely related), but C and D share traits 7 and 8, making a stronger case for the link between C and D.

ESTABLISHING SISTER GROUPS

There are many text books that provide excellent primers in cladistics (Hennig, 1966; Wiley et al., 1990; Brooks and McLennan, 1991). This is not the goal of this chapter. Nevertheless, it would be useful to quickly summarize a few of the techniques that have been most important to the research described in this chapter.

When characteristics are identified on extant and fossil specimens (the identification and definition of "characters" is an entire subject of its own, better left for some other time), they must be analysed to determine their significance to the function and evolutionary relations of the taxa that possess them. From the perspective of systematics, the primary concern in this chapter, the attributes of an organism are divided into two hierarchical categories. At the higher level is the character, which is a broadly and theoretically defined homologous structure. Homologous structures, or homologues, at this level of analysis, are usually anatomical complexes (hindlimbs), whole bones (femur, tibia, etc.), or major parts of bones (proximal femur, femoral head, femoral shaft, etc.), about which there is general agreement about commonality of descent, or homology. Homology is a rather nebulous and somewhat circular concept easier to use than to define. Homology is the quality that the parts of two different organisms share of being ultimately traceable back to a single part in a single organism, like the tibiae of birds, frogs, dogs, spider monkeys, and humans but not the tibiae of grasshoppers. Tetrapods all derive their tibiae from an early lobe-finned vertebrate ancestor, while insect tibiae have a completely different invertebrate origin. Likewise, the humeri, radii and ulnae of humans, elephants, mice, chickens, and fruit bats are all homologous, as are the larger anatomical regions they comprise (forelimbs). However, the reorganization of the forelimb that results in wings in bats and chickens is not homologous, having evolved independently in bat ancestors and bird ancestors. The big problem with homology is that you need to know evolutionary relations to be certain that two characters are homologous, but you need to identify homologies to establish evolutionary relations. This is a limitation of the evidence about which we can do nothing but maintain vigilance. In most cases, problems do not arise, but occasionally, when uncertainty persists, an error in basic homology attribution may be the culprit. One example of this may be the case of the hominoid frontal sinus (see below).

The list of homologous characters to be included in an analysis is then further refined into lists of character states within each taxon included in the analysis. For the character femoral head, different states may be, for example, round, ovoid, or flat. Or, femoral head could be further subdivided, as the need arises, into femoral head shape and femoral head size, with such character states as very large, intermediate, or small.

Characters for each taxon in the analysis are assigned character states in this manner. Sometimes, as with discrete shapes, assignment is not too difficult, but in other cases, usually involving size differences alone, it becomes difficult to determine the boundary between categories, for example, large and intermediate. Transforming continuous variables such as length into discrete variables such as long or short can often be accomplished by using some discontinuity in the distribution of sizes corresponding to taxonomic differences (i.e., all non-human hominids have canines above a certain size relative to their molars, while all humans have smaller canines). Sometimes statistical constructs such as means or standard deviations can be used to transform continuous into discontinuous variables. Again, it is best to recognize that there are limits to these approaches, and to scrutinize these characters severely when difficulties in an analysis arise. Finally, some character states are continuous in the sense that they go from least to most strongly developed, and it is sometimes difficult to break these down into discrete states. This is particularly true of the behavioural characters used in this chapter (see below). Where different character states are recognized, as for example in the case of behavioural flexibility, I am relying on the assessments of field primatologists, who speak (and publish) in these terms, which incorporate numerous observations of numbers of food items, variability in ranging patterns and groups size, group formation and dissolution, and ecological distribution. While these character states could be considered continuously distributed, they are generally discussed as discrete differences (see references below) and are presented as such here.

Once characters and character states have been identified, a character analysis must be performed to assess the significance of each character state to interpretations of evolutionary history. The first step in a character analysis is to designate an outgroup. An outgroup is an organism or group of organisms that are not within the group under analysis (the ingroup), and that are more closely related to the ingroup taxa than are any other forms. In other words, outgroups share with ingroups a common ancestor. Characters present in some ingroup taxa that are also present in the outgroup can be assumed to have been present in the ancestor of both, and thus in the ancestor of all the ingroup forms. These characters are designated primitive characters (plesiomorphies), or when they are shared between two taxa, symplesiomorphies (Hennig, 1966). Characters that define groups having evolved after the common ancestral forms (which are by definition not present in the outgroups) are called

196

apomorphies, or derived characters, of that group (synapomorphies when they are shared among two or more different organisms within a group, and autapomorphies when they are unique to a particular group). In this analysis, character analysis consists of determining whether character states are primitive, being found in the outgroup, or derived, being unique to the ingroup. This is referred to as the outgroup criterion of polarity (primitive vs derived) determination. There are other criteria used for character polarization (ontogenetic, paleontologic, commonality), but these require additional assumptions and have not been used in this analysis.

Once characters have been polarized (assigned to either primitive or derived), they can be used to reconstruct evolutionary history, or phylogeny. Shared derived characters (synapomorphies) indicate close evolutionary relationship, because these characteristics appear after the divergence from the outgroup, which is why the outgroup lacks them. Shared primitive characters (symplesiomorphies) indicate only a relationship to the outgroup, without the more specific relations within the ingroup defined. Usually, different patterns of relationship are suggested by different combinations of characters. The pattern of relationship suggested by the largest number of synapomorphies is the preferred hypothesis, as a starting point. This is only because it is the simplest explanation for the distribution (a pattern) of observable characters, not because we know *a priori* that evolution takes the simplest path. However, when the answer to a question is not known, and when many possible explanations are feasible, the simplest feasible explanation, given the known constraints of the system in question, is to be preferred. In the case of evolution, the simplest explanation is the one that requires the fewest number of evolutionary changes, in other words, the one that maximizes parsimony. In this sense, parsimony is *not* an attribute of the evolutionary process, it is simply a criterion derived from the theory of logic for choosing among competing hypotheses. In the absence of a reason to believe otherwise, the simplest solution is the best.

For nearly every preferred hypothesis of relationship there are a number of characters that contradict that hypothesis. The hypothesis is not falsified if the number of contrary characters is less than in any other hypothesis, but there are always a few. These are characters that have evolved in parallel in separated lineage, and misleadingly suggest these lines to be more closely related than they really are. In systematics, these characters are known as homoplasies (parallelisms and convergences). A classic example of a homoplasy is the convergence in form of sharks and dolphins, which evolved their similar forms independently (one evolved from an aquatic vertebrate and the other from a terrestrial form with legs!). There are many examples in primate evolution, ranging from orang, gorilla and baboon-like sub-fossil prosimians, to the independent acquisition of bilophodonty, mandibular symphyseal fusion, elongated forelimbs, postorbital closure and large brains in numerous different lineages. Homoplasies may be the most interesting phenomenon in evolutionary biology, because they combine the studies of systematics (to detect them) and functional morphology (to explain how they could happen). But, for the purposes of systematics, they are just noise.

BACKGROUND

Another advantage to identifying ancestors via their descendants is that sisters can potentially be anywhere, whereas ancestors have to be exactly where their descendants originate. Humans and their closest relatives originate in Africa, but the best known fossil great apes are from Eurasia. These forms are not ancestors of humans, but they are sisters. Historically there have been many attempts to identify human ancestors in the fossil record.

Looking for human origins in all the wrong places

Hesperopithecus haroldcookii was an early candidate for human ancestry (Osborn, 1922). Two facts are immediately striking about this potential human ancestor. The first is that it is represented only by a single molar tooth of Miocene age, roughly 12 million years old. This is older than we now know our earliest direct ancestors to have been, but at the time this was considered a reasonable time frame. The second odd thing about *Hesperopithecus haroldcookii*, other than the name itself, is that it was found in Nebraska, and is in fact named for the fellow who discovered it (Harold Cook), who was from the area. I know of nothing inherently odd about Nebraska, but there is something inherently unlikely about finding human origins there. Where are the other anthropoids from which this form evolved? How did it get there? In fact, these mysteries all came to a swift resolution shortly after the initial descriptions of this specimen when it was revealed by more detailed work to belong to a tapir (a close relative of pigs), and not a primate at all. This sounds unlikely, but the fact is that the specimen misled numerous luminaries in paleontology, partly because humans do have somewhat pig-like teeth, but perhaps more because many of these scholars wanted to find evidence of human origins in North America, as opposed to Africa.

Eoanthropus dawsoni was another early candidate for human ancestry (Dawson and Smith-Woodward, 1913). *Eoanthropus dawsoni* was a primitive human form from the lower Pleistocene (roughly 1–2 million years ago) of England. The age of this specimen is perhaps closer to that which we expect today for the first human, but the location is little more likely than Nebraska. *Eoanthropus dawsoni*, like *Hesperopithecus haroldcookii*, offered confirmation for preconceptions of the time regarding the likely place for humans to have originated and the likely morphology of the first humans. The worst part was that unlike *Hesperopithecus haroldcookii*, which was basically a silly mistake in retrospect, *Eoanthropus dawsoni*, or "Piltdown Man", was a fraud (Weiner, 1955).

In contrast to these first two cases, *Ramapithecus*, another candidate for human ancestry, is both a primate and an actual fossil organism (Lewis, 1934). Fossils that were attributed to *Ramapithecus* do in fact resemble humans much more closely than *Hesperopithecus*. They are primarily from Asia, though many were also identified in Africa. Furthermore, they occur at about the right time in geological terms to represent a legitimate human ancestor. So, the majority, if not the nearly universal view, was that *Ramapithecus* was a human ancestor, or, the first member of the human lineage, and this view was based on some solid evidence (Pilbeam, 1972). However, the *conviction* that *Ramapithecus* was our ancestor did lead to a number of unjustified assumptions about such behaviours as tool use, bipedalism, and canine reduction, all of which characterize early true humans, and none of which was actually directly inferable from the available fossil evidence, consisting of fragmentary jaws and teeth. Eventually, it was recognized that the similarities between *Ramapithecus* and early humans (*Australopithecus*) were also to be found in other much more "ape-like" forms, and were therefore probably present in the common ancestor of all the great apes and humans (Greenfield, 1979). Although none of the postcranial remains attributed to *Ramapithecus* actually suggested bipedalism, and there was never any convincing evidence of tool use, small canines did characterize most specimens for which the canine was known. In fact, it turned out that the small canines of *Ramapithecus* specimens were small because they were all female canines, and females of sexually dimorphic species such as the great apes have small, "human-like" canines (Greenfield, 1979). That all the *Ramapithecus* fossils were females was revealed by more complete discoveries of both the small females and the larger males, most of which had originally been attributed to the genus *Sivapithecus*. Since *Sivapithecus* was named first, by the rules of taxonomic nomenclature it has priority over *Ramapithecus*, which is no longer used today. But, even more significantly, the face of *Sivapithecus* turns out to look strikingly orang-like (Andrews and Cronin, 1982). The modern consensus is that *Sivapithecus* is a close but extinct relative of the modern orang, and the only fossil great ape with a known specific relationship to a living form.

MODERN SISTERS: RECONSTRUCTING THE HUMAN ANCESTOR

In retrospect, there have been many good reasons to be cautious in attempting to identify human ancestors in the fossil record. But, the impact of the *Ramapithecus* story continues to influence human origins research. For example, most researchers now feel that the last common ancestor of humans and their closest relatives looked something like *Sivapithecus*, but without the specialized features of the orang lineage (Andrews and Martin, 1987; Ward and Pilbeam, 1983). Modern African apes look different from this. They have differing molar teeth, in terms of the shapes of the cusps and the crest among them, and the enamel layer covering their teeth is much thinner (Martin, 1985; Kay, 1981). Their mandibles are also more slender in overall construction, and their mode of posture and locomotion (positional behaviour) is decidedly different. We do not really know how *Sivapithecus* got around, but we know it was not a knuckle-walker, like African apes, or for that matter a quadrumanous clamberer, like orangs. *Sivapithecus* was more likely some sort of more primitive climbing arboreal quadruped (Rose, 1983, 1988, 1989), unlike any living form, and that is what human ancestors are considered to have been as well (Fleagle, et al., 1981; Susman et al., 1984). Knuckle-walking, a highly specialized mode of locomotion consisting of placing body weight on the middle part of the middle fingers, is considered by most to be unique to the African apes and not characteristic of any human ancestor (Tuttle, 1967, 1969). Quadrumanous clambering, in which the hands and feet function similarly in the deliberate clambering movements of the modern orang (Cant, 1987a,b), is unique to this genus and evolved after the separation from *Sivapithecus*. The result of this, which is again part of the legacy of the *Ramapithecus* story, is that African apes are widely considered to be two or three branches of a specialized off-shoot of the common ancestor of the great apes and humans, more closely related to each other than to any other primate. *Sivapithecus* has become a sister as opposed to an ancestor, but continues to inform us about human origins with indications of the anatomy of the last common ancestor of humans and our close kin. However, other sisters are worthy of consideration. These, when analysed, call into question some of the conclusions based on the analysis of *Sivapithecus*.

There are in fact two well known Eurasian fossil great apes that should both be considered as possible sisters to living great apes and humans. Two forms, one of which diverged from the last common ancestor of the African apes and humans and then went extinct, preserved at least some of the anatomy of this last common ancestor since lost in ourselves. One of these Eurasian forms is *Sivapithecus*, and the other is *Dryopithecus*. *Dryopithecus*, from Europe alone, is very different in details of dental and skull morphology from the South Asian *Sivapithecus*.

**Figure 3. Great Ape and Human Relations Suggested
by the *Sivapithecus* Sister Group**

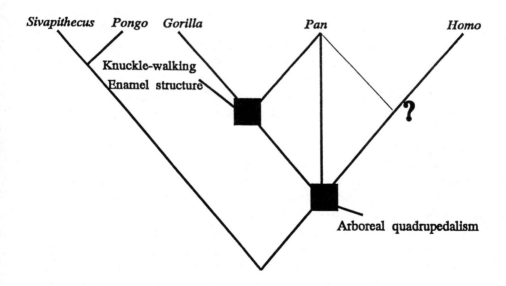

Most favor the chimp (Pan)-gorilla lineage, identified by knuckle-walking and details of tooth structure. The common ancestor of African apes and humans would have been an arboreal quadruped according to this view.

The anatomy of *Sivapithecus* currently forms the basis for reconstructing the ancestral African ape and human (Figure 3). If this is correct, then characters present only in African apes, like those related to knuckle-walking, evolved after they diverged, which in turn implies that humans diverged from some generalized suspensory quadruped before these other traits evolved. But there is another important implication. The characters known to be shared by chimps and gorillas, including knuckle-walking and other traits of the skull and teeth not found in other primates, are considered as further evidence of a period of common ancestry for the African apes exclusive of humans. That is, chimps and gorillas are more closely related to one another than either is to either the orang or to humans. Humans diverged from a common ancestor of both the chimp and gorilla before specifically African ape traits evolved. The characters known to be shared by chimps and humans, and there are a few (see below), are considered to have evolved in parallel. This line of reasoning is the basis for the often cited preference of paleoanthropologists who study fossils and modern anatomy to link chimps and gorillas (Groves, 1986; Andrews and Martin, 1987; Andrews, 1988), in contrast to the increasing number of molecular biologists who have found evidence either favouring an even three-way split or who actually believe that humans and chimps are closer to one another than are chimps and gorillas (Ruvolo, et al., 1991; Marks, 1992; Rogers, 1993).

Figure 4. Great Ape and Human Relations Suggested by the
***Dryopithecus* Sister Group. See text for discussion.**

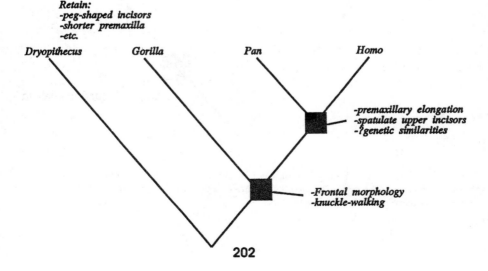

202

What is the alternative if *Dryopithecus* is considered to be the sister group, the last known genus to diverge from the common ancestor of the African apes and humans (Figure 4). It turns out that *Dryopithecus* looks much more like an African ape than *Sivapithecus*.

This is true for two reasons. One is that *Sivapithecus* shares numerous derived features with orangs, especially in details of facial morphology (Pilbeam, 1982; Andrews and Cronin, 1982; Ward and Pilbeam, 1983). The other is that *Dryopithecus* shares derived characters with African apes and humans not found in *Sivapithecus* (Begun, 1992a; Dean and Delson, 1992, and see below). This means that many of the characters still found in modern African apes were present when *Dryopithecus* lived, and thus in the common ancestor of African apes and humans, or hominines. In essence, this means that the last common ancestor humans shared with something else was much more like *Dryopithecus*, and by extension more like living African apes. In fact, *Dryopithecus* looks not only African ape-like, but more gorilla-like than chimp-like, in most characters except overall size. So, it appears that gorillas retain a surprising number of the ancestral hominine traits also found in *Dryopithecus*, while chimps and humans appear to share a larger number of characters not found in *Dryopithecus* or gorillas. This does not mean that *Dryopithecus* is closely related to gorillas, but simply that gorillas have changed less in certain characters. But this conclusion does suggest that the characters shared by chimps and humans were inherited from a form that lived after the gorillas diverged, in other words, that chimps and humans share derived characters of their own, suggesting that they are most closely related.

As we can see, selection of the correct sister group can have far reaching implications not only for reconstructing the anatomy and behaviour of our ancestors but also for deciding the issue of our place among primates. Are we an ancient off-shoot of a general African ape ancestor or do we share a specific and much closer evolutionary relationship with a single living form, the chimpanzee? Furthermore, much as the identity of the sister of the African apes and humans helps to reconstruct the common ancestor of these forms, the identity of the sister of humans will help to flesh out details of the anatomy of the common ancestor of chimps and humans, that from which we evolved, and this will prove very useful in understanding why we evolved.

The case for *Dryopithecus*

A strong case for *Sivapithecus* as the sister of living African apes and humans has been made based primarily on gnathic morphology (the jaws and teeth) (Andrews and Cronin, 1982; Pilbeam, 1982; Ward and Pilbeam, 1983; Ward and Kimbel, 1983; Andrews and Martin, 1987; Andrews, 1992). *Sivapithecus* is well known, represented by a large collection of specimens, including reasonably well preserved cranial pieces and post-crania. Until recently, *Dryopithecus* was much more poorly known. The sample consisted mostly of mandibles, preserving too little evidence to be sure about relationships to other forms. Now there is much more material, in particular from Hungary and Spain, and this greatly clarifies relationships to other forms.

Dryopithecus is a European great ape that lived between about 12.5 to maybe 9.5 million years ago (Mein, 1986, 1990; Bernor et al., 1987; Steininger et al., 1990). It evolved, flourished and died out in Europe, without leaving any identifiable descendants. It is an extinct northern side branch of the great apes. However, as an early branch of this group, it is potentially very informative of their evolutionary history. *Dryopithecus* shares many derived features with other great apes not found in the lesser apes (hylobatids). These include, to name just a few, modified, thick upper and lower incisors for food processing like those seen in modern frugivorous (fruit eating) apes, reduced canines in cross section, probably also related to diet, and elongated premolars and molars, as opposed to the broader molars of more primitive forms (Andrews and Martin, 1987; Begun, 1987, 1992a; Begun and Kordos, 1993). In the skull *Dryopithecus* is characterized by such great ape characters as enlarged premaxilla (the front part of the upper jaw of non-human primates and many other animals, housing the roots of the incisor and canine teeth), a modified palate with the premaxilla and the maxilla overlapping to produce a canal, a modified nasal floor lacking a large opening (incisive fenestration, common in other animals), prominent cheek bones, and probably an enlarged brain case (Begun, 1987, 1992a). The limbs of *Dryopithecus* are similar to that of other great apes in bearing a number of important modifications of the upper arm and elbow joint permitting a wide range of motions typical of hominoids (Begun, 1992b). It also had long, powerfully built finger bones, for suspensory movement in the trees, with their bodies positioned below branches, as with apes generally, instead of above them, as in monkeys (Begun, 1993).

While there can be little doubt that *Dryopithecus* is a great ape, i.e., a hominid, its place among the great apes is more controversial. It is more like living great apes in the features mentioned earlier than most other fossil apes from the Miocene (including, for example, *Proconsul* and *Afropithecus*, from the early Miocene, and *Kenyapithecus*, from the middle Miocene) (Begun, 1987, 1992a,b; Martin and Andrews, 1993). *Sivapithecus*, however, does share many of these features. *Dryopithecus*, unlike *Sivapithecus*, does not closely resemble the modern orang in many details of facial anatomy (Andrews and Cronin, 1982; Pilbeam, 1982). However, as noted above, *Dryopithecus* does shares many characters found only in African apes and humans among living forms, which are missing from *Sivapithecus*. Some of these include a large frontal sinus (an air-filled cavity between and above the eyes), a projecting brow, a longer skull, some details of palatal and nasal floor morphology, and several important details of jaw joint and temporal bone morphology (Begun, 1992a).

The story of the frontal sinus is an interesting one and worth a slight digression. Frontal sinuses occur in many primates (a number of prosimians, New World Monkeys, hominines and rarely in orangs and hylobatids). The name frontal sinus implies a basic level of homology (like femur implies homology of that limb bone in all vertebrates). Yet, the different frontal sinuses are not homologous across taxa. They occur as a result of different processes in different animals, and usually have different forms or positions as a result, though they are always, by definition, in the frontal bone (Cave and Haines, 1940). When a frontal sinus was identified in the skull of *Proconsul*, a primitive hominoid from the early Miocene of Kenya (Andrews, 1978; Walker and Pickford, 1983; Walker and Teaford, 1989), it was concluded that frontal sinuses must be primitive for all hominoids, because they are found in the outgroup to living hominoids, *Proconsul*. However, this frontal sinus, despite its name, is not homologous to hominine frontal sinuses. In size, shape, position, and connection to other sinuses, the frontal sinus of *Proconsul* is very similar to that of a few New World Monkeys, like *Cebus* (the capuchin, or organ grinder monkey) and *Saimiri* (the squirrel monkey), whereas in *Dryopithecus* it is very similar to that of hominines, though much smaller. Like the superficial similarity of sharks and dolphins, the frontal sinuses of *Proconsul* and *Dryopithecus* are the result of homoplasy, and are intriguing from a functional point of view but misleading from the point of view of systematics.

In the rest of the skeleton the differences with *Sivapithecus* are less marked, though the upper arm bone (humerus) in *Dryopithecus* generally

205

more closely resembles that of living great apes and humans than does that of *Sivapithecus* (Pilbeam, et al., 1990; Begun, 1994). All of these traits are from diverse anatomical and functional regions, the braincase, dentition, face, jaw joint, and postcranial skeleton. In contrast, *Sivapithecus* does share with African apes and early humans (*Australopithecus*) a much smaller number of characters, including some details of the incisor teeth and premaxilla. More traits link *Dryopithecus* to African apes and *Australopithecus*. So, here is where the logic of the parsimony criterion comes in. It requires fewer evolutionary changes to go from a *Dryopithecus*-like form to the hominines than it takes starting with a *Sivapithecus*-like form. All the African ape-like characters in *Dryopithecus* would have to have evolved twice, if we were in fact more closely related to *Sivapithecus* than to *Dryopithecus*. Note, however, that the most parsimonious hypothesis is not without some complexity. A small number of characters did indeed evolve twice; those that are shared by *Sivapithecus* and hominines. This is more likely because they are fewer in number than those shared between *Dryopithecus* and hominines. However, there is no avoiding the conclusion that parallel evolution did occur. In fact, all cladistic analyses with which I am familiar require some amount of parallelism, ironically demonstrating, through the logic of parsimony, that evolution is anything but parsimonious. The characters shared by *Sivapithecus* and African apes and humans are primarily from the same anatomical area (the front of the face), so in addition to the fact that they are less numerous, it is also more likely that they evolved in parallel in both lineages than it would be to have a larger number of characters from a larger diversity of anatomical regions all evolving independently. This is the simplest explanation, but it also makes sense given some of the specializations of the orang lineage, with their highly distinctive faces and differences in facial growth patterns (Ward and Pilbeam, 1983; Brown and Ward, 1988; Krogman, 1930), suggesting that the similarities with African apes and humans are superficial and achieved independently.

The most straight-forward conclusion to be reached from the new evidence of *Dryopithecus* is that it is more likely to be the sister to African apes and humans than is *Sivapithecus*. This has far reaching implications for interpretations of human origins (see above). The common ancestor of the African apes probably more closely resembled living African apes than previously thought, and this appears to be the case for *Dryopithecus*. It is possible to further refine a reconstruction of the common ancestor of the African apes and humans because they all share traits not found in

206

Dryopithecus, which most likely were also present in their last common ancestor. These include much stronger brow ridges, larger, more extensive frontal sinuses, a more horizontally oriented frontal bone, and a flatter, longer brain case. These characters are not found in any Miocene hominoid. This suggests a period of common ancestry in Africa between 12 million years ago, when *Dryopithecus* first appears, and 5 million years ago, when the first human fossils appear. In addition to the traits shared among all great apes and humans, a number of characters are found only in chimps and humans. Chimps and humans share further elongation and other detailed similarities of the premaxillary bones and other attributes of the face, spatulate or shovel-shaped upper lateral incisors, changes in eye socket shape, even longer skulls, and certain details of postcanine tooth shape.

As if to make things more complicated, chimps and gorillas also share a few traits not found in *Dryopithecus* or *Australopithecus*. These characters, including such things as still more horizontal frontal bones and more projecting brows, probably evolved independently in each African ape lineage, again, because by the parsimony criterion this is more likely, since they are less numerous than are the similarities between chimps and humans. However, one striking and highly specialized similarity within the African apes remains their habit of knuckle-walking. African apes are the only great apes, or for that matter the only animals, to move with their body weight transmitted to the ground via the second knuckles of their middle three fingers. No known Miocene hominoid was a knuckle-walker, nor for that matter were any known Miocene forms bipedal. Both these strategies of positional behaviour are unique to the African apes and humans, and it is likely that one was characteristic of the last common ancestor of African apes and humans. In fact, there are many more anatomical similarities between knuckle-walkers and other primates than between bipeds and other primates. The extreme anatomical uniqueness of bipedal humans strongly suggests that knuckle-walking is the more primitive of the two patterns. And, since the evidence discussed above favours the view that chimps and humans are more closely related to one another than either is to the gorilla, this implies that knuckle-walking evolved before the three taxa split. The common ancestor of the African apes and humans was a knuckle-walker, and this pattern of mobility is retained in two of the three descendants. Since chimps are also knuckle-walkers, and are most closely related to humans, humans must have evolved from a knuckle-walker as well. In fact, a careful analysis of the structure of the human hand and wrist reveals a number of similarities to African apes that are probably related to a period of knuckle-walking in human ancestry. The reduction of the number of bones in our wrists, the shortness of our hands and fingers, and the stability of the joints of our wrists are all vestiges of a knuckle-walker that supported its body weight by standing on its fingers.

THE HUMAN ANCESTOR AND HUMAN ORIGINS

The view of the ancestor from which humans evolved as a basically terrestrial, knuckle-walking, chimp-like form differs from most reconstructions, which stress arboreal behaviour and more general ape-like characters. The significance of this conclusion is that it provides an adaptive framework from which to test hypotheses of human origins. The more detailed the reconstruction of the ancestor of humans, the better we should be able to understand the processes that contributed to the initial changes that characterize the first members of our lineage.

The origins of the human lineage appear to have been characterized by an initial phase following the divergence of the gorilla but prior to the separation of the ancestral chimp and human. The chimp-human phase was characterized by features that in large part are still characteristic of the chimpanzee behavioural repertoire (Teleki, 1974, 1975, 1981; Wrangham, 1977; Goodall, 1986; Ghiglieri, 1984; Nishida and Hiraiwa-Hasegawa, 1986; Nishida and Hiraiwa, 1982). This form was knuckle-walker, probably spending a large percentage of its time on the ground as opposed to in the trees, as most other primates prefer. It lived in relatively open or mosaic environments (woodlands with scattered trees) and probably ranged over substantial distances during the day and seasonally. It was probably eclectic or very broad-based in its feeding habits, eating fruit and other tree products but also invertebrates, small vertebrates and grassland resources like grasses and roots. Its body size was reduced compared to other great apes (gorillas and orangs), possibly in connection with the habit of ranging greater distances in search of separated clusters of food resources. Changes in the lower face and incisors are related to the wide diversity of feeding choices, with large incisors and robust jaws allowing them to process many differing food types (Kay, 1981; Kay and Hylander, 1978; Hylander, 1975; Kay and Covert, 1984). Like living chimps, this phase of human origins was probably characterized by more complex patterns of behaviour involving food sharing (or tolerated scrounging), dynamic changes in group size and composition, rudimentary tool use (Goodall, 1986; Boesch and Boesch, 1981; Ghiglieri, 1984; Nishida and Hiraiwa, 1982; McGrew, 1987) . All of these characteristics are in fact still shared by living chimps and humans, in one form or another (Figure 5).

Figure 5. Cladogram with Hominine (African Ape and Human) Anatomical and Behavioural Attributes At Their Likely Points of Origin

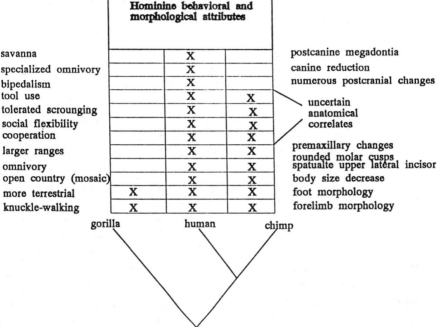

Traits marked off in the left hand column were present in the common ancestor of the African apes and humans, those in the middle in early humans, and those on the right in the common ancestor of chimps and humans.

The above description of the last common ancestor of humans and chimps closely resembles the common perception of the first humans, as rudimentary tool users still dependent on woodlands for food and to a lesser extent mobility (e.g., Lovejoy, 1981; Susman et al., 1984). However, if this scenario explains still existing similarities between chimps and humans, additional factors are needed to explain the human divergence from this form, and to explain the morphological and behavioural uniqueness of our lineage. The human lineage itself separated following a likely shift to much more open, grassland or savanna environments accompanied by a more specialized form of omnivory in these settings. There was likely selection for the ability to survive in more open habitats. This resulted in bipedalism as a response to the demands of efficiently traveling great distances in open country (Taylor and Rowntree, 1973; Wheeler, 1991a). This would also have included postcanine megadontia, or increases in chewing tooth size beyond that expected for a primate of human ancestor size, and the development of a very powerful masticatory apparatus, resulting in an enhanced ability to process tough or gritty foods characteristic of grassland (Dart, 1924; Robinson, 1956; Tobias, 1967; Rak, 1983). In addition, selection may have favoured those individuals physiologically capable of surviving in open environments with enhanced mechanisms of heat loss, including comparative hairlessness and increases in sweat output, both characteristic of modern humans today (Wheeler, 1991b). By the time humans with complex tool kits evolved, with *Homo erectus*, close to 2 million years ago, they had achieved the large body size characteristic of modern humans. The correspondence of large body sizes, more complex tool kits, and also larger brains, may have made possible dusk or night time activity, and eventually migration to colder climates. Both are unusual for anthropoids, especially naked anthropoids that would be particularly prone to heat loss. But, with increases in body size, which cuts down on heat loss, and possibly the invention of controlled fire, further increases in ecological and behavioural flexibility became possible, and the human lineage expanded out of the tropics. All of these changes are explicable given the hypothesis of initial behavioural flexibility characteristic of the common ancestor of chimps and humans, and the view that much of human evolution represents a trend toward the increase in this adaptability.

Finally, the view that humans are most closely related to chimps is in line with at least some current thought in molecular systematics. The genetic evidence is unclear about relations among great apes and humans, except that they are so closely related that it is not yet possible to tease apart the order of their divergence from one another. There has been substantial morphological divergence only in the human lineage. African apes seem to have mostly undergone stabilizing selection and differ genetically from one another and from humans primarily due to stochastic factors that produce random changes in gene frequencies. African apes, particularly gorillas, do have some specializations of their own, such as very large body size and changes in the skull and teeth associated with increases in folivory (leaf-eating), but these pale in comparison to the changes that have occurred in the human lineage. Humans have undergone more intensive selection, as implied by dramatic morphological changes, including those related to brain size, facial and dental reduction, bipedalism, and basic changes in growth and development. Changes in the human lineage are suggested by documented environmental shifts, species range increases, and human lineage diversification (splitting into a number of species). The phenomenon of splitting has added implications for genetic change via the mechanisms of genetic drift (founder effect, bottle neck effect, etc.), which would further contribute to the genetic differences among hominines. The human lineage may have speciated as many as ten times given current estimates of fossil human species diversity (Grine, 1993; Stringer, 1990; Wood, 1991; Aiello, 1993).

Yet, the genetic differences among African apes and humans is close to the same for any paired comparison (chimp-human, chimp-gorilla, human gorilla) (Goodman, 1963; Sarich and Wilson, 1967; Marks, 1992; Rogers, 1993). Even if overall genetic distances are sometimes found to be slightly less between chimps and humans than between either and gorillas (Sibley and Alquist, 1984, 1987), the differences are trivial in comparison to the morphological differences. Molecular studies suggest that little genetic divergence, in terms of total number of genetic changes, has occurred since the branching of the three African ape and human lineages, despite the implications of human morphological uniqueness and human evolutionary tree bushiness (i.e., the many branches of fossil humans) (e.g., King and Wilson, 1975). In reality, since the divergence of gorillas from chimps and humans, and of chimps from humans, very few of the genetic changes that have occurred have been detected. The inability of molecular systematists to even demonstrate the uniqueness of humans that is so obvious to an anatomist is striking, and should send cautionary shivers down their collective spines (contra Wilson and Cann, 1992). Genetic change during hominine evolution has obviously not been general, but highly specific, focussed on a small number of changes in genes that have a profound influence on morphology and behaviour (such as so called regulatory genes (King and Wilson, 1975)). For every nucleotide sequence that reveals information on relations among hominines (synapomorphies) there are hundreds if not thousands that represent noise, that is, that have not changed (sympleisiomorphies) or that have changed in parallel in different lineages (homoplasies). The same rules apply to both molecular and morphological methods of phylogeny inference (Andrews, 1988).

CONCLUSIONS

Though we lack any fossil evidence, we have some idea of what the human ancestor looked like, based on the likely relations we share with our closest relatives. We evolved from an African, tropical forest-mosaic dwelling frugivorous knuckle-walker. Our lineage diverged as a result of responses to environmental changes favouring behaviour flexibility, including the ability to exploit a wider array of resources in a greater diversity of ecological settings. The similarities between African apes and australopithecine postcrania are related to the vestiges of a knuckle-walking ancestry, and not to selection for arboreality in our ancestors, as suggested by some authors (Susman, et al., 1984). Continued research on Miocene hominids is providing new insights into human relations to other primates, into the anatomy and behaviour of hypothetical human ancestors, and into the anatomy and behaviour of early humans like *Australopithecus*. If it is true that chimps are most closely related to us, this may change our opinion of chimps, but it will surely change our perception of ourselves and our origins.

REFERENCES

Aiello, LC (1993) The fossil evidence for modern human origins in Africa. A revised view. *Am. Anthropol.* 95: 73-95.

Andrews, P (1978) A revision of the Miocene Hominoidea from East Africa. *Bull. Br. Mus. Nat. Hist.* (Geol.) 30(2): 85-224.

Andrews, P (1987) Aspects of hominoid phylogeny. In C Patterson (ed.): *Molecules and Morphology in Evolution: Conflict or Compromise.* Cambridge: Cambridge University Press, pp. 23-53.

Andrews, P (1988) Hominoidea. In I Tattersall, E Delson and J Van Couvering (eds.): *Encyclopedia of Human Evolution and Prehistory.* New York: Garland, pp. 248-255.

Andrews, P (1992) Evolution and environment in Miocene hominoids. *Nature* 360: 641-646.

Andrews, P and Cronin, J (1982) The relationships of *Sivapithecus* and *Ramapithecus* and the evolution of the orang-utan. *Nature* 297: 541-546.

Andrews, P and Martin, L (1987) Cladistic relationships of extant and fossil hominoids. *J. Hum. Evol.* 16: 101-118.

Begun, DR (1987) A Review of the genus *Dryopithecus*. Ph.D. Thesis, University of Pennsylvania.

Begun, DR (1992a) Miocene fossil hominids and the chimp-human clade. *Science* 257: 1929-1933.

Begun, DR (1992b) Phyletic diversity and locomotion in primitive European hominids. *Am. J. Phys. Anthropol.* 87: 311-340.

Begun, DR (1993) New catarrhine phalanges from Rudabánya (Northeastern Hungary) and the problem of parallelism and convergence in hominoid postcranial morphology. *J. Hum. Evol.* 24: 373-402.

Begun, DR (1994) Relations among the great apes and humans: New interpretations based on the fossil great ape *Dryopithecus*. *Yrbk. Phys. Anthropol.* 37: 000-000.

Begun, DR and Kordos, L (1993) Revision of *Dryopithecus brancoi* SCHLOSSER 1910 based on the fossil hominoid material from Rudabánya. *J. Hum. Evol.* 25: 271-286.

Brooks, DR and McLennan, DA (1991) *Phylogeny, Ecology and Behavior.* Chicago: University of Chicago Press.

Bernor RL, Brunet M, Ginsburg L, Mein P, Pickford M, Rögl F, Sen S, Steininger F, and Thomas H (1987) A consideration of some major topics concerning old world Miocene mammalian chronology, migrations and paleogeography. *Geobios* 20:431-439.

Boesch, C and Boesch, H (1981) Sex differences in the use of natural hammers by wild chimpanzees: a preliminary report. *J. Hum. Evol.* 10: 585-593.

Brown, B and Ward, S (1988) Basicranial and facial topography in *Pongo* and *Sivapithecus*. In Schwartz, J.H (ed.): *Orang-utan Biology*. New York: Oxford University Press, pp. 247-260.

Cant, JGH (1987a) Positional behavior of female bornean orangutan (*Pongo pygmaeus*). *Am. J. Primatol.* 12: 71-90.

Cant, JGH (1987b) Effects of sexual dimorphism in body size on feeding postural behavior of sumatran orangutans (*Pongo pygmaeus*). *Am. J. Phys. Anthropol.* 74: 143-148.

Carroll, RL (1988) *Vertebrate Paleontology and Evolution.* New York: W.H. Freeman.

Cave, AJE and Haines, RW (1940) The paranasal sinuses of the anthropoid apes. *J. Anat.* London 74: 493-523.

Dart, RA (1924) *Australopithecus africanus*: The man-ape of South Africa. *Nature* 115: 195-199.

Dawson, C and Smith-Woodward, A (1913) On the discovery of a palaeolithic human skull and mandible in the flint-bearing gravel overlying the Wealden (Hastings Beds) at Piltdown, Fletching (Sussex). *Quart. J. Geol. Soc.* 69: 117-151.

Dean, D. and Delson, E (1992) Second gorilla or third chimp? *Nature* 359: 676-677.

Fleagle, J. G. Stern, JT, Jungers, WL, Susman, RL, Vangor, AK, and Wells, JP (1981) Climbing: A biomechanical link with brachiation and with bipedalism. In MH Day (ed.): *Vertebrate Locomotion*. Symp. Zool. Soc. Lond. 48: 359-375.

Ghiglieri, MP (1984) *The Chimpanzees of Kibale Forest.* New York: Columbia University Press.

Goodall, J (1986) *The Chimpanzees of Gombe.* Cambridge: Harvard University Press.

Goodman, M (1963) Man's place in the phylogeny of the primates as reflected in serum proteins. In Washburn, SL (ed.) *Classification and Human Evolution*. Chicago: Aldine Press, pp. 204-234.

Goodman, M (1973) The chronicle of primate phylogeny contained in proteins.

213

Symp. Zool. Soc. Lond. 33: 339-375.

Greenfield, LO (1979) On the adaptive pattern of "*Ramapithecus*". *Am. J. Phys. Anthropol.* 50, 527-548.

Grine, FE (1993) Australopithecine taxonomy and phylogeny: Historical background and recent interpretation. In RL Ciochon and JG Fleagle (eds.): *The Human Evolution Source Book.* Englewood Cliffs: Prentice Hall, pp. 198-210.

Groves, CP (1986) Systematics of the great apes. In DR Swindler and J Erwin (eds.): *Comparative Primate Biology, Volume 1: Systematics, Evolution, and Anatomy.* New York: Alan R. Liss, pp. 187-217.

Hennig, W (1966) *Phylogenetic Systematics.* Chicago: University of Illinois Press.

Huxley, TH (1863) *Evidence as to Man's Place in Nature.* London: Williams and Norgate.

Hylander, WL (1975) Incisor size and diet in anthropoids with special reference to the cercopithecidae. *Science* 189: 1095-1098.

Kay, RF (1981) The nut-crackers — a theory of the adaptations of the *Ramapithecinae. Am. J. Phys. Anthropol.* 55: 141-151.

Kay, RF and Covert, HH (1984) Anatomy and behavior of extinct primates. In DJ Chivers, BA Wood, and A Bilsborough (eds.): *Food Acquisition and Processing in Primates.* Cambridge: Cambridge University Press, pp. 467-508.

Kay, RF and Hylander, WL (1978) The dental structure of mammalian folivores with special reference to primates and phalangeroidea. In GG Montgomery (ed.), *The Ecology of Arboreal Folivores.* Washington: Smithsonian Institution Press, pp. 173-192.

King, M-C, and Wilson, AC (1975) Evolution at two levels in humans and chimpanzees. *Science* 188: 107-113.

Krogman, WM (1930) Studies in growth changes in the skull and face of anthropoids. II Ectocranial and endocranial sutures closure in anthropoids and apes. *Am. J. Anat.* 46: 315-353.

Lewis, GE (1934) Preliminary notice of new man-like apes from India. *Am. J. Sci.* Ser. 5 27: 161-179.

Lovejoy, CO (1981) The origin of Man. *Science* 211: 341-350.

Marks, J (1992) Genetic relationships among the apes and humans. *Curr. Opinion Gen. Develop.* 2: 883-889.

Martin, RD (1990) *Primate Origins and Evolution.* Princeton: Princeton University Press.

Martin, RD (1993) Primate origins: plugging the gaps. *Nature* 363: 223-234.

Martin, L and Andrews, P (1993) Renaissance of Europe's ape. *Nature* 365: 494.

Martin, L (1985) Significance of enamel thickness in hominoid evolution. *Nature* 314: 260-263.

McGrew, WC (1987) Tools to get food: the subsistants of Tasmanian aborigines and Tanzanian chimpanzees compared. *J. Anthropol. Res.* 43: 247-258.

Mein, P (1986) Chronological succession of hominoids in the European Neogene. In Else, JG and Lee, PC (eds.): *Primate Evolution.* Cambridge: Cambridge University Press, pp. 58-70.

Mein, P (1990) Updating of the MN zones. In Lindsay, EH, Fahlbusch, V and

Mein, P (eds.): *European Neogene Mammal Chronology*. New York: Plenum Press, pp. 73-90.

Nishida, T. and Hiraiwa-Hasegawa, M (1986) Chimpanzees and bonobos: Cooperative relationships among males. In Smuts, BB, Cheney, DL, Seyfarth, RM, Wrangham, RW, and Struhsaker, TT (eds.): *Primate Societies*. Chicago: University of Chicago Press, pp. 165-177.

Nishida, T and Hiraiwa, M (1982) Natural history of a tool-using behavior by wild chimpanzees in feeding upon wood-boring ants. *J. Hum. Evol.* 11: 73-99.

Osborn, HF (1922) *Hesperopithecus*, the first anthropoid primate found in America. *Am. Mus. Nov.* 37: 463-465.

Pilbeam, DR (1972) *The Ascent of Man*. New York: Macmillan.

Pilbeam, DR (1982) New hominoid skull material from the Miocene of Pakistan. *Nature* 295: 232-234.

Pilbeam, DR, Rose, MD, Barry, JC, Shah, SMI (1990) New *Sivapithecus humeri* from Pakistan and the relationship of *Sivapithecus* and *Pongo*. *Nature* 348: 237-239.

Rak, Y (1983) *The Australopithecine Face*. New York: Academic Press.

Robinson, JT (1956) The dentition of the *Australopithecinae*. *Trans. Mus. Mem.* 9: 1-179.

Rogers, J (1993) The phylogenetic relationships among *Homo, Pan* and *Gorilla*: A population genetics perspective. *J. Hum. Evol.* 25: 201-216.

Rose, MD (1983) Miocene hominoid postcranial morphology: Monkey-like, ape-like, neither, or both?. In RL Ciochon and RS Corruccini (eds.): *New Interpretations of Ape and Human Ancestry*. New York: Plenum Press, pp. 405-417.

Rose, MD (1988) Another look at the anthropoid elbow. *J. Hum. Evol.* 17:193-224.

Rose, MD (1989) New postcranial specimens of catarrhines from the Middle Miocene Chinji Formation, Pakistan: Description and a discussion of proximal humeral functional morphology in anthropoids. *J. Hum. Evol.* 18: 131-162.

Ruvolo, M, Disotell, TR, Allard, MW, Brown, WM, and Honeycutt, R.L. (1991) Resolution of the African hominoid trichotomy by use of a mitochondrial gene sequence. *Proc. Natn. Acad. Sci.* USA 88: 1570-1574.

Sarich, VM and Wilson, AC (1967) Immunological time-scale for hominoid evolution. *Science* 158: 1200-1203.

Sibley, CG and Alquist, JE (1984) The phylogeny of the hominoid primates as indicated by DNA-DNA hybridization. *J. Mol. Evol.* 20:2-15.

Sibley, CG and Alquist, JE (1987) DNA hybridization evidence of hominoid phylogeny: Results from an expanded data set. *J. Mol. Evol.* 26: 99-121.

Steininger FF, Bernor RL, and Fahlbusch V (1990) European Neogene marine/continental chronologic correlations. In EH Lindsay, V Fahlbusch, and P Mein (eds.): *European Neogene Mammal Chronology*. New York: Plenum Press, pp. 15-46.

Stringer, CB (1990) The emergence of modern humans. *Sci. Am.* December, 1990, 98-104.

Susman, RL, Stern, JT and Jungers, WL (1984). Arborality and bipedality in the

Hadar hominids. *Folia Primatol.* 43: 113-156.

Tattersall, I, Delson, E, and Van Couvering, J (1988) *Encyclopedia of Human Evolution and Prehistory.* New York: Garland.

Taylor, CR and Rowntree, VJ (1973) Running on two or four legs: Which consumes more energy? *Science* 179: 186-187.

Tobias, PV (1967) *Olduvai Gorge, vol. 2: The Cranium and Maxillary Dentition of Australopithecus (Zinjanthropus) boisei.* Cambridge: Cambridge University Press.

Teleki, G (1974) Chimpanzee subsistence technology: Materials and skills. *J. Hum. Evol.* 3: 575-594.

Teleki, G (1975) Primate subsistence patterns: Collector-predators and gatherer-hunters. *J. Hum. Evol.* 4: 125-184.

Teleki, G (1981) The omnivorous diet and eclectic feeding habits of chimpanzees in Gombe National Park, Tanzania. In Harding, R and Teleki, G (eds): *Omnivorous Primates.* New York; Columbia University Press, pp. 303-343.

Tuttle, RH (1967) Knuckle-walking and the evolution of hominoid hands. *Am. J. Phys. Anthropol.* 26: 171-206.

Tuttle, R (1969) Knuckle-walking and the problem of human origins. *Science* 166: 953-961.

Walker, AC and Pickford, M (1983) New postcranial fossils of *Proconsul africanus* and *Proconsul nyanzae.* In RL Corruccini and RS Ciochon (eds.): *New Interpretations of Ape and Human Ancestry.* New York: Plenum Press, pp. 325-352.

Walker, A and Teaford, MF (1989) The hunt for *Proconsul. Scientific American* 260: 76-82.

Ward, SC and Pilbeam, DR (1983) Maxillofacial morphology of Miocene hominoids from Africa and Indo-Pakistan. In RL Corruccini and RS Ciochon (eds.): *New Interpretations of Ape and Human Ancestry.* New York: Plenum Press, pp. 211-238.

Ward, SC and Kimbel, WH (1983) Subnasal alveolar morphology and the systematic position of *Sivapithecus. Am. J. Phys. Anthropol.* 61: 157-171.

Weiner, JS (1955) *The Piltdown Forgery.* Oxford: Oxford University Press.

Wheeler, PE (1991a) The thermoregulatory advantages of hominid bipedalism in open equatorial environments: The contribution of increased convective heat loss and cutaneous evaporative cooling. *J. Hum. Evol.* 21: 107-115.

Wheeler, PE (1991b) The influence of bipedalism on the energy and water budgets of early hominids. *J. Hum. Evol.* 21: 117-136.

Wiley, EO, Siegel-Causey, DJ, Brooks, DR, and Funk, VA (1990) *The Compleat Cladist: A Primer of Phylogenetic Procedures.* Lawrence: Museum of Natural History, Univ. of Kansas.

Wilson, AC and Cann, RL (1992) The recent African genesis of humans. *Sci. Am.* April: 68-73.

Wood, BA (1991) *Koobi Fora Research Project Volume 4: Hominid Cranial Remains.* Oxford: Clarendon Press.

Wrangham, RW 1977 Feeding behavior of chimpanzees in Gombe National Park, Tanzania. In Clutton-Brock (ed.): *Primate Ecology.* New York: Academic Press, pp. 503-538.

10

The Species Problem
An Approach to Studying Hominid Diversity in the Plio-Peistocene

Jennifer L. Thompson

The fossil record indicates considerable diversity in early hominid forms but there is a lack of consensus on the number of species represented. Determination of the number of species, however, is fundamental to the interpretation of evolutionary relationships and to the reconstruction of past lifeways. In order to facilitate the recognition of distinct species, the amount of within- and between-group variation across species must be assessed. This paper uses morphological variability in the crania of extant hominoid species (Homo, Pan, Gorilla and Pongo) as a guide to variation to be expected within a sample of fossil hominid crania from the Plio-Pleistocene (A. afarensis, A. africanus, A. robustus, A. boisei, H. habilis and H. erectus). The analysis revealed traits of relatively low variability and low sexual dimorphism that were held in common by all four modern groups. The method presented here provides a systematic way of assessing a measurement's ability to discriminate between fossil samples using the coefficient of variation (CV). The method may prove to be a powerful tool with which to assess variability in fossil hominid samples and so help to begin to resolve the "species problem" encountered in the study of hominid diversity in the Plio-Pleistocene.

INTRODUCTION

Human palaeontologists are interested in how humans evolved from their non-human primate origins to the present. This evolution involves shifts in morphology (what species looked like) and changes in behaviour over time. Questions that become important therefore, are, What did the different hominids eat? Which, if any, used tools? Were all equally at home on the ground? When did language evolve? Evolution also involves changes in physiology and life history parameters: How fast did hominids grow? When did the human pattern of growth appear? How long did the average individual in a species live, what was their lifespan and so on. The answers to these questions ultimately depend on identifying which, and how many, species are present in the fossil record. With this knowledge, we can then examine differences and similarities between species over time and come to a better understanding of the evolutionary relationships between them.

Identifying the number of species present in the fossil record is no easy matter. The task is complicated because we do not know how many species actually lived, nor can we be certain that all species that existed are represented in the fossil record. Furthermore, the fossil record is composed of fragments of individuals from populations that are represented at several sites and time periods and thus whole populations are never preserved. There are also several definitions of the concept of *species* and no single method for determining the number of species present in the fossil record.

This chapter addresses some of the problems in identifying hominid species in the fossil record with a particular focus on the genus *Australopithecus* and with special attention to variation within the hominid species, *Australopithecus boisei*. The chapter begins with a discussion of the concept of species, then describes the problem of variability in the hominid fossil record, and proceeds to an analysis of species diversity using the coefficient of variation (CV).

THE SPECIES PROBLEM

Since this chapter is concerned with identifying fossil hominid species, it is important to understand the concept of *species* (for a detailed treatment of the species concept see, for example, Kimbel and Martin, 1993). A species can be considered to be the lowest taxonomic level in the Linnaean Classification system. Another common way of thinking about species employs the concept of *biospecies*, put forward by Ernst Mayr in 1944. Biospecies are groups of actually or potentially interbreeding natural populations, which are reproductively isolated from other such species. But because the criterion for recognizing a species is reproduction, this definition can only be applied to living species; we cannot know if hominids actually interbred. We assume that if the morphology of fossil hominids was similar, they were capable of interbreeding.

Paleoanthropologists therefore basically work with *morphospecies*, species defined on the basis of morphological characteristics.

The biospecies definition implies that speciation only takes place when populations become reproductively isolated from one another and precludes other methods of speciation, like anagenetic evolution (transformation of a single species into another species over time), from having a role in the evolutionary process.

The biospecies concept also fails to address the fact that species can exist over long periods of time. *Palaeospecies* and *chronospecies* both refer to species within a single lineage that succeed each other in time. The problem here is to determine species boundaries: where does one species end and another begin?

Species are also dispersed over geographical space and show variations in their biology and behaviour, even though they consist of a series of populations that possess similar morphological, physiological, and ecological characteristics (Mayr, 1963). So *populations*, not individuals, must be identified and classified. But, since whole populations do not fossilize, one must make inferences from relatively few fossilized specimens to the once-living population as a whole.

The extent of variation within fossil species, over time and through geographical space, was poorly understood or appreciated until relatively recently. In the early days of human paleontology, there was a tendency for each new specimen to be given a distinct species or genus name. This is because small differences in shape were taken to indicate species differences rather than normal within-species variation. The lack of adequate fossil samples contributed to this tendency but, over time, an increased appreciation of within-species variation led many paleoanthropologists to resist virtually *any* proposed new species, this resistance was demonstrated by the chilly reception received by the new taxon *Homo habilis* in the 1960s and by *Australopithecus afarensis* in the 1980s.

Tattarsall (1986), however, wrote an influential article on the subject of species recognition. He argues that in closely related but distinct living species, differences are more likely to be found in soft tissue or other features like coat colour, rather than in the skeleton. It follows, therefore, that when distinct differences are found between fossil skeletons, even in a few characters, the specimens should be assigned to separate species. Recent acceptance of this way of thinking has led some paleoanthropologists to more readily accept diversity in the fossil record and, hence, more species.

219

The fossil record has expanded enormously over the past ten years and indicates that hominid evolution was very complex. Despite the recognition of many taxa, there is no firm agreement about the number of species represented; neither is there agreement about how the evolutionary relationships between hominid species should be interpreted, nor about their relationship to modern humans.

ADDITIONAL PROBLEMS

In addition to the problem of trying to develop an adequate and comprehensive definition of fossil species, there are other factors that need to be considered when trying to sort out the number of species of hominids that lived in the past:

(1) *Chronology*: The fossil record consists of many individuals from different time periods. These specimens do not necessarily represent a single breeding population that was alive at one time.

(2) *Fragmentary remains*: Until recently, many of the fossils, especially those from East Africa, were subject to a number of taphonomic processes prior to their discovery, such as weathering, cracking, or trampling by animals.

(3) *Uncertainty about the amount of variation within a species*: At the very least, variation within a species includes both individual variation, variation by age and sex, and over time within a lineage. The latter includes small differences that may develop over time without speciation, but that distinguish earlier and later forms of the same species.

(4) *Sample representativeness*: It is extremely difficult to determine how representative a fossil sample might have been of the extinct populations they are derived from. Furthermore, fossil samples do not contain all elements of the skeletons. They are usually composed predominantly of elements of the skull due to the fact that teeth and jaws are the most likely to survive to be fossilized.

Despite these problems, paleontologists continue to evaluate the number of species present in the fossil record, approaching the problem from different angles, and/or attempting to apply new techniques or methods to try to resolve the issue. Without such attempts, one cannot go on to ask questions about diet and lifespan and other important biological and behavioural questions (e.g., Helmuth and Thompson 1989; Thompson 1986).

SPECIES DIVERSITY IN THE HOMINID FOSSIL RECORD

Most researchers currently recognize four or five species of "Australopithecine" from the Plio-Pleistocene: *Australopithecus afarensis, A. africanus, A. robustus* (and *A. crassidens)* and *A. boisei*. The relatively new specimen from the West of Lake Turkana, KNM-WT 17000, may represent a new, sixth, species of robust Australopithecine, *A. aethiopicus*. However, each of the above "species" is composed of samples of specimens that show morphological variation and some authors believe this indicates greater diversity within the fossil record than previously suspected. For instance, some researchers argue that *A. afarensis* is really comprised of two species (e.g. Senut and Tardieu, 1985). Indeed, the homogeneity of each of these Australopithecine species has been questioned (see Brown, et al., 1993; Grine, 1981, 1988; Clarke, 1988; Delson, 1986, 1987; Kimbel and White, 1988; Tobias, 1988; Walker et al., 1986; Wood, 1988; Trinkaus, 1990; Skelton and McHenry, 1992).

Arguments over species diversity are not limited to the genus *Australopithecus*. For years researchers have argued that *Homo habilis* consists of several species (e.g. Stringer, 1986; Tobias, 1991; Wood, 1991; see also Thompson, 1993b) and *Homo erectus* has also been the centre of dispute (Bilsborough, 1992; Kramer, 1993; Andrews, 1984; Wood, 1984, 1991). Much has also been written about the composition of *Homo sapiens* (see Stringer and Andrews, 1988; Stringer, 1990; Thorne and Wolpoff, 1992; Smith, 1992; Aiello, 1993). It is difficult to resolve whether there are eight or more species in the human lineage when there is no agreement regarding methods for determining the extent of species diversity.

ADDRESSING THE ISSUE OF VARIATION IN THE FOSSIL RECORD

One way to address the question of the nature of the diversity present in a hominid sample is to examine both within- and between-species variation in modern species. Measurement of such variation can be used as a set of criteria against which to compare variation within fossil samples.

The range of variation in a sample can be assessed by evaluating measurements (metric traits), such as the maximum length of the skull, or by assessing the presence, absence or relative size of various attributes (non-metric traits), such as the presence or absence of a chin, using subjective categories like small, intermediate, or large.

Non-metric traits must be analysed with great care, especially those that require subjective labels, such as small, intermediate, or large. This is because fossil collections are housed in different countries and, even if a whole sample is located in one place, researchers are rarely permitted to view dozens of specimens at one time. Consider the following scenario: the researcher examines three specimens but must return each one before examining the next. The first specimen's attribute is listed as small, specimen two's as large, and specimen three's as intermediate. Had the order of examination been different, the researcher might have listed the traits as small (specimen one), large (specimen three), and [very] large (specimen two). Clearly, the usefulness of these characters is enhanced when they can be quantified. Even if the boundaries between the categories are the subjective decision of the researcher, this allows meaningful comparisons between specimens or between the results of different researchers to be made, as long as everyone knows what the boundaries are (see Rak, 1988 and Tobias, 1989 regarding the use of non-metric traits in cladistic analyses).

When analysing metric traits, one must be careful to measure between homologous points, that is, features that have the same evolutionary origin in different individuals or species. By taking a measurement between two homologous points, the researcher ensures that the same measure is being compared between individuals or species.

One way to control for within-species variation is to concentrate on measurements that are stable within modern species, ones that do not show individual, sexual, or geographical differences. Characters that have low variability within groups but high variability between groups are said to have *phyletic valence* and are best used to discriminate between species of fossil hominids (Robinson, 1960; Tobias, 1967).

The variability in any measurement can be examined by listing the smallest and largest values *within* a sample, or by examining the mean (average) and standard deviation (the dispersion of the scores around the mean value). However, if one wishes to compare values *between* samples, then other statistics must be calculated.

The Coefficient of Variation

The *coefficient of variation* (CV) is one method for assessing species diversity. It is a simple statistic used extensively to compare measurements. It represents the relative dispersion of values for a sample around the mean. The coefficient of variation is expressed mathematically as:

$$CV = \text{Standard Deviation} / \text{Mean} \times 100$$

The CV makes it possible to compare samples whose values differ in absolute size since it is independent of any unit of measurement if the variables are homologous or if they all belong to the same category (i.e., linear dimensions).

Sokal and Rohlf (1981) suggest the use of 95% confidence limits when comparing CV values. The CV value of a sample, +/- its 95% confidence limits, indicates how likely this estimate is to be close to that of the true population value of CV. In other words, using the confidence limits indicates that there is a 95 percent probability that the true population CV value lies within the given sample CV values' confidence intervals. If two CV values (+/- 95% confidence limits) do not overlap, then the two samples differ considerably in their degree of variation. This is useful, for example, when comparing an unknown sample's CV value to that of a living primate species.

Several studies of fossil hominid samples have used the CV as a tool of analysis and, recently, researchers have used living primate species as a guide to the expected amount of variation within a fossil species. The logic is as follows: if a fossil sample has a CV value that is equivalent to or less than that obtained for a modern species, then the fossil sample likely represents one species. Conversely, if the fossil CV value exceeds the CV value of any single living species, then the fossil sample is variable enough to accommodate more than one species.

Unfortunately, if applying the simple logic outlined above, one cannot really determine whether large CV values for a fossil sample are caused by individual variation, sexual dimorphism, other causes of within-species variation, or between-species variation. Also, small sample sizes combined with sample bias can artificially inflate fossil CV values (see Sokal and Braumann, 1980 about dealing with small sample size bias: see Martin, 1983; Martin and Andrews, 1984; Millar 1991; and Cope and Lacey, 1992 for a discussion of the advantages and disadvantages of using CV).

ONE ATTEMPT TO ADDRESS THE VARIATION PROBLEM: AN EXAMPLE FROM THE PLIO-PLEISTOCENE

As part of my research on early hominid cranial variation I wanted to isolate individual cranial metric measurements that were not very variable within a number of modern species but that could discriminate between those species. I decided to use the coefficient of variation as one way to evaluate that variation. I reasoned that if I could find measurements that varied little (low values of CV) *within* species but could discriminate *between* species (high values of CV if more than one species was represented) then these characters could then be applied to fossil samples to assess their homogeneity. For instance, if the fossil sample was extremely variable (large CV value) for a measurement that showed little variability in each of the modern species, then this might mean that the fossil sample contained more than one species.

I chose humans (HO=Homo), Chimpanzees (PA=Pan), Gorillas (GO) and Orangutans (PO=Pongo) as my modern yardsticks against which to compare the variation in my fossil samples. I measured fossil specimens of the currently recognized Plio-Plesitocene species: *A. afarensis*, *A. africanus*, *A. robustus*, *A. boisei*, *H. habilis*, and *H. erectus*. Where possible I measured the original fossils; otherwise casts (plastic or plaster copies) were used.

The measurements on modern skulls were taken at the British Museum of Natural History in London, England. I measured the original fossils at the Kenya National Museum in Nairobi, Kenya and at the University of the Witwatersrand in Johannesburg and the Transvaal Museum in Pretoria, in the Republic of South Africa. The majority of the specimens included in this study were judged to be adult on the basis of dental eruption.

Ninety-six measurements were taken on each specimen (when possible), from five regions of the skull: mandible, palate, base, vault, and face. The measurements were chosen to circumscribe the whole skull and were chosen from each region to ensure that even fragmentary fossil specimens could be included since many fossils are incomplete (see Thompson, 1991).

Of the 96 measurements, I isolated 21 characters/measurements that, in each modern comparative sample, met the criteria of being relatively invariant and showed little sexual dimorphism. I assumed that these measurements might be better at discriminating between samples of fossil hominids because many causes of within-species variation are controlled for.

The next step was to determine whether any of these 21 measurements could discriminate between modern species. I reasoned that if I combined my modern data into a larger sample, one representing several species and if, for that sample, the CV value for any of the 21 measurements was larger than what was found in each of the modern species individually, then that particular measurement was actually able to discriminate between the modern species (the large CV value reflecting the fact that the larger sample was, indeed, heterogeneous). If a measurement could do this for three or four modern species, then it was likely that it could also do so for fossil species.

In order to test if any of the 21 measurements had the ability to discriminate between modern species the data for Homo, Pan, Gorilla, and Pongo were pooled to obtain values of CV for each measurement. I named this sample Pooled Sample 1 (PS1). The data for apes alone were pooled (Pan, Gorilla, Pongo) to obtain a second set of CVs for each measurement and this sample was called Pooled Sample 2 (PS2). Pooling the data of the modern comparators into two data sets (humans and apes in one; apes only in the second data set) gives values of the CV that I KNOW represent two taxonomically diverse samples (Thompson, 1993a).

If the CV values of PS1 and PS2 are very large (especially if they are larger than those of each of the four modern species), then we know that the CV value is accurately reflecting the fact that PS1 and PS2 are composed of several different species and, hence, heterogeneity. If the CV value of a particular measurement actually indicates a heterogeneous sample of modern species, then logically, it has a better chance of distinguishing between fossil samples.

On the other hand, if the CV value of an invariant and undimorphic character fails to indicate a multi-species sample (heterogeneity), even when that sample is known to contain three or four species of several genera (!), then that character is of little use for fossil species. Note, however, that a sample could be heterogeneous, but the CV value for a particular measurement may not reveal this fact. It is only when a CV value for a particular measurement is *large* that it is possible to detect a heterogeneous sample. According to Martin and Andrews (1984:27): "...CV can only be used to say that it is likely that more than one species is present, it cannot be used to demonstrate that a single species is present, or to determine the number of species present."

The following criteria were used to assess the ability of the 21 measurements to indicate that PS1 (pooled human and ape sample) and PS2 (pooled ape sample) were, indeed, heterogeneous samples:

> **Criterion 1**: the CV value of a measurement from the PS1 and/or PS2 sample should be greater than the CV value of the same measurement in each of the modern samples; and
>
> **Criterion 2**: the CV value of a measurement from the PS1 and/or PS2 sample should also exceed the 95% confidence intervals of the same measurement in each of the four modern samples.

RESULTS

Nineteen of the twenty-one measurements had the ability to discriminate between the modern samples, but only eight (the first eight measurements in Table 2) were able to discriminate between the modern samples according to criterion one and two listed above. The last eleven measurements listed in Table 2, however, only met criterion one (larger CV values than each of the modern comparators). Thus the first eight of the nineteen measurements have more "power" to discriminate between samples than do the remaining eleven, but all can be used in the assessment of fossil samples.

Table 1. P5: Palatal Length: Coefficient of Variation Data for PS1, PS2, and Modern Samples

Sample	CV	N	INT
PS1	23.2	69	19.0–27.4
PS2	15.3	55	12.3–18.3
HO	6.5	14	3.8–9.1
PA	6.2	18	4.0–8.4
GO	9.8	18	6.3–13.2
PO	7.6	19	5.0–10.1

N=   Number in sample
INT =   95% confidence interval

I will illustrate this analytical process using the example of P5-PALATE ARCADAL LENGTH (see Table 1) to explain how the two criteria are assessed and to apply the results to the fossil species problem. For the measurement P5:

(1) the CV values of the pooled samples PS1 and PS2, are greater than those of any of the modern groups; and

(2) these values also exceed the 95% confidence intervals of each of the four modern groups. This means that there is little possibility that any of the modern groups could have such a high CV value by chance alone.

With regard to measurement P5, we know that if an unknown sample has a CV value of 13.2 or less for the character P5 the homogeneity of the sample cannot be questioned *on the basis of that particular character* because

Measurement	N	CV	CV*	CV Flag	AB
M9	4	6.8	13.6	8.6	>
P5	4	10.9	21.9	13.2	>
B4	4	6.3	12.6	10.5	>
B8	7	**15.4**	——	**10.8**	>>
B18	6	**15.2**	——	**13.8**	>>
F1	4	8.4	16.7	12.4	>
F4	4	7.9	15.8	11.0	>
F17	4	**13.3**	**26.6**	**13.1**	>>
P4	5	6.4	14.3	11.0	>
P6	3	10.2	17.8	10.6	>
B1	3	2.2	3.9	15.7	<<
B2	4	8.8	17.7	12.4	>
B5	3	9.9	17.4	11.7	>
B6	6	**17.3**	——	**14.5**	>>
B9	6	9.1	——	12.8	<
V2	5	6.8	15.3	8.2	>
V8	3	3.7	6.5	15.5	<<
V9	3	9.6	16.8	10.2	>
V10	5	**29.9**	**67.0**	**11.5**	>>

Table 2. Status of Australopithecus Boisei When Assessed Against the CV Flag for Each Character

When n< or = 5, the following formula was used to correct for bias: $CV^* = (1+.25n)$ x CV (Sokal and Braumann, 1980)

AB=A. boisei
M9=Maximum external breadth from alveolar margins of the mandible
P5 =Arcadal length of palate
B4=Bistylomastoid width
B8=Biforamen ovale breadth
B18=Bimastoid breadth
F1=Maximum biorbital breadth
F4=Maximum orbit height
F17=Bizygomatic tubercle breadth
P4=Maximum external breadth of palate between outer margins
P6=Maximum palatal arcade breadth
B1=Foramen magnum length
B2=Foramen magnum width
B5=Bistyloid width
B6=Bicarotid canal width
B9=Biinfratemporal fossa width
V2=Maximum biparietal breadth
V8=Occipital chord
V9=Basi-bregmatic height
V10=supraglabella-bregma chord (see Thompson, 1991 for defining landmarks)

the sample in question is no more variable than any of the modern primate samples *for that character*. But a value of greater than 13.2 may indicate a heterogeneous sample and certainly warrants closer attention. The value of 13.2 for P5 thus becomes its *CV FLAG*. If a fossil sample has a CV value of greater than 13.2 *for this character*, we may begin to suspect that more than one species may be present in the sample.

This methodology was applied to each measurement to produce measurement-specific CV FLAG values. Then the CV values of various fossil species were assessed to see if they exceeded (were greater than: >) or fell below (were less than: <) the CV FLAG values for these measurements.

I will briefly summarize the results for the *Australopithecus boisei* sample (see Thompson, 1991 for more details).

Table 2 lists: 1) the measurements; 2) the number of fossil specimens measured for each measurement (N); 3) the CV value; 4) the CV* value (when N is less than or equal to 5); 5) the CV FLAG for each measurement; and 6) the status of the *A. boisei* sample when assessed against the CV FLAG for each measurement (ie. whether the fossil sample's CV was greater than or less than the CV FLAG value). Recall that the first eight measurements in Table 2 have more "power" to discriminate a heterogeneous sample since they met both criterion 1 and 2 listed above. For sixteen of the measurements, the CV* value (or CV value if N > 5) was larger than the CV Flag and thus the results indicate that the *A. boisei* sample is heterogeneous.

Recall that when the sample size is small, numbering five or less, the CV* formula is used because population variability may not be adequately represented. For eleven of the sixteen measurements in Table 2, the CV FLAG value is exceeded only when the CV* value is calculated. However, for five of the measurements the CV value exceeds the CV FLAG value. These measurements are emphasized in **boldface** and indicated under the AB column by two greater than signs (>>). For these measurements, either N is greater than five and/or both the CV value and the CV* value indicate a great deal of variability in the *A. boisei* sample.

The underlying sources of the large CV and CV* values cannot be assessed without examining the original data, so I examined the raw data for each of the five measurements. This procedure indicated that certain fossil specimens were producing the variability. In many cases, specimen KNM-ER 732, possibly a female *A. boisei*, was the source of the variability. In some cases it was KNM-ER 407 and 732 (both possible females of *A. boisei*) and in some cases it was KNM-WT 17000 (see Thompson, n.d.).

My results indicate that if KNM-ER 732 is included in the *A. boisei* sample, and if it is a female, then the level of sexual dimorphism is extremely high in this species. It is so high, in fact, that it exceeds that found in the two most sexually dimorphic primates: Gorillas and Orangutans. While this is certainly possible, I need to do more work in order to evaluate its likelihood. It is also possible that KNM-ER 732, and possibly even KNM-ER 407 and KNM-WT 17000, may belong to a separate species.

It is important to remember that none of the modern comparative samples were highly variable or sexually dimorphic for any of these measurements. Consequently, the assumption I am making is that early hominid species should also show little variability or sexual dimorphism for these measurements.

On the basis of these results, there are a number of different inferences that one could make about *A. boisei*:

(1) We either accept that the *A. boisei* sample consists of a number of different species; or

(2) We assume that *A. boisei* was more variable for these measurements than modern hominoids (to include KNM-WT 17000 in the *A. boisei* sample); we also must assume that the level of sexual dimorphism in *A. boisei* was much higher than in modern hominoids (to include KNM-ER 732 and 407 in the *A. boisei* sample); or

(3) We are detecting within-species variability due to change in the species over time, not to differences between individuals or between the sexes. Some of the specimens in the *A. boisei* sample are separated by as much as .5 million years, some by much less. In any case, it is extremely unlikely that any of these specimens come from the same breeding population, living in the same area, at the same time.

Thus while I may suspect that the *A. boisei* sample is heterogeneous and possible contains more than one species, in particular that KNM-ER 732 may belong to a separate species, the fact that the sample size is so small means that I must corroborate this hypothesis using other methods (see Thompson and Moggi Cecchi, 1994, for example). The analysis and results provide the background information I need to construct the working hypothesis that the *A. boisei* sample consists of more than one species.

229

CONCLUSIONS

The fossil record indicates considerable diversity in early hominid forms but there is a lack of consensus on the number of species represented. In order to facilitate the recognition of distinct species, the amount of within- and between-group variation across species must be assessed. This paper demonstrates how morphological variability in the crania of extant hominoid species (Homo, Pan, Gorilla and Pongo) can be used as a guide to variation to be expected within a sample of fossil hominid crania from the Plio-Pleistocene. The analysis of a sample of hominoid crania (humans and apes) revealed traits of relatively low variability and low sexual dimorphism, which were held in common by all four modern groups. Application of this variability to a sample of *A. boisei* crania suggested that there may be considerably more variability within the sample than would be predicted from variation in measurements from contemporary hominoid samples. Clearly, we need to re-think the *A. boisei* taxon and re-examine the specimens that have been assigned to it, notably KNM-ER 732.

The research presented here offers a systematic way of assessing a measurement's ability to discriminate between fossil samples using the coefficient of variation (CV). This method may prove to be a powerful tool with which to assess variability in other fossil hominid samples and so help to begin to resolve the "species problem" encountered in the study of hominid diversity in the Plio-Pleistocene.

ACKNOWLEDGEMENTS

This research was supported by a Commonwealth Scholarship. Travel grants for the support of research in Africa were made by the Boise Fund, The Commonwealth Commission, The Department of Anthropology, Durham, The Fawcus Travel Fund, Durham, and the Graduate Society, Durham. I am grateful to Dr. R. Leakey, Dr. C. K. Brain, and Professor P. V. Tobias for giving me access to the fossil hominids in their care. Thanks should also go to the staff at the Kenya National Museum, The Transvaal Museum, and the University of the Witwatersrand for their assistance. I thank the governments of Kenya and South Africa for giving me permission to study in their respective countries. Also, thanks should go to P. D. Jenkins and R. Kruszynski, who gave me access to primate and human skeletal material in their care at the British Museum (Natural History) in the U. K. I am extremely grateful to Professor Bernard Wood (The University of Liverpool), Dr. Leslie Aiello (University College London) and, in particular, Professor Alan Bilsborough (Durham University) for their support and advice as well as their valuable comments on an earlier version of this work. I would like to thank the anonymous reviewer of this manuscript for his/her constructive criticisms/comments. Finally, special thanks should go to the editors of this volume for their helpful suggestions and for inviting me to contribute to this volume.

REFERENCES

Aiello, L 1993 Fossil evidence for modern human origins in Africa: A revised view. *American Anthropologist* 95(1): 73-96.

Andrews P (1984) An alternative interpretation of the characters used to define Homo erectus. *Cour Forsh. Inst. Senkenberg* 69: 167-175.

Bilsborough A (1992) *Human Evolution*. Glasgow: Blackie Academic and Professional.

Brown B, Walker A, Ward CV, and Leakey RE (1993) New Australopithecus boisei calvaria from East Lake Turkana, Kenya. *American Journal of Physical Anthropology* 91: 137-159.

Clarke R J (1988) A new Australopithecus cranium from Sterkfontein and its bearing on the ancestry of Paranthropus. In FE Grine (ed.): *Evolutionary History of the "Robust" Australopithecines*. New York: Aldine, pp. 285-292.

Cope DA and Lacy MG (1992) Falsification of a single species hypothesis using the coefficient of variation: a simulation approach. *American Journal of Physical Anthropology* 89: 359-378.

Delson E (1987) Evolution and palaeobiology of robust australopithecines. *Nature* 327: 654-655.

Delson E (1986) Human phylogeny revised again. *Nature* 322: 496-497.

Grine FE (1981) Trophic differences between 'gracile' and 'robust' australopithecines: A scanning electron microscope analysis of occlusal events. *South African Journal of Science* 77: 203-230.

Grine FE (1988) Evolutionary history of the "robust" australopithecines: A summary and historical perspective. In FE Grine (ed.): *Evolutionary History of the "Robust" Australopithecines*. New York: Aldine, pp. 509-520.

Helmuth H and Thompson JL (1989) Lebens- und Entwicklungsdauer bei den plio-pleistozanen Hominiden Ostrafikas. *Ethnographisch-archaeologische Zeitschrift*. 30: 479-491.

Kimbel WH and Martin LB (1993) *Species, Species Concepts, and Primate Evolution*. New York: Plenum.

Kimbel WH and White TD (1988) Variation, sexual dimorphism and the taxonomy of Australopithecus. In FE Grine (ed.): *Evolutionary History of the "Robust" Australopithecines*. New York: Aldine, pp. 175-192.

Kramer A (1993) Human taxonomic diversity in the Pleistocene: does Homo erectus represent multiple hominid species? *American Journal of Physical Anthropology* 91: 161-171.

Martin L (1983) The relationships of the later Miocene Hominoidea. Ph. D. thesis, University of London.

Martin L and Andrews P (1984) The phyletic position of Graecopithecus freybergi KOENIGSWALD. *Cour. Forsch. Inst. Senckenberg* 69: 25-40.

Mayr E (1963) *Populations, Species, and Evolution.* Cambridge: Harvard University Press.

Mayr E (1944) On the concepts and terminology of vertical subspecies and species. *Natl. Res. Council Bull.* 2: 11-16.

Millar JA (1991) Does brain size variability provide evidence of multiple species in Homo habilis? *American Journal of Physical Anthropology* 84: 385-398.

Rak Y (1988) On variation in the masticatory system of A. boisei. In FE Grine (ed.): *Evolutionary History of the "Robust" Australopithecines.* New York: Aldine, pp.193-198.

Robinson JT (1960) The affinities of the new Olduvai australopithecine. *Nature* 186: 456-458.

Senut B and Tardieu C (1985) Functional aspects of Plio-Pleistocene hominid limb bones: Implications for taxonomy and phylogeny. In E Delson (ed.) *Ancestors: the hard evidence.* New York: Alan R. Liss, pp. 193-201.

Skelton R and McHenry H (1992) Evolutionary relationships among early hominids. *Journal of Human Evolution* 15: 165-175.

Smith FH (1992) The role of continuity in modern human origins. In Brauer G and Smith FH (eds.) *Continuity or Replacement? Controversies in Homo sapiens evolution.* Rotterdam: Balkema, pp. 145-156.

Sokal RR and Braumann CA (1980) Significance tests for coefficients of variation and variability profiles. *Syst. Zool.* 29: 50-66.

Sokal RR and Rohlf FJ (1981) *Biometry. The Principles and Practice of Statistics in Biological Research.* San Francisco: Freeman.

Stringer CB (1990) The emergence of modern humans. *Scientific American.* December 10th edition, pp. 68-74.

Stringer CB (1986) The credibility of Homo habilis. In BA Wood, R Martin, and P Andrews (eds.) *Major Topics in Primate and Human Evolution.* Cambridge: Cambridge University Press, pp. 266-294.

Stringer CB & Andrews P (1988) Genetic and fossil evidence of the origin of modern humans. *Science* 239:1263-1268.

Tattersall I (1986) Species recognition in human paleontology. *Journal of Human Evolution* 15: 165-175.

Thompson JL (n.d.) The use of computed values of the coefficient of variation in the analysis of Australopithecine cranial variability. *Proceedings* of the conference: Four Million Years of Hominid Evolution in Africa: An International Congress in Honour of Dr. Mary D. Leakey's Outstanding Contribution in Palaeoanthropology. August 8-14, 1993. (Submitted)

Thompson JL (1993a) The use of the coefficient of variation in the assessment of early hominid cranial variability. *American Journal of Physical Anthropology.* Special Supplement 16: 195.

Thompson JL (1993b) The unusual cranial attributes of KNM-ER 1805 and their implications for studies of sexual dimorphism in Homo habilis. *Human Evolution* 8 (4): 255-63.

Thompson JL (1991) The significance of early hominid cranial variability. Unpublished PhD thesis. University of Durham, U.K.

Thompson JL (1986) A paleodemographic analysis of the East African Plio-Pleistocene Hominidae. Unpublished MA thesis, Trent University.

Thompson JL and Moggi Cecchi J (1994) Advances in morphometrics: Analysis of the size and shape of organisms using Geometric Morphometrics. Report on the NATO Advanced Study Institute held at Il Ciocco, Lucca, Italy 18-30 July, 1993. *Human Evolution* 9 (1): 73-77.

Thorne AG and Wolpoff MH (1992) The multiregional evolution of humans. *Scientific American* 266(4): 28-33.

Tobias PV (1991) *Olduvai Gorge Volume 4. The Skulls, Endocasts and Teeth of Homo habilis.* Cambridge: Cambridge University Press.

Tobias PV (1989) Hominid variability, cladistic analysis and the place of Australopithecus africanus. In G. Giacobini (ed.): *Hominidae: Proceedings of the Second International Conference of Human Palaeontology.* Milan: Jaca Book, pp. 119-127.

Tobias PV (1988) Numerous apparently synapomorphic features in Australopithecus robustus, Australopithecus boisei and Homo habilis: support for the Skelton-McHenry-Drewhorn hypothesis. In FE Grine (ed.): *Evolutionary History of the "Robust" Australopithecines.* New York: Aldine, pp. 293-308.

Tobias PV (1967) *Olduvai Gorge, Volume 2. The Cranium and Maxillary Dentition of Australopithecus (Zinjanthropus) boisei.* Cambridge: Cambridge University Press.

Trinkaus E (1990) Cladistics and the hominid fossil record. *American Journal of Physical Anthropology* 83: 1-11.

Walker A, Leakey REF, Harris JM, and Brown FH (1986) 2.5-Myr Australopithecus boisei from west of Lake Turkana, Kenya. *Nature* 322: 517-522.

Wood BA (1991) *Koobi Fora Research Project Volume 4. Hominid Cranial Remains.* Oxford: Clarendon Press.

Wood BA (1988) Are "robust" australopithecines a monophyletic group? In FE Grine (ed.): *Evolutionary History of the "Robust" Australopithecines.* New York: Aldine, pp. 269-284.

Wood BA (1984) The origin of *Homo erectus.* Cour. Forsh. Inst. Senkenberg 69: 99-111.

Thompson JL and Moggi Cecchi J (1994) Advances in Morphometrics: Analysis of the size and shape of organisms using Geometric Morphometrics. Report on the NATO Advanced Study Institute held at Il Ciocco, Lucca, Italy 18-30 July, 1993. *Human Evolution* 9 (1): 73-77.

Thorne AG and Wolpoff MH (1992) The multiregional evolution of humans. *Scientific American* 266(4): 28-33.

Tobias PV (1991) *Olduvai Gorge Volume 4. The skulls, endocasts and teeth of Homo habilis.* Cambridge: Cambridge University Press.

Tobias PV (1988) Numerous apparently synapomorphic features in Australopithecus robustus, Australopithecus boisei and Homo habilis: support for the Skelton-McHenry-Drewhorn hypothesis. In FE Grine (ed.): *Evolutionary History of the "Robust" Australopithecines.* New York: Aldine, pp. 293-308.

Tobias PV (1967) *Olduvai Gorge, Volume 2. The Cranium and Maxillary Dentition of Australopithecus (Zinjanthropus) boisei.* Cambridge: Cambridge University Press.

Trinkaus E (1990) Cladistics and the hominid fossil record. *American Journal of Physical Anthropology* 83: 1-11.

Walker A, Leakey REF, Harris JM, and Brown FH (1986) 2.5-Myr Australopithecus boisei from west of Lake Turkana, Kenya. Nature 322: 517-522.

Wolpoff MH (1969) Crania capacity and taxonomy of Olduvai Hominid 7. *Nature* 223: 182-183.

Wood BA (1991) Koobi Fora Research Project Volume 4. *Hominid Cranial Remains.* Oxford: Clarendon Press.

Wood BA (1988) Are "robust" australopithecines a monophyletic group? In FE Grine (ed.): *Evolutionary History of the "Robust" Australopithecines.* New York: Aldine, pp. 269-284.

Wood BA (1984) *The origin of Homo erectus.* Cour. Forsh. Inst. Senkenberg 69: 99-111.

11

The Origin and Dispersal of Modern Humans

Pamela R. Willoughby

In 1987, a group of geneticists proposed that Africa was the continent in which anatomically modern Homo sapiens sapiens *developed, sometime between 100,000 and 200,000 years ago. This "out of Africa", "mitochondrial Eve" or "replacement" model stands in stark contrast to the traditional "multiregional" or "continuity" view that modern humans first appeared around 35,000 to 40,000 years ago, developing from archaic* Homo sapiens *populations throughout Eurasia and Africa by means of local selection and gene flow. For some palaeoanthropologists, the genetic model fits the available fossil evidence quite well, but it is opposed by others, especially by those working in the Far East. As a result of this argument, Upper Pleistocene fossil and archaeological research has become a major focus of current work.*

This paper reviews the fossil, archaeological and molecular evidence for modern human origins within the framework of current models. It also discusses current field research in the Western Rift Valley of Tanzania, which examines the behavioural changes associated with the appearance of modern humans.

UNDERSTANDING MODERN HUMAN ORIGINS

In 1987, three human geneticists studying mitochondrial DNA (mtDNA), Rebecca Cann, Mark Stoneking and Alan Wilson, proposed that Africa was the only continent that gave rise to anatomically modern humans, *Homo sapiens sapiens*, and that the last common ancestor of living people existed between 100,000 and 200,000 years ago (Cann et al., 1987; Cann, 1987, 1988, 1992; Wilson and Cann, 1992). This "mitochondrial Eve", "Garden of Eden" or "out of Africa" model provided a new line of support for the idea that there was a single geographic centre of origin of modern humans, called the "Noah's ark" (Howells, 1976) or "replacement" model (Bräuer and Smith, 1992). From this African centre, it was proposed, modern humans spread out to all other regions completely replacing or possibly interbreeding with the hominids already living there (Stringer, 1990, 1992a, 1992b; Stringer and Andrews, 1988a, 1988b; Bräuer, 1984, 1989, 1992). It was a viable alternative to the "multiregional", "continuity" or "candelabra" model that suggested that parallel evolution, local selection and gene flow between populations led to the gradual appearance of modern humans by 35,000 years ago wherever earlier hominids existed (throughout Europe, Asia and Africa) (Wolpoff, 1989, 1992; Wolpoff et al., 1988; Wolpoff and Thorne, 1991; Thorne and Wolpoff, 1981, 1992; Frayer, 1992; Frayer et al., 1993; Pope, 1991, 1992; Smith, 1992a, 1992b).

A new argument had begun in paleoanthropology; as in the case of the debate about the relationship of Miocene apes to hominid origins, which took place in the 1960s and 1970s (Lewin, 1987:85-127, see Begun, this volume), geneticists and palaeontologists presented very different interpretations. But, unlike the Miocene problem, many palaeontologists immediately accepted the conclusions of the mtDNA study. Within a year of the original article, Christopher Stringer and Peter Andrews (1988a:1268) wrote that "palaeoanthropologists who ignore the increasing wealth of genetic data on human population relationships will do so at their peril", presumably because they believed that these data explain what happened as well as, if not better than, the fossil evidence. Despite this apparent capitulation, the debate has not been any less acrimonious than earlier ones. In back to back articles in *Scientific American*, proponents of the mtDNA model recently argued that "biologists trained in modern evolutionary theory must reject the notion that the fossils provide the most direct evidence of how human evolution actually proceeded" (Wilson and Cann, 1992:68), while the multiregional supporters stated that "mitochondrial DNA is useful for guiding the development of theories, but only fossils provide the basis for refuting one idea or the other" (Thorne and Wolpoff, 1992:77).

It is true that the facts of human evolution are the fossils, their anatomical or morphological characteristics, and their position in time and space, along with associated archaeological and palaeoenvironmental data. The study of genetic relationships among living people provides a new way to collect information. What is not always clear is the need to distinguish the facts from the interpretations. Much of paleoanthropology is interpretive and subjective, including classification, decisions over which morphological traits are used to link fossils into types and species, and behavioural reconstructions. The facts remain the same for all researchers; they only change when a new fossil is discovered, a date for a known fossil is revised, or when there is a fundamental shift in our understanding of the ones already recovered. Such a shift is currently underway in the interpretation of modern human origins. While it makes understanding the data very difficult, the debate clearly illustrates the range of opinions characteristic of current palaeoanthropological research.

The basic models of modern human origins have different expectations. The replacement model argues that there was a single centre of modern human origins, Africa. There should be no evidence of transition from an earlier hominid to modern humans except in Africa, and there was no interbreeding of early moderns with more archaic forms elsewhere. The date of the first appearance of modern humans should vary from region to region, as populations migrated further from their original source, and overall genetic differences within and between populations should be low (Smith, 1992a:146). Proponents of the "multiregional" model believe that population features evolved over long periods in the regions where these groups are found today; transitional forms should exist everywhere, and genetic differences should be greatest between geographic areas (Smith, 1992a:146). Some gene flow was maintained between separate regions, so this accounts for the degree of genetic or morphological overlap between them. A blend of the two models is Bräuer's (1984:395) "replacement with hybidization" or gene flow model. Here, an African origin is postulated, but interbreeding can still occur (for example, in Eastern Europe); therefore, mixed or hybrid forms could be present in more than one area.

In this paper I will review the genetic and fossil evidence for modern human origins, as it is currently understood. Towards the end I will concentrate on the archaeological and behavioural problems that are the focus of my own research. Over the course of hominid evolution in the Pliocene and Pleistocene, increasingly complex cultural systems developed; the culmination of these is the technology associated with early modern humans, the Upper Palaeolithic. In Western Europe, modern humans are clearly immigrants, replacing local neandertals between 30,000 and 35,000 BP. Throughout Europe, this replacement or change is marked by the archaeological transition from the Middle Palaeolithic (dominated by flake tools) to the Upper Palaeolithic (characterized by long, straight, parallel-sided flake tools known as blades) (Klein, 1992).

A number of other things change as well. For the first time, archaeological sites have substantial numbers of bone, antler and ivory artifacts, including the first examples of personal adornment such as beads and animal teeth drilled for suspension as pendants. The number and variety of stone tool types increases, and these tools appear more standardized. Regional tool cultures make their appearance, and archaeologists propose that major changes in economic and social organization of human groups occurred (Mellars, 1991, 1992). The earliest Upper Palaeolithic associated with modern humans in Europe is the Aurignacian; "its remarkable uniformity and synchroneity over a vast area clearly suggest that it was the product of a rapidly expanding population" (Klein, 1992:8) rather than a local development.

Archaeologists have stressed that the Upper Palaeolithic represents a cultural explosion, one associated with the appearance of modern humans, and/or with the development of new patterns of linguistic and symbolic communication (Mellars, 1991:64). Most researchers explain the course of human evolution as a product of a feedback system operating among biology, environment and culture. In general, changes in technology seem to occur at the same time that new hominid species appear. But the move to alter the timing and pattern of modern human origins forces us to re-examine this fundamental assumption. Outside of Europe, there is growing evidence that modern human anatomy developed well before modern human technology (represented by the Upper Palaeolithic). If the biological and behavioural transition that produced modern humans occurred at different times, then no single process was responsible for both. In addition, the pattern of human biocultural evolution in the Upper Pleistocene may vary from place to place, so it is necessary to examine events throughout Eurasia and Africa. My own research, described below, examines some of these questions using data from Upper Pleistocene archaeological sites in East Africa.

GENETIC EVIDENCE FOR MODERN HUMAN ORIGINS

Mitochondrial DNA is found in small two-strand rings in mitochondria, organelles within cells that convert food and water into energy;

mtDNA is composed of around 16,000 base pairs that encode for 37 genes, as opposed to several hundred million base pairs coding for around 100,000 genes in nuclear DNA (Wilson and Cann, 1992:69; Cann, 1988:34). The sections of mtDNA measured for historical research evolve quickly and steadily through neutral mutation. The fact that mtDNA is inherited only from one's mother means that it is not subject to recombination from generation to generation; changes are only due to copying mistakes or mutations (Stringer, 1990:99). The amount of difference between two individuals, combined with a known constant rate of change, gives a date for the last common ancestor they share. With a number of individuals sampled, lines of descent can be traced and used to produce the ultimate in family trees.

The initial mtDNA study examined 145 individuals and two cell lines composed of 20 sub-Saharan Africans, 34 Asians, 46 Caucasians, 21 Australian aborigines and 26 New Guinea aborigines (Cann et al., 1987:32). However, only two of the 20 Africans were born in sub-Saharan Africa; the remainder were African Americans. Only 133 different mtDNA types were found. Using a computer and a method called parsimony analysis, these researchers produced a tree of descent, much like a genealogy. Parsimony analysis involves selecting the least number of branches needed to account for the observed genetic differences. The preferred tree had two branches at the base: one with seven African mtDNA types and one composed of all others (Cann et al., 1987:33).

The Africans in the first group were as different from each other as all the rest put together. Based on these results, Cann and her co-authors argued that Africa was the centre of origin for all living people and the last common ancestor for all people studied existed between 100,000 and 200,000 BP (Cann et al., 1987; Cann, 1987, 1988, 1992; Stoneking and Cann, 1989; Wilson and Cann, 1992). If the amount of difference between two individuals is known, it can be combined with a constant rate of mutation (here between 2 and 4% mutations per million years) to give a date for their last common ancestor. The rate of change is calculated by examining the degree of difference between populations with an estimated or known date of divergence. For instance, archaeological data show that New Guinea was most likely first settled between 50,000 and 60,000 years ago, when, due to low sea levels during the last glacial, it was joined to Australia as part of a supercontinent called Sahul (Cann, 1988:37). The amount of evolution in mtDNA that has taken place in Papua New Guinea is one-third of that of the whole human species. Therefore, the

239

last common ancestor existed 3 x (50,000-60,000) years ago or 150,000 to 180,000 BP (Wilson and Cann, 1992:72).

Results of the various mitochondrial DNA samples analysed since the original study was completed (Stoneking, 1993; Stoneking et al., 1992; Vigilant et al., 1991) reconfirm the results and implications of the original model, but introduce new complications. The methods used in the original study, such as how the tree chart was produced, were questioned as well as the conclusions drawn from them. Since most of the Africans sampled were African Americans, it was possible their mtDNA was not typical of Africans at all. A restudy by Vigilant et al. (1991) addressed some of the problems. Here 189 people, including 121 Africans, were sampled. A new estimate of the age of the last common ancestor was computed using an "outgroup" method. The mtDNA sequence of a common chimpanzee was compared to that of the human samples. From genetic and fossil studies we known that chimpanzees and humans share a common ancestor who lived around 5 to 6 million years ago; the number of mutations between the human samples was less than 1/25th of the chimpanzee to human one, implying that the last common ancestor of the humans ("mitochondrial Eve") lived less than 200,000 BP (Vigilant et al., 1991; Wilson and Cann, 1992:72).

This study led to new complaints about the statistical methods used, as well as about the wisdom of comparing DNA sequences from two different species. David Maddison (1991) and Alan Templeton (1992, 1993) both showed that they could produce many more trees of descent that had fewer branches (and therefore were more parsimonious) than the one chosen; many of these did not have an African ancestor. Templeton (1993:69) also argued that genetic studies can be used to argue for recurring gene flow over time rather than a single origin.

Recently there has been a new twist provided by some of the mtDNA researchers themselves. Henry Harpending and his colleagues (Harpending et al., 1993) suggest that the mtDNA evidence shows at least two population movements rather than just one. The first occurred around 100,000 years ago; it would have involved populations spreading from a restricted source (which can still be Africa), but not necessarily a major expansion. Around 50,000 years ago, there is evidence of dramatic population growth in groups descended from this initial migration, but who had then become isolated from one another over the next several thousand years (Harpending et al., 1993:495). They note that this expansion coincides with the Middle-Upper Palaeolithic transition, the traditional marker of the appearance of modern humans.

Nuclear and mitochondrial DNA studies produce similar patterns of relationship. Early work on the distribution of classical genetic markers such as blood group frequencies showed a split between Africans and Europeans on one hand and Asians, Australians, and Melanesians on the other (Cavalli-Sforza, 1991; Howells, 1976:630). In studies of nuclear DNA polymorphisms, the greatest differences are always between Africans and non-Africans (Wainscoat et al., 1986, 1989; Mountain et al., 1992). Studies of genes on the Y-chromosome, inherited through the male line, provide a similar picture to those drawn from maternally-linked mtDNA (Lucotte, 1989, 1992).

In general, the genetic data do not agree with a multiregional model, but do provide support for a single African centre of origin. Whether or not the last common ancestor is anatomically modern cannot be determined by genetic analysis. Some researchers feel that their results "could reflect a migration out of Africa either 1–1.5 Mya, 100,000 years ago, or both. Nuclear genetic data alone provide no time scale" (Mountain et al., 1992:163) and must be correlated to palaeontological or archaeological information to yield an estimate of when the founder population existed and what taxonomic group it belonged to.

FOSSIL EVIDENCE FOR MODERN HUMAN ORIGINS

In the last few years there has been a movement to split hominid fossils into more and more groups, as researchers increasingly favour speciation via cladogenesis and "punctuated equilibrium", the rapid appearance of new species followed by long periods of no change, as a model of evolution (Eldredge and Gould, 1972). Whereas the genus *Homo* was once presented as having only one species at a time, gradually evolving from *Homo habilis* through *H. erectus* to *H. sapiens*, now more than one form is said to exist at a specific time (e.g., *H. rudolfensis* along with *H. habilis* between 2.5 and 1.5 Mya, *H. ergaster* in Africa followed by *H. erectus* from 1.7 Mya to 300,000 years ago, and *H. heidelbergensis*, *H. neandertalensis* and *H. sapiens* after 300,000 BP) (see Tattersall, 1993:93).

Table 1 is an attempt to place the fossil evidence for later Pleistocene human evolution in a coherent time and space framework. This is not an easy task, since many dates are not well established. Many specimens come from a time period that is too early for radiocarbon dating and too recent for potassium-argon. So a number of different methods have to be relied on including uranium-series dating, electron spin resonance (ESR) and thermoluminescence.

241

Table 1: Distribution of Fossil Hominids in Key Regions
(Dates in Thousands of Years Before Present)

Europe	Middle East	Africa	China	SE Asia and Australia	Pattern
					10k
modern Cro-Magnon Predmost Mladeč	modern	modern	Zhoukoudian Upper Cave	Kow Swamp	modern *Homo sapiens sapiens* everywhere
			?Liujiang	L. Mungo(26k) Niah	
Wurm III+IV					35k
Saint-Césaire					
	Shanidar				neandertals in Europe and Mid East;
classic	Tabun?				moderns in Mid-East
neandertals	Amud				and Africa; archaic in
(Wurm I + II)	Kebara				Far East?
La Chapelle	(60k)				
La Ferrassie	neandertals				
Neandertal					
Gibraltar					
Krapina		Florisbad			
		Irghoud		Wadjak?	
		Border Cave	Xujiayao		
generalized	"proto-Cro	(100k)	?Liujiang		
neandertals	Magnons"	Klasies RM	Maba (125k)		
(Riss-Wurm)	Qafzeh (92k)	(80-115k)			
interglacial):	and 115k				
Fontéchevade	Skhūl (100k)	Ngaloba		Ngandong (Solo)	archaic *Homo sapiens*
Ehrinsdorf	+ Tabun (100k)	(120k)		Sambungmachan	
	neandertal?	Omo Kibish 1		(125k)	
		Omo-Kibish 2			
Bianche		(130k)			
Pontnewydd		Kabwe (130k)			
La Chaise					
	Zuttiyeh		Dincun		
			(140k)		
			Jinniushan (200k)		
Swanscombe		Eyasi (200k)	Dali (230k)		
Steinheim					
Atapuerca			Hexian (250k)		
Bilzingsleben					
Arago					
Verteszöllös			Zhoukoudian		
(200-300k)		Bodo (300k)	locality 1		
		Ndutu (300k)	(250-500k)		
				Sangiran	
Petralona (280k)				Trinil	
				Djetis	
		archaic *Homo sapiens*			*Homo erectus*
	Homo erectus				

Uranium-series dating is done on calcium carbonate deposits (e.g., cave deposits such as travertines, stalagmites and stalactites) that are no more than 350,000 years old (Schwarcz, 1992). For electron spin resonance (ESR) and thermoluminescence, one measures trapped electronic charges produced by the bombardment by radioactive particles from the surrounding sediments (Schwarcz and Grün, 1992:145; Grün and Stringer, 1991). ESR works on the principle that the amount of uranium in dental enamel increases over time as it is absorbed from the surrounding environment; the amount of uranium provides the age of a sample. How uranium is absorbed into enamel is not clear, and two models are proposed. Early uptake (EU) assumes that it is absorbed soon after burial, then remains at the concentration seen today. Linear uptake (LU) states that uranium is taken up at a constant rate over time. If only a little uranium is present in the sample, the EU date will be the same as the LU date; otherwise, two dates are published.

The earliest anatomically modern humans outside of Africa are the "proto-Cro Magnons" of Jebel Qafzeh and the Mugharat-es-Skhūl, Israel. At Skhūl, more modern looking human remains were excavated in the 1930s in association with Middle Palaeolithic artifacts. Dates for Qafzeh are 100,000 ± 10,000 (EU) and 120,000 ± 8,000 (LU), while at Skhūl they are 81,000 ± 15,000 (EU) and 101,000 ± 12,000 (LU) (Grün and Stringer, 1991:174-6), well before most of the neandertals in the same area (such as Kebara with an EU of 60,000 ± 6,000 BP and a LU of 64,000 ± 6,000 BP) (Schwarcz and Grün, 1992; Bar-Yosef, 1992; Bar-Yosef and Vandermeersch, 1993; Bar-Yosef, et al., 1992). Thermoluminescence (tl) measures electrons trapped in the crystal lattice of minerals, and their change over time from a time when they were heated (Aitken and Valladas, 1992). Dating burned flint artifacts through thermoluminescence provided the first direct evidence that modern humans predate neandertals in the Middle East (Valladas et al., 1987, 1988; Aitken and Valladas, 1992:143).

The first hominid to be found outside of Africa was *Homo erectus*, possibly around 1.0 Mya. While the earliest *H. erectus* (or *H. ergaster*) fossils are from East Africa and are about 1.7 Myr old, the best described ones come from Asian sites (Trinil, Djetis and Sangiran in Java and Zhoukoudian in China where they may be no older than half a million years (Rightmire, 1990; Klein, 1989a:196-8), or, alternately, equally as old (Swisher et al., 1994). By 400,000 years ago, the earliest "archaic" *Homo sapiens* (or *H. heidelbergensis*) are present in Africa as well as in Europe (where they may be the earliest hominids).

If the dates are accurate, a basic east-west split of hominids appears for the first time (Stringer and Andrews, 1988a:1265), since *H. erectus* is still present in the Far East until around 250,000 BP. Archaic *Homo sapiens* specimens generally have a larger, rounder cranium than *H. erectus* and the size is within the modern range (from 1000 to 2000 cc. with an average of 1350 cc.). In Europe, they gave rise directly to neandertals (*Homo sapiens neandertalensis* or *H. neandertalensis*) by 150,000 BP, while in Africa they may lead directly to modern humans.

Neandertals have unique anatomical characteristics, including short stocky bodies, long low braincases and large faces. Several reasons have been proposed for this. It could have been local selection for musculoskeletal hypertrophy: "the high-water mark for the genus *Homo* in favoring the brawn approach to environmental adaptation" according to Fred Smith (1991:225). Or it could represent a long-term adaptation to the cold conditions of glacial Europe; shorter distal limb segments mean that blood does not have to flow as far to keep an individual warm, and the deep set sinuses of the large protruding face might also have helped in cold weather. Erik Trinkaus (1989:57) suggested that the large neandertal face developed in order to conserve moisture while dissipating excess body heat. Neandertals are present throughout Europe and the Middle East. Except for Tabun, which may be significantly older, the Middle Eastern neandertals are in the range of 60,000 years old or younger. This makes them substantially younger than the "proto-Cro Magnons" of Qafzeh and Skhūl (Vandermeersch, 1982, 1989).

Modern humans (*Homo sapiens sapiens* or *H. sapiens*) are generally characterized by having a less robust cranial and postcranial skeleton than all earlier hominids. The cranium is large and rounded with a vertical forehead and rounded occipital area. The face is reduced and flat, teeth are much smaller, and a chin is present (Klein, 1989a:349-350). All researchers accept that modern humans were present by 35,000 to 40,000 years ago throughout Eurasia and Africa; the question relates to what occurred before this time (Mellars et al., 1992:127).

Africanist researchers have argued for years that anatomically modern humans were present in Africa quite early (Bräuer, 1984, 1989, 1992; Hublin, 1992; Rightmire, 1984, 1989). Possible modern humans come from sites such as Border Cave (cranium, mandible and infant skeleton) and Klasies River Mouth (at least 10 individuals, represented by cranial elements, upper and lower jaws, and isolated teeth) in South Africa, both dated to around 100,000 BP (Deacon, 1989; Beaumont et al., 1978; Grün et al., 1990; Deacon and Shuurman, 1992; Rightmire and Deacon, 1991). In East Africa, one cranial specimen from the Kibish Formation at Omo around 100,000 BP (Omo-1) is said to be anatomically modern, yet another from the same general time period (Omo-2) is called an archaic *H. sapiens*. Specimens from Ndutu (Olduvai Gorge), Ngaloba (Laetoli) and near Lake Eyasi, all in northern Tanzania are classified as either archaic *H. sapiens* or as fully modern (Bräuer, 1984, 1989; Rightmire, 1989; Klein, 1989b; Mehlman, 1987, 1991; Aiello, 1993; Clark, 1989), largely on whether or not they show skeletal robusticity.

Most of the East and Southern African forms are found with Middle Stone Age (MSA) artifacts, the cultural period in sub-Saharan Africa that spans the period between 200,000 and 30,000 BP (Clark, 1988; Thackeray, 1992; Willoughby, 1993b; Allsworth-Jones, 1993). Early modern fossils (two crania, one with a face, a juvenile mandible, and a humerus) associated with Middle Palaeolithic artifacts are also found at Jebel Irghoud in Morocco (Hublin, 1992), as well as at Skhūl and Qafzeh in Israel.

The situation in Europe is a little clearer. The earliest modern humans appear after 35,000 BP, and are associated with Upper Palaeolithic industries. In Western Europe, neandertals exist very recently. At Saint-Césaire, France, dated to 36,000 BP, a neandertal skeleton is associated with the Châtelperronian, a transitional industry that is usually considered to be the earliest Upper Palaeolithic. Few modern human fossils are known from the transitional period; the Cro Magnon skeleton, the type specimen for *Homo sapiens sapiens*, may be no more than 30,000 years old (Gambier, 1989:197). But the early Upper Palaeolithic hominids known from France (30 individuals, including 10 non-adults) have no perceptible neandertal characteristics (Gambier, 1989:195).

The situation in central Europe is markedly different. Fred Smith (1984) has traced a continuous line from early neandertals through late neandertals to early modern humans. Early neandertals are represented by forms from Krapina rockshelter in Croatia. Associated with Middle Palaeolithic artifacts, they exhibit the classic features of neandertals described above. Succeeding them are forms such as those from nearby Vindija Cave. These neandertals share a number of features with modern humans, including a reduced supraorbital torus and the presence of a chin. Some of the earliest moderns here are also morphologically intermediate. At Mladeč in Moravia, they have modern postcranial bones, but the skulls on some show neandertal-like traits including an occipital hemi-bun, a flattened area in the back of the skull reminiscent of (but not identical to) the neandertal *chignon* (Smith, 1984:175). There is enough time between these populations for local evolution to have occurred (Smith, 1984:196), but hybridization or interbreeding may also explain the shared features.

Hominids from East and Southeast Asia are most often cited in support of the multiregional model (Pope, 1991, 1992; Thorne and Wolpoff, 1981, 1992; Wolpoff, 1989), as they show morphological continuity from *H. erectus* (e.g., Sangiran, Trinil in Java and Zhoukoudian in China) to archaic *H. sapiens* (represented by Ngandong and Sambungmachan in Java and Jinniushan, Dali, Dincun and Maba in China). But few fossils have secure dates. Various researchers from Franz Weidenreich onwards have presented a list of traits said to be unique to this region such as a congenital absence of third molars and the retention of a metopic suture into adulthood (Thorne and Wolpoff, 1981; Habgood, 1989, 1992). But others say that many of these are retained from *H. erectus* and have no regional significance whatsoever (Groves, 1989; Brown, 1992). Still others see continuity from *H. erectus* to archaic *H. sapiens* but not from archaics to early modern humans (represented by Zhoukoudian Upper Cave and Liujiang).

ARCHAEOLOGICAL AND BEHAVIOURAL ISSUES

In Europe, the replacement of neandertals by modern humans is marked by the archaeological transition from the Middle to the Upper Palaeolithic. But the earliest Upper Palaeolithic industries, such as the Châtelperronian of France, the Szeletian of Central Europe and the Ahmarian of the Middle East (Mellars, 1992; Klein, 1992), have closer typological and technological affinities to the preceding Middle Palaeolithic than to the Aurignacian that follows them. In fact, the Châtelperronian is associated with neandertal skeletal remains at two French sites: Saint-Césaire and Arcy-sur-Cure (Lévêque et al., 1993). The "real" Upper Palaeolithic, the one produced by modern humans, only begins with the Aurignacian (Mellars, 1992:225).

Many prehistorians recognize that variation exists within and between Middle Palaeolithic assemblages. But they believe that it reflects functional constraints rather than culture-historical or stylistic ones. In other words, there are no cultures or ethnic groups until the Upper Palaeolithic when modern human behaviour, including symbolism and true language, begins. If there are regional differences in the Middle Palaeolithic, they are a product of technology and environment rather than of culture. Earlier hominids are not considered to have been capable of adding symbolic meaning to artifacts and assemblages precisely because they were not modern (Binford and Binford, 1966; Chase, 1991; Chase and Dibble, 1987; Hayden, 1993; Lindly and Clark, 1990, 1991; Noble and Davidson, 1993; Sackett, 1982).

No regional or cultural differences in assemblages are supposed to exist before 35,000 to 40,000 BP. But if African and some Middle Eastern Middle Palaeolithic assemblages up to 100,000 years old were manufactured by anatomically modern humans, it creates a problem. Their capacity for culture does not seem to be much different than that of neandertals. Can there be modern humans with Middle Palaeolithic minds? It is possible that modern human anatomy developed well before modern ("Upper Palaeolithic") cultural behaviour appears. Or, in other words, "perhaps early Upper Pleistocene man [in Africa] had modern biological hardware, but simply lacked the software—the cumulative body of knowledge and tradition—required to make effective use of a technology not yet invented" (Ambrose and Lorenz, 1990:28). If so, the cultural significance of the archaeological material found with the earliest modern humans remains unclear.

In graduate school, I concentrated on the study of Palaeolithic archaeology, the study of cultural evolution from the origins of stone tool making (around 2.5 million years ago) up until the end of the Pleistocene (10,000 BP). The archaeological record shows major technological changes co-occurring with the appearance or diversification of hominid taxa. Not surprisingly, Palaeolithic archaeologists frequently borrow ideas and models from hominid palaeontologists, and in exchange contribute information about cultural and behavioural evolution.

When I was a student, the issue of modern human origins was not a major concern. Those of us working in sub-Saharan Africa were excited about pushing the cultural record farther and farther back; we wanted to establish the nature of the earliest technologies, rather than those that accompanied the emergence of our own species. In courses in archaeology and hominid palaeontology, the subject of modern human origins was quickly glossed over at the end. It was generally agreed that there was no real problem to investigate. A multiregional model predicting the appearance of modern humans with special kinds of blade and bone tools (belonging to the Upper Palaeolithic) around 35,000 to 40,000 BP seemed to fit the available data. The discovery of modern human skeletal material in association with Middle Palaeolithic (in North Africa) and MSA (in sub-Saharan Africa) tools was used to illustrate how far behind Africa was from the (supposedly contemporary) European Upper Palaeolithic. Once hominids left Africa, it was presumed, the focus of biological and cultural innovation became Western Europe. It seemed that little of major interest awaited the archaeologist who chose to work on Upper Pleistocene matters anywhere else.

With the redating of key sites and the first mtDNA publications, the problem of modern human origins resurfaced. The genetic data offered another model, one where African developments were critically important. It also seemed to fit new data better, data derived from reassessing the age of fossils and archaeological sites in the Middle East and Africa. The traditional multiregional model could not explain some of this new information, but the out of Africa model could.

I have always been interested in the history of ideas concerning human evolutionary theory, so the growing debate attracted me to this issue. At the same time as the mtDNA papers first came out, I was initiating archaeological field research in southwestern Tanzania (Map 1) (Willoughby, 1992, 1993a, 1993b). This area may not contain any really early archaeological sites, but has many Middle Stone Age (MSA) ones.

In sub-Saharan Africa, the MSA is the cultural period in which modern humans developed. Whether or not these modern humans are ancestral to living populations world-wide is a separate but obviously related issue. Defined by distinctive retouched flake tools like scrapers and points made on radial, discoidal or Levallois cores and by the absence of large bifacial tools characteristic of the earlier Acheulean, the MSA extends from 200,000 to 30,000 years ago. Its basic technology retains many features in common with the coeval Middle Palaeolithic of Eurasia and North Africa. The incidence of Levallois technology varies region by region, and certain shaped tool types are found in some regions and not others. In South Africa, for example, substantial numbers of blade tools are found in MSA contexts, as well as in special industries such as the Howieson's poort where large geometric pieces (such as crescents) are a major component (Thackeray, 1992). Both are more characteristic of the subsequent Later Stone Age (LSA) than of this earlier period.

Map 1: Archaeological and Geological Localities in Southwestern Tanzania

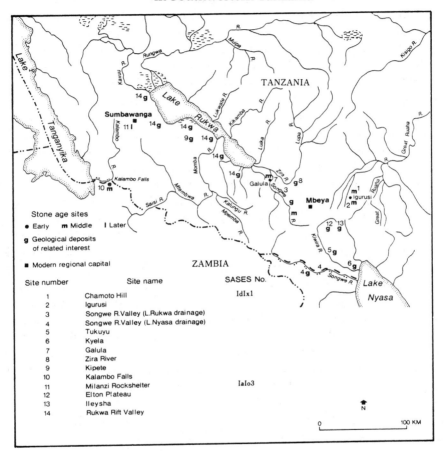

Throughout North Africa, later Middle Palaeolithic occurrences belong to the Aterian, where up to a quarter of shaped tools have a bifacial retouched tang at the base, presumably for hafting (Clark, 1992:204). This is a clear stylistic signature. In addition, blade tool industries both precede (Pre-Aurignacian) and follow (Dabban) a typical Middle Palaeolithic industry at the deeply stratified site of Haua Fteah in Libya, one of the few North African sites with occupation dating to the early Upper Palaeolithic period (Close, 1986:175). In summary, African evidence shows that the Middle-Upper Palaeolithic transition is a much more complicated issue than previously recognized.

With the permission of the Tanzanian Department of Antiquities and the Tanzania Commission on Science and Technology, a field project was initiated to study the prehistoric occupation of southwestern Tanzania (Map 1). It began with an intensive survey of the Songwe River valley in 1990. The Songwe drains north off of volcanic highlands into Lake Rukwa. It traverses a large part of the Rukwa Rift, a regional extension of the Western or Albertine Rift valley system. Twenty-three new archaeological sites were identified, and a number of others were relocated (Willoughby, 1992, 1993a, 1993b).

This area exhibits a variety of habitats most of which contained evidence of human occupation: volcanic highlands, old lake deposits, river terraces and hills containing rockshelters. MSA sites were present throughout the study area, primarily associated with the old Songwe river terraces. Surface collections were made at each site identified. While few fossils were collected, many stone artifacts were analysed.

The MSA sites contained a number of retouched flake tools: scrapers were most common, and some points, burins, awls, and geometric pieces such as crescents were also recorded. Core tools (choppers, core scrapers and bifaces such as picks and small handaxes) occur in small numbers throughout the series, and are most abundant in the northernmost sites. Technological studies still in progress reveal that the flakes used for tool production were almost always selected from the final stages of reducing cores before their discard. Only in some sites were cortical flakes later shaped into tools. Many cores were initially small pebbles that were discarded well before all possible flakes were removed. Most flaking involved radial working, striking flakes off from around the perimeter of spherical pebbles. While radial preparation is also a preliminary step in Levallois reduction, few cores in the Songwe were secondarily shaped to become Levallois pieces. A variety of raw materials were employed including quartz, quartzite, chert and volcanic rocks.

So far what we see is pretty typical of the MSA in East Africa, but so little is known of basic culture history here that the local sequence must be established through excavation of stratified, datable sites before any firm conclusions can be offered. There are few signs of the kinds of technological differences seen in other parts of Africa at the same time, but this issue will be examined in future fieldwork. The Rukwa Rift valley was probably densely settled during the MSA. It lies between regions of East and Southern Africa that have been the focus of most MSA research to date. Based on the initial survey, it is clear that what is now needed is a detailed examination of the prehistoric occupation of this area within its palaeoenvironmental context.

The major question presented to Africanist archaeologists by the replacement or mtDNA model is when and where did modern human technology and behaviour develop? Must we expect to see major changes along the lines of the Middle-Upper Palaeolithic transition in Europe, or is the pattern in Africa on a different order? Can industries such as the Howieson's poort of South Africa be explained as part of the transition? There is always the worst case scenario for archaeologists: is it possible that modern human behaviour develops with no technological or cultural sign at all? If the African MSA represents the beginning of regional variation and modern human behaviour (Clark, 1988, 1989; Allsworth-Jones, 1993; Willoughby, 1993b), it is still different from the Eurasian Upper Palaeolithic. But at least we now know that the pattern of cultural evolution does not (and should not) have to replicate that of Europe. Clearly a lot of work remains to be done, but African research will be critical for the resolution of the question of modern human cultural development.

CONCLUSIONS

The issue of modern human origins has become of central importance to paleoanthropology. Differing lines of evidence exist: genetic, fossil and archaeological data, and new geochronological methods have led to the reassessment of the age of several key sites. Rather than one species at a time, more than one form apparently existed, possibly in the same places at the same times. Regions once thought peripheral to the centre of action in later human evolution (Africa and Asia) may instead be critically important. The African and Middle Eastern data favour a replacement model, while that from East Asia best fits the continuity one. The early modern hominids of central Europe show that some hybridization could have occurred, but it is unlikely that the recent neandertals of Western Europe evolved into modern humans. Only a replacement with hybridization model can account for all of the evidence as is currently understood.

Paleoanthropology consists of a number of competing explanations of human evolution based on an often limited fossil sample. While it has been possible to produce general, synthetic perspectives on modern human origins, only a first-hand re-examination of the data in all regions or the discovery of new evidence will let us decide which model is most plausible. One unexpected but positive outcome of the replacement model is the renewed focus of attention on Upper Pleistocene African pre-history. As J. Desmond Clark (1975) predicted long ago, the continent is of paramount importance for understanding all stages of human evolution.

ACKNOWLEDGEMENTS

I would like to thank Ann Herring and Leslie Chan for assistance with this article. The field research described here was conducted under permits from the Department of Antiquities of Tanzania and the Tanzania Commission on Science and Technology. It has been funded by research grants from SSHRCC, the L.S.B. Leakey Foundation, the Boise Fund of Oxford University, and from two University of Alberta sources: the Support for the Advancement of Scholarship Fund, Faculty of Arts, and the Central Research Fund.

REFERENCES

Aiello L (1993) Fossil evidence for modern human origins in Africa: A revised view. *American Anthropologist* 95(1): 73-96.

Aitken MJ and Valladas H (1992) Luminescence dating relative to human origins. *Philosophical Transactions of the Royal Society* 337B(1280): 139-144.

Allsworth-Jones P (1993) The archaeology of archaic and early modern *Homo sapiens*: An African perspective. *Cambridge Archaeological Journal* 3(1): 21-39.

Ambrose SH and Lorenz KG (1990) Social and ecological models for the Middle Stone Age in Southern Africa. In P Mellars (ed.) *The Emergence of Modern Humans*. Ithaca: Cornell University Press, pp. 3-33.

Bar-Yosef O (1992) Middle Palaeolithic chronology and the transition to the Upper Palaeolithic in southwest Asia. In G Bräuer and F Smith (eds.) *Continuity or Replacement*. Rotterdam: A.A. Balkema, pp. 261-272.

Bar-Yosef O and Vandermeersch B (1993) Modern humans in the Levant. *Scientific American* 268(4): 94-100.

Bar-Yosef O, Vandermeersch B, Ahrensburg B, Belfer-Cohen A, Goldberg P, Laville H, Meignen L, Rak Y, Speth JD, Tchernov E, Tillier AM and Weiner S (1992) The excavations in Kebara Cave, Mt. Carmel. *Current Anthropology* 33(5): 497-550.

Beaumont PB, de Villiers H and Vogel JC (1978) Modern man in sub-Saharan Africa prior to 49,000 years BP: A review and evaluation in particular reference to Border Cave. *South African Journal of Science* 74: 409-419.

Binford LR and Binford SR (1966) A preliminary analysis of funtional variability in the Mousterian of Levallois facies. In JD Clark and FC Howell (eds.) Recent Studies in Palaeoanthropology. *American Anthropologist* 68(2)(2): 238-295.

Bräuer G (1984) A craniological approach to the origin of anatomically modern *Homo sapiens* in Africa and implications for the appearance of modern

Europeans. In FH Smith and F Spencer (eds.) *The Origins of Modern Humans*. New York: Alan R. Liss, pp. 327-410.

Bräuer G (1989) The evolution of modern humans: A comparison of the African and non-African evidence. In P Mellars and CB Stringer (eds.) *The Human Revolution*. Princeton: Princeton University Press, pp. 123-154.

Bräuer G (1992) Africa's place in the evolution of *Homo sapiens*. In G Bräuer and F Smith (eds.) *Continuity or Replacement*. Rotterdam: A.A. Balkema, pp. 83-98.

Bräuer G and Smith F (eds.) (1992) *Continuity or Replacement: Controversies in Homo Sapiens Evolution*. The Hague: A.A. Balkema.

Brown P (1992) Recent human evolution in East Asia and Australasia. *Philosophical Transactions of the Royal Society* 337B(1280): 235-242.

Cann, RL (1987) In search of Eve. *The Sciences* Sept./Oct., pp. 30-37.

Cann, RL (1988) DNA and human origins. *Annual Review of Anthropology* 17: 127-143.

Cann RL (1992) A mitochondrial perspective on replacement or continuity in human evolution. In G Bräuer and F Smith (eds.) *Continuity or Replacement*. Rotterdam: A.A. Balkema, pp. 65-73.

Cann RL, Stoneking M and Wilson AC (1987) Mitochondrial DNA and human evolution. *Nature* 325(6099): 31-36.

Cavalli-Sforza LL (1991) Genes, peoples and languages. *Scientific American* 265(5): 104-110.

Chase P (1991) Symbols and Palaeolithic artifacts: Style, standardization and the imposition of arbitrary form. *Journal of Anthropological Archaeology* 10: 193-214.

Chase P and Dibble HL (1987) Middle Palaeolithic symbolism: A review of current evidence and interpretations. *Journal of Anthropological Archaeology* 6: 263-296.

Clark GA and Lindly JM (1989) Modern human origins in the Levant and Western Asia. *American Anthopologist* 91(4): 962-985.

Clark JD (1975) Africa in prehistory: Peripheral or paramount? *Man* 10: 175-198.

Clark JD (1988) The Middle Stone Age of East Africa and the beginnings of regional identity. *Journal of World Prehistory* 2(3): 235-305.

Clark JD (1989) The origins and spread of modern humans: A broad perspective on the African evidence. In P Mellars and CB Stringer (eds.) *The Human Revolution*. Princeton: Princeton University Press, pp. 565-588.

Clark JD (1992) African and Asian perspectives on the origins of modern humans. *Philosophical Transactions of the Royal Society* 337B(1280): 201-215.

Close AE (1986) The place of the Haua Fteah in the Late Palaeolithic of North Africa. In GN Bailey and P Callow (eds.) *Stone Age Prehistory*. Cambridge: Cambridge University Press, pp. 169-180.

Deacon HJ (1989) Late Pleistocene palaeoecology and archaeology in the Southern Cape, South Africa. In P Mellars and CB Stringer (eds.) *The Human Revolution*. Princeton: Princeton University Press, pp. 547-564.

Deacon HJ and Shuurman R (1992) The origins of modern people: the evidence from Klasies River. In G Bräuer and F Smith (eds.) *Continuity or Replacement*. Rotterdam: A.A. Balkema, pp. 121-129.

Eldredge N and Gould SJ (1972) Punctuated equilibria: An alternative to phyletic gradualism. In TJM Schopf (ed.) *Models in Paleobiology*. San Francisco: Freeman, Cooper and Co., pp. 82-115.

Frayer DW (1992) The persistence of Neanderthal features in post-Neanderthal Europeans. In G Bräuer and F Smith (eds.) *Continuity or Replacement*. Rotterdam: A.A. Balkema, pp. 179-188.

Frayer DW, Wolpoff MH, Thorne AG, Smith FH and Pope G (1993) Theories of modern human origins: the palaeontological test. *American Anthropologist* 95(1): 14-50.

Gambier D (1989) Fossil hominids from the early Upper Palaeolithic (Aurignacian) of France. In P Mellars and CB Stringer (eds.) *The Human Revolution*. Princeton: Princeton University Press, pp. 194-211.

Groves CP (1989) A regional approach to the problem of the origin of modern humans in Australasia. In P Mellars and CB Stringer (eds.) *The Human Revolution*. Princeton: Princeton University Press, pp. 274-285.

Grün R and Stringer CB (1991) Electron spin resonance dating and the evolution of modern humans. *Archaeometry* 33(2): 153-199.

Grün R, Beaumont P and Stringer CB (1990) ESR dating evidence for early modern humans at Border Cave in South Africa. *Nature* 344(6266): 537-539.

Habgood PJ (1989) The origin of anatomically modern humans in Australasia. In P Mellars and CB Stringer (eds.) *The Human Revolution*. Princeton: Princeton University Press, pp. 245-273.

Habgood PJ (1992) The origin of anatomically modern humans in east Asia. In G Bräuer and FH Smith (eds.) *Continuity or Replacement*. Rotterdam: A.A. Balkema, pp. 273-288.

Harpending H, Sherry ST, Rogers AR and Stoneking M (1993) The genetic structure of ancient human populations. *Current Anthropology* 34(4): 483-496.

Hayden B (1993) The cultural capacities of Neandertals: A review and re-evaluation. *Journal of Human Evolution* 24(2): 113-146.

Howells WW (1976) Explaining modern man: Evolutionists versus migrationists. *Journal of Human Evolution* 5: 77-95.

Hublin JJ (1992) Recent human evolution in northwestern Africa. *Philosophical Transactions of the Royal Society* 337B(1280): 185-191.

Klein RG (1989a) *The Human Career*. Chicago: University of Chicago Press.

Klein RG (1989b) Biological and behavioural perspectives on modern human origins in Southern Africa. In P Mellars and CB Stringer (eds.) *The Human Revolution*. Princeton: Princeton University Press, pp. 529-546.

Klein RG (1992) The archaeology of modern human origins. *Evolutionary Anthropology* 1(1): 5-14.

Lévêque F, Backer AM, and Guilbaud M (1993) Context of a late neandertal. *Monographs in World Archaeology* 16. Madison: Prehistory Press.

Lewin R (1987) *Bones of Contention*. New York: Simon and Schuster.

Lindly JM and Clark GA (1990) Symbolism and modern human origins. *Current Anthropology* 31(3): 233-261.

Lindly JM and Clark GA (1991) Cognitive changes and the emergence of modern humans. *Cambridge Archaeological Journal* 1(1): 63-76.

Lucotte G (1989) Evidence for the paternal ancestry of modern humans: Evidence from a Y-chromosome specific sequence polymorphic DNA probe. In P Mellars and CB Stringer (eds.), *The Human Revolution*. Princeton: Princeton University Press, pp. 39-46.

Lucotte G (1992) African pygmies have the more ancestral gene pool when studied for Y-chromosome DNA haplotypes. In G Bräuer and F Smith (eds.) *Continuity or Replacement*. Rotterdam: A.A. Balkema, pp. 75-81.

Maddison DR (1991) African origin of mitochondrial DNA reexamined. *Systematic Zoology* 40(3): 355-363.

Mehlman MJ (1987) Provenience, age and association of archaic *Homo sapiens* crania from Lake Eyasi, Tanzania. *Journal of Archaeological Science* 14: 133-162.

Mehlman MJ (1991) Context for the emergence of modern man in eastern Africa: Some new Tanzanian evidence. In JD Clark (ed.) *Cultural Beginnings*. Bonn: Dr. Rudolf Habelt GMBH, pp. 177-196.

Mellars P (1991) Cognitive changes and the emergence of modern humans in Europe. *Cambridge Archaeological Journal* 1(1): 63-76.

Mellars P (1992) Archaeology and the population-dispersal hypothesis of modern human origins in Europe. *Philosophical Transactions of the Royal Society* 337B(1280): 225-234.

Mellars P, Aitken MJ and Stringer CB (1992) Outlining the problem. *Philosophical Transactions of the Royal Society* 337B(1280): 127-130.

Mountain JL, Lin AA, Bowcock AM and Cavalli-Sforza LL (1992) Evolution of modern humans: evidence from nuclear DNA polymorphisms. *Philosophical Transactions of the Royal Society* 337B(1280): 159-165.

Noble W and Davidson I (1993) Tracing the emergence of modern human behavior: Methodological pitfalls and a theoretical path. *Journal of Anthropological Archaeology* 12: 121-149.

Pope G (1991) Evolution of the zygomaticomaxillary region in the genus *Homo* and its relevance to the origin of modern humans. *Journal of Human Evolution* 21(3): 189-213.

Pope G (1992) Craniofacial evidence for the origin of modern humans in China. *Yearbook of Physical Anthropology* 35: 243-298.

Rightmire GP (1984) *Homo sapiens* in sub-Saharan Africa. In FH Smith and F Spencer (eds.) *The Origins of Modern Humans*. New York: Alan R. Liss, pp. 295-325.

Rightmire GP (1989) Middle Stone Age humans from Eastern and Southern Africa. In P Mellars and CB Stringer (eds.) *The Human Revolution*. Princeton: Princeton University Press, pp. 109-122.

Rightmire GP (1990) *The Evolution of Homo erectus*. Cambridge: Cambridge University Press.

Rightmire GP and Deacon H (1991) Comparative studies of late Pleistocene human remains from Klasies River Mouth, South Africa. *Journal of Human Evolution* 20(2): 131-156.

Sackett JR (1982) Approaches to style in lithic archaeology. *Journal of Anthropological Archaeology* 1: 59-112.

Schwarcz HP (1992) Uranium-series dating and the origin of modern man. *Philosophical Transactions of the Royal Society* 337B(1280): 131-137.

Schwarcz HP and Grün R (1992) Electron spin resonance (ESR) dating of the origin of modern man. *Philosophical Transactions of the Royal Society* 337B(1280): 145-148.

Smith FH (1984) Fossil hominids from the Upper Pleistocene of Central Europe and the origin of modern Europeans. In FH Smith and F Spencer (eds.) *The Origins of Modern Humans.* New York: Alan R. Liss, pp. 137-209.

Smith FH (1991) The neandertals: Evolutionary dead ends or ancestors of modern people? *Journal of Anthropological Research* 47(2): 219-238.

Smith FH (1992a) The role of continuity in modern human origins. In G Bräuer and F Smith (eds.) *Continuity or Replacement.* Rotterdam: A.A. Balkema, pp. 145-156.

Smith FH (1992b) Models and realities in modern human origins: the African fossil evidence. *Philosophical Transactions of the Royal Society* 337B(1280): 243-250.

Stoneking M (1993) DNA and recent human evolution. *Evolutionary Anthropology* 2(2): 60-73.

Stoneking M and Cann RL (1989) African origin of human mitochondrial DNA. In P Mellars and CB Stringer (eds.) *The Human Revolution.* Princeton: Princeton University Press, pp. 17-30.

Stoneking M, Sherry ST, Redd AJ and Vigilant L (1992) New approaches to dating suggest a recent age for the human mtDNA ancestor. *Philosophical Transactions of the Royal Society* 337B(1280): 167-175.

Stringer CB (1990) The emergence of modern humans. *Scientific American* 263(6): 98-104.

Stringer CB (1992a) Replacement, continuity and the origin of *Homo sapiens.* In G Bräuer and F Smith (eds.) *Continuity or Replacement.* Rotterdam: A.A. Balkema, pp. 9-24.

Stringer CB (1992b) Reconstructing recent human evolution. *Philosophical Transactions of the Royal Society* 337B(1280): 217-224.

Stringer CB and Andrews P (1988a) Genetic and fossil evidence for the origin of modern humans. *Science* 239(4845): 1263-1268.

Stringer CB and Andrews P (1988b) Modern human origins. *Science* 241(4867): 773-774.

Swisher CC, Curtis GH, Jacob T, Getty AG, Suprijo A, and Widiasmoro (1994) Age of the earliest known hominids in Java, Indonesia. *Science* 263(5150): 1118-1121.

Tattersall I (1993) *The Human Odyssey: Four Million Years of Human Evolution.* New York: Prentice Hall.

Templeton AR (1992) Human origins and analysis of mitochondrial DNA sequences. *Science* 255(5045): 737.

Templeton AR (1993) The Eve hypothesis: a genetic critique. *American Anthropologist* 95(1): 51-72.

Thackeray AI (1992) The Middle Stone Age south of the Limpopo River. *Journal of World Prehistory* 6(4): 385-440.

Thorne AG and Wolpoff MH (1981) Regional continuity in Australasian Pleistocene hominid evolution. *American Journal of Physical Anthropology* 55: 337-348.

Thorne AG and Wolpoff MH (1992) The multiregional evolution of humans. *Scientific American* 266(4): 76-83.

Trinkaus E (1989) The Upper Pleistocene transition. In E Trinkaus (ed.) *The Emergence of Modern Humans.* Cambridge: Cambridge University Press, pp. 42-66.

Valladas H, Joron JL, Valladas G, Arensburg B, Bar-Yosef O, Belfer-Cohen A, Goldberg P, Laville H, Meighen L, Rak Y, Tchernov E, Tillier AM, and Vandermeersch B (1987) Thermoluminescence dates for the Neanderthal burial site at Kebara in Israel. *Nature* 330(6144): 159-160.

Valladas H, Reyss JL, Joron JL, Valladas G, Bar-Yosef O, and Vandermeersch B (1988) Thermoluminescence dating of Mousterian "Proto-Cro Magnon" remains from Israel and the origin of modern man. *Nature* 331(6157): 614-616.

Vandermeersch B (1982) The first *Homo sapiens sapiens* in the Near East. In A Ronen (ed.) *The Transition from the Lower to the Middle Palaeolithic and the Origin of Modern Man.* BAR International Series #151: 297-300.

Vandermeersch B (1989) The evolution of modern humans: Recent evidence from Southwest Asia. In P Mellars and CB Stringer (eds.) *The Human Revolution.* Princeton: Princeton University Press, pp. 155-164.

Vigilant L, Stoneking M, Harpending H, Hawkes C and Wilson AC (1991) African populations and the evolution of human mitochondrial DNA. *Science* 253(5027): 1503-1507.

Wainscoat JS, Hill AVS, Boyce AL, Flint J, Hernandez M, Thein SL, Old JM, Lynch JR, Falusi AG, Weatherall DJ and Clegg JB (1986) Evolutionary relationships of human populations from an analysis of nuclear DNA polymorphisms. *Nature* 319(6053): 491-493.

Wainscoat JS, Hill AVS, Thein SL, Flint J, Chapman JC, Weatherall DJ, Clegg JB and Higgs DR (1989) Geographical distribution of alpha- and beta-globin gene cluster polymorphisms. In P Mellars and CB Stringer (eds.) *The Human Revolution.* Princeton: Princeton University Press, pp. 31-38.

Willoughby PR (1992) An archaeological survey of the Songwe River, Lake Rukwa Basin, Southwestern Tanzania. *Nyame Akuma* 27: 28-35.

Willoughby PR (1993a) Culture, environment and the emergence of *Homo sapiens* in East Africa. In R.W. Jamieson, S. Abonyi and N.A. Mirau (eds.) *Culture and Environment: A Fragile Coexistence.* Calgary: Chacmool Archaeological Society, pp. 135-143.

Willoughby PR (1993b) The Middle Stone Age in East Africa and modern human origins. *The African Archaeological Review* 11: 3-20.

Wilson AC and Cann RL (1992) The recent African genesis of humans. *Scientific American* 266(4): 68-73.

Wolpoff MH (1989) Multiregional evolution: The fossil alternative to Eden. In P Mellars and CB Stringer (eds.) *The Human Revolution.* Princeton: Princeton University Press, pp. 62-108.

Wolpoff MH (1992) Theories of modern human origins. In G. Bräuer and F. Smith, (eds.) *Continuity or Replacement.* Rotterdam: A.A. Balkema, pp. 25-63.

Wolpoff MH, Spuhler JN, Smith FH, Radovcic J, Pope G, Frayer DW, Eckhardt R and Clark G (1988) Modern human origins. *Science* 241(4867): 772-773.

Wolpoff MH and Thorne AG (1991) The case against Eve. *New Scientist* 130(1774): 37-41.

12

The Mummies of Dakhleh

Megan A. Cook

Skeletal, natural and artificially mummified human remains were excavated from two cemeteries (designated east and west) that were associated with the town site of Ismant el-Kharab, located in the Dakhleh Oasis, Egypt during the 1992 field seasons. Ismant el-Kharab, dated at the 1st to the 5th century AD is a fascinating site as three early Christian churches, four temples of stone and/or mud brick, a Roman bath, and two groups of well preserved above-ground mausolea have been found. This community spans the threshold of conversion to Christianity from the earlier Egypto-Roman pagan tradition. The east cemetery, presumed to be early Christian, contains single burials in graves and most are orientated east-west. The west cemetery has rock cut tombs containing groups of individuals and is pagan.

Age-at-death and sex determinations, gross pathologies, stature, thin sectioning of bone and soft tissue were carried out on the 41 skeletal remains from the east cemetery and 16 intact naturally mummified remains from the west cemetery. Inter-individual differences in mortuary practice between those interred in the tombs were evident. There was strong evidence suggesting that some individuals were reburied. As this was a relatively closed population an understanding may be reached of the cultural and social transition period of Ismant by careful examination and interpretation of the known occupations and preserved habits of the individuals and their mortuary practices as they relate to the biological anthropological data. The immense value of a multi-disciplinary project such as the Dakhleh Oasis Project is clearly evident as so much more than just what the remains tell us, is known about the past inhabitants of this town.

INTRODUCTION

In the low lying hills overlooking the town site of Ismant el-Kharab, Dahkleh Oasis, Egypt, depressions were observed in the hillsides. Further examination revealed half buried mummy bandages and sun bleached human bones. Likewise, human bones were found eroding out of depressions in the undulating plain east of Ismant. Thus the west and east cemeteries of Ismant were discovered, surveyed, and excavated in the field seasons of 1992.

The objectives of this chapter are to: (1) present the mortuary practices of two different social and religious groups of people living in Ismant between the 1st to the 5th centuries A.D.; (2) present a case study outlining the procedures used for the analyses of the Mummies of Dakhleh; (3) convey to the reader the value of a multi-disciplinary project for research into the lifeways, health and disease of past and present populations of the Dakhleh Oasis; (4) discuss how information from different specialities can be utilized and integrated into biological anthropological data to form a complete picture of the people's lives; (5) discuss future research.

The Dakhleh Oasis is situated approximately 660km south west of Cairo and 270km from the Nile Valley (Fig. 1) and is part of a string of depressions around the south and west edges of the Libyan Plateau. It is surrounded by a 300m escarpment on the north and east side. The long history of human occupation and adaptation to this arid region is being investigated by the Dakhleh Oasis Project (DOP).

THE DAKHLEH OASIS PROJECT

The Dakhleh Oasis Project (DOP) is a multi-disciplinary investigation, which has been operating field seasons since 1978, with the following objectives:

(1) study the entire oasis; hence, the necessity for a group of specialists to collaborate. Investigators of the DOP include an archaeobotanist, an archaeozoologist, prehistoric and historic archaeologists, geologists, physical anthropologists and conservators. Dakhleh is not large enough to be unwieldy for study but large enough to have had a continuing independent existence;

(2) study the interrelated archaeological and environmental contexts from the Pleistocene to the present;

(3) investigate past patterns of land and water resource exploitation to provide lessons for modern land planning for population growth;

260

(4) carry out geological investigations into local and regional environments;

(5) conduct faunal and floral studies that contribute to environmental reconstructions and information on past subsistence strategies;

(6) translate texts, excavate and preserve several temples for the historic period;

(7) carry out biological anthropology of burial practices, analyses of human remains, health and disease in the past and present populations.

Figure 1. Location of Dakhleh Oasis

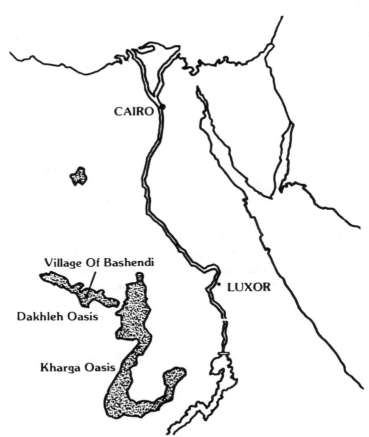

The project is co-sponsored by the Society for the Study of Egyptian Antiquities (SSEA) and by the Royal Ontario Museum (ROM) with Anthony Mills as the director. The DOP operates under a Concession Licence from the Egyptian Antiquities Organization (EAO), which gives the project exclusive rights to conduct archaeological research in the Oasis. Through the DOP's multi-disciplinary research efforts Africanists are becoming aware of Dakhleh's cultural and environmental connections to the south and west so that the Nile Valley should no longer be considered typical of northeast Africa. Indeed, as more and more of the unearthed textual materials are translated, the trade, social and/or cultural connections to the Nile Valley, Kharga, Dakhleh and Africa west and south are and will be made clearer. For example, some ancient medical texts, found earlier in Kharga, have similar ideas and myths concerning reproduction as those translated from the Nile Valley. It is thought by some investigators that these ideas may well have originated in Africa (Ghalioungui, 1973).

MORTUARY PRACTICES

For many people the ancient Egyptians are symbolized and synonymous with their funerary remains — pyramids, tombs, mastabas, exotic grave goods and mummies. Ancient Egyptians had an all pervasive belief in life after death; they believed that death was not final, life afterwards continued in a different form. Three spirits were created at the same time as the body: *Ka*, symbolized by two outstretched arms, represented the vital force and genius; *Ba*, symbolized by a human headed bird, represented the embodiments of the soul and witnessed the heart being weighed in the underworld; and *Ankh*, symbolized by the crested, ibis represented immortality. For the spirits to survive death it was essential for the physical body (after death) to be preserved in a recognized form (Andrews, 1984). During the Pre-dynastic period, i.e., before Upper and Lower Egypt were united under Narmer (circa 3000 BC), preservation was natural as individuals were buried in shallow sandy desert graves, usually in a flexed position. The quick desiccation of the bodies in the hot sand largely prevented any post-mortem bacterial infestations that normally occur during decomposition in more humid climates. (For more information on the faunal succession in human corpses consult Harrison, (1986)). Later, wealthier individuals, probably as a status indicator, were buried in coffins. Ironically, the coffins that were supposed to preserve the body, served only to hasten the deterioration of the mortal remains.

To remedy this situation some method of artificial preservation (embalming or mummification) was instituted with elaborate rituals and practices.

Mummification started at least as early as the Fourth Dynasty (2600 BC) and was practised until the early Coptic period, a time span of nearly 3000 years. Wrapped remains, perhaps indicating some sort of artificial preservation, were found by Petrie dating to the 1st Dynasty at Abydos in a royal tomb. The technology peaked in the 21st Dynasty (1045–945 BC). The deceased were embalmed using unguents, resins and oils. Natron, found at Wadi Natrun, is a mixture of sodium salts — carbonates, bicarbonates, sulphates and chlorides. It was the principal substance used as a preservative. In the Old Kingdom it was used as a ritual purifier. *Neteryt* is the Egyptian word for natron and means "belonging to the God". This mixture absorbs water and is also mildly antiseptic. Even as late as the Coptic Period, it was used on 3 monks from the monastery of St. Mark at Gournet Mar ei Nord near Deir el-Medineh (Prominska, 1986). After the Late Period (600 BC) molten resin was utilized in the process resulting in blackened and brittle mummies that suggested that they were dipped in bitumen. (The English word mummy is derived from the Arabic *mummiya* meaning bitumen or pitch).

The embalming profession was highly organized on the same principles as the temple priesthood. Generally, the embalming process went as follows:

(1) After death the body was washed with a solution of natron symbolizing the rebirth of the dead just as the sun was reborn each day after bathing in the ocean.

(2) During and after the 18th Dynasty the brain was removed through either the nostrils, eye sockets or a hole in the back of the head. The brain was never preserved. The lungs, stomach, intestines and liver were removed, preserved in natron and placed in canopic jars under the protection of 4 minor gods called the Sons of Horus. Imsety (human headed) looked after the liver; Hapy (baboon headed) the lungs; Duamutef (jackal headed) the stomach; Qebehsenuef (falcon headed) the intestines. The heart was left in the body as it was believed to be the seat of intelligence.

(3) To remove water, natron was heaped over the body that was stretched out on a low stone table at the embalmer's workshop. The body cavities were packed with material, such as natron soaked linen, straw etc. to hold the body's shape.

(4)   After dehydration the body was bandaged carefully, even the fingers and toes were individually bandaged. Saffron dyed shrouds were used. Red and yellow ochre was also used. (For more information on the bandaging consult Andrews 1984)

(5)   In the Greco-Roman Period (after 350 BC) gold leaf was sometimes applied to the cheeks, chest and nails. Name tablets, usually wooden, tied around the neck identified the individual at the embalmer's workshop.

(6)   So far no embalming tables or name tablets have been found at Dakhleh. Red and yellow ochre impregnated shrouds were found. A few mummies had gold leaf on their cheeks and on the backs of their hands.

Skeletal, natural and artificially mummified human remains were excavated from two cemeteries (designated east and west) that were associated with the town site of Ismant el-Kharab.

ISMANT EL-KHARAB

The DOP has been studying this site since 1981. The site measures approximately 900m x 1200m and is in the middle of a large plain of agricultural land. The main temple, although badly damaged, is important as it is the only known one in Egypt dedicated to the god Tutu. The domestic buildings are generally well preserved and filled with wind-borne sand. The floor deposits contain large quantities of midden material as well as various texts on papyrus and wooden writing tablets. Several languages have been identified — Greek, Coptic and Syriac.

Ismant's West Cemetery

Six rock cut tombs were excavated in the 1992 field seasons. The tombs contained varying numbers of skeletal, resin treated (i.e., artificially mummified) and non-resin treated human remains, a dog and grave goods. All the tombs were disturbed in antiquity, consequently there were many broken, dis-articulated and partially skeletonized/mummified mixed up human remains. The human remains were numbered with tags indicating tomb and individual to determine the minimum number of individuals (MNI). In Dakhleh, the artificial mummification of individuals was sporadic, and apparently random, i.e., there was no obvious pattern, determined by age, sex, and/or status for any particular individual to be or not to be mummified. Another distinct possibility is that these resin treated bodies belonged to family units, but this is still to be determined. Table 1 summarizes the West Cemetery. There was evidence of secondary burial practice in Tombs 2, 3, and 4.

Secondary Burials
Tomb # 2:

Body J consists of a torso; the legs and hips are missing. It was partially skeletonized and was treated with resin. The head was wrapped in orange-coloured bandages. On removing the bandages, a wooden stick measuring 25 cms long was observed to be holding the head onto the rest of the body by passing through the cervical vertebrae and into the foramen magnum. Two skulls, # 1 (partially covered with soft tissue and the eye sockets plugged with resin soaked bandages) and # 10, were also found with palm rib sticks in their skulls. Body P was resin treated and tied to a palm rib rack. Visible again, was a palm rib stick passing into the foramen magnum and holding the head onto the body.

Tomb # 3:

Body D, an adult male, skeletonized with some adherent soft tissue on the arms, was placed on a palm rib rack that was lashed together with rope. The bones on the rack were anatomically incorrect; the fibulae were placed with their distal ends towards the face; the calcaneus was next to the first rib; 15 extra ribs were found placed in what would have been the abdominal cavity. There was also a wooden stick anchoring the head to the rest of the body by passing distally first through the 7th cervical, then through the first 3 thoracic vertebrae and into the skull by way of the foramen magnum (Fig. 2).

Tomb # 4:

Body D was a young adult male (about 25 years old) that was disarticulated with the lower limbs tied to the femurs with bandages. The left leg was bent up onto the body with one foot tied to the distal tibia; the right upper arm was also tied with bandages to a palm rib stick.

More data need to be collected before any interpretations can be made. One can conjecture that the individuals were either: 1) interred, visited sometime later and as the bodies were perhaps falling apart they were then tied together; 2) not interred, left out for some time then tied up and interred permanently in the tombs; or 3) the stick in the foramen magnum served to pull out the brain before mummification. However, usually it was done through the nostrils and therefore hypothesis #3 is less likely. The sticks were found after unwrapping the face and head. It does not seem possible that the grave robbers would have taken so much trouble and care to keep body and soul together!

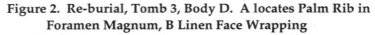

Figure 2. Re-burial, Tomb 3, Body D. A locates Palm Rib in Foramen Magnum, B Linen Face Wrapping

Ismant's East Cemetery

This cemetery was identified and described by Peter Sheldrick of the DOP during the 1991/1992 field seasons. It is situated on a low undulating rise 200m east of the present day guard hut. The surface is littered with potsherds, some sun bleached bones and the occasional eroding grave containing bones. In 1992 excavations were begun on an area on top and around a small knoll (Tomb # 9). Mud brick walls of the grave shafts were evident and some were covered with white plaster. Forty-one individuals were removed from individual graves. Most were supine and orientated E-W with the head at the west end. This cemetery is assumed to contain early Christians who, as part of their separation from the old religion, were buried in another place. Table 2 summarizes the differences in mortuary practice between the West and East cemeteries. Table 3 summarizes the East Cemetery.

Table 1. Summary of West Cemetery*

Tomb #	I.D.	Age	Sex	Pathology, Comments
1	A	4**	F	-
2	A	-	-	wavy red hair, organs carbonized, little lipping on lumbar vertebrae.
	B	adult***	F	resin treated, otherwise intact.
	D	adult	M	resin treated.
	E	child	M	resin treated.
	G	adult	-	resin treated.
	H	adult	M	-
	I	adult	-	-
	J	adult	-	resin treated, ? reburied.
	L	child	F	organs carbonized.
	M	adult	-	right club foot
	P	adult	-	resin treated.
	R	adult	M	sand pneumoconiosis
	S	old	-	edentulous, severe alveolar bone loss, osteoporotic, insect damage.
	T	subadult	M	resin filled wrappings stuffed into head.
3	A	young	M	resin treated.
	B	old	M	resin treated.
	C	8	-	lung region carbonized.
	D	adult	M	osteoarthritis elbow, ? reburial
	E	old	M	severe alveolar bone loss, edentulous, insect damage, two fused thoracic vertebrae.
4	A	old	M	edentulous with severe alveolar bone loss, skull sutures obliterated, entire bowel region filled with coprolites, samples taken for parasitic examination, ? constipation as cause of death ? bowel obstruction.
	B	young	F	entirely wrapped in tunics of linen, no evidence of pathology.
	C	old	F	edentulous, insect damage, sand pneumoconiosis
	D	20	M	evidence of reburial, legs tied up together
	E	-	F	resin treated, nostrils dilated, resin penetrated all organs.
	F	20	M	dental abcess in maxilla
5	A	old	F	sand pneumoconiosis, no evidence of TB
	B	adult	M	sand pneumoconiosis, osteophytosis on lumbar vertebrae.
	C	adult	M	sand pneumoconiosis, ? atherosclerosis, cirrhosis
	D	adult	M	resin treated.
	E	adult	-	resin treated.

Table 1. Summary of West Cemetery*   (cont.)

	F	old	F	prolapsed uterus, osteoporotic, some carbonization lung region.
	G	-	-	resin treated.
	H	9	M	no gross pathologies
	I	-	-	resin treated.
6	A	-	-	resin treated.
	B	old	F	osteoporotic, sand pneumoconiosis
	C	-	-	resin teated.
	D	51	M	spondololysis, erosion, porosity and osteoarthritis of vertebral column.
	I	-	-	short-faced dog

*   only intact remains are summarized in this table, so where there is a gap in the numbers, the remains were fragmentary.

**   children were aged by dental eruption and long bone lengths.

***   osteon aging of adults still in progress.

Table 2. Differences in Mortuary Practice Between West and East Cemeteries

	East Cemetery	West Cemetery
Architecture	Grave shafts lined with mud brick	Rock cut tombs, entrances lined with mud brick
Individuals	Single burials	Burials in groups
Mummified	None	Many artificially
Body Decoration	None	Gold leaf on hands, cheeks
Body Orientation	E-W	None noticeable
Grave Goods	Potsherds	Pottery, Statues, Horis, Anubis
Reburials	None	Likely

ANALYSES OF HUMAN REMAINS.

The mummified remains usually had genitalia present and therefore presented no problems regarding their sex. Their ages were determined by osteon aging of the rib (Stout, 1992) and/or tibia (Thompson and Paine, 1978). J.E. Molto analysed the remains from the East Cemetery using Suchey (1979), dental attrition and pathology for age-at-death estimations, and Phenice (1969) for sex determination. Autopsies were performed on the naturally mummified remains by sawing through the ribs laterally, then exposing the chest and abdominal cavities. Some mummies were tightly wrapped in many layers of hardened resin soaked bandages so that determination of their sex, or any other analyses, was impossible. Dilated nostrils and damaged nasal bones indicated that artificial mummification was done (Fig. 3). When hot molten resin was used for artificial mummification all the soft tissue was destroyed and it even penetrated the bones; if poured through the nose, pools of solidified resin were found in the skulls.

Soft tissue samples were taken from the heart/lung, the abdominal and kidney regions. Hair, muscle and bone were also sampled. The soft tissue was processed according to standard histological practice and 30μm sections of bone were prepared as well. Stains for parasites, tubercle bacilli, muscle striations, glycoproteins and polysaccharides were applied. These sections were examined under the microscope with polarized, UV and ordinary white light. Any coprolite material was also processed and examined to determine if any parasites were present.

With one or two exceptions all the skeletal remains are extremely well preserved, i.e., the bone's microstructure is intact; the naturally mummified remains are in general also very well preserved. The excellent preservation adds validity to any chemical analyses, histological aging techniques and diagnosis. Some organs (liver, kidney, brain and endocrine glands) with high metabolic rates show some degree of deterioration, which makes diagnosis difficult. Data have to be interpreted with a great deal of caution when the preservation of the remains is bad. In fact, often no meaningful results are obtained. As an example, the artificially mummified remains could not be analysed at all. If the ages-at-death in a population are consistently incorrect then it follows that the demography is also inaccurate. If the remains are not well preserved then the results of any chemical analyses must also be viewed with caution. A report of a case study (autopsy) follows. All the mummies were autopsied in the same way.

Table 3. Summary of East Cemetery Burials*

Burial #	Age	Sex	Pathology
1	1mn*	-	-
2	25	F	cribra orbitalia
3	1.5	-	? hydrocephalic, cribra orbitalia
4	38	M	osteoarthritis
5	40+	F	multiple fractures, cribra orbitalia
6	30	M	? leprosy
7	1mn	-	-
8	55+	F	edentulous, osteoarthritis
9	25	M	-
10	1.5	-	cribra orbitalia
11	6mn	-	-
12	6	-	cribra orbitalia
13	4	-	cribra orbitalia
14	6mn	-	cribra orbitalia
15	9mn	-	spina bifida, cribra orbitalia
16	30	M	spina bifida
17	2mn	-	-
18	1.5	-	cribra orbitalia
19	30	F	-
20	45	F	healed fracture scapula
21	45	F	-
22	25	F	spina bifida, cribra orbitalia
23	3	-	? hydrocephalic, cribra orbitalia
24	7	-	cribra orbitalia
25	22	F	spina bifida, cribra orbitalia, sponylolysis
26	22	F	-
27	30	F	-
28	fetus		-
29	2mn	-	-
30	30	F	-
31	9mn	-	-
32	45	F	dental attrition
33	35	F	dental attrition
34	1.8	-	-
35	1	-	cribra orbitalia
36	n.b.	-	-
37	n.b.	-	-
38	7.5	-	cribra orbitalia
39	10mn	-	porotic hyperostosis
40	6mn	-	-
41	62	F	healed fracture femur

mn = months old
n.b. = neonate
All other ages are given in years.
* Data summarized from J.E. Molto's end of season report. Data may not be final.

Figure 3. Dilated Nostrils of Body C, Tomb 3

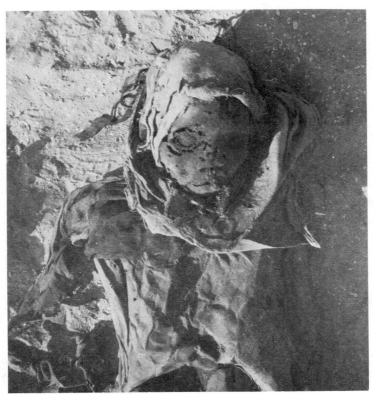

Anaylsis of Tomb 5; Body C; Site 31/420 - C5 - 1/5/C

This individual is a large-framed male with a beard and long black curly hair. The fingers and toes are each individually wrapped and tied separately. The right ring finger is missing. This appears to be a post mortem amputation. The height is approximately 170 cms. The sex organs are present. Skull measurements were made with the soft tissue present, so they are approximate only.

Circumference	700 (mm)
Max. Breadth	140
Max. Length	193
Bizygomatic Breadth	129
Upper Facial Height	65
L. Orbital Height	35

L. Orbital Breadth	41
R. Orbital Height	35
R. Orbital Breadth	48
Nasal Height	47
Nasal Breadth	27
Total Facial Height	126
Min. Frontal Breadth	103
Symphyseal Height	37

On opening the chest cavity a heart-like structure was observed and in the right upper quarter of the abdominal cavity a large amorphous mass was noted that could have been the liver. No evidence of any pathology was observed apart from the presence of several small osteophytes (bony abnormal outgrowths on spine) on all the lumbar vertebrae. Three round structures were observed in the bowel region, one was sampled and the others were left in the body. Tissue samples were taken from all the body cavities. Hair and a bone sample from the tibia were also taken. All spare tissue was placed back into the body. Photographs were taken.

Microscopic Report

Heart/Lung: The lungs show patchy consolidation and there appears to be some aspirated plant material as well as sand pneumoconiosis (Fig. 4). Silica particles and anthracotic pigment is present, no *tubercle bacilli* (bacteria causing tuberculosis) were observed; the heart muscle was not well preserved. Some artery walls are slightly thickened indicating mild hardening of the arteries.

Gastro-Intestinal System: The liver has fibrosis, possibly cirrhosis. Many diseases cause cirrhosis; the most likely cause here is hepatitis. The round structure in the bowel was found to be feces. No parasites or parasite eggs were found so far.

Ureto-Genital System: The kidneys were not well preserved, the genitalia were normal; no bladder wall could be identified.

Diagnosis: Respiratory failure, ? pneumonia

DISCUSSION
Multi-disciplinary Projects

The great value of a multi-disciplinary project such as this is that so much information is gathered about the ecology of the entire oasis in every facet imaginable and this has been immensely helpful in unfolding the story of Ismant's inhabitants:

- the environment — (a) the climate, both past and present. Ground water, in the past was traditionally obtained by shallow wells, now is obtained by drilling deep boreholes. The effect of wells drying up on the settlement patterns can be documented. (b) the ever present sand, which works its way into everything and is actually a biological hazard as realized by the paleopathology analyses on the mummified soft tissue.
- the ecology — the type of fauna and flora surviving the arid conditions gives more insight into diet and nutrition of the human inhabitants of the region.
- the architectural remains — the type of houses the people lived in; the temples and churches tell stories too about domestic arrangements and society.
- the written words giving us information about their myths, beliefs, religion, economics (the *Farm Accounts Book*), and finally their mortuary practices.
- The translation of the *Farm Accounts Book* has proved an invaluable source of information about the kinds of foods that were available to the people (Wagner, n.d.). Pigs, goats, sheep, chickens, and pigeons were sources of protein; barley and wheat were the important cereals; beans, dates, honey, and perhaps wild chickling were also available food.
- Other sources of information about food comes from the architecture of the Roman Period sites. Two-roomed buildings with large pigeon lofts suggest that there was a great dependence on pigeons (Mills, 1984). The diets of the people, taken from the documentary evidence of what was grown and traded, were really well balanced.
- In the search for pathological parasites the importance of a multi-disciplinary project is realized. It is pointless searching for parasites that could not possibly live in dry environments. For example, the Nile flooding its banks created an environment ideal for such parasites as bilharzia (schistosomiasis) and/or the strongyloides larvae to penetrate the hands and feet of the people working in the inundated fields. According to Churcher (1983) the snail vector for bilharzia (*Bulinus contortus*) is not and was never present in the Dakhleh Oasis. But, if perchance it is found in some individual then one can safely conclude that the person came from another place. Other possibilities for parasitic infestations in the Oasis population are from the trichinella and taenia species. As pigs were in the Oasis, the parasite causing "measly" pork, aptly named as the parasite forms cysts in the skeletal muscle (of the pigs) is another possibility as well as *Echinococcus*

granulosis (hydatid cyst), Guardia lambia, *Entamoeba histolytica* and *Enterobius vermicularis* (Meyer and Olsen, 1971). If any ova are found they will be photographed and measured for identification. No parasites have been identified in the human remains, but importantly, it has to be remembered that this does not mean that there are no parasites present in these remains.

The arid, dry, sandy and windy environment has affected and still does affect the health of the population. Almost without exception the thin sections of lung show evidence of sand pneumoconiosis. When examined under polarized light, the sections show particles of silica mixed with anthracotic pigment in the lung tissue (Fig. 4). This condition could lead to pneumonia, fibrosis and consolidation of the lungs. Individuals could also be predisposed to cancer and infections. There is a high probability, to-day, for the present inhabitants of the Oasis to suffer from various respiratory ailments. During the still nights one can hear some individuals coughing and hacking for long periods of time! The abrasive sand also effects dental attrition so care must be taken if aging techniques solely rely on dental attrition for the estimations. (My dentist always says " Been to Egypt again eh!" as there are always new chips on my teeth).

The human occupation and adaptations to this desert region can be documented from prehistoric times to the present day. This is quite remarkable and unique!

FUTURE RESEARCH PLANS

The Dakhleh Oasis has been inhabited by human beings from the Pleistocene onwards. Descendent populations have adapted from a wetter early environment to that of the desert over time. Three prehistoric cultural units have been identified and their settlement patterns delineated. The "epipaleolithic" *Masara* unit was followed by the *Bashendi* unit, putative pastoral nomads who aggregated in Dakhleh, and by the Sheikh Muftah unit, the "Neolithic" oasis dwellers who survived to overlap with the Old Kingdom immigrants (Mills, 1987). Funding has been requested for research into the evolution of the past Dakhleh Oasis populations and the descendent population by using modern molecular biology technology.

Figure 4. Thin Section of Lung AShowing: A the Anthracotic Pigment and Silica, B Brinchial Lumen. Polarized Light 100x

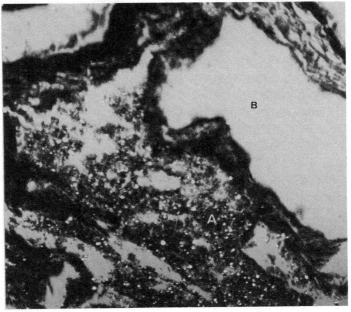

Comparisons of DNA sequences of what may be ancestral and descendent populations in this isolated region would indicate changes in gene frequencies, genetic drift, variations in population size, and migration patterns between the Nile Valley, Dakhleh and Africa, south and west of the Sahara. DNA from individuals from four cemeteries; 'Ein Tirghi (circa 2133 – 1786 B.C. and 36 B.C. – 400 A.D.), east and west Ismant (circa 1 – 500 A.D., and a Neolithic cemetery (circa ? 5000 B.C.) may then be extracted, amplified, sequenced, and compared. Another area of future research concerns the modern population of Dakhleh. A survey will be conducted into the health status of the people of the village of Bashendi in the coming field seasons. As life for the oasis dwellers (at present), in many ways, has not changed too much from the past it would be valuable to document diet, family history and present health status, i.e., dental, age, height, weight and respiratory and gastric problems. The data collected could be related back to the skeletal and mummified remains from the old cemeteries.

In the study of past populations, for example the inhabitants of the

Dakhleh Oasis, several variables must always be kept in mind:

(1) a multifactorial (i.e., use as many of the current techniques as possible) approach to age and sex determination must be taken. Many other variables such as demography depend on the accuracy of age and sex determination.

(2) the degree of preservation both macroscopic and microscopic must be assessed for the individual remains. Bone and soft tissue that are not well preserved tend to warp the results of any kind of chemical analyses that may be subsequently performed. Such results have to be interpreted with caution. There should always be controls for testing the methods.

(3) any analyses beyond one investigator's scope should be done by experts in that particular field, e.g., the histology of the bones and soft tissue should be done by a histotechnologist.

(4) a multi-disciplinary approach is invaluable for obtaining other information about the population under investigation. The fauna and flora, the ecology and settlement patterns are important facets of life and should always be considered as part of the entire tapestry of the people's lives.

(5) collaboration with other disciplines is very important as the analyses of the human condition covers so many different facets.

We have learnt, through the excavations, research and analyses at Ismant that:

- the people were not as tall as modern individuals
- they suffered the pain of losing infants and children, and the pain of broken bones, arthritis, dental disease, respiratory ailments and age-related diseases
- there were two different social/cultural systems (Christian and Egypto-Roman pagan) operating. Individuals depending on their religious affinities were either buried in the east or west cemetery
- there was a fairly wide variety of food available and that their diets would have been well balanced
- during the 1st to the 5th century AD, 270km from the nearest point to the Nile Valley (at Manfalut), in this isolated Oasis, Ismant was a thriving community. There was trade between the Nile Valley and Africa west and south
- there were scholars, story tellers and accountants. The ancient name of Ismant has been identified as *Kellis*.

ACKNOWLEDGEMENTS

The author wishes to thank Anthony Mills, Director of the Dakhleh Oasis Project for his information on the Dakhleh Oasis, past and present, advice, and humour (which is greatly appreciated). To Peter Sheldrick, the unsung hero of the Oasis, for his devotion to the Project, and enthusiasm, thank you. Thanks also go to Mandy Marlowe, Scott Fairgrieve and El Molto for additional information. A special thank you to Jessica Goodwin and Wayne Pitchford of Henry Ford Hospital, Detroit, for the prints.

REFERENCES

Andrews Carol (1984) *Egyptian Mummies*. Cambridge, Mass.: Harvard University Press, pp. 5-8.

Churcher CS (1983) Dakhelh Oasis Project Palaeontology: Interim report on the 1988 field season. *Journal of the Society for the Study of Egyptian Antiquities*. X111(3): 178-187.

Ghalioungui Paul (1973) *Magic and Medical Science in Ancient Egypt*. Amsterdam: BM Israel, pp. 110-111.

Harrison IR (1986) Arthropod Parasites associated with Egyptian Mummies with special reference to 1770 (Manchester mummies). In *Science in Egyptology*. R. David (ed.) Manchester: Manchester University Press, pp. 171-173.

Meyer MC and Olsen O.W.(1971) *Essentials of Parasitology*. Dubuque, Iowa: W.C. Brown, pp. 28-250.

Mills AJ (1987) Neolithic Cultural Units and Adaptations in the Dakhleh Oasis, Egypt. In AJ Mills (ed.) *The Dakhleh Oasis Project; Interim Reports* Vol. 1, Royal Ontario Museum, Toronto.

Mills AJ (1984) Research in the Dakhleh Oasis. In L Krzyzaniak, and M. Kobusiewicz (eds.) *Origin and Early Development of Food Producing Cultures in North-Eastern Africa*. Poznan: Polish Academy of Sciences. pp. 205-210.

Phenice TW (1969) A newly developed method of sexing the os pubis. *Am. J. of Phys. Anthrop.* 30:297-301.

Prominska Elzbieta (1986) Ancient Egyptian Tradition of Artificial Mummification in the Christian Period in Egypt. In *Science in Egyptology*. R David (ed.), Manchester: Manchester University Press, pp. 113-121.

Suchey JM(1979) Problems in the aging of females using the os pubis. *Am. J. of Phys. Anthrop.* 51: 467-470.

Stout S and Paine R (1992) Brief communication: Histological age estimation using Rib and clavicle. *Am. J. Phys. Anthrop.* 87: 111-115.

Thompson DD (1979) *Age-related Changes in Osteon Remodeling and Bone Mineralization*. PhD Thesis, Farmington: University of Connecticut.

Wagner G (nd) Prepublication French translation of the *Farm Accounts Book* of Ismant el-Kharab, Dakhleh Oasis Project.

13

Dietary Dental Pathology and Cultural Change in the Maya

Christine D. White

The human dentition is our primary food-processing unit. As such, it provides a reliable means of reconstructing diet in ancient populations. Teeth also preserve better than bone, making them a particularly important source of information for Maya remains that are generally quite poorly preserved because of the hot, moist tropical environment. Previous stable carbon and nitrogen isotope analysis on bone collagen from Lamanai, Belize has demonstrated significant shifts in the consumption of maize. These dietary changes have occurred in association with cultural change from the Preclassic period (~1250 B.C.) to early Colonial times (1670 A.D.). In this study, caries and enamel hypoplasia are analysed for the entire sample (N=122). The results support the chemical data for temporal trends and intrapopulational variables of social status, sex and age, and augment previous interpretations.

INTRODUCTION

Knowledge of diet and subsistence (or food procurement) has become increasingly important in the research of most anthropological fields. From the biological perspective, food consumption is crucial to our understanding of human behavioural and biological evolution, ontogeny and development, physiological adaptation and human variability, and the relationship between nutrition and disease. From the cultural perspective, food has ideological and metaphorical significance. Its distribution is determined by social, political and economic factors, and its procurement is reflective of technological status.

The "menu" from which we all make dietary choices is context-specific, determined by the resources available in our physical and cultural environments (Bumsted, 1985). In any environment, biotic and abiotic systems interact to create a potential inventory of consumable foods. Procurement technology (e.g., techniques and tools used for agriculture, horticulture, gathering, hunting and fishing), determines which resources can be captured, and processing technology (e.g., techniques and tools used for cooking, grating, grinding, roasting, drying, etc.) determines which resources can be converted into edible foods and/or stored. The foods or "meals" that are selected from the available "menu" are largely culturally determined. Reconstructing the "meal" in ancient populations is highly problematic because the traditional methods used by archaeologists have, in fact, only been able to write the "menu". Subsistence and dietary information has been largely indirect, dependent on preserved plants and animals, evidence for food procurement and processing, written and artistic records, and the presence of pathology (disease). Only rare instances of fine preservation such as coprolites (preserved faeces) or stomach contents, give us a glimpse of actual meals.

This chapter discusses the ancient Maya diet at Lamanai, Belize based on information derived from skeletal remains from the site, and interpreted in the light of ethnohistoric accounts and observations about subsistence and food practices among living Maya. Indirect evidence of diet derived from patterns of disease in teeth (dental pathology) is compared with direct evidence for diet derived from the chemical analysis of skeletal remains recovered from Lamanai (for more details, see White and Schwarcz, 1989). The analysis of dental pathology centres on the incidence of caries (focal areas of enamel destruction) and enamel hypoplasia (lesions resulting from disturbances during tooth growth) in the teeth, while the chemical analysis focusses on stable carbon and nitrogen isotope measurements of bone collagen from the skeleton. By using a combination of indirect and direct indicators of diet, this chapter illustrates the usefulness of integrated research designs for improving our ability to reconstruct in greater detail the components of ancient meals and patterns of food consumption.

ANALYSING DENTAL PATHOLOGY AND THE CHEMICAL CONSTITUENTS OF HUMAN BONE

Dental pathology is one of the most sensitive of the indirect indicators of diet. Teeth are our primary food processing units, and anything we consume must pass over them before being used by the rest of the body. Dental pathology is, therefore, a function of diet, and provides good indirect evidence of food consumption.

Chemical analysis of human bone, on the other hand, provides direct information on actual food consumed and thus, helps to separate the "meal" from the "menu" (Bumsted, 1985). Stable carbon and nitrogen isotope analyses are done here on the major organic fraction of bone (collagen) and determine the ratio of the two stable isotopes C^{12} and C^{13}. Interpretations of isotopic data are based on two main principles: 1) the ability to divide plants, which form the base of the food chain, into isotopically distinct categories, and 2) our position in the food chain (i.e., herbivore, carnivore, omnivore).

In the case of the Maya, carbon isotope studies allow us to measure the relative quantities of maize in the diet. This is because maize (and a few other tropical grasses, such as millet and sorghum) photosynthesizes carbon from the atmosphere differently than virtually all other food plants available to the Maya. Maize is a C-4 plant and, as such, uses more carbon-13 than other possible Maya plant staples (including fruits, nuts, and vegetables), which are C-3 plants. C-3 plants use a different kind of photosynthesis that results in a different ratio of carbon-12 to carbon-13 than C-4 plants. This is known as an *isotopic signature*, which is expressed in per mil (o/oo) values as $\delta^{13}C$.

A plant's "signature" is passed on to its consumers through the different levels of the food chain. As we move from one level in the food chain to the next (e.g., plant to herbivore, herbivore to carnivore) some of the carbon-12 is lost. Because the amount lost is constant for every tissue and between species, we can also determine what position in the food chain the consumer occupies (i.e., herbivore, carnivore, omnivore).

Nitrogen isotope analysis works on the same principles, but in addition to identifying the consumer's level in the food chain, it is used to determine the kind of protein in the diet (e.g., legumes, marine vs. terrestrial). It is particularly important to analyse nitrogen isotopes in situations where the diet could include both a C-4 plant staple (e.g., maize) and marine resources, because the carbon signature of marine resources can mimick that of C-4 plants. In the case of the Maya, both marine resources and C-4 plants could have been important dietary components. Thus, chemically, we really are what we eat. (For reviews, see Van der Merwe, 1982; DeNiro, 1987; Schoeninger and Schwarcz, 1991; Katzenberg, 1992; Schoeninger and Moore, 1992; Ambrose, 1993).

DIET AND SUBSISTENCE AMONG THE MAYA

My interest in studying the Maya arose from my participation in an undergraduate archaeology fieldschool in Belize, and reconstruction work as a research assistant for Dr. Hermann Helmuth of Trent University on the bones recovered from Lamanai. During a course on Mesoamerican Prehistory taught by Dr. Paul Healy (also from Trent University), I became aware of how crucial subsistence is to our interpretation and understanding of Maya history. This led me to begin to investigate ways of reconstructing diet that would yield the greatest amount of reliable information, incorporating newer methods of chemical analysis in conjunction with more traditional osteological (bone) and odontological (tooth) analyses.

The ancient Maya represent an excellent case for studying the interaction between environment and culture in food choice. Questions about subsistence among the Maya initially arose from the need to understand how they maintained such high population densities and in a fragile tropical ecosystem. More recently, archaeological concern has tended to focus on the role played by intensive agriculture in the so-called "collapse" or depopulation of many Classic Maya sites.

'Slash and burn' or 'milpa' agriculture is the only subsistence technique used today in this area. The milpa system involves controlled burning of vegetation to create fields made temporarily fertile from the burned residue. In tropical areas where there is only a thin layer of fertile soil, heavy rainfalls can cause massive soil depletion. As milpa plots are only fertile for a limited amount of time, new fields must be created regularly, while the old ones are left to regenerate. Clearly, this is not a form of intensive agriculture, but it was the only technique observed among the Maya by the Spanish Conquistadors upon their arrival in Mesoamerica in the sixteenth century (Landa, 1566, in Tozzer, 1941).

Archaeologists hypothesized that this kind of extensive agricultural system could have eventually caused ecological degradation of the region that ultimately could have led to the collapse of the Maya culture in the Late and Terminal Classic periods (Willey and Shimpkin, 1973).

However, we now know that the pre-Conquest Maya practised alternate forms of agriculture that would have been more intensive, more productive, and ecologically more sound than milpa agriculture alone. Crop yields were improved by effective water control methods such as terraced hillsides, and lowland swamp areas were transformed into highly productive raised fields (Harrison and Turner, 1978; Flannery, 1982; Healy et al., 1983; Chase and Chase, 1987; Pohl, 1988). The technology of Maya agriculture has thus been well investigated, but the reconstruction of diet continues to present a challenge. Analysis of plant and animal remains excavated from Maya sites has provided some evidence for subsistence (Pohl, 1985). However, because the preservation of organic remains in the wet tropics is so poor, such traditional reconstructions provide only limited information on the composition of the diet.

It has long been assumed that maize was the staple food throughout Maya history. Not only does it appear in Maya iconography and codices, but its social and religious importance is also described by the Spanish in ethnohistoric records (e.g., Bishop Landa, 1566, in Tozzer, 1941). Skeletal and dental pathology in the form of iron deficiency anemia, heavy calculus deposits, and high caries rates also suggest high maize consumption at several ancient sites (Hooton, 1940; Saul, 1972; Kennedy, 1983; Danforth et al., 1985; Whittington, 1989; Storey, 1992). Furthermore, research on living populations has shown that dependence on maize has created serious nutritional disease, particularly anemia (Shattuck, 1938; Béhar, 1968; Scrimshaw and Tejeda, 1970).

The first dietary models for the Maya were therefore created from a combination of ethnohistoric records and from studies of subsistence and food use among living Maya populations (ethnographic analogy). More recent dietary models draw attention to the ecological potential of the Maya region. Controversy over which resources were actually exploited centres on the relative importance of possible staples, the degree of change over time and regional differences in their consumption. Models of food consumption include "monotonous" staple diets, as well as those that suggest diversity in food resource use. In addition to maize, both root crops (*Manihot esquelenta* - Bronson, 1966) and ramon nuts (*Brosimum alicastrum* - Puleston, 1982) have been proposed as staples. Resource diversity models include backyard (kitchen) gardening and the "artificial rain forest" (Wiseman, 1973), and multi-species horticulture (Sanders and Price, 1968; Wilkin, 1971; Harris, 1978; Marcus, 1982). As implied by their names, these models suggest that the Maya were less reliant on maize

283

agriculture than previously supposed because they incorporated a number of other plants such as beans, cucurbits, peppers, tomatoes, and so forth into their diets.

In spite of the resource diversity of the area, most archaeologists nevertheless accept maize as the main staple in the ancient Maya diet. In 1989, Dr. Henry Schwarcz (McMaster University) and I tested alternate hypotheses about food consumption among the Maya using isotopic analysis on the skeletons from the site of Lamanai, Belize. Our study established the predominance of maize in the ancient Maya diet from the Preclassic (~1500 B.C.) to Historic (A.D. 1670) periods. However, the results of the isotopic analysis also indicated that there had been significant changes in the amount of maize consumed at the site, over time. As will be demonstrated later in this chapter, the dental indicators of diet provide further support for this finding.

THE SUBSISTENCE ENVIRONMENT AT LAMANAI

Lamanai is located in Northern Belize on the north-western shore of the New River Lagoon about 70 km inland from the Caribbean coast (see Figure 1). It was excavated by Dr. David Pendergast of the Royal Ontario Museum (Toronto, Ontario) between 1974 and 1985. The environment of the site and its surrounding area is characterized by wide diversity in both terrestrial and aquatic ecozones, making it a microcosm of the Maya Lowlands. Virtually all of the possible food staples identified for the Maya so far could have been grown on or near the site.

The potential for maize agriculture at Lamanai is remarkable. Agronomic research indicates that the ancient population there could have produced far more maize than was needed, even at the peak of the site's occupation (Lambert et al., 1984). Milpa fields tended by the modern inhabitants of the area are a testament to the likelihood that they existed in the past. There is also evidence for ancient raised fields and an alluvial shoreline, which are possible ancient areas of food production. These may date to the Early Preclassic (2500 to 1250 BC) or Classic (250 to 900 AD) periods (Lambert et al., 1984).

Raised fields are made by creating hillocks from the nitrogen-rich muck at the bottom of swamps. Their fertility is extremely high and is maintained by regular dumping of excavated mud onto the top of the mounds. Raised fields are self-irrigating and, unlike other subsistence systems, can produce several crops per year. Analysis of pollen cores also indicates that maize was being grown on the site in the Preclassic period, perhaps as early as 1500 BC (Pendergast, personal communication). In addition, kitchen equipment for processing maize (manos and metates) is common at the site, and the use of alkali to improve its nutritional value is implicated by the existence of many lime-lined pots and colanders.

Figure 1. Map of Belize Showing Location of Lamanai

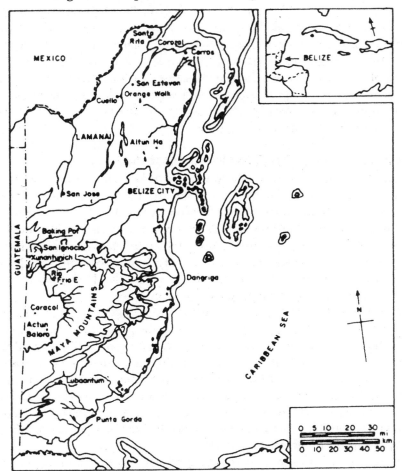

THE SKELETAL SAMPLE

The site of Lamanai offers one of the longest continuous occupations in Mesoamerica, (Pendergast 1986) and the skeletal material excavated from it spans the most of Maya history:

Preclassic (1250 B.C. – 250 A.D.),
Early Classic (250 – 400 A.D.),
Late Classic (650 – 900 A.D.),
Terminal Classic (900 – 1000 A.D.),
Postclassic (1000 – 1520 A.D.)
Historic (1520 – 1670 A.D.).

Because of differences in the quality of preservation and in excavation design, the number of skeletons available for study varies by time period. All of the individuals of known age and sex from Preclassic to Late Classic periods have been analysed chemically, but because the Terminal Classic and Historic periods yielded very large samples, individuals were selected randomly for study.

The sample of teeth comes from a much greater number of individuals (N=167), and essentially includes all of the teeth available as of the end of the 1985 field season. Most of the skeletal material comes from the ceremonial core, or the central area of the site, where the temples and elite residences are found. Because of this, I assume that most of the individuals in the sample come from a fairly high socio-economic status.

The skeletal sample from the Early Classic consists of a set of very elite (possibly royal) tomb burials (one male, one female). These are the only individuals who can be used definitively to mark possible social contrast in differential access to resources.

DENTAL PATHOLOGY
Caries

Caries are focal areas of dental enamel destruction. A carious lesion is any macroscopically observable lytic defect large enough to insert the tip of a dental explorer. The development of caries involves complex interrelationships between many types of organisms, their oral environments and the morphology and tissue intregity of the host tooth (Newbrun, 1982). The solubility of enamel, which creates caries, is promoted by the consumption of carbohydrates, especially sugars and refined carbohydrates (Sobel, 1960; Jenkins, 1970). Carbohydrate consumption has been used in modern dentistry to explain spatial and temporal patterns in modern caries incidence, as well as patterns related to socio-economic status and life-style (Bibby, 1970; Moore and Corbett, 1975; Keene, 1981).

Caries can provide the most reliable data for ancient populations because they are easily observed and well preserved. Anthropologists have used caries as a means of demonstrating shifts in the amounts of carbohydrates consumed or changes in cereal refinement (Patterson, 1984; Larsen, 1983; Cohen and Armelagos, 1984). Caries data have also been used elsewhere to support stable carbon and nitrogen isotope values indicating terrestrial/marine shifts in diet (Walker and Erlandson, 1986; Sealy and Van der Merwe, 1988).

Figure 2. An Example of Caries

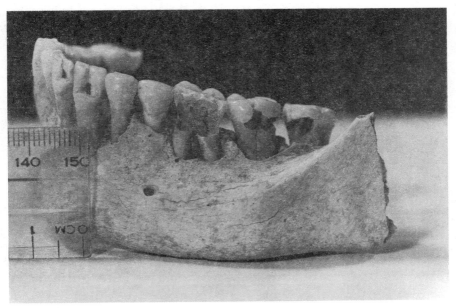

At Lamanai, analysis of caries is not only an important means of confirming dietary shifts, but also has potential for addressing the problem of differentiating between the various C-3 plants available to the Maya. In the Maya region, virtually all plants other than maize are C-3 plants, with the exception of amaranth, which is not suspected to have been an important food item. Isotopic analysis alone cannot clearly disriminate between the consumption of root crops versus mixed plants (both C-3 plant regimes). However, if we assume that root crops produce a greater amount of sticky carbohydrates than mixed plants, caries frequency should be lower among people exploiting a mixed plant diet.

To determine the extent of caries at Lamanai and to document changes in their frequency over time, I examined all the surfaces of all the teeth from the site for the presence or absence of caries. Figure 2 illustrates the degree of cavitation found in many dentitions. Because the frequency of caries depends on the age of the individual, only teeth from adults were analysed in this study. I calculated the total number of carious lesions per individual as a percent of the number of preserved teeth. From the individual means, a mean percent was calculated for each time period, sex, and social status group.

The major potential source of error in this study is tooth loss, which can occur both before and after death. Unlike other research on caries among the Maya (e.g., Saul, 1972), however, I did not assume that teeth lost before death had contained caries.

Enamel Hypoplasia

Enamel hypoplasia is a dental lesion indicative of a non-specific growth disturbance. It results from abnormal metabolism and development of the enamel-forming cells (ameloblasts) and is observed as horizontal lines of under-developed enamel (see the canine in Figure 3). The nature and frequency of lesions in a population can be characteristic of several health problems, including infectious disease and malnutrition. Consistency in the occurrence and developmental timing of hypoplasia within members of agricultural populations, generally has been interpreted as a record of stress during the period when children are weaned from breast milk. The phenomenon of weanling diarrhea is known to be an indirect cause of linear hypoplasia, as are acute protein-calorie malnutrition and iron deficiency anemia (Nikiforuk and Fraser, 1981).

Both of these conditions are associated with maize-dependent diets (Katz et al., 1974). As native North American populations became increasingly dependent on maize agriculture, the incidence of hypoplasia rose accordingly (Rose et al., 1978; Cook and Buikstra, 1979). Similarly, there is a decrease in enamel hypoplasia in Nubia concomitant with an improvement in nutrition (Rudney, 1982). Because of this link with nutritional deficiency, enamel hypoplasia can only be used as in indicator of dietary stress and as a useful companion to the more direct dietary indicators. Interestingly, Saul's (1972) study of the Maya site of Altar de Sacrificios shows a peak in enamel hypoplasia in the Late and Terminal Classic periods and appears to coincide with the age of weaning.

I examined all of the teeth from Lamanai macroscopically, looking for the presence of linear grooves, shown in Figure 3, that characterize enamel hypoplasia. A mean was calculated from the number of observable teeth for each individual, then a mean of these individual means was calculated for each time period. Attrition can obliterate hypoplastic lines that might have originally existed and missing teeth can result in an underestimate of enamel hypoplasia for both the individual and the population. Furthermore, there is considerable variability in the methodology used to analyse enamel hypoplasia, so the data in this study are not necessarily comparable to those from other studies.

Figure 3. An Example of Enamel Hypoplasia

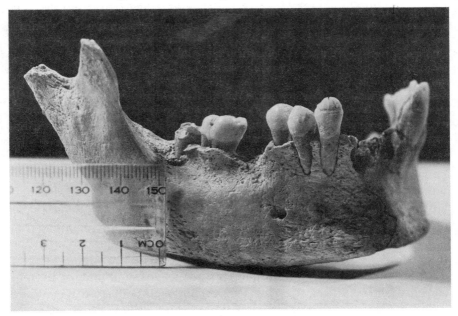

Social Status and Diet at Lamanai

Social status is often a major determinant of diet. Higher status individuals not only have access on a more regular basis to more food, but also to the most socially valued foods. Although all of the burials at Lamanai are assumed to be of relatively high status, the male and a female found in the Early Classic tombs, mentioned previously, provide a source of true social distinction and potential dietary contrast to non-elite members of the population.

Interestingly, the carbon isotope ratios ($\delta^{13}C$) for both of these individuals strongly suggest that they consumed *less* maize than the rest of the population. The tomb male is further distinguished by a nitrogen isotope ratio ($\delta^{15}N$) uncharacteristic of the rest of the population, but typical of those found in the Bahamian reef fisher-agriculturalists described by Schoeninger et al. (1983). It is reasonable to speculate that this elite male had access to coastal reef resources that were available at the mouth of the New River, whereas the elite female did not.

The two tomb individuals are also markedly different in their caries frequency. In fact, they experienced *no caries* at all, further suggesting that they consumed far less maize than the other individuals from the same time period (n=2), who had a high caries rate. This elite couple also had the same style of intentional pre-mortem carving on their upper central incisors. This apparent status difference in the frequency of caries at Lamanai is consistent with that found at Copan, Honduras (Hodges, 1985) and at the nearby site of Tipu (Bennett and Cohen, 1985).

Gender and Diet at Lamanai

Females in archaeological populations often have more caries than males (Hillson, 1979). This could be due either to gender differences in diet or to the earlier eruption of teeth among females (Walker, cited in Larsen, 1987). It was only possible to determine whether there were sex differences in the frequency of caries at Lamanai for the Postclassic and Historic time periods because a larger sample with a more equal sex ratio is available for study, compared to the earlier periods.

The analysis revealed that there were basically no differences in the frequency of caries between the sexes. This conclusion is supported by the isotopic data that suggest gender equality in plant and/or protein consumption (see Table 1). Archaeological and ethnohistorical evidence indicates, moreover, that Maya women were not excluded from high status positions and thus should have had access to high status foods. Analysis of enamel hypoplasia further suggests that female children at Lamanai did not suffer any more developmental stresses than males during infant and early childhood years (see Table 1).

This apparent picture of 'dietary equality' by gender is probably not as simple as this, however. For example, the Early Classic tomb female at Lamanai evidently did not consume the seafood eaten by her elite male counterpart. This suggests that dietary differentiation by gender occurred at the elite level, even if it does not exist further down the social scale. In addition, regional variation in gender-based dietary differences appears to be emerging from other studies of the ancient Maya. Data from Pacbitun, Belize , for example, do indicate significant sex differences in diet at both the elite and common levels (White et al., 1993), whereas data from Copan, Honduras (Reed, 1991) do not.

Table 1. Comparisons by sex and age for dietary measures

		Male	n	Female	n	Juvenile	Adult (N=6)	(N=13)
Enamel Hypoplasia	mean[*]	0.39	61	0.34		50	-	-
	sd	0.49		0.48				
Caries	mean%	17.82	61	22.33		50	-	-
	sd	29.61		37.57				
$\delta^{13}C$	(o/oo)	-9.6	16	-9.4		13	-9.2	-9.3
	sd	1.1		0.5			0.6	0.8
$\delta^{15}N$	(o/oo)	9.7	16	9.4		13	-9.8	-9.4
	sd	0.6		0.7			1.3	0.7

[*]   mean here is really a mean of individual means
sd =   standard deviation

Age and Diet at Lamanai

Weaning is often a physiologically and dietarily stressful period for children and is known to cause enamel hypoplasia. Analysis of enamel hypoplasia at Lamanai suggests that 2- to 4-year-olds experienced the most stress throughout the entire study period. In fact, there is no change in the frequency of hypoplasia over time, which indicates that infants in all periods suffered equally. Although infants must have begun receiving solid food supplements to breast milk much earlier than the age of two, the Bishop Landa's (1566, in Gates, 1978) sixteenth-century account of life among the Maya documents a three-year breast feeding period. A two-year breast feeding period is common among the modern Maya (Shattuck, 1938). Prolonged milk feeding is associated with chronic parasitic and gastrointestinal disease, which is blamed for roughly 40% of infant deaths today (Scrimshaw et al., 1969; Shattuck, 1931) and may have been a major factor underlying disease and death in the past.

The transition from breast feeding to weaning is often reflected in age differences in $\delta^{15}N$ values (Fogel et al., 1989; White and Schwarcz, 1993). Breast feeding infants in both modern and archaeological populations have more of the nitrogen-15 isotope than infants who are not breast feeding due to a food chain effect. Because they are feeding off their mothers, they are essentially one level higher in the food chain than their mothers, as well as the rest of the population.

In the Lamanai skeletal sample, only two of the children analysed isotopically were young enough to have been breast feeding. One, who is 9 months to a year old, has values similar to the older members of the population, whereas the 2-year-old is more enriched in $\delta^{15}N$. This suggests that there was probably variability in the timing and degree of solid food supplementation of suckling infants..

From the isotopic analysis, it appears that children and adults at Lamanai were consuming the same proportions of plants and proteins (see Table 1). The diet of both groups was dominated by C-4 (maize) plants and protein was derived mostly from plants and terrestrial animals. The consistency in diet found here is significant for two reasons: 1) it means that individuals of different ages could be used to test changes over time in the isotopic data and, 2) it has profound implications for childhood health and nutritional status because children have greater protein and iron demands, which might not have been met with a maize staple. The similarity between adult and juvenile diets cannot be generalized to all Maya populations however. For example, at the site of Pacbitun, children are consuming much more maize than are the adults are (White et al., 1993).

Time Trends in the Diet at Lamanai

It is clear that the diet and the extent of maize consumption among the Maya at Lamanai changed over time. Examination of the graphs in Figure 4 and the values in Table 2 shows that the frequency of dental caries and $\delta^{13}C$ values fluctuated markedly from 1250 B.C. to 1670 A.D. These dietary shifts can be interpreted in light of archaeological and ethnohistoric information on the relationship between maize consumption, the development of Maya civilization, and changes in population density and pressure in the region.

In the ancient and sacred Quiche book, the *Popul Vuh*, the Maya describe maize not only as the resource upon which their civilization was

Table 2. Temporal Means of Enamel Hypoplasia and Caries

Cultural Period	Enamel Hypoplasia		Caries	
	Mean*	sd	Mean%	sd
Preclassic (n=5)	0.40	0.51	20.0	44.7
Early Classic (n=4)	0.20	0.44	24.5	24.2
Late Classic (n=5)	0.20	0.44	17.1	21.0
Terminal Classic (n=6)	0.44	0.52	1.8	3.2
Postclassic (n=50)	0.39	0.49	17.6	37.5
Historic (n=42)	0.31	0.46	20.5	28.5

    enamel hypoplasia and caries are status adjusted
    caries is age adjusted
*   enamel hypoplasia mean is really a mean of individual means

built, but also as the material from which humans were physically mould-ed (Béhar, 1968). Dental data also suggest the prominent role of maize in the diet during the Preclassic period (Figure 4). Caries incidence is high and typical of populations dependent on high carbohydrate foods (Patterson, 1984). Similarly, Preclassic levels of C-4 (maize) consumption measured isotopically are even higher than those for North American populations that experienced the transition to maize agriculture later on (see Schwarcz et al., 1995 and Lynott et al., 1986). This means that in the earliest phase of Maya civilization maize agriculture was already full-blown, lending credence to the idea that maize had a particularly early development in this region.

Figure 4. Temporal Trends in Caries, $\delta^{13}C$ and $\delta^{15}N$ Values

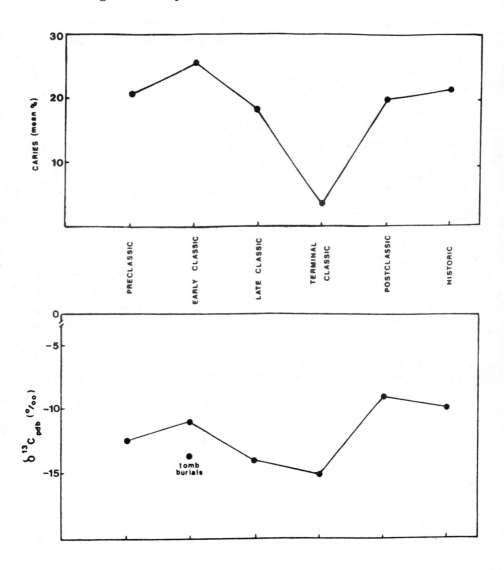

At the neighbouring site of Cuello, where some of the earliest Maya remains occur, the genetic and morphological development of maize is documented over the 3,000 year Preclassic period (Hammond, 1980). Maize was apparently being artificially selected for increasingly better yields. The high level of maize consumption in the Preclassic could also be a reflection of the increased population density that is hypothesized for the middle to late Preclassic period at Lamanai (Weaver, 1981), but we need more data from earlier periods to test this idea. Research for later time periods at Pacbitun suggests that there may well be an association between maize consumption and agricultural intensification (White et al., 1993).

Although both the dental and isotopic data suggest that there was little change in the diet during Preclassic times, the caries rate drops off during the Late Classic, however, and caries become almost non-existent during the Terminal Classic period. The incidence of dental caries is so low, in fact, that it approaches levels more characteristic of non-agricultural populations (Turner, 1979; Sealy and Van der Merwe, 1988).

The chemical data in Figure 4 also reflect the same pattern, with the percentage of maize in the diet dropping to its lowest point in the sequence during the Terminal Classic. The isotopic data cannot clearly indicate whether the C-3 plants being substituted for maize at this time were root crops or a mixed plant regime. The dental data, however, suggest that it is unlikely that root crops were used extensively. Given that root crops are starchy carbohydrates with caries producing properties, they could not have been consumed in significant amounts during this time period without leaving the tell-tale signs of caries. By process of elimination, it appears that the remaining proportion of the Terminal Classic diet likely consisted of wild and/or cultivated C-3 plants, typical of the mixed plant models.

We do not know why maize consumption declined so dramatically during this period. Similar evidence for reduced maize production at this time has been documented in pollen profiles for Lowland sites in the Peten, Guatemala (Vaughan et al., 1985; Wiseman, 1985). Shifts in food consumption can be due to either changes in production, or changes in availability of other resources. Agricultural production at the site could have been affected by cultural, rather than environmental, events. During the 100 year Terminal Classic Period, the inhabitants of Lamanai expended vast amounts of energy in building monumental architecture. Unlike many contemporary sites in lowland Guatemala, for many of which this was a period of decline, the Terminal Classic at Lamanai represents a period of cultural flourescence. It also stands in stark contrast with Altar de Sacrificios, in the Peten, Guatemala, where caries incidence rose significantly just before the site was abandonned (Saul, 1972).

At Lamanai, the drop in maize consumption, which begins in the Late Classic period, is *not* the harbinger of cultural collapse that it appears to be at Altar de Sacrificios. Instead, Lamanai appears to have been in the process of switching its cultural and trade affinities from the Peten to the Yucatan. The flurry of Terminal Classic construction at the site may be evidence of political and economic survival strategy. Such monumental building activity could have created a scarcity of human resources for maintaining the maize fields. Alternately, changing patterns of trade could have altered diet by making more diverse resources available to the people at the site.

The downward trend in maize consumption during the Late and Terminal Classic reversed with the abrupt Postclassic return to a strongly dominant maize diet. During the Postclassic, caries incidence also rebounds to levels characteristic of the Preclassic and Early Classic periods and the high incidence of lesions in the Postclassic continues into the Historic period without significant change. Chemical data are again consistent with the dental data. Carbon isotope ratios indicate that maize consumption doubled within a 100 year period. In the Postclassic, maize constitutes an even greater proportion of the diet than that found in the Preclassic and Early Classic periods. These high levels of consumption also persisted into and throughout the Historic period. In fact there is some reason to believe that diet has not changed significantly since then. Ethnographic research on the modern Maya has quantified the proportion of maize in the diet to be between 65–86% (Benedict and Steggerda, 1936).

The resurgence of maize production and consumption during the Postclassic period supports a growing body of research that challenges previous ideas that the Postclassic was simply a continuation of the "decline, decadence and depopulation" exhibited at some sites in the Late and Terminal Classic (Chase and Rice, 1985; Pendergast, 1986). Furthermore, the uniformity of Maya diet at Lamanai throughout the period of European conquest also provides evidence that the presence of the Spaniards in this area had no immediate or significant dietary impact.

CONCLUSIONS

Lamanai represents an ideal test case for the usefulness of an integrated research design in addressing major issues of Maya diet and subsistence. The most basic data come from understanding the composition of the diet for each cultural period in their history. The interpretation of dietary patterns in the ancient Maya at Lamanai is enriched by combining the direct evidence from chemical analysis with data for dental pathology that resulted from exposure to different dietary regimes. Isotopic analysis provided the inferential baseline for determining the proportions of C-4 plants (maize) and the source of protein in the diet. The use of isotopes alone, however, limits the depth of paleodiet reconstruction when there are several significant C-3 plant options. Because maize is considered one of the few significant C-4 plants used as a staple in North America it becomes important to be able to distinguish between C-3 alternatives. Some discrimination between the C-3 options was made possible with the use of caries data, which can indicate whether the plants consumed were high carbohydrate or not. Quite simply, by using integrated research designs, we improve our potential to reconstruct more of the components of ancient "meals".

Issues of greater social complexity in Mesoamerican archaeology range from the relationship between diet and the development of Maya culture, to changes in food consumption associated with culture, technology, population pressure, and the environment. The Maya at Lamanai do demonstrate remarkable shifts in their plant food regime that seem to be related to these factors. We find status differences in food consumption, and within the very elite, gender differences. In addition, it is clear that as Maya culture changed, so did their diet. At the same time, they appear to have been highly selective of the extensive menu available to them. Assuming their economy was based mainly on agriculture, as it is for most pre-industrial societies, maize consumption is a sensitive indicator of cultural and environmental disruptions. We are reminded not only of the saying "you are what you eat", but also of the wisdom of the *Popul Vuh*, which said that the Maya were made from maize.

ACKNOWLEDGEMENTS

I would like to thank Hermann Helmuth and Paul Healy, Department of Anthropology, Trent University for their help in Maya osteology and archaeology. I also thank Henry Schwarcz, Department of Geology, McMaster University for his significant contribution to the isotopic analysis, and David Pendergast, Royal Ontario Museum, who graciously allowed access to the site and the skeletal material. Technical support was provided by Martin Knyf, McMaster University. I would also like to recognize Stanley Ambrose, University of Illinois, Anne Katzenberg, University of Calgary, and George Armelagos, University of Florida, Gainsville for their theoretical contributions. This research was supported by an Ontario Graduate Scholarship and an NSERC scholarship to C. White, an NSERC grant to H. Schwarcz and by the Department of Anthropology, Trent University.

REFERENCES

Ambrose SH (1993) Isotopic analysis of paleodiets: Methodological and interpretive considerations. In MK Sandford (ed.): *Investigations of Ancient Human Tissue*. Langhorne, PA: Gordon and Breach, pp. 59-130.

Béhar M (1968) Food and nutrition of the Maya before the Conquest and at the present time. In *Biomedical Challenges Presented to the American Indians, Scientific Publication No.165*. Washington, D.C.: Pan American Health Organization, pp. 114-119.

Benedict FG and Steggerda M (1936) *The Food of the Present-day Maya Indians of the Yucatan*. Carnegie Institute Contributions to American Archaeology No. 18, Vol. III. Washington, D.C.

Bennett S and Cohen MN (1985) Social patterns in the colonial population from Tipu. Paper presented at the American Anthropological Association, Washington.

Bibby BG (1970) Inferences from naturally occurring variations in caries prevalence. *Journal of Dental Research* 49:1194-1199.

Bronson B (1966) Roots and the subsistence of the ancient Maya. *Southwestern Journal of Anthropology* 22:251-279.

Bumsted MP (1985) Past human behaviour from bone chemical analysis: Respects and prospects. *Journal of Human Evolution* 14:539-551.

Chase AF and Rice PM (1985) *The Lowland Maya Postclassic*. Austin: University of Texas Press.

Chase AF and Chase DZ (1987) *Investigations at the Classic Maya City of Caracol, Belize: 1985-1987*. Pre-Columbian Art Institute, Monograph 3. San Francisco: Pre-Columbian Art Institute.

Cohen MN and Armelagos GJ (eds.) (1984) *Paleopathology at the Origins of Agriculture*. Orlando: Academic Press.

Cook DC and Buikstra JE (1979) Health and differential survival in prehistoric populations: Prenatal defects. *American Journal of Physical Anthropology* 51:649-664.

Danforth ME, Bennett S, Cohen MN and Melkunas H (1985) Femoral cortical involution in a colonial Maya population. *American Journal of Physical Anthropology*. 66:162 (abstract).

DeNiro MJ (1987) Stable isotopy and archaeology. *American Scientist* 75:182-191

Flannery KV (ed.)(1982) *Maya Subsistence*. New York: Academic Press.

Fogel ML, Tuross N, Owsley D (1989) Nitrogen isotope tracers of human lactation in modern and archaeological populations. *Carnegie Institution of Washington Yearbook*. Washington: Geophysical Laboratory.

Gates Wm, (1978) *Yucatan Before and After Conquest*. N.Y.: Dover.

Goodman, AH and Rose JC (1990) Assessment of systemic physiological perturbations from dental enamel hypoplasias and associated histological structures. *Yearbook of Physical Anthropology 33*:59-110.

Hammond N (1980) Early Maya ceremonial centre at Cuello, Belize. *American Antiquity 54*:176-190.

Harris D (1978) The agricultural foundations of Lowland Maya Civilization. In PD Harrison and Turner BL (eds.): *Pre-Hispanic Maya Agriculture*. Albuquerque: University of New Mexico Press, pp. 301-324.

Harrison PD and Turner BL (eds.) (1978) *Pre-Hispanic Maya Agriculture*. Albuquerque: University of New Mexico Press.

Healy PF, Lambert J, Arnason T and Hebda R (1983) Caracol, Belize: Evidence of ancient Maya agricultural terraces. *Journal of Field Archaeology 10*:397-410.

Hillson SW (1979) Diet and dental disease. *World Archaeology 11*:147-162.

Hodges DC (1985) Dental pathology in a Late Classic sample from the Copan Valley, Honduras. Paper presented at the American Anthropological Association, Washington.

Hooton EA (1940) Skeletons from the Cenote of Sacrifice at Chichen Itza. In CL Hay, Linton RL, Lothrop SK, Shapiro HL and Vaillant CG (eds.): *The Maya and Their Neighbours*. New York: Dover, pp. 270-280.

Jenkins GN (1970) Enamel protective factors in food. *Journal of Dental Research 49*:1318-1325.

Katz SH, Hediger ML and Valleroy MA (1974) Traditional maize processing techniques in the New World. *Science 184*:763-765.

Katzenberg MA (1992) Advances in stable isotope analysis of prehistoric bones. In SR Saunders and MA Katzenberg (eds.): *Skeletal Biology of Past Peoples: Research Methods*, New York: Wiley-Liss, pp. 105-119.

Katzenberg MA and Saunders SR (1993) Age differences in stable carbon and nitrogen isotope ratios in a population of prehistoric maize horticulturalists. *American Journalof Physical Anthropology 90*:267-282.

Keene HJ (1981) History of dental caries in human populations: The first million years. In JM Tanzer (ed.): *Animal Models in Cariology*. Washington: Information Retrieval Inc., pp 23-40.

Kennedy GE (1983) Skeletal remains from Sartajena, Belize. In RV Sidrys (ed.): *Archaeological Excavations in Northern Belize, C.A. Monograph XVII*. L.A.: Institute of Archaeology, University of California, pp. 353-365.

Lambert JDH, Arnason JT and Siemens AH (1984) Ancient Maya drained field agriculture: Its possible application today in the New River flood-plain, Belize, C.A. *Agriculture, Ecosystems and Environment 11*: 67-84.

Larsen CS (1987) Bioarchaeological interpretations of subsistence economy and behavior from human skeletal remains. In M Schiffer (ed.): *Advances in Archaeological Method and Theory, Vol. 10*. San Diego: Academic Press, pp. 339-445.

Larsen CS (1983) Behavioural implications of temporal change in cariogenesis. *Journal of Archaeological Science 10*:1-8

Lovell NC, Nelson DE and Schwarcz HP (1986) Carbon isotope ratios in paleodiet: Lack of age or sex effect. *Archaeometry 28*:51-55.

Lynott MJ, Boutton TW, Price JE and Nelson DE (1986) Stable carbon isotopic evidence for maize agriculture in Southeast Missouri and Northeast Arkansas. *American Antiquity 51*:51-65.

Marcus J (1982) The plant world of the 16th and 17th Century Maya. In K Flannery (ed.): *Maya Subsistence*. New York: Academic Press, pp. 239-273.

Moore WJ and Corbett ME (1975) The distribution of dental caries in ancient British populations. *Caries Research 9*:163-179.

Newbrun E (1982) Sugar and dental caries: A review of human studies. *Science 217*: 418-423.

Nikiforuk G and Fraser D (1981) The etiology of enamel hypoplasia: A unifying concept. *Journal of Pediatrics 98*:888-893.

Patterson DK (1984) *Diachronic Study of Dental Pathology and Attritional Status of Prehistoric Ontario Pre-Iroquois and Iroquois Populations*. Mercury Series, No. 22. Ottawa: National Museums of Man.

Pendergast DM (1986) Stability through change: Lamanai, Belize, from the 9th to the 17th Century. In JA Sabloff and EW Andrews (eds.): *Late Lowland Maya Civilization*. Albuquerque: School of American Research, University of New Mexico Press, pp 223-249.

Pohl M (ed.) (1985) Prehistoric Lowland Maya environment and subsistence economy. *Papers of the Peabody Museum of Archaeology and Ethnology, No. 77*. Harvard University, Cambridge.

Pohl M (ed.) (1988) *Ancient Maya Wetland Agriculture*. Boulder: Westview Press.

Puleston DE (1982) The role of ramon in Maya subsistence. In K Flannery (ed.): *Maya Subsistence:* New York: Academic Press, pp. 353-367.

Reed DM (1991) *Stable Isotopes and Ancient Maya Diet at Copan, Honduras*. Paper Presented at the Annual Meeting of the Society for American Archaeology, New Orleans.

Rose JC, Armelagos GJ and Lallo JW (1978) Histological enamel indicator of childhood stress in prehistoric skeletal samples. *American Journal of Physical Anthropology 49*:511-516.

Rudney JD (1982) Dental indicators of growth disturbances in a series of ancient Nubian populations: Changes over time. *American Journal of Physical Anthropology 60*:463-470.

Sanders WT and Price BJ (1968) Mesoamerica: The Evolution of a Civilization. New York: Random House.

Saul FP (1972) The human skeletal remains of Altar de Sacrificios. *Papers of the Peabody Museum of Archaeology and Ethnology Vol. 63, No. 2*. Harvard University, Cambridge, Massachusetts.

Schoeninger MJ and Moore K (1992) Bone stable isotope studies in archaeology. *Journal of World Prehistory 6*:247-296.

Schoeninger MJ, DeNiro MJ and Tauber H (1983) Stable isotope ratios of bone collagen reflect marine and terrestrial components of prehistoric human diet. *Science 220*:1381-1383.

Schwarcz HP, Melbye J, Katzenberg MA and Knyf M (1985) Stable isotopes in human skeletons of Southern Ontario: Reconstructing paleodiet. *Journal of Archaeological Science* 12:187-206.

Schoeninger MJ and Schwarcz HP (1991) Stable isotope analysis in nutritional ecology. *Yearbook of Physical Anthropology* 34:283-321.

Scrimshaw NS and Tejeda C (1970) Pathology of living Indians seen in Guatemala. In TD Stewart (ed.): *Handbook of Middle American Indians, Vol. 9*: Austin: University of Texas Press, pp. 203-225.

Scrimshaw NS, Béhar M, Guzman A and Gordon JE (1969) Nutrition and infection field study in Guatemalen villages, 1959-1964, IX: An evaluation of medical, social and public health benefits, with suggestions for future field study. *Archives of Environmental Health* 18:51-62.

Sealy JC and Van der Merwe NJ (1988) Social, spatial and chronological patterning in marine food use as determined by $\delta^{13}C$ measurements of Holocene human skeletons from the southwestern Cape, South Africa. *World Archaeology* 20:87-102.

Shattuck GC (1938) *A Medical Survey of the Republic of Guatemala*. Carnegie Institution of Washington Publication no. 499. Washington, D.C.

Shattuck GC (1931) *Medical Survey of Yucatan*. Carnegie Institution of Washington Publication no. 30. Washington, D.C.

Sobel AA (1960) Inter-relationships of tooth composition, body fluids, diet and caries susceptibility. *Annals of the New York Academy of Science* 85:96-109

Storey R (1992) The children of Copan: Issues in paleopathology and paleodemography. *Ancient Mesoamerica* 3:165-171.

Tozzer AM (translation) (1941) Landa's Relacion de los Cosas de Yucatan. *Papers of the Peabody Museum of Archaeology and Ethnology*, Vol. 4, No. 3. Harvard University Press, Cambridge, Massachusetts.

Turner BLII, Hanham RQ and Portararo AV (1977) Population pressure and agricultural intensity. *Annals of the Association of American Geographers* 67: 384-396.

Turner CG (1979) Dental anthropological indications of agriculture among the Jomon people of central Japan, X; Peopling of the Pacific. *American Journal of Physical Anthropology* 51:619-636.

Ubelaker DH (1978) Human skeletal remains: Excavation, analysis, interpretation. *Manuals in Archaeology*, No.2. Washington, D.C.: Taraxacum.

Van der Merwe NJ (1982) Carbon isotopes, photosynthesis, and archaeology. *American Scientist* 70:596-606.

Vaughan HH, Deevy AS Jr. and Garrett-Jones SE (1985) Pollen stratigraphy of two cores from the Peten Lake District, with an appendix on two deep-water cores. In *Prehistoric Lowland Maya Environment and Subsistence: Papers of the Peabody Museum of Archaeology and Ethnology*. Harvard University Press, Cambridge, Massachusetts, pp. 73-89.

Walker PL, Erlandson JM (1986) Dental evidence from prehistoric dietary change on northern Channel Islands, California. *American Antiquity* 51:375-383.

Weaver MP (1981) *The Aztecs, Maya, and their Predecessors*. 2nd edition. New York: Academic Press.

White CD (1986) Paleodiet and nutrition of the ancient Maya at Lamanai, Belize: A study of trace elements, stable isotopes, nutritional and dental pathology. M.A. Thesis, Trent University.

White CD and Schwarcz HP (1993) Temporal trends in stable isotopes for Nubian mummy tissues. *American Journal of Physical Anthropology* 33:165-187.

White CD and Schwarcz HP (1989) Ancient Maya diet: As inferred from isotopic and elemental analysis of human bone. *Journal of Archaeological Science* 16:451-474.

White CD, Healy PF and Schwarcz HP (1993) Intensive agriculture, social status and Maya diet at Pacbitun, Belize. *Journal of Anthropological Research* 49:347-375.

White CD, Wright LE, Pendergast DM (1993) Biological disruption in the Early Colonial period at Lamanai. In CS Larsen and GR Milner (eds.): *In the Wake of Contact: Biological Responses to Conquest.* N.Y.: Wiley & Sons, pp. 135-145.

Whittington S (1989) Characteristics of demography and disease in low-status Maya from Classic Copan, Honduras. Ph.D. Dissertation, Pennsylvania State University.

Wilken GC (1971) Food-producing systems available to the ancient Maya. *American Antiquity 36:*432-448.

Willey GR and Shimkin DB (1973) The Maya collapse: A summary view. In TP Culbert (ed.): *The Classic Maya Collapse.* Albuquerque: University of New Mexico Press, pp. 457-503.

Wiseman FM (1973) The artificial rain forest. Paper presented at the Annual Meeting of the Society for American Archaeology, San Fransisco.

Wiseman FM (1985) Agriculture and vegetation dynamics of the Maya collapse in Central Peten, Guatemala. In *Pre-historic Maya Environment and Subsistence: Papers of the Peabody Museum of Archaeology and Ethnology.* Harvard University Press, Cambridge, Massachusetts, pp. 63-71.

14

Nutritional Ecology and Energetics of the Evenki Herders of Central Siberia

William R. Leonard and Peter T. Katzmarzyk

Methodological advances are now allowing biological anthropologists to more effectively study the ecology, energy expenditure and nutritional status of anthropological populations. This chapter provides an overview of the methods of human nutritional ecology and energetics, drawing on examples from recent work on the Evenki reindeer herders of Russia. Results indicate that the Evenki's traditional herding lifestyle remains a successful and sustainable strategy. Levels of energy and protein consumption are high during the late summer, and are sufficient to meet predicted metabolic requirements. The maintenance of a traditional lifestyle requiring high levels of energy expenditure explains why health and nutritional status remains relatively good in the Evenki in contrast to indigenous northern populations of the New World. Evenki women show greater evidence of obesity than men, a difference that appears to reflect recent changes in activity and fertility patterns.

The Evenki are quite small in stature, even relative to other indigenous arctic populations. Small adult body size is attributable to slow rates of growth during late childhood and adolescence. We believe that elevated resting and total metabolic rates along with seasonal constraints on food availability are responsible for limiting growth. Future research will monitor seasonal changes in the energy dynamic between the Evenki and their environment, and its impact on physical growth and health status.

The study of diet and nutrition has become increasingly important within all areas of biological anthropology. Nutrition is central to the discipline because it shapes so many aspects of biological variation in our species, such as physical growth, health status and patterns of fertility and mortality. Studies of the human fossil record suggest that ecological changes in food availability have been an important selective force throughout our evolutionary history (Gordon, 1987; Leonard and Robertson, 1992). Today, food availability and nutrition continue to influence strongly the biology of human populations throughout the world (Huss-Ashmore, 1988; de Garine and Harrison, 1988). Among developing countries, limited food availability and nutrient deficiencies contribute to poor growth and high mortality rates among infants and young children (Martorell, 1985). In the developed world, on the other hand, "overnutrition" (food consumption in excess of biological needs) contributes to high rates of obesity and other chronic diseases (e.g., heart disease, hypertension) (Eaton and Konner, 1985).

Nutrition encompasses the study of macronutrients (protein, fat and carbohydrates) and micronutrients (vitamins and minerals). Macronutrients are required in relatively large amounts, and provide the energy and key building blocks for sustaining life. Vitamins and minerals are required in much smaller amounts, and are important for regulating biological function. Nutritionists tend to focus on how nutrients influence function at the individual level (Huss-Ashmore, 1992). Biological anthropologists, on the other hand, generally approach the study of nutrition from an "ecological" perspective, examining how human populations go about extracting and utilizing food from different environments. This approach focusses largely on energy as a general measure of nutrient availability, since for most non-industrial societies, energy is the primary nutritional constraint. Once it is consumed, food energy can be allocated for a variety of different biological needs: 1) basic maintenance (resting metabolism), 2) thermoregulation (heating or cooling the body), 3) activity (exercise or work), 4) growth, and 5) reproduction (e.g., pregnancy, lactation). Obviously, if food is chronically limited within an environment, little energy will be available for "non-maintenance" needs. Thus, in the short run, an individual's or population's nutritional well-being (nutritional status) can be measured in terms of energy balance, that is the number of calories (kcal) consumed relative to number expended. Over longer time frames, measures of growth and body size, such as height and weight are often used as indices of nutritional status since they, in part, reflect the amount of food energy that has been allocated above maintenance requirements.

The strength of this ecological approach is that it explicitly attempts to link key environmental variables with human biological parameters that are of adaptive and evolutionary importance. To date, a major limitation of this type of research has been the tendency to focus exclusively on the influence of the physical and biotic stressors on food availability, while ignoring the impact of social and cultural factors. Consequently, biological anthropologists are now becoming more interested in incorporating social, cultural and economic variables into these models.

This chapter will provide an overview of the theory and methods of human nutritional ecology and energetics, focussing on our work with the Evenki reindeer herders of the central Siberian region of Russia. We will first present some background information on the research project and a brief ethnographic description of the Evenki. Next, we will outline the methods used to assess energy intake, energy expenditure and physical nutritional status in the Evenki. Finally, we will present our results to date, highlighting how the Evenki compare to other indigenous arctic populations and proposing future avenues of research.

RESEARCH BACKGROUND

Recent social and political changes in the former Soviet Union have opened up many new research opportunities for scholars interested in the biology of arctic populations. Our research on the Evenki is an international collaboration that is exploring the ecology and genetic heritage of this population. The work is being conducted in collaboration with population geneticists Michael Crawford (University of Kansas) and Rem Sukernik (Russian Academy of Science), and is the first detailed study of the ecology and population biology of indigenous Siberians. The ecological and nutritional component of our research is examining 1) how the Evenki biologically and behaviorally adapt to the marginal ecosystem in which they live (the northern boreal forest or *taiga*), and 2) how ongoing cultural and ecological changes in Siberia are influencing their health and nutrition.

Arctic populations are of particular interest to nutrition researchers because of the severe dietary and physiological constraints posed by harsh northern environments. In general, northern populations such as the Inuit derive a large proportion of their diet from animal foods. Despite these high meat and high fat diets, traditional[1] arctic populations tend to have low rates of cardiovascular disease (Draper, 1980). With acculturation[2] and the shift to a diet high in simple carbohydrates and

305

refined foods, Inuit populations have shown dramatic increases in body weight, fatness, and risk for diabetes and other chronic metabolic diseases. It therefore appears that northern populations may display distinct metabolic adaptations to diets high in animal protein and fat that make them susceptible to dietary changes associated with acculturation.

Previous research has also shown that northern populations have high resting (maintenance) energy expenditure, presumably in response to the severe cold stress of their environments (Itoh, 1980; Roberts, 1978). What remains unclear, however, is whether these elevated metabolic rates reflect a genetic adaptation, or a short term physiological adjustment. Consequently, research on Siberian groups such as the Evenki can allow us to address a number of important questions about human adaptation to arctic environments.

The Population

The Evenki population is among the largest of any indigenous Siberian group. Today, there are approximately 30,000 Evenki in Central Siberia, most of them (79.8%) continuing to live in isolated rural areas (Hannigan, 1991). The biological and cultural origins of the Evenki are unclear. However, it appears likely that they were once reindeer hunters who, over time, adopted a breeding and herding subsistence (Vasilevich, 1946). Until the 1930s, the Evenki remained socially organized into named, family lineages (or clans) that served as herding units. During Stalinist times, they were forcibly reorganized into cooperative settlements and herder groups called *brigades* (Forsyth, 1992; Uvachan, 1975). As a result of collectivization, the clan-based herding structure and much of the Evenki's indigenous culture was lost. Additionally, the reindeer herds were no longer held by families, but rather were placed into communal herds and controlled by the cooperatives. Collectivization also resulted in the construction of permanent settlements with their own health care and educational facilities.

Today, most of the Evenki speak Russian as their first language, with only the more elderly members of the population continuing to speak the native Tungusic language with any regularity. Evenki collectives are typically composed of 600–800 individuals who control about 10,000–15,000 head of reindeer. During the spring and summer, each collective divides into 8–10 herding brigades that disperse over the *taiga*, living in temporary tepee-like shelters known as *chums* (see Figure 1). In the *brigades*, the men are responsible for herding the reindeer and building fences to delimit pasture. Women, on the other hand, tend to remain in and around the encampment and spend much of their day preparing and cooking food, looking after the young children, and collecting wild plant foods such as blueberries and pine nuts. In the winter, entire collectives congregate in the central villages, which have wooden houses with access to heat and electricity. A small proportion of the population (especially the elderly and the very young) remains in the central villages year round.

Figure 1. Evenki Family and Russian Researcher (R.I. Sakernik) Standing in Front of a Traditional Dwelling Known as a *Chum*

Our research was conducted among Evenki settlements on and around the Stony Tunguska river. During July-September of 1991 and 1992, we collected data among the Evenki cooperative settlements of Surinda and Poligus, and eight of their associated herding *brigades* (see Figure 2). The Surinda and Poligus collectives are quite isolated within Central Siberia, lying in the central portion of the Evenki Autonomous Territory of Central Siberia (63° N latitude; 97° E longitude). We travelled into the collective villages by bush plane, and from there, were transported by helicopter into the herding brigades. Mean monthly temperatures range from a high of +15° C in July to a low of -32.5° C in January. According to 1991 census information, there are approximately 600 individuals in each of the Surinda and Poligus cooperatives (Irwin, n.d.).

Figure 2. Map Showing the Locations of the Evenki Villages of Surinda and Poligus in the Tunguska Region of Central Siberia

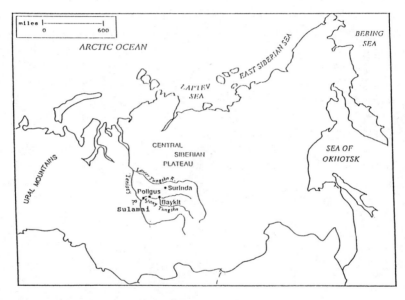

METHODS OF NUTRITIONAL ECOLOGY
Measuring Dietary Consumption

Data on dietary consumption are often difficult to obtain among anthropological populations. Having subjects keep their own diet records is obviously not feasible in non-literate societies. Consequently, quantification of food consumption in traditional populations most often involves direct measurement or recall techniques. Direct food weighing is the most accurate method for measuring dietary intake, but it is very time and labour intensive and often disruptive for the participating subjects (Gibson, 1990). With this approach, the researcher normally weighs and measures all ingredients of the meal while it is being prepared, as well as the individual portions during the meal itself.

More often, anthropological studies use daily or weekly recall questionnaires to quantify nutritional consumption. Dietary recalls are of limited accuracy for estimating dietary intakes at an individual level; however, they do appear to be effective for assessing mean group-level intakes (Quandt, 1987). By collecting multiple recalls on the same subject, more precise estimates of 'usual' dietary intake can be obtained.

Among the Evenki, we measured food consumption using standard 24-hour dietary recalls. Undergraduate biology students from the Russian Academy of Science were trained to administer the dietary recalls. The interviewers asked subjects about the types and amounts of food consumed during the previous day. From this dietary information, daily energy and macronutrient intakes were calculated by referring to standard food composition tables for central Asia compiled by the Food and Agriculture Organization of the United Nations (FAO, 1972). These tables present detailed data on the calorie and nutrient content of foods found in this region of the world.

Measuring Energy Expenditure

Activity patterns and energy expenditure are also difficult to quantify in anthropological groups. Traditional approaches for assessing energetics in the field frequently involve time allocation methods in which a subject's activity pattern is monitored either through direct observation or recall. Once an activity profile is obtained, caloric costs are assigned to each activity based on standard reference data (e.g., Durnin and Passmore, 1967; FAO/WHO/UNU, 1985), allowing for the calculation of daily energy expenditure. The direct observation approach is very burdensome, since it requires the researcher to follow a subject for an entire day. It is, therefore, quite time consuming for the researcher and may interfere with the subject's activity patterns. Recall techniques are also problematic since traditional human groups do not live their lives "by the clock" as we do in the industrialized world. Moreover, all time allocation approaches are of questionable accuracy because the caloric reference data may not be appropriate due to differences in body size or metabolic efficiency between the reference and study populations.

To address some of these problems, nutritional researchers have recently developed the use of heart-rate (HR) monitoring for measuring energy expenditure (Spurr and Reina, 1990; Livingstone et al., 1990). This technique uses the strong relationship between HR and oxygen consumption to quantify daily energy expenditure from a minute-by-minute HR profile. Relative to time allocation methods, the HR-monitoring technique is much less burdensome for the subjects and researcher, and based on recent validation studies, provides more accurate estimates of energy expenditure (Livingstone et al., 1990).

Our research among the Evenki was the first to apply the HR monitoring technique to a traditional subsistence-level population (Katzmarzyk, 1993). The first step of this technique involves simultaneously measuring HR (beats per minute) and energy expenditure (EE, in kcal per minute) for each subject under resting (i.e., lying, sitting, standing) and exercising conditions. Energy expenditure is determined through the use of the Douglas bag method. This technique requires the subject to breathe into a gas collection bag for a specified period of time (3 minutes for the resting positions, and 1 minute for the exercising levels). Once an expired air sample has been collected, its volume and oxygen concentration (% O_2) are measured. From this information, energy expenditure (kcal/min) can be calculated.[3]

After these data have been collected, an EE vs. HR relationship similar to the one shown in Figure 3a is constructed for each subject. In the second part of the protocol, the subject wears a portable HR monitor[4] for an entire waking day to collect minute-by-minute HRs (see Figure 3b for an example). These HR data are then converted into energetic equivalents using the HR vs. EE relationship for that particular subject.

In general, the daily HR monitoring method proved to be a feasible method for assessing activity patterns and energy expenditure in the Evenki. Wearing the HR monitor for an entire active day did not pose a problem for any of our subjects, and several even wore their monitors while sleeping. In a few cases, individuals accidentally turned off their monitors; therefore, we tried to periodically check up on subjects to make sure the monitors were still working. We also discovered that interference can be created if two people with monitors are close to each other. Consequently, it is generally wise not to have members of the same family wearing monitors on the same day.

When a subject returned with his/her monitor at the end of a day, the data were directly transferred to a laptop computer. The data transfer usually went smoothly, although there were several cold mornings when the laptop had to be "coaxed" into booting up! Subjects were also questioned about food consumption and activities over the course of the day. We found that graphically displaying a subject's HR profile greatly facilitated the activity recall, since it clearly identified the periods of high work intensity.

Figure 3. Components of the Flex-HR
Method For Assessing Energy Expenditure.
a) A Plot of Energy Expenditure vs. HR for a Single Subject

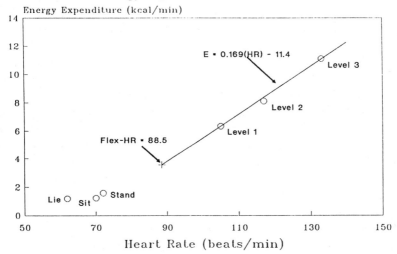

Subject #19

3. b) A Typical Minute-by-minute HR Profile for the Same Subject for a 4-hour Period. Data Derived from Katzmarzyk et al. (in press)

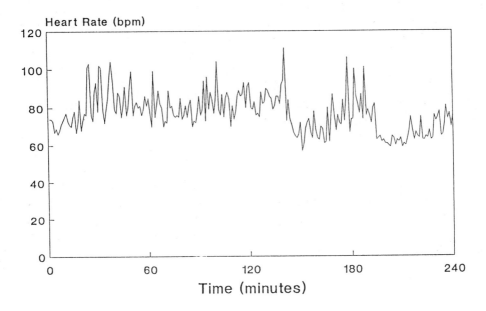

311

Growth and Nutritional Status

The long term balance between energy intake and expenditure is reflected in physical growth rates and achieved adult body size. Consequently, basic anthropometric measurements, such as height, weight, limb circumferences and fatfolds (skinfolds), can provide important information about overall nutritional status of a population. In using anthropometric dimensions to evaluate nutritional status, measurements are compared to reference standards derived from well-nourished populations of the developed world. Over the last decade, standards derived from large health surveys in the United States (the first and second National Health and Nutrition Examination Surveys [NHANES I and II]) have become the preferred criteria for assessing growth and nutritional status (see Hamill et al., 1979; Frisancho, 1990). These standards allow the researcher to assess whether a child is sufficiently small to indicate that his/her growth has been compromised by poor nutrition or disease. Comparisons to these norms are generally made through the use of percentiles. For anthropometric indices such as height-for-age and weight-for-age, individuals falling below the 3rd percentile are considered to be nutritionally "at risk". Low height-for-age, or "stunting", is thought to reflect chronic, mild-moderate nutritional stress. Low weight-for-age and weight-for-height (known as "wasting") are thought to reflect more severe, acute nutritional problems.

Among the Evenki, anthropometric measurements were taken on a sample of 478 individuals (247 males; 231 females) ranging in age from 1 month to 76 years. These measurements included: stature (centimeters [cm]), weight (kilograms [kg]), mid arm circumference (cm), and skinfold thicknesses on the mid arm (triceps) and back (subscapular) (millimeters [mm]). All subjects were measured in light clothing without shoes. Stature was measured 0.1 cm using a field anthropometer. Weight was determined to the nearest 0.2 kg using a hanging scale for children under 2 years, and a standing scale for all other subjects. Mid arm circumference was measured to the nearest 0.1 cm using plastic tape measures developed by Ross Laboratories.

From the above measurements, two additional indices were calculated: the body mass index (BMI) and upper arm muscle area (UMA). The BMI is a weight-for-height index that is frequently used as a measure of obesity. It is calculated as weight/height,[2] with weight being expressed in kg, and height in meters. In adults, BMI values between 20 and 25 kg/m^2 are considered optimal. Estimated UMA is an index of muscular development and is calculated from the arm circumference and triceps skinfold dimensions.[5]

Birth dates were obtained directly from each subject (or from their parent) before they were measured so that precise fractional ages could be calculated. Birth dates were validated against demographic records kept by the cooperatives. In cases of discrepancies, the information from the formal records was used.

DIETARY CONSUMPTION AND ENERGY BALANCE

Table 1 presents average anthropometric measures, dietary consumption and energy expenditure of the 36 Evenki adults (26 males, 10 females) who participated in the energy balance portion of the research. Overall, energy expenditure levels are high, especially in light of the Evenki's small body size. Total daily energy expenditure (TDEE) is significantly higher in men, averaging 2800–2900 kcal/day, as compared to 2000–2100 for women. When these values are expressed as a proportion of basal (minimum maintenance) energy requirements, this index of physical activity level (PAL) for Evenki is 1.80, placing them in the "highly active" category as defined by the World Health Organization's (1985) most recent protein and energy recommendations. Evenki women have an average PAL of 1.61, which places them in the "moderately active" category. By comparison, sedentary adults of the developed world typically have PALs of 1.3–1.4.

Despite their high energy demands, the Evenki appear to be in positive caloric balance during the late summer months. Energy consumption exceeds 3200 kcal/day in men, and is between 2000 and 2100 in women. These energy intake levels are comparable to those reported for Canadian Inuit populations (Draper, 1980).

Protein intakes are also quite high (see Table 1). Adult males and females consume 125 and 60 grams of protein per day, respectively, which are 237% and 134% of the predicted requirements from the most recent World Health Organization recommendations (FAO/WHO/UNU, 1985). Fat intakes, on the other hand, are relatively modest. Fat contributes only 18–19% of the Evenki's dietary energy, about 65 grams/day for men and 43 grams/day for women.

As for diet composition, animal products obtained from the reindeer, wild game and fish make up a substantial portion of the Evenki diet (about 30–35% of calories). Foraged plant foods such as wild blueberries and pine nuts contribute some 10% of energy intake, while the remainder of the diet is derived from non-local foods, such as rice, flour and sugar, that are brought in periodically by supply helicopter.

313

TABLE 1. Anthropometric dimensions, dietary consumption and energy expenditure among adult male and female Evenki herders

Measure	Males (n=26)		Females (n=10)	
	Mean	SD	Mean	SD
Age (years)	28.5	8.4	23.0*	6.1
Anthropometric Measures:				
Stature (cm)	160.1	4.8	150.5‡	4.3
Weight (kg)	59.9	7.6	52.2‡	4.0
BMI (kg/m^2)	23.4	2.9	23.0	1.4
Sum of Skinfolds[1] (mm)	29.8	11.9	55.9‡	15.2
Dietary Consumption:				
Energy (kcal/day)	3207	1315	2036†	813
Protein (g/day)	126	58	61‡	24
Fat (g/day)	65	50	43	27
Energy Expenditure:				
Total (kcal/day)	2846	679	2095‡	499
PAL[2] (TEE/BMR)	1.80	0.42	1.61	0.40
RMR (kcal/min)	1.66	0.38	1.24†	0.31
Dietary Adequacy:				
Energy[3]	1.19	0.57	1.00	0.42
Protein[4]	2.37	1.14	1.34‡	0.55

Male and female means are significantly different at: *$p < 0.05$; †$p < 0.01$; ‡$p < 0.001$.
1 Sum of triceps, biceps, subscapular and supra-iliac skinfolds.
2 PAL = Physical Activity Level
3 Adequacy = [Energy Intake]/[Energy Expenditure].
4 Adequacy = [Protein Intake]/[WHO Protein Requirement]

In addition to their high activity levels, elevated resting metabolic rates (RMR) also contribute to the high levels of total energy expenditure seen in the Evenki. Table 1 shows that RMRs for the Evenki average 1.66 kcal/min in males and 1.24 kcal/min in females. These values are 19%

above predicted levels for males and 7% above for females. Therefore, the Evenki are similar to other northern populations in displaying increased resting energy needs. Our data also suggest that this elevation is a proximate physiological response rather than a genetic adaptation, since Evenki living in the *brigades* (who are exposed to greater cold stress) show substantially higher RMRs than those living in the central villages.

The very large gender difference in energy expenditure appears to reflect current patterns of sexual division of labour within the Evenki. Under the present collectivized system, the Evenki are no longer nomadic, but rather tend to remain in a single encampment area for most of the spring and summer months. Also, with the transition away from clan-based herding parties, the current herding brigades function essentially as work groups in which the males are almost exclusively responsible for herding the reindeer and building fences to delimit pasture, while women are responsible for maintenance of the encampment. Consequently, daily activity budgets are much higher for males, who often walk 6–10 km/day in herding the reindeer.

PHYSICAL GROWTH AND NUTRITIONAL STATUS

The gender differences in daily energy expenditure appear to be reflected in differences in relative body size and fatness between Evenki men and women. These differences are shown in Table 2, which presents selected anthropometric measurements and their corresponding US percentile values for Evenki adults (ages 20 years and older). Evenki men and women are both quite diminutive in stature. Men are, on average, about 158 cm tall (about 5 ft. 2 in.), while women are about 147 cm (4 ft. 9 in.). Thus, Evenki men and women are equally short relative to their US counterparts, as both fall below the 3rd US percentile.

For body weight, Evenki women average 53.4 kg (118 lbs.), and approximate the 25th percentile relative to US women. Men, on the other hand, average 56.8 kg (125 lbs.) and achieve only the 5th percentile relative to their US peers. Therefore, in terms of weight, Evenki women are significantly closer to their US counterparts than Evenki men. In other words, Evenki women are *relatively heavier* than Evenki men.

This point is also evident when body weight is standardized for height using the BMI. Women have significantly higher BMIs than men (24.6 vs. 22.8 kg/m^2, Table 2). Average BMIs for Evenki women *exceed* the US 50th percentile, while those for men achieve the 20th percentile.

Women also display both absolutely and relatively higher levels of body fatness. Table 2 shows that the sum of the triceps and subscapular skinfolds for Evenki women is more than double that of Evenki men (38.8 mm vs. 16.6 mm). These values place males at the 15th US percentile, while women approximate the 40th percentile.

Muscularity, as estimated by the upper-arm muscle area (UMA) index, is absolutely greater in Evenki men (47.8 vs. 35.0 cm^2); however, compared to the US norms, women appear relatively better muscled, achieving the 25th percentile, while men are at the 5th percentile.

TABLE 2. Anthropometric Dimensions and Corresponding US Percentile Values for Adult Male and Female Evenki

	Actual Measures[1]		Percentiles[2]	
	Males	Females	Males	Females
Stature (cm)	157.8±6.8	147.2±4.8‡	< 3rd	< 3rd
Weight (kg)	56.8±7.4	53.4±10.7*	5th	25th‡
BMI (kg/m^2)	22.8±2.3	24.6±4.6†	20th	50th‡
Sum of Skinfolds[3] (mm)	16.6±6.1	38.8±14.8‡	15th	40th‡
UMA (cm^2)	47.8±7.3	35.0±7.4‡	5th	25th‡

Male and female means are significantly different at: *$p < 0.05$; †$p < 0.01$; ‡$p < 0.001$.
1   All measurements are presented as Mean±SD (n=118 males, 70 females)
2   Approximate placement of average Evenki values relative to US percentiles compiled by Frisancho (1990)
3   Sum of triceps and subscapular skinfolds.

Overall, these data indicate that Evenki adults are small bodied, and that women are relatively heavier and have greater nutritional reserves than men. Evenki women also show age-related increases in both weight and fatness, while men display slight declines with age. These differences in relative weight and body composition appear to be consistent with the marked differences in energy expenditure and activity patterns outlined previously. Furthermore, they suggest that social changes associated with collectivization have had a greater impact on the health and nutrition of women. While obesity is not currently a major problem for the Evenki, the risk of becoming obese is clearly greater in women than men[6].

Children
Despite their diminutive adult size, Evenki children are not

remarkably small early in life, but are characterized by slow growth in stature and body weight, especially during late childhood and adolescence. Figures 4a and 4b present statural growth profiles of Evenki males and females relative to the US 5th and 50th percentiles (from Frisancho, 1990). As seen in Figure 4a, Evenki boys track at around the 15th percentile until age 6–7 years when they drop below the 5th percentile where they will remain for through adulthood. A similar pattern is seen for females (Fig. 4b), with substantial declines relative to the normative data occurring between 8 and 10 years.

Body weight follows a growth pattern comparable to stature, as seen in Figures 5a and 5b. Male track at about the 15th percentile until 11–12 years when they decelerate to below the 5th percentile (Fig. 5a). Females, on the other hand, approximate the US norms more closely, falling between the 10th and 25th percentiles throughout most of their growth.

Evenki children and adolescents appear to have adequate energy reserves, as indicated by their skinfold measurements. Figures 6a and 6b present the sum of triceps and subscapular skinfolds for Evenki males and females relative to the US 5th and 50th percentiles. Among the males, although there is considerable variation in fatness over the growth period, the Evenki never fall below US 5th percentile. The same is true for females; however, they differ from their male counterparts in more closely approaching, or in some cases exceeding, the US median. As noted previously, this gender difference continues into adulthood as Evenki men fall at about the 15th percentile for sum of skinfolds, while Evenki women closely approximate the US median.

Comparison to Other Northern Populations

The Evenki also appear to be small relative to other indigenous northern populations. Figures 7a and 7b compare adult stature and body weight among the Evenki, the Canadian and Alaskan Inuit, and the Finnish Lapps. We find that both Evenki men and women are, on average, 5–7 cm shorter than their Canadian Inuit and Lapp counterparts, and some 8–9 cm shorter than their Alaskan Eskimo peers. The differences in weight are even more striking. Evenki males are an average of 17 kg lighter than Alaskan Inuit males, and about 7–9 kg lighter than the Canadian Inuit and Lapps. For women, the differences are relatively less, with there being about a 2–3 kg difference relative to the Lapps and Canadian Inuit and a 10 kg deficit in comparison to the Alaskan Inuit.

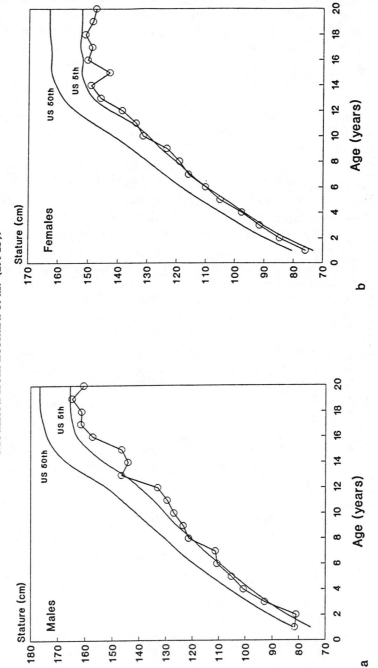

Figure 4. Comparison of Statural Growth in Evenki Males (a) and Females (b) to the US 5th and 50th Percentiles from Frisancho (1990). Modified from Leonard et al. (1994b).

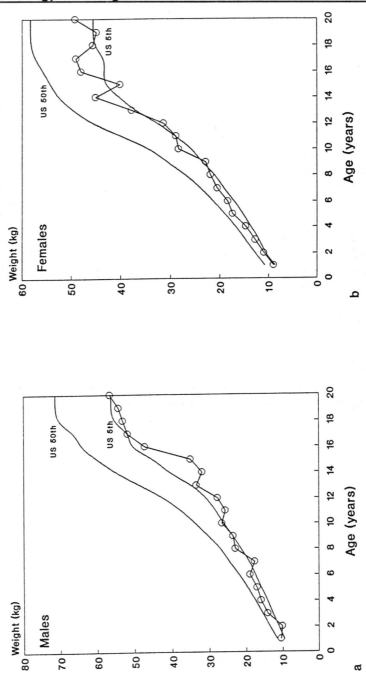

Figure 5. Comparison of Body Weight Growth in Evenki Males (a) and Females (b) to the US 5th and 50th Percentiles from Frisancho (1990). Modified from Leonard et al. (1994b).

Figure 6. Comparison of the Sum of Triceps and Subscapular Skinfolds in Evenki Males (a) and Females (b) to the US 5th and 50th Percentiles from Frisacho (1990).

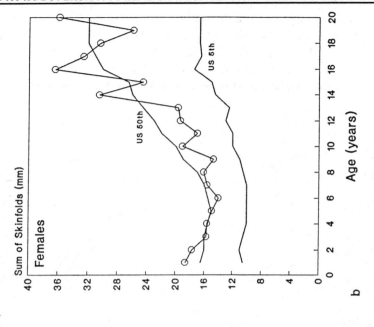

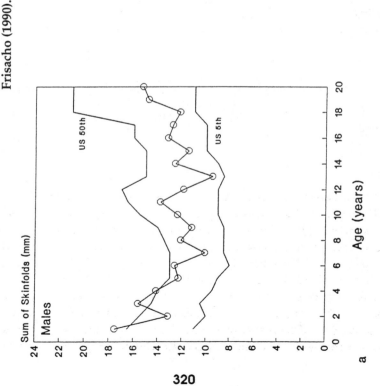

Figure 7. Comparison of Adult Stature and Body Weight in Males (a) and Females (b) of Four Indigenous High Latitude Populations: 1) the Evenki, 2) Alaskan Eskimo, 3) Foxe Basin (Canadian) Eskimo, and 4) Finnish Lapps. Comparative data were derived from Auger et al. (1980)

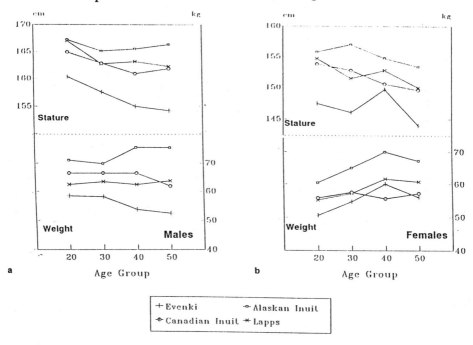

These comparisons suggest that the level of acculturation of the Evenki is substantially less than that of comparative European and North American arctic populations. While increases in stature and body weight (secular trends in growth) have been widely demonstrated among Inuit populations that have adopted a more "Westernized" lifestyle (see Rode and Shephard, 1984), the limited data on the Evenki suggest that there has been little or no secular trend in recent years. Data compiled by Franz Boas as part of the Jessup expedition at the turn of the century show height for Evenki men and women to be only 1–2 cm less than it is today (155.8 cm for men; 146.0 cm for women) (Comuzzie, 1993). Therefore, the

Evenki sharply differ from northern populations of Europe and North America in showing essentially no secular trend in stature over the last century.

In summary, small adult body size in the Evenki reflects slow rates of physical development, a pattern that characterizes many traditional human populations. Statural growth is compromised to a much greater extent than weight gain; this type of growth "stunting" is indicative of chronic mild to moderate nutritional stress, rather than severe and acute undernutrition. The diminutive size of the Evenki relative to other indigenous arctic groups, and the lack of a secular growth trend seem to reflect their relative isolation within Siberia. The increased risk of obesity among women, however, suggests that they are on the leading edge of health declines associated with ongoing cultural change.

DISCUSSION AND CONCLUSIONS

Recent advances in the methods of nutritional anthropology are now allowing human biologists to more effectively evaluate energy dynamics and nutritional status in anthropological populations. Our work among the Evenki indicates that daily HR-monitoring is an accurate method for measuring daily energy expenditure even in remote field settings. This approach has broad applications for the study of subsistence behaviour and energy balance among traditional populations.

For the Evenki, our data demonstrate that they remain isolated, and have maintained a relatively traditional lifestyle. Herding is a successful and sustainable lifeway for many Evenki, one that requires high levels of activity and energy expenditure. Despite the high energy demands of the herding lifestyle, dietary energy consumption during the late summer appears to meet or exceed expenditure levels. The large reindeer herds (15,000 head for a population of 600) serve as an important source of dietary energy, and also provide the income necessary for purchasing and importing non-local foods. Thus, the cooperative system, which provides for the sale and exchange of reindeer products, facilitates the flow of additional energy into this ecosystem.

The Evenki of Surinda and Poligus also show little evidence of the diminished health status seen among arctic populations of the New World. Body weight and skinfold data indicate that obesity is not currently a major problem. Cholesterol and triglyceride levels in the Evenki are extremely low, especially considering their high meat diet. Total cholesterol averages 140 mg/dl in men and 148 mg/dl in women, some 50 mg/dl less than the average for N. Americans and 70–80 mg/dl less than the most recent values for Inuit and Lapp populations (Leonard et al., 1994a). It appears that their herding lifestyle, which requires high levels of energy expenditure, largely explains why the Evenki do not show the "diseases of civilization" that are now so common among Inuit and other native Canadian populations.

Although the overall level of acculturation is low among the Evenki, social and cultural changes associated with collectivization have had a greater impact on the biology and health of Evenki women. Women are more likely to become obese and show strong age-related increases in both weight and fatness. We believe that these trends are attributable to changes in activity and reproductive patterns. As outlined previously, the markedly lower energy expenditure levels in Evenki women relative to men reflects a more sedentary lifestyle that appears to have resulted from changes associated with collectivization. Additionally, preliminary analyses of reproductive histories indicate that fertility rates and length of breast feeding have both been declining among Evenki women (Irwin, n.d.). These reproductive changes are important from a nutritional standpoint since they are associated with reduced energy requirements. Such gender differences in health and nutritional status have been documented in other populations (Baker et al., 1986; Darlu et al., 1984) and suggest that, in general, women may show greater health declines in the early stages of acculturation.

The slow growth of Evenki children and the resulting small adult size seems inconsistent with the high energy intakes observed from the dietary analyses. However, it is likely that data from the late summer present an overly favourable picture of annual energy availability for the Evenki. We expect that food availability will be more marginal during the winter when little food is brought in from the outside. Moreover, we expect that energy requirements are likely to be quite high during the winter due to high activity and elevated resting metabolism in response to the severe cold and short day lengths. Indeed, recent experimental studies have demonstrated increases in resting metabolism of 40% in response to conditions of arctic winter. Therefore, we hypothesize that a seasonal imbalance between energy demands and availability is responsible for shaping the slow growth and small adult size of the Evenki.

In the next phases of our work with the Evenki, we will examine seasonality in energy expenditure and energy balance since this will be critical for understanding the slow rates of growth observed in the Evenki. We also hope to expand our sample to Evenki living in more urban environments to evaluate the energetic and health effects associated with acculturation. Because of their wide geographic distribution within Siberia (from the isolated *taiga* to larger urban centres in Siberia), the Evenki encompass a much wider range of acculturation than arctic populations of the New World. Thus, the Evenki can provide a unique window on the evolution of chronic disease problems among high latitude populations.

ACKNOWLEDGEMENTS
We are extremely grateful to the participants in this study. Without their assistance and cooperation, this work would not have been possible. Special thanks go to Mary McNally, Mark Builder, Leslie James and Al Ross for assistance with data entry and library research. We also appreciate the comments and suggestions of Ann Herring, Leslie Chan, Marcia Robertson and an anonymous reviewer. This work was supported by grants from the Natural Sciences and Engineering Research Council (NSERC) of Canada (#OGP-0116785), the US National Science Foundation (BSR-99101571), and the US Man and the Biosphere Program.

ENDNOTES

1   By "traditional" we are referring to populations that are involved in the production of their own food, and who retain distinct aspects of their own indigenous lifestyle.

2   Acculturation refers to the adoption of aspects of culture and lifestyle from another group.

3   From the measurements of the volume and oxygen content of a sample of expired air, energy expenditure is calculated as follows:

$$E = 4.92(V)(20.93 - O^2)/100.$$

where:

E = energy expenditure (kcal/min)

V = volume of expired air (liters/min)

O^2 = percent (%) oxygen in the expired air

4.   The monitor consists of a transmitter, that is attached to a strap worn around the chest, and a receiver that is worn as a wristwatch.

5.   Estimated upper arm muscle area is calculated as:

$$UMA = (C - T\pi)^2/4\pi$$

where:

C = mid arm circumference (cm)

T = triceps skinfold (cm)

6.   For example, 6% of men have BMIs over 27 kg/m^2, as compared to 24% of women.

REFERENCES

Augur F, Jamison PL, Balslev-Jorgensen J, Lewin T, de Pexa JF, Skrobak-Kaczynski J (1980) Anthropometry of circumpolar populations. In: Milan FA (ed.): *The Biology of Circumpolar Populations*. Cambridge: Cambridge Univ. Press, pp. 213-255.

Baker PT, Hanna JM, and Baker TS (eds.) (1986) *The Changing Samoans: Behavior and Health in Transition*. Oxford: Oxford University Press.

Comuzzie AG (1993) Genomic, genetic and morphological variation in a sample of modern Evenki, and their relationship with other indigenous Siberian populations. Ph.D. thesis, University of Kansas.

Darlu P, Couilliot MF and Drupt F (1984) Ecological and cultural differences in the relationship between diet, obesity and serum lipid concentrations in a Polynesian population. *Ecol. Food Nutr.* 14:169-183.

de Garine I and Harrison GA (eds.) (1988) *Coping with Uncertainty in Food Supply*. Oxford: Oxford University Press.

Draper HH (1980) Nutrition. In Milan FA (ed.) *The Human Biology of Circumpolar Populations*. Cambridge: Cambridge University Press, pp. 257-284.

Durnin JVGA and Passmore R (1967) *Energy, Work and Leisure*. London: Heineman.

Eaton SB and Konner M (1985) Paleolithic nutrition: a consideration of its nature and current implications. *N. Engl. J. Med.* 312:283-289.

FAO (1972) *Food Composition Tables for use in East Asia*. Bethesda, MD: National Institutes of Health.

FAO/WHO/UNU (1985) *Energy and Protein Requirements*. Report of joint FAO/WHO/UNU expert consultation. WHO technical report series no. 724. Geneva: WHO.

Forsyth J (1992) *A history of the peoples of Siberia*. Cambridge: Cambridge University Press.

Frisancho AR (1990) *Anthropometric Standards for the Sssessment of Growth and Nutritional Status*. Ann Arbor: University of Michigan Press.

Gibson RS (1990) *Principles of Nutritional Assessment*. Oxford: Oxford University Press.

Gordon K (1987) Evolutionary perspectives on the human diet. In Johnston FE (ed.): *Nutritional Anthropology*. New York: Alan R. Liss, pp. 3-39.

Hamill PVV, Drizd TA, Johnson CL, Reed RB, Roche AF, and Moore WM (1979) Physical growth: National Center for Health Statistics percentiles. *Am. J. Clin. Nutr.* 32:607-629.

Hannigan J (1991) *Statistics on the Economic and Cultural Development of the northern Aboriginal People of the USSR* (for the period of 1980-1989). Ottawa: Bureau of Indian and Northern Affairs.

Huss-Ashmore R (ed.) (1988) *Coping with Seasonal Constraints*. MASCA Research Papers 5:1-141.

Huss-Ashmore R (1992) Introduction: Nutrition and diet as issues in human biology. *Am. J. Hum. Biol.* 4:155-157.

Irwin M (n.d.) Surinda age structure and fertility: Preliminary results. ms.

Itoh S (1980) Physiology of circumpolar populations. In Milan FA (ed.): *The Biology of Circumpolar Populations*. Cambridge: Cambridge University

Press, pp. 285-303.

Katzmarzyk PT (1993) The adaptive significance of energy expenditure among indigenous Siberian populations. M.Sc. Thesis. University of Guelph.

Katzmarzyk PT, Leonard, WR, MH Crawford and RI Sukernik (in press) Resting metabolic rate and daily energy expenditure among two indigenous Siberian populations *Am. J. Hum. Biol.*.

Leonard WR Crawford MH, Comuzzie AG and Sukernik RI (1994a) Correlates of low serum lipid levels among the Evenki herders of Siberia. *Am. J. Hum. Biol.* 6(3):333-350.

Leonard, WR, Katzmarzyk PT, AG Comuzzie, Crawford MH and Sukernik RI (1994b) Growth and nutritional status of the Evenki reindeer herders of Siberia. *Am. J. Hum. Biol.* 6(3):in press.

Leonard WR and Robertson ML (1992) Nutritional requirements and human evolution: A bioenergetics model. *Am. J. Hum. Biol.* 4:179-195.

Livingstone MBE, Prentice AM, Coward WA et al. (1990) Simultaneous measurement of free-living energy expenditure by the doubly labelled water method and heart rate monitoring. *Am. J. Clin. Nutr.* 52:59-65.

Martorell R (1985) Child growth retardation: A discussion of its causes and its relationship to health. In Blaxter K and Waterlow JC (eds.): *Nutritional Adaptation in Man*. London: John Libbey, pp. 13-30.

Quandt SA (1987) Methods for determining dietary intake. In Johnston FE (ed.): *Nutritional Anthropology*. New York: Alan R. Liss, pp. 67-84.

Roberts DF (1978) *Climate and Human Variability (2nd Ed.)*. Menlo Park, CA: Cummings Publishers.

Rode A and Shephard RJ (1984) Growth, development and acculturation — a ten year comparison of Canadian Inuit children. *Hum. Biol.* 56:217-230.

Spurr GB and JC Reina (1990) Estimation and validation of energy expenditure obtained by the minute-by-minute measurement of heart rate. In Schurch B and Scrimshaw NS (eds.) *Activity, Energy Expenditure and Energy Requirements of Infants And Children*. Lausanne, IDECG, Switzerland.

Uvachan VN (1975) *The Peoples of the North and their Road to Socialism*. Moscow: Progress Publishers.

Vasilevich, GM (1946) Drevneyshiye etnonimy Azii nazvaniya evenkiyskikh rodov. *Sovetskaya Etnografiya*, No. 4.

15

Lifestyle and Health of Voyageurs in the Canadian Fur Trade

Nancy C. Lovell and Ping Lai

The Seafort Burial Site is a Fur Trade Period cemetery located near the town of Rocky Mountain House, Alberta. Fourteen skeletons were recovered during salvage excavations between 1969 and 1971, and our recent analysis of the remains suggests that three males were voyageurs in the employ of the Hudson's Bay Company. Arthritis of the spine, shoulder girdle and elbow, herniated spinal discs, and robust muscle attachments provide evidence for carrying, lifting, and paddling or rowing. The presence of accessory joints in the sacroiliac region also may be due to weight-bearing stress. In addition, modifications to joints of the toes may be the result of habitually bending the toes backwards when kneeling in river canoes. This study demonstrates that the complementary nature of historical writings and osteobiographies can lead to a better understanding of the biological histories of people in their cultural setting.

INTRODUCTION

Osteobiography is an application of the analysis of human skeletal remains with the purpose of identifying a person's life history from their bones (Saul, 1976). Decades of research have provided physical anthropologists with the means for estimating how old a person was when he or she died, whether the person was male or female, approximately how tall they stood, and whether their health and nutritional status was good or bad. The age of children can be determined with some precision because their teeth develop and erupt in the jaws at fairly standard times, while indicators of age in adults tend to represent less exact degenerative morphological changes. The determination of the sex of a skeleton is most reliable with adult remains because sex differences in size and shape, expressed particularly in the pelvis due to its relationship to child-bearing, are firmly established only after puberty. Living stature may be estimated within several inches from a calculation based on the measured lengths of limb bones. Health status may be reconstructed by noting the presence of healed fractures, arthritis, the lingering effects of chronic infectious diseases or cancer, or defects in bones and teeth that are due to malnutrition. The teeth can tell much about diet, too, from the presence of cavities, abscesses, bone responses to gum disease and the wearing down of tooth surfaces.

One type of osteobiographic data of special interest to medical professionals, forensic anthropologists, and archaeologists is skeletal indicators of occupational stresses and other habitual activities. Clinical studies, for example, often address occupational hazards that predispose workers to degenerative joint disease and debilitating pain and disability, particularly in the lower back (Anderson and Duthie, 1963; Hagberg, 1984; Lawrence, 1955; Lee, et al., 1974). In contrast, forensic applications aim to document features of the skeleton that may relate to occupation or habitual recreational activity and which therefore may assist in the personal identification of human remains (Kennedy, 1983, 1989; Kennedy, et al., 1986). Similarly, attempts have been made to reconstruct aspects of ancient lifestyles, such as details of food preparation and habitual activity patterns, or to examine the physical effects of changes in lifestyle due to a shift in subsistence pattern (Bridges, 1991; Edynak, 1976; Jurmain, 1977, 1980; Merbs, 1983; Molleson, 1989; Pickering, 1979, 1984; Satinoff, 1972; Trinkaus, 1975; Ubelaker, 1979; Walker and Holliman, 1989). In this paper we employ clinical and forensic approaches to describe features of three archaeological skeletons that provide evidence for occupationally-related physical stress in the Canadian fur trade.

HISTORICAL CONTEXT

The skeletal remains are from the Seafort Burial Site, which is located approximately one and one-half miles southwest of the town of Rocky Mountain House, Alberta (Fig. 1). Five forts, or trading posts, were operated by the Hudson's Bay Company in the Rocky Mountain House region between 1799 and 1875, and a series of excavations have identified the

Figure 1. Map of the Rocky Mountain House Region, Showing the Location of the Seafort Burial Site and Nearby Hudson's Bay Forts

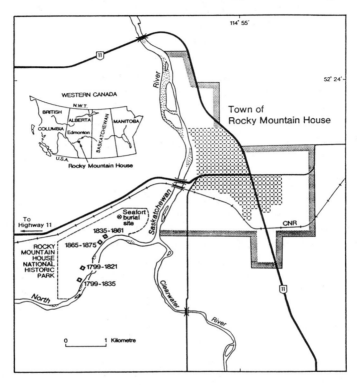

ruins of four of them along a two-kilometre stretch of the North Saskatchewan River (Dempsey, 1973; Noble, 1973; Skinner, 1971, 1972; Smyth, 1976; Steer, 1976; Steer and Rogers, 1976a, 1976b, 1978). The cemetery is only 750 m away from the nearest fort. The cemetery was discovered in 1969 during construction activities of Seafort Petroleum Limited, and the skeletal remains of 14 individuals (five adult males, one adult female, and eight subadults of unknown sex, ranging in age from newborn to approximately 14 years) were recovered during salvage excavations over a two-year period (Skinner, 1971). The age at death and the sex of each individual was determined by the application of standard osteological methods (Bass, 1989; Katz and Suchey, 1986; White, 1991). All but two skeletons are nearly complete and were found in their original position in the cemetery; one adult male and the adult female were represented by crania only, perhaps indicating secondary burial. All of the remains were well preserved although some were damaged by construction equipment. The Rocky Mountain House National Historic Park was established in 1979 to protect these sites.

Based on skeletal shape and size, which were assessed according to standardized quantitative and qualitative criteria (Bass, 1989), three of the four complete male skeletons in the sample are either Indian or Métis. The term "Métis" refers to those of mixed European and Indian ancestry; intermarriages and interbreeding were common during the Fur Trade Period (Brown, 1980; Parker, 1987). Although the inhabitants of the Rocky Mountain House area were primarily Indians, many European settlers also lived in the region, including the French who were already well settled in Quebec. Although a distinction between Indian and Métis cannot be made on the available skeletal evidence, we believe that the three men were Métis since they had adopted European cultural practices: they were buried in European clothing, were interred as primary inhumations in wooden coffins, and one of them was wearing a crucifix. Plains Indians who had not adopted European ways, by contrast, did not bury their dead immediately after death but placed their bodies on scaffolds, hills or cliffs, or in trees or abandoned tipis (Brink, 1988; Kidd, 1986; Wissler, 1911).

Indians were traded with, for furs and provisions, but were not often employed by the Hudson's Bay Company. The northwest plains groups, the Peigan, Sarsi, Blackfoot and Blood Indians traded at Rocky Mountain House, and a few Indians would live at or near the posts, employed as hunters. Two or three hunters, typically Cree or Stoney Indians, Métis, or Iroquois, were usually attached to Rocky Mountain House, but it was not until the late 19th century that Indians began to join the Hudson's Bay Company as part-time labourers (Dickason, 1992). The Company employed Métis as canoeists or labourers throughout western Canada (Brown, 1980; Howard, 1952; Parker, 1987; Williams, 1983). Men as young as 14 years of age often joined the Company as labourers and typically signed initial five-year contracts that often were renewed indefinitely (Brown, 1980).

In addition to the three Indian or Métis males, the complete skeleton of another male was recovered. This skeleton does not resemble the others in its shape or size, and it was buried with grave goods that suggest Scottish heritage (Skinner, 1971). Orkneymen, Orcadians, and Highland Scots were employed in a variety of occupations in the fur trade. This man may have been relatively new to fur trade service since he was a young adult (20–25 years of age) at the time of his death and he lacked obvious skeletal markers of occupational stress. We believe that he habitually smoked a pipe, however, because of the unusual wear on his teeth (Fig. 2), which is consistent with clenching a pipe stem in the mouth. Clay pipes have been recovered from many archaeological sites dating to this time period.

**Figure 2. Wear of the Teeth that Results from the
Habitual Clenching of a Pipe Stem**

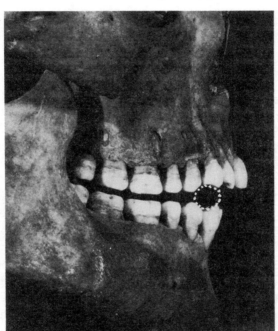

The deaths of officers of the Company were usually recorded, and since there is no known reference to any officers having died at Rocky Mountain House we have concluded that none of the Seafort skeletons represent deceased officers. We have been unable to identify any of these four men by name. Labourers at the forts were infrequently mentioned in Company records, and since the cause of death of these men is not apparent in their skeletal remains we do not know how they died. We speculate that acute infectious disease, such as the smallpox epidemic of 1837–38 or the measles epidemic of 1865, or repeated food shortages, especially in later years with the decline of buffalo herds and scarcity of other game, may have been responsible for one or more of these deaths. Other causes of death, however, such as misadventure or interpersonal violence, cannot be ruled out.

At the time the Seafort sites were occupied, the governor and London committee of the Hudson's Bay Company dominated fur trade society, followed by the chief factors, other officers and clerks, tradesmen, and labourers (Hamilton, 1985). Officers were mostly European or of European descent, predominantly English or Scottish, while labourers were variously Indian, Métis, French Canadian, or European. The number of employees at Rocky Mountain House was usually 12 to 18 men, and although the wives and families of the men often travelled with them in the yearly trading cycle, Company policy discouraged traders from having families at posts and hence the ratio of men to women at Rocky Mountain House was approximately 3:1 (Smyth, 1978:2). By the mid-19th century, most fur trade wives were Métis women, the daughters of earlier unions between traders and Indian women (Brown, 1980; Van Kirk, 1980). Regrettably, we were unable to reconstruct the health status of fur trade period women since their skeletal remains have not been recovered. Indian and Métis women may have been given traditional, non-European style burial outside the cemetery since they were not encouraged to live at the post, but the lack of female skeletons is not unusual given the male to female ratio at Rocky Mountain House and may be due simply to the small size of our sample. A small sample may not adequately represent the population from which it came, particularly if the cemetery was incompletely excavated, as may be the case with this site. The subadults recovered from the Seafort cemetery were probably children of the men and women who lived at the fort, since they were given European style burials.

SKELETAL INDICATORS OF PHYSICAL STRESS

The skeletons of the Indian or Métis males exhibit a variety of indicators of physical stress and are described in detail here. Figure 3 illustrates the bones of the human skeleton to facilitate understanding of the descriptions that follow. Two of these three males were about 35 to 45 years of age at their time of death, while the third was 30 to 40 years old. Arthritic lipping around the intervertebral discs is prevalent, affecting one-third of cervical and thoracic vertebrae, and two-thirds of lumbar vertebrae. This lipping is similarly common around the posterior cartilaginous joints, where it is often accompanied by localized 'pitting' destruction of the joint surface. Eburnation, a polished appearance that results from bone rubbing on bone after the cartilage has been worn away, is seen in two males and affects both cervical and thoracic vertebrae. New bone growth also occurs at the junction of the vertebrae with the ribs in one individual.

Figure 3. Elements of the Human Skeleton

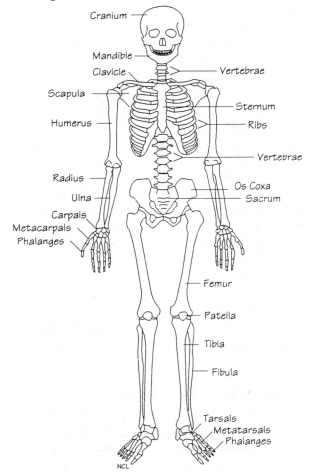

Herniated intervertebral discs (Fig. 4) typically result from torsional and compressional injuries through the sudden application of loading stresses (Bullough and Boachie-Adjei, 1988), and evidence of these is found in all three males, affecting 22% of observable thoracic vertebrae

and 47% of observable vertebrae in the lower back. Other evidence of rup-
tured discs is seen on two vertebrae of the neck in one of these men. A
final indicator of vertebral loading stresses is the compression of two vertebrae in one man, with no evidence of a predisposing pathological condition, such as the poor bone mineralization that is associated with the disease called osteoporosis, that could have weakened the bone.

**Figure 4. Evidence for Herniated Discs on the
Bodies of Thoracic Vertebrae**

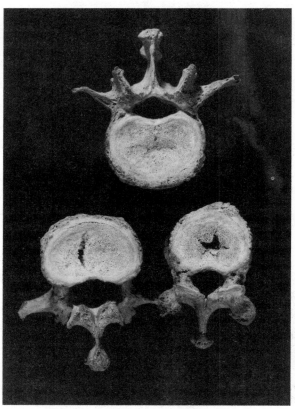

Although the most obvious bony changes affect the spine, arthritic
involvement is also found in the shoulder, elbow, hip, knee and ankle
joints. All three men display arthritis at their shoulder and elbow joints.
Lipping of the hip joint is observed in two males, and is quite severe in
one. Arthritis is also prevalent at the knee.

Figure 5. Pronounced Attachment for Platysma on the Inferior-Anterior Mandibular Margin, and for Masseter on the Gonial Angle

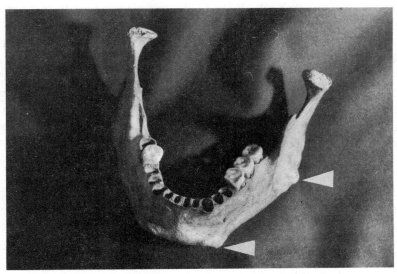

Figure 6. Accessory Articular Facets on the First Metatarsals

The three males also display extreme skeletal robusticity and bony growths on the tendinous insertions of muscles on the clavicle, sternum and limb bones. Most of the body's movements are generated through the skeletal lever system, in which muscles contract to produce power at their point of attachment on a bone in order to move another part of the body across a joint, which serves as a fulcrum. Thus, strenuous muscle activity can lead to a bony reaction at the point where the muscle attaches. The humeri in all three males display new bone formation at the insertions for muscles that control movements of the shoulder joint (i.e., Deltoid, Teres major, Pectoralis major and Latissimus dorsi). Similarly, there is pronounced robusticity at the origins of the muscles that control flexion and extension at the elbow (Triceps brachii, Anconeus, and Brachioradialis). The radii and ulnae in two males show marked attachments for the insertions of muscles that rotate the forearm, and the attachments for muscles that flex the fingers are also exaggerated. The leg bones of all three males are similarly robust and display pronounced attachment areas for the muscles of the calf, buttocks, and hamstrings.

Another likely indicator of physical stress is the ossification of ligaments that hold bones together at joints; the ossification occurs in response to stress or strain that threatens to separate the bones. This evidence of microtrauma can be seen in one individual where the spinous ligament, which joins the vertebrae along the back in the midline, has ossified in the lower region.

Only two of these males have mandibles that were not damaged postmortem, but both exhibit pronounced squaring of the chin as well as an outward flaring of the bone's posterior angle (Fig. 5), features that are likely due to stresses caused by muscle actions.

Accessory joint surfaces or extensions of joints were observed on several skeletal elements. Two males exhibit accessory joints in the sacroiliac region of the lower back (the sacrum of the third man was not recovered in excavation), while all three males display enlargement of toe joints (Fig. 6).

RECONSTRUCTING LIFESTYLE AND HEALTH

Debate over the reliability of expressions of osteoarthritis and hyperdevelopment of muscle attachment areas for indicating specific occupations or habitual activities has emerged in recent years. Jurmain (1990) has cautioned that the correlation of specific physical stressors with skeletal characteristics is virtually impossible for prehistoric groups and may not be possible even for people for which historical records and ethnographic analogy are available. Cohen (1989) was unable to make even broad distinctions between subsistence patterns when reviewing the published evidence for arthritis in hunter-gatherers and agriculturalists. Clinical investigations similarly have provided conflicting evidence for relating particular skeletal features to specific activities. Some skeletal samples are able to overcome these problems to a certain extent, however, by virtue of good skeletal preservation, an established time frame, and documented cultural associations and physical activities. The combined features of arthritis, muscle origin robusticity and accessory joint surfaces described above appear to reflect a lifestyle that involved habitual physical stress, and we believe that the pattern of these features in this skeletal sample results specifically from the occupation of *voyageur* [1] in the Fur Trade. *Voyageurs* engaged in manual labour that required both endurance and physical strength (Howard, 1952). The transportation of furs and provisions as well as of officers of the Company was by canoes and boats on swift-flowing rivers. Messages and visiting dignitaries were transported in lightweight "express" canoes made of birch bark, which could be paddled rapidly by the *voyageurs*, usually four to a boat. Prior to 1821, furs and provisions were transported by freight canoes, also of birch bark construction but much larger. The *Canot du Nord* of the rivers of the Plains was about 24 ft. long and 4 ft. broad at its widest point and tapered fore and aft, with a capacity of between five and eight men and one to two tonnes of provisions (Newman, 1987; Parker, 1987). *Voyageurs* paddled at a steady pace of about 40 to 50 strokes per minute, covering up to six miles in an hour, and journeys for these men involved 17 or 18 hours, with only six or seven hours of rest in a day (Bryce, 1902; Newman, 1987).

After the amalgamation of the North West Company and the Hudson's Bay Company in western Canada in 1821, the birch bark freight canoes were largely replaced by "York" boats, which had been introduced earlier in eastern Canada. These wooden boats were large, heavy, and originally designed for lake travel, but carried more freight and were less expensive than the boats made of bark (Innis, 1956; Newman, 1987). The two types of boats required different styles of maneuvering, since although the birch bark canoes could be carried on overland excursions to bypass hazardous waterways (*portages*), the York boats were usually pushed or towed over pre-cleared paths of logs, or were towed through the rapids themselves. As well, the larger boats were rowed instead of paddled.

In addition to the physical stresses associated with paddling canoes or rowing York boats, the *portages* required that men carry packs of provisions or merchandise on their backs (Ballantyne, 1859; Bryce, 1902; Parker, 1987; Newman, 1987). Each pack, or *pièce*, of goods weighed about 45 to 50 kgs, and was slung onto a man's back with a belt-like tumpline looped around his forehead. The average load on longer *portages* was two packs, and usually more on shorter ones. This task often turned competitive and men would carry three or four packs at a time, jogging along the portage trail (Newman, 1987).

Muscle origin robusticity and new bone formation at ligament attachments of the arms and axial skeletons, accompanied by arthritis at the elbow and shoulder joints, provide evidence for carrying, lifting, and paddling. The marked muscle attachments on the ulnae for example, can be interpreted as resulting from the habitual twisting of the forearm and hand that occurs when rowing or paddling. As well, the pronounced attachments for flexor muscles on the finger bones may be due to grasping, against resistance, a paddle or oar for hours at a time and days on end. As well, the marked muscle attachments on the leg bones may reflect the stresses of jogging along the portage trail, often up and down steep inclines, while carrying a canoe or packs of goods. Further, the squaring of the jaw may be less a secondary sex characteristic in these men than the result of facial tension due to tumpline force; the affected area of the mandible is the insertion area for the muscle Platysma, which can be seen as "cords" in the neck when the jaw is tensed or thrust forward. The pronounced attachments of the Masseter muscle on the angle of the mandible may similarly result from jaw tension.

Although it is not uncommon for some arthritic changes to appear in young and middle-aged adults, we believe that the nature and prevalence of the degenerative lesions displayed by these males, particularly when viewed in the context of other skeletal markers, are attributable to more than simple aging processes. Although the Seafort sample size is so small that any comparison with frequencies or severities of similar conditions found in other studies is problematic, it is worth noting that the patterns of arthritis displayed in the Seafort males are not inconsistent with those found in the Sadlermuit Eskimo and attributed to habitual paddling of kayaks or rowing of umiaks. Further, the patterns of degenerative changes in the spines of the Seafort males echo those thought to result from tumpline use and the carrying of heavy loads in the Eskimo (Merbs, 1983). As well, the new bone formation at ligament attachments in the shoulder girdle of one male and the bone defects at the same site in another closely resemble lesions described by Stirland (1991) among 16th-century sailors of the ship the *Mary Rose* and attributed to the intense mechanical stresses associated with their working environment. Bone defects such as these also have been found in a skeletal sample of soldiers who fought and died in the British-American War of 1812 and who were documented to have engaged in a variety of activities that required repeated and pronounced muscular exertion (Owsley, et al., 1991). The presence of accessory sacroiliac joints in two males also may be stress-related, since several studies have found a relationship between these and load-carrying on the back (reviewed by Trotter, 1964).

Finally, the enlargement of joint surfaces on the toes may also indicate occupational stress since habitual kneeling can cause the toes to be bent back severely, in what is called hyperdorsiflexion. This condition has been described by Ubelaker (1979) for a habitual resting posture of prehistoric Ecuadorians and by Molleson (1989) for Neolithic agriculturalists in Syria who kneeled while grinding grain. In the Seafort males, the activity that involved kneeling was probably river canoeing, which requires that the individual kneel in order to keep the centre of gravity low in the canoe to maintain balance in turbulent water (Newman, 1987). Indian canoeists, for example, were observed to sit on their heels while paddling (Glover, 1958). As is clear from many artists' depictions of the early Fur Trade canoeists (e.g. Hopkins, National Archives of Canada C-2774 and C-13585), a bowsman stood in the bow of the canoe to guide it, a steersman sat or stood in the stern, and the rest of the crew knelt on one or both knees, usually two abreast, in the middle (Innis, 1956; Newman, 1987; Parker, 1987).

CONCLUSIONS

Although caution must be exercised when attributing causation to joint changes and other skeletal modifications, the alterations to the skeleton that are displayed by the three Indian or Métis males in this sample are consistent with the habitual lifting, carrying, and paddling or rowing performed by *voyageurs*. Hyperdevelopment of muscle and ligament attachments in the trunk and limbs may indicate repeated strenuous activity; more diverse, prevalent, and severe joint changes than perhaps would be predicted for men of this age suggest weight-bearing functional stress; and accessory joint surfaces reflect eccentric joint action beyond the normal range of motion.

Although the Seafort skeletal sample is small, it meets the criteria for a study of activity-induced pathology since there are a limited number of known, specialized activities involved, skeletal preservation is good, the time span to which the remains are attributed is narrow, and the cultural and genetic associations are reasonably well documented. Although archaeological data and historical documents have provided a relatively comprehensive picture of aspects of lifestyle in the fur trade, the examination of the effects of occupationally-related physical stresses on the skeleton has not previously been the focus of study. This reconstruction of the lives of these men of the Fur Trade has examined their cultural and social associations and has provided new information on the physical stresses of Fur Trade life. Through an interdisciplinary investigation incorporating historical, archaeological and osteological data, we have augmented the limited documentary evidence for health and living conditions during the Fur Trade period in western Canada.

ACKNOWLEDGEMENTS

We thank Kenneth A. R. Kennedy and Marcella Sorg for helpful comments on the markers of occupational stress, and John Foster and Heinz Pyszczyk for critiques of our discussion of the Fur Trade in an earlier version of this manuscript. Arne Carlson kindly provided us with several helpful references; interested readers may wish to consult his analysis of environmental and cultural sources of lead at Rocky Mountain House and the implications of lead ingestion and toxicity for health at the trading post (Carlson, 1993).

ENDNOTES

1   The term actually refers to canoeists in the St. Lawrence/Great Lakes fur trade circa 1650-1700, who shared in the profits of the fur trading companies. After 1700, the term *engagés* is used, which refers to wage employees. *Voyageur* survived as an honorific term of address for *engagés*, and it appears that the latter preferred it (John Foster, pers. comm.).

REFERENCES

Anderson JAD and Duthie JJR (1963) Rheumatic complaints in dockyard workers. *Ann. Rheum. Dis.* 22:401-409.

Ballantyne RM (1859) *Hudson's Bay; or Everyday Life in the Wilds of North America.* Boston: Phillips, Sampson

Bass W (1989) *Human Osteology*, 3rd Edition. Columbia: Missouri Archaeological Society.

Bridges PS (1991) Degenerative joint disease in hunter-gatherers and agricultural-ists from the southeastern United States. *Amer. J. Phys. Anthropol.* 85:379-391.

Brink J (1988) The Highwood River site: A Pelican Lake phase burial from the Alberta Plains. *Can. J. Archaeol.* 12:109-136.

Brown J (1980) *Strangers in Blood.* Vancouver: University of British Columbia Press.

Bryce G (1902) *The Remarkable History of the Hudson's Bay Company.* London: Sampson Low Marston and Company.

Bullough PG, and Boachie-Adjei, O (1988) *Atlas of Spinal Disease.* New York: Gower Medical Publishing.

Carlson AK (1993) Lead analysis of human skeletons from the 19th century Seafort Burial Site, Alberta. Edmonton: University of Alberta [Unpublished M.A. thesis, Department of Anthropology]

Cohen MN (1989) *Health and the Rise of Civilization.* New Haven: Yale University Press.

Dempsey HA (1973) A history of Rocky Mountain House. Occasional Papers in Archaeology and History No. 6. Ottawa: National Historic Sites Service, pp 7-53.

Dickason OP (1992) *Canada's First Nations: A History of Founding Peoples from the Earliest Times.* Toronto: McClelland and Stewart.

Edynak GJ (1976) Life-styles from skeletal material: a Medieval Yugoslav example. In E Giles and JS Friedlander (eds.): *The Measures of Man.* Cambridge: Peabody Museum Press, pp 408-432.

Glover R (ed.) (1958) *A Journey from Prince of Wales's Fort in Hudson's Bay to the Northern Ocean, 1769, 1770, 1771, 1772.* By Samuel Hearne. Toronto: Macmillan Company of Canada Limited.

Hagberg M (1984) Occupational musculoskeletal stress and disorders of the neck and shoulder: a review of possible pathophysiology. *Int. Arch. Occ. Environ. Health* 53:269-278.

Hamilton JS (1985) The Social organization of the Hudson's Bay Company, Formal and informal social relations in the context of the inland fur trade. Edmonton: University of Alberta [Unpublished M.A. Thesis, Department of Anthropology]

Howard JK (1952) *Strange Empire: A Narrative of the Northwest.* New York: Morrow.

Innis HA (1956) *The Fur Trade in Canada.* Toronto: University of Toronto Press.

Jurmain RD (1977) Stress and the etiology of osteoarthritis. *Amer. J. Phys. Anthropol.* 46:353-366.

Jurmain RD (1980) The pattern of involvement of appendicular degenerative joint disease. *Amer. J.Phys. Anthropol.* 53:143-150

Jurmain RD (1990) Paleoepidemiology of a central California prehistoric popula-tion from CA-ALA-329: II. Degenerative Disease. *Amer. J. Phys. Anthropol.* 83:83-94.

Katz D, and Suchey JM (1986) Age determination of the male Os Pubis. *Amer. J.Phys. Anthropol.* 69:427-435.

Kennedy KAR (1983) Morphological variations in ulnar Supinator crests and fos-sae as identifying markers of occupational stress. *J. For. Sci.* 28:871-876.

Kennedy KAR (1989) Skeletal markers of occupational stress. In MY Iscan and KAR Kennedy (eds.): *Reconstruction of Life from the Skeleton.* New York: Alan R. Liss, pp 129-160.

Kennedy KAR, Plummer J, and Chiment J (1986) Identification of the eminent dead: Penpi, a scribe of ancient Egypt. In K Reichs (ed.): *Forensic Osteology: The Recovery and Analysis of Unknown Skeletal Remains.* Springfield: Charles C. Thomas, pp 290-307.

Kidd KE (1986) *Blackfoot Ethnography. Archaeological Survey of Alberta* Manuscript Series No.8. Edmonton: Alberta Culture.

Lawrence JS (1955) Rheumatism in coal miners Part III: Occupational factors. *Brit. J. Indus. Med.* 12:249-261.

Lee P, Rooney PJ, Sturrock RD, Kennedy AC, and Dick WC (1974) The etiology and pathogenesis of osteoarthrosis: a review. *Sem. Arthritis Rheum.* 3:189-218.

Merbs CF (1983) *Patterns of Activity-Induced Pathology in a Canadian Inuit Population.* Ottawa: National Museums of Canada.

Molleson T (1989) Seed preparation in the Mesolithic: the osteological evidence. *Antiquity* 63:356-62.

Newman PC (1987) *Caesars of the Wilderness.* Volume II of Company of Adventurers. Markham, Ont.: Penguin Viking.

Noble WC (1973) The excavation and historical identification of Rocky Mountain House. Occasional Papers in Archaeology and History No. 6. Ottawa: National Historic Sites Service, pp 54-163.

Owsley D, Mann RW, and Murphy SP (1991) Injuries, surgical care and disease. In S Pfeiffer and RF Williamson (eds.): *Snake Hill: An Investigation of a Military Cemetery from the War of 1812.* Toronto: Dundurn Press, pp 198-226.

Parker J (1987) *Emporium of the North: Fort Chipewyan and the Fur Trade to 1835.* Alberta Culture and Multiculturalism/Canadian Plains Research Centre.

Pickering RB (1979) Hunter-gatherer/agriculturalist arthritic patterns: a preliminary investigation. *Henry Ford Hosp. Med. J.* 27:50-53.

Pickering RB (1984) An examination of patterns of arthritis in Middle Woodland, Late Woodland, and Mississippian skeletal series from the Lower Illinois Valley. PhD dissertation, Department of Anthropology, Northwestern University.

Satinoff M (1972) Study of the squatting facets of the talus and tibia in ancient Egyptians. *J. Human Evol.* 1:209-212.

Saul FP (1976) Osteobiography: Life history recorded in bone. In E Giles and JS Friedlander (eds.): *The Measures of Man.* Cambridge: Peabody Museum Press, pp 372-382.

Skinner MF (1971) Seafort Burial Site (FcPr100), Rocky Mountain House, Alberta. Edmonton: University of Alberta [Unpublished Honors Paper, Department of Anthropology]

Skinner MF (1972) The Seafort Burial Site (FcPr100), Rocky Mountain House (1835-1861): Life and death during the Fur Trade. *West. Can. J. Anthropol.* 3:126-143.

Smyth D (1976) The Fur Trade Posts at Rocky Mountain House. Manuscript

Report Series No. 197. Ottawa: Parks Canada.

Smyth D (1978) Provisioning of a Fur Trade Post: The Case of Rocky Mountain House. Research Bulletin No. 99. Ottawa: Parks Canada.

Steer DN (1976) Archaeological Survey Methods Applied at Rocky Mountain House National Historic Park, 1975 and 1976. Manuscript Report Series No. 194. Ottawa: Parks Canada.

Steer DN, and Rogers, HJ (1976a) Archaeological Research at Rocky Mountain House, 1976. Research Bulletin/Bulletin de Recherches, No. 41. Ottawa: Parks Canada.

Steer DN, and Rogers HJ (1976b) 1975 Archaeological Excavations at Rocky Mountain House National Historic Park. Manuscript Report Series No. 180. Ottawa: Parks Canada.

Steer DN, and Rogers HJ (1978) Archaeological Research at Rocky Mountain House, 1977. Research Bulletin/Bulletin de Recherches, No. 80. Ottawa: Parks Canada.

Stirland A (1991) Diagnosis of occupationally-related paleopathology: Can it be done? In DJ Ortner and AC Aufderheide (eds.): *Human Paleopathology*. Washington: Smithsonian Institution Press, pp 40-47.

Trinkaus E (1975) Squatting among the Neandertals: a problem in the behavioral interpretation of skeletal morphology. *J. Archaeol. Sci.* 2:327-351.

Trotter M (1964) Accessory sacroiliac articulations in East African skeletons. *Amer. J. Phys. Anthropol.* 22:137-142.

Ubelaker DH (1979) Skeletal evidence of kneeling in prehistoric Ecuador. *Amer. J. Phys. Anthropol.* 51:679-686.

Van Kirk S (1980) *Many Tender Ties, Women in Fur-Trade Society in Western Canada 1670-1870*. Winnipeg: Watson and Dwyer Publishing Ltd.

Walker PL, and Holliman SE (1989) Changes in osteoarthritis associated with the development of a maritime economy among southern California Indians. *Int. J. Anthropol.* 4:171-183.

White TD (1991) *Human Osteology*. Orlando: Academic Press.

Williams G (1983) The Hudson's Bay Company and the fur trade: 1670-1870. *The Beaver* Autumn:4-86.

Wissler C (1911) Social organization and ritualistic ceremonies of the Blackfoot Indians. *Anthropol. Pap. Amer. Mus. Nat. Hist.* 7:3-64.

16

Occupational Hazards in 19th-Century Upper Canada

Susan B. Jimenez

Indicators of traumatic injuries in human skeletal remains can provide information about occupational hazards within a specific time period, and, along with evidence of infectious disease, can be used to help reconstruct the health status of a community.

An analysis of 250 adults, removed from an archaeological excavation of cemetery interments associated with St. Thomas' Anglican Church in Belleville, Ontario was examined for traumatic injuries. The interments, dating from 1820 to 1874, reflect some of the occupational hazards associated with the pioneer lifestyle of early United Empire Loyalists that settled in this, and other regions, of Upper Canada.

Traumatic injuries are common within the sample, and differences between males and females are evident in terms of healed fractures and traumatic injuries in general. The data were compared to historical documentation from the period, since inferences about mortality rates and causes of death among groups of individuals are often made on the basis of observations of the skeletal material alone. The results of the study suggest that a combination of both historical documentation and skeletal analysis provides a comprehensive picture of the occupational hazards of nineteenth-century Upper Canada.

INTRODUCTION

There are relatively few opportunities for the osteologist to examine the skeletal remains from historic populations of the eighteenth and nineteenth centuries, and it is rare to be able to analyse such skeletal material within the context of archival documentation. Yet, we frequently make inferences about mortality rates and the disease stresses on a population on the basis of observations from skeletal remains alone. If one is trying to reconstruct the health status of an earlier group of individuals, the picture that results from skeletal analysis by itself may be incomplete. This is due to the fact that many fatal infectious diseases do not leave any evidence of their existence in bone tissue. Since acute infectious diseases played a role among populations of early pioneers of nineteenth-century Upper Canada, it is helpful to be able to compare historical records, newspaper accounts, parish documents, etc., to the actual skeletal material in order to round out the picture of the health status of a community.

Traumatic injuries are also an important aspect of skeletal studies, since they reflect both occupational and personal events that occur during the lifetime of the individual. Within the context of nineteenth-century Ontario, occupational hazards reflect any kind of injury sustained through the daily activities of pioneer existence. By analysing fractures, dislocations, etc. it is possible to reconstruct the overall picture of health and the stresses endured by nineteenth-century settlers and their descendants in Upper Canada.

THE ST. THOMAS' ANGLICAN CHURCH SKELETAL SAMPLE

A unique opportunity to study a pioneer population from Upper Canada was provided when, in 1989, skeletal remains associated with St. Thomas' Anglican Church cemetery in Belleville, Ontario were removed. Northeastern Archaeological Associates were contracted to conduct the archaeological excavation of the burials in order to facilitate an expansion to the church. The cemetery, in use from 1820 to 1874, represents United Empire Loyalists who settled in this region of Upper Canada, as well as immigrants from Scotland, England, and Ireland. I was interested in examining the 250 adult skeletons (146 males/104 females) in this sample for evidence of infectious disease and traumatic injuries in order to reconstruct the health status of the population, comparing it to historical accounts of the time.

The collection of skeletal remains and associated parish records have been the focus of numerous studies, including testing techniques used in sex determination (Rogers, 1991; Gibbs, 1991), age estimations (Rogers,

1991; Saunders et al., 1993; Saunders et al., 1992), growth studies (Saunders, 1992) and paleodemography (structure of the community by age and sex) (Saunders and Herring, 1991; Herring, Saunders and Boyce, 1994; McKillop et al., 1989). Other analyses focusing on dental disease, skeletal variation and joint disease have also been undertaken. The information gleaned from these analyses has enabled us to piece together a comprehensive picture of nineteenth century pioneer life in Ontario.

During the mid-nineteenth-century, immigration into both Upper and Lower Canada reached a peak, most of it the result of scores of people trying to escape the Irish potato famine of the 1840s (Westwood, 1980). At this time typhoid fever, smallpox, tuberculosis and cholera were prevalent in European communities. It takes no stretch of the imagination to see the implications for disease transmission to this side of the Atlantic! Ships carrying infected passengers arrived in Lower Canada in large numbers, and since quarantine measures at the time were often inadequate, infections spread quickly as disembarking passengers travelled to points throughout Lower and Upper Canada. Within the St. Thomas' sample, evidence of active and healed infections was found, including tuberculosis, syphilis, and non-specific infections. Although infectious diseases certainly played a role in the lives of these Loyalist pioneers, evidence of traumatic injuries are more frequently found within the sample. Healed fractures and perimortem (occurring at or around the time of death) fractures are present in both males and females in all age groups. Dislocations and spondylolysis (separation of the neural arch from the vertebral body) are observed within the sample, and there are several cases of pseudarthroses (false joint) formation. While some of these injuries can be attributed to simple accidents such as falls, many are occupation induced traumas. As Steinbock (1976) has noted, the cases of trauma within a population are of interest to osteologists because of what they say about the culture and lifestyles of that population. Traumatic injuries from occupational hazards will be discussed within the context of nineteenth-century Belleville and medical practices at the time. The methodology utilized and the role of historical documentation in supplementing the skeletal evidence will also be investigated.

METHODOLOGY

Adults were chosen for this analysis because they can provide the best information about traumatic injuries and infectious diseases by both sex and age groups and this is important for reconstructing the health status of the community. Sex determination from the sub-adult skeleton

(<18 years of age) is unreliable since the skeletal characteristics that differentiate males from females do not begin to be manifested until puberty. In adults there are numerous areas of the skeleton that differ between males and females, primarily in the hips and the skull. In addition, stature differs (on a continuum) between the sexes and so does robusticity, or the degree of muscle markings and general size of the bone. The osteologist has a variety of techniques that can be employed to discriminate adult males and females with a very high degree of accuracy (as high as 95% for some techniques).

Bone is a dynamic tissue and as such, is continually being modified throughout life. A number of complicated processes contribute to the maintenance of healthy bone. This balanced state, however, is upset by some pathological conditions that cause visible changes to the bone (Steinbock, 1976). By recognizing the appearance of "normal" bone, the osteologist is able to identify what is "abnormal" and can then try to determine the cause of the abnormality. Just as the physician attempts to diagnose the cause of symptoms of illness in the patient, the osteologist endeavours to obtain as much information as possible from the skeleton in order to identify the process that has caused changes to the bone.

Since different diseases may produce similar types of changes to bone, determining the cause is facilitated by a thorough analysis of not only the type of bony change, but the pattern and distribution of those changes throughout the skeleton. Many observable "non-specific" infections are not caused by a specific disease syndrome such as tuberculosis, but are reactions to trauma to the bone, such as fractures. Specific infections including tuberculosis and syphilis often leave distinct types of bone lesions and each disease demonstrates an affinity for particular areas of the skeleton.

Fractures occurring at or around the time of death (perimortem), will not demonstrate any evidence of the normal healing processes that occur in living bone. These can be distinguished from fractures sustained during the lifetime of the individual that manifest bony changes as healing takes place. Other types of traumatic events may be chronic in nature such as dislocations. A fracture that does not heal properly can sometimes result in the formation of a new joint called a "pseudoarthrosis" (false joint).

BELLEVILLE DURING THE NINETEENTH CENTURY

Belleville is located in Hastings County, Ontario, on the north shore of Lake Ontario's Bay of Quinte. The Moira River, which empties in the bay, was the site of the earliest settlers of European origin to the region, in 1785 (Mika & Mika, 1986). In 1789, approximately fifty Loyalist families arrived in the area and founded Thurlow Village; by the early nineteenth century, the community had become a major farm market centre (Mika & Mika, 1986).

Because of its location between the Town of York (Toronto), and Kingston, Belleville's population increased rapidly in the 1820s. Early settlers in the area encouraged others to move into the region, describing Belleville as "...a place where job and business opportunities were plentiful" (Mika & Mika, 1986:17). A steamship service operated between Kingston, Prescott, and Belleville, facilitating trade in items such as flour, lumber and wheat; numerous saw and grist mills were established and small businesses flourished.

By the 1840s, Belleville had become a major centre for lumber manufacturing; iron foundries were built to supply machinery and equipment for the various manufacturing industries in the town (Mika & Mika, 1986). In 1856, the Grand Trunk Railway began to provide service between Montreal and Toronto, passing through Belleville enroute. The arrival of the railway further stimulated business; locomotive shops employed many townspeople, and manufacturers could export their goods to other centres.

Information obtained from Canada Census statistics includes the nature of the industries located in Belleville during the time that the St. Thomas' cemetery was in use. These included grist and saw mills, woollen factories, tanneries, foundries, and breweries (Census of the Canadas, 1853). Not listed in the census, but also operating in Belleville during this time were lath factories, carriage factories, sash and shingle factories, a paper mill, and a factory that produced shoe lasts (wooden forms for shoe manufacture). It is no surprise that occupational injuries are common within the St. Thomas' sample.

MEDICAL CARE IN NINETEENTH-CENTURY UPPER CANADA

Despite the growth of industry in Belleville during the early part of the nineteenth century, the area was essentially a rural farming community. Although medical practitioners were located in the region during the time that the individuals from St. Thomas' were alive (1821–1874), in many cases, particularly in the case of traumatic injuries, medical care was limited by the practical aspects of accessibility. It is also likely that there were a number of opportunistic unlicensed "practitioners" who

349

were consulted by the sick. In the early nineteenth century in Canada there were very few regulations governing the practice of medicine. At the time of the War of 1812 there were numerous "licensed quacks" (Jack, 1981:37), and "Unqualified persons with no training..." (Holling, 1981:39). Attempts to impose admission standards to practise medicine at this time were largely ineffective because they could not be enforced. A Provincial Act in 1839 incorporated the College of Physicians and Surgeons of Upper Canada (this later became the province of Ontario), thereafter having the authority to examine candidates before issuing medical licences (Godfrey, 1979).

Writing in 1915 about pioneer life among the United Empire Loyalists, Herrington (1915:96) discusses the state of medicine and its availability to the settlers noting that it was:

> ...not at all uncommon for a plain and simple farmer, with no pretension to a knowledge of medicine or surgery, to acquire a reputation as a specialist in some particular branch of the profession. Perhaps in some emergency he would set a broken limb, with results so satisfactory that his services would be requisitioned in the next case of a similar character.

Pioneer settlers in most areas of Upper Canada, Belleville included, were very much "...on their own when illness or accidents struck them" (Holling, 1981:33). Since most of the settlers lived in rural areas, the distance from the closest town or village likely prohibited access to treatment. Of the few medical practitioners available at the time, most settlers could not afford to pay the fees that were charged: many bartered for medical care by supplying property or farm animals to the attending physician (Holling, 1981). It was far more customary in nineteenth-century Upper Canada for people to self-doctor or rely on neighbours for assistance (Guillet, 1963).

One tale of such doctoring is related by Guillet (1963:98) about a woman in Haliburton whose neighbour treated her husband after he was injured while felling trees:

> One (tree) had rolled on him breaking his left leg at the thigh, crushing three ribs, and splitting his throat open, exposing the windpipe. She sewed up the throat with darning needle and thread, but the leg was not set, and though he lived to be over a century old, one leg remained two inches shorter than the other. Later he broke the same leg below the knee, but...reset it himself...

Only in the most extreme of cases, such as accidents resulting in life-threatening fractures or crushed limbs was the medical practitioner summoned. However, local road conditions were often a hindrance to physicians attempting to visit rural patients, especially in spring when the roads became impassable.

Hospitals were generally rare during this time period in Ontario. Two hospitals, on average, were being constructed in Ontario by 1855, but nursing staff were not available until the early 1880s when the Toronto General nursing school began training individuals for positions in areas outside Toronto (Godfrey, 1979). Serious traumatic injuries that resulted from occupational accidents might have been survivable in some instances, however, the infection that often accompanied the injury complicated matters. This was the pre-antiseptic era: it was not until the late nineteenth century that the preventative approach to medicine began to gain acceptance (MacDougall, 1983). Before Lister's antiseptic treatment came into general usage many deaths occurred as the result of infection. Compounding the problem was the lack of anaesthesia during surgery: according to one historian, two of every three surgical patients died! (Jack, 1981). Preparations containing small amounts of opium or substantial quantities of whisky were the only anaesthetic available, and the patient was usually tied or held down (Holling, 1981). Not surprisingly it must have been difficult to convince a patient to submit to surgical procedures under these circumstances, and explains why the medical practitioner was only summoned as a last resort!

INJURIES ASSOCIATED WITH OCCUPATIONAL HAZARDS

The hazards of daily life in 19th-century Belleville can be seen in the fact that thirty percent (seventy-six individuals) of the adults in the St. Thomas' sample show evidence of either healed or perimortem fractures! Multiple fractures occur in twelve individuals (males and females combined); one individual sustained thirteen fractures in his lifetime, yet all of them had healed. Table 1 illustrates the distribution of traumatic injuries by sex and age group. It appears that males in the thirty to fifty-nine year age group are at high risk for fractures; females between the ages of forty and sixty are also at risk, compared to other age groups. Occupational risks may account for the differences between the sexes in regard to the peak decade in which fractures are most common.

Twenty-three females within the St. Thomas' sample exhibit healed fractures. According to nineteenth-century Canadian medicine, however, many physicians held the belief that "...women were susceptible to ill

Table 1. Traumatic Injuries - St. Thomas' Skeletal Sample
(Number of Individuals)

Males (68 of 146)

Age	17-29	30-39	40-49	50-59	60-69	70-79	80+	Ttl.
Healed Fractures	2	16	17	14	6	1	2	58
Perimortem Fractures		1	1	1				3
Pseudarthroses				1				1*
Dislocations			1	1				2
Spondylolysis	1	1	2					4
TOTAL:								68

Females (29 of 104)

Age	17-29	30-39	40-49	50-59	60-69	70-79	80+	Ttl.
Healed Fractures		2	2	8	7	4		23
Perimortem Fractures					2			2
Pseudarthroses								*
Dislocations						1	1	2
Spondylolysis		1				1		2
TOTAL:								29

*   One individual with a pseudarthroses could not be identified as to either age or sex health because they were women, that is, female" (Mitchinson, 1984:383). This "...vague form of environmentalism..." as Mitchinson (1984:385) describes it, did little to advance the cause of medicine where women were involved. Oddly enough, the numerous cases of healed fractures in females from the St. Thomas' sample suggests that the image of the frail female does not reflect the pioneer way of life in this community. Fractures are important because they reveal information about behaviour and occupation (Knowles, 1983). Traumatic injuries to the ankle and foot occur frequently among individuals involved in occupations that place heave stresses on the knee and hip (Knowles, 1983). One particular type of fracture seen in the St. Thomas' skeletal sample is the "march" fracture of the long tubular bones in the feet (metatarsals). This type of fracture typically occurs historically as the result of long marches by soldiers (Revell, 1986). Parish records for St. Thomas' indicate that several individuals within the sample had participated in the Rebellion of 1837 (Boyce, 1990), suggesting that this type of fracture might be expected to occur within this sample.

Another fracture, thought to be associated with occupational hazards, is a type of "fatigue" fracture of the ribs. Fatigue fractures result when a particular bone is subjected to some form of chronic physical stress over a period of weeks, or months (Ortner and Putschar, 1985). Kitchen (cited in Revell, 1986), notes that these fatigue fractures of the ribs can occur from the continual forking of farm manure. Numerous healed rib fractures are common among the St. Thomas' skeletal sample and some may represent the stresses associated with the more unpleasant aspects of pioneer life!

Another injury thought to be associated with physical activity is a pseudarthrosis. After a long bone is fractured, (for example, the femur or thigh bone), the healing process may be interrupted. Instead of uniting, the two fragments of the bone remain separate and continue to move around independently of each other. The causes are numerous: normal healing of the bone may be hindered by the aging process with its subsequent reduction in the ability of the body to recuperate from injury (Weinmann and Sicher, 1955). Or, the bone fragments may simply be too far from each other to permit healing to occur. This non-union of a fractured bone is usually the result of a failure to immobilize the broken bone, or immobilizing it for an insufficient period of time, or could result from a simple misalignment of the fragments during setting (Lichtenstein, 1970). There are two cases of pseudarthroses within the St. Thomas' sample (one is from a male, aged 54 and the other occurs in an individual whose age and sex are undetermined), and these may reflect the rigours of pioneer life. Fracture healing must have been incomplete in these individuals when daily activities recommenced.

There are at least four examples of hip dislocations within the sample, two males and two females. Dislocations can occur as the result of a fracture, congenitally (predisposed to the condition at birth), or through traumatic force to the joint (Ortner and Putschar, 1985). Individuals who have congenital dislocations usually have distinctive features of the hip bones that reflect the condition. It appears that none of these features were present in any of the individuals suffering from dislocations within the St. Thomas' sample, suggesting that traumatic injuries or some sort of extreme physical stress may have caused the problem.

Another condition seen in several individuals from the St. Thomas' sample is spondylolysis. In spondylolysis, the neural arch (the bony portion that forms the back of the spine) separates from the body of the vertebra. Although it may be a congenital condition (Ubelaker, 1989; Turkel, 1989), physical stress appears to be a factor that may contribute to the condition (Merbs, 1989; El-Najjar and McWilliams, 1978). Two females and four males within the St. Thomas' sample are affected. All cases involve the fifth lumbar vertebra, the last vertebra in the spinal column, and the one most often subjected to strain.

In general, there appears to be a trend of more healed fractures in males, particularly in the region of the thorax. Age does not seem to be a major factor in the occurrence of traumatic injuries since there are no significant differences between males and females in the incidence of trauma when analyzed by age groups of under fifty years or over fifty years of age. (For a complete discussion of the statistical analyses see Jimenez, 1991). Figures 1 to 8 illustrate some examples of the types of traumatic injuries observed in the sample.

Figure 1. Spondylolysis of the 5th Lumbar Vertebra

Figure 2. Compression Fracture of the 12th Thoracic Vertebra

Figure 3. Healed Displaced Fracture of Right Head of
Femur with Fracture Callus (Healing)

Figure 4. Healed Depressed Fracture of the
Left Parietal Bone of Skull

Figure 5. Complete Shearing Fracture of Head of Right
Femur with Pseudarthrosis

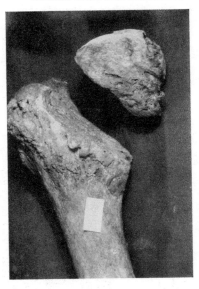

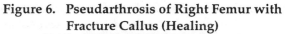

Figure 6. Pseudarthrosis of Right Femur with
Fracture Callus (Healing)

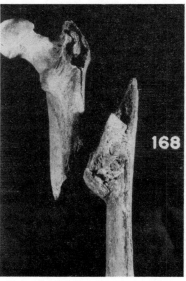

Figure 7. Radiograph of Healed, Misaligned
Fracture of the Right Tibia

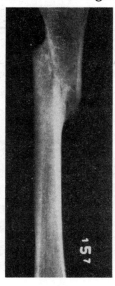

Figure 8. Radiograph of Healed, Misaligned Fractures
of the Left Tibia and Right Fibula

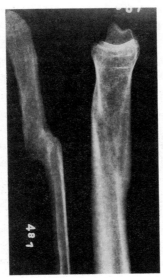

CORRELATION BETWEEN SKELETAL EVIDENCE
AND HISTORICAL DOCUMENTATION

Thomas Burke was 39 years of age when he died on December 12th, 1867 as the result of a mining accident. Parish records indicate that the fatal accident occurred as the result of an encounter with a crushing machine (Boyce, 1990). According to an article that appeared in *The Daily Intelligencer*, December 16, 1867:

> It appears that Burke, who was employed as an engineer at the crushing works of Messrs. Scott & Taylor, had occasion to examine some of the higher parts of the machinery, and losing his balance, fell on to the belt, which was revolving at a rapid rate, carrying him down with such force to the ground as to break his neck. Death was instantaneous.

The skeletal remains of Mr. Burke corroborate this event: extensive radiating fractures of several skull bones were evident, with no indication of healing, suggesting they occurred around the time of death. In addition, several well healed fractures were present and likely reflect injuries Mr. Burke sustained in other industrial accidents prior to his death.

Several other individuals have been identified within the sample, but accounts of their deaths are not able to be correlated to the skeletal remains because of poor bone preservation in several cases. However, newspaper accounts and obituaries relate stories surrounding the deaths of some of them. *William Coleman* died November 13, 1869 when the horse that was pulling his carriage bolted, throwing him to the ground. The newspaper account notes that he died instantly of a broken neck and that one of his legs was fractured below the knee (*Belleville Intelligencer*, 1869). Mr. Coleman was buried in a cemented tomb that retained moisture at the time of excavation. As a result, his tomb was moved to Belleville Municipal Cemetery without osteological examination. However, it is likely that evidence of perimortem trauma would have been observable in the skeletal remains.

Several cases of death were recorded for individuals within the St. Thomas' skeletal sample as the result of railroad construction accidents, and traumatic injuries were undoubtedly sustained by others. In addition, although not part of the St. Thomas' sample, other local individuals suffered injury and death from such accidents. Reviewing them helps to give an overall picture of some of the hazards to which the community was exposed. One such example concerns an accident that took the life of a brakeman from Belleville, in May of 1856. As a result of serious injuries sustained, his left leg was amputated; however, he did not survive the operation (*The Intelligencer*, 1856). Another report in the July 11, 1856 edition of *The Intelligencer* tells of an accident involving a workman on the railroad. Typical of the time, the newspaper accounts left very little to the imagination of the reader. Accounts of personal injury accidents were graphic:

> We regret to learn that on Tuesday last, one of the workmen on the Grand Trunk Railroad in this vicinity, was seriously injured, by having one of the dirt cars run over him, so mangling both legs that amputation was necessary. We learn that one of the legs was so nearly cut off, that it hung by a few threads of the skin.

These horrific accidents were not confined only to construction: there are numerous reports of passenger deaths or other accidents involving individuals within the vicinity of passing trains. Railway accidents, resulting either in serious injury or loss of life were frequent in Belleville and environs during the mid-nineteenth century.

CONCLUSIONS

Within the St. Thomas' skeletal sample there is some correlation between historical documentation and what is exhibited in the skeletal remains in terms of traumatic injuries. Obituaries and accounts of accidents causing either death or serious injury are common in the local newspapers of the time. In some cases, this information can be matched to known individuals within the sample. In other cases, it completes the picture of occupational hazards in nineteenth-century Ontario, and illustrates some of the challenges associated with a pioneer existence. Industrial accidents associated with logging, mining and saw mills, were common occurrences and caused injury and death. Healed fractures, the result of either accidents or occupationally induced stresses, also occur with frequency and are generally more common in males. Many individuals suffered multiple fractures as well.

The St. Thomas' sample reflects the arduous nature of pioneer life, including the industrialization that occurred in the Belleville area during the mid-nineteenth century. During the 1850s there are numerous cases of traumatic injuries as lumber, saw, and grist mills began to appear within the locale. The construction of the Grand Trunk Railway in 1856 accounted for a number of accidents, many of them documented in historical and parish records. Belleville was essentially a rural community during the time that the individuals from St. Thomas' were alive (1821–1874), and medical care was limited by the practical aspects of accessibility or time. The cases of both misaligned fractures and pseudoarthroses suggest that, perhaps, the pioneer lifestyle did not permit the luxury of the time necessary or the expertise to immobilize fractured limbs. Additionally, there were undoubtedly a number of opportunistic unlicensed "practitioners" who were consulted by the sick. The quality of medical service provided to these individuals may be reflected within the St. Thomas' sample.

In attempting to reconstruct the health status of the community by examining the St. Thomas' skeletal sample, it is important to note the limitations of such analyses. As indicated in the introductory remarks of this discussion, some diseases do not leave traces on bone and any analysis of infectious disease needs to be supplemented by archival documentation in the form of death records, newspaper accounts, obituaries, etc. In addition, parish records cannot always be considered absolute in terms of information: data for some periods may have been lost over the years, or unavailable as a result of inadequate record-keeping. Cultural attitudes

361

also play a role in medical history. Because of the stigma associated with certain diseases such as syphilis, cases often went unreported (Jimenez, 1991). Analyses of the St. Thomas' parish records, however, indicate that they appear to be reliable (DeVito, 1991).

Reconstructing the health status of a population contributes not only to our knowledge of the past, but offers insights into the future as well. By studying the human skeleton and the processes that modify it, we can learn much about the ways in which we adapt (or fail to adapt) to both internal and external influences that modify our biology. Our genetic makeup may predispose us to certain diseases. Poor nutrition puts stresses on the body that may result in susceptibility to infections. Some diseases appear to be associated with certain age groups. By studying the skeletal remains of past populations we can augment our knowledge about human diversity and adaptation and perhaps, in doing so, apply this to some of the contemporary biological and environmental issues facing us. While sufficient skeletal material is available from this sample, when this is supplemented by supporting historical documentation, a reconstruction of the occupational stresses on a community can be made with some confidence.

ACKNOWLEDGEMENTS

I thank St. Thomas' Anglican Church, Belleville, for permission to study the skeletal remains. I also thank the three reviewers of this paper for their suggestions, and Ann Herring and Leslie Chan for their comments. The original research upon which this paper is based was funded in part by a grant from the Ontario Heritage Foundation.

REFERENCES

Belleville Intelligencer (1869) Melancholy Accident. November 19. Belleville, Ontario.

Boyce G (1990) Personal communication. Preliminary notes - August 20, 1990.

Census of the Canadas 1851-52 (1853) *Personal Census, Vol. I.* Quebec: Printed by John Lovell, at his Steam Printing Establishment.

DeVito C (1991) Personal communication re: Parish Records from St. Thomas' Anglican Church.

El-Najjar MY, and McWilliams KR (1978) *Forensic Anthropology.* Springfield, Ill: Charles C. Thomas.

Gibbs, LM (1991) What's sex in the East is not necessarily sex in the West: Citrate, sex and human skeletal remains. MA Thesis, Hamilton: McMaster University, Ontario.

Godfrey CM (1979) *Medicine for Ontario — A History*. Belleville: Mika Publishing Company.

Guillet EC (1963) The Pioneer Farmer and Backwoodsman, Vol. I. Toronto: The Ontario Publishing Co. Ltd.

Herring DA, Saunders SR, and Boyce GE (1994) Bones and burial registers: Reconstructing a 19th-century pioneer community from skeletal evidence and cemetery records. *Northeast Historical Archaeology*, 20:54-70.

Herrington WS (1915) *Pioneer Life Among the Loyalists in Upper Canada*. Toronto, at St. Martin's House: The MacMillan Company of Canada.

Holling SA (1981) Each family its own doctor. In S Holling, J Senior, B Clarkson, and DA Smith (eds.): *Medicine for Heroes — A Neglected Part of Pioneer Life*. Erin: Boston Mills Press, pp. 31-49.

Jack D (1981) *Rogues, Rebels, and Geniuses — The Story of Canadian Medicine*. Toronto: Doubleday Canada Ltd.

Jimenez SB (1991) Analysis of patterns of injury and disease in an historic skeletal sample from Belleville, Ontario. M.A. Thesis. McMaster University, Hamilton, Ontario.

Kitchen (1948) Fatigue fractures of the ulna. *J. Bone Joint Surgery* (BR) 30: 622-623. Cited in PA Revell (1986) *Pathology of Bone*. Berlin: Springer-Verlag.

Knowles AK (1983) Acute traumatic lesions. In DG Hard (ed.): *Disease in Ancient Man*. Toronto: Clarke Irwin, pp. 61-83.

Lichtenstein L (1970) *Diseases of Bone and Joints*. St. Louis: The C.V. Mosby Co.

MacDougall H (1983) Epidemics and the environment: The early development of public health activity in Toronto, 1832-1872. In RA Jarrell, and AE Roos (eds.): *Critical Issues in the History of Canadian Science, Technology and Medicine*. Thornhill: HSTC Publications, pp. 135-151.

McKillop H, Marshall S, Boyce G, and Saunders S (1989) Excavations at St. Thomas Church', Belleville: A nineteenth-century cemetery. Paper presented at the Annual Meeting of the Ontario Archaeological Society, London, Ontario.

Merbs CF (1989) Trauma. In MY Iscan and KAR Kennedy (eds.): *Reconstruction of Life from the Skeleton*: New York: Alan R. Liss, Inc., pp. 161-189.

Mika N, and Mika H (1986) Belleville — Seat of Hastings County. Belleville: Mika Publishing Company.

Mitchinson W (1984) Causes of disease in women: The case of late 19th-century English Canada. In CG Roland (ed.): *Health, Disease and Medicine Essays in Canadian History*. The Hannah Institute for the History of Medicine. Toronto: Clarke Irwin, pp. 381-395.

Ortner DJ, and Putschar WGJ (1985) *Identification of Pathological Conditions in Human Skeletal Remains*. Washington: Smithsonian Institution Press.

Revell PA (1986) *Pathology of Bone*. Berlin: Springer-Verlag.

Rogers, T (1991) Sex determination and age estimation: Skeletal evidence from St. Thomas' Cemetery Belleville, Ontario. Master's thesis. McMaster University, Hamilton, Ontario.

Saunders SR (1992) Subadult skeletons and growth related studies. *Skeletal Biology of Past Peoples: Research Methods*. New York: Wiley-Liss, pp. 1-20.

Saunders SR, and Herring DA (1991) Testing theory and method in paleodemography: The St. Thomas' Anglican Church Cemetery. Paper presented to the Canadian Archaeological Association Meetings, St. John's, Nfld.

Saunders SR, Fitzgerald C, Rogers T, Dudar C, and McKillop H (1992) A test of several methods of skeletal age estimation using a documented archaeological sample. *Can. Soc. Forens. Sci. J.*, Vol. 25, No. 2,: 97-118

Saunders SR, DeVito C, Herring A, Southern R, and Hoppa R (1993) Accuracy tests of tooth formation age estimations for human skeletal remains. *Am. J. Phys. Anthropol.* 92:173-188

Steinbock RT (1976) *Paleopathological Diagnosis and Interpretation.* Springfield, Ill: Charles C. Thomas.

The Intelligencer (1856) Railway Accident. May 30. Belleville, Ontario.

The Intelligencer (1856) Accident. July 11. Belleville, Ontario.

The Daily Intelligencer (1867) Inquest. December 16. Belleville, Ontario.

Turkel SJ (1989) Congenital abnormalities in skeletal populations. In MY Iscan and KAR Kennedy (eds.): *Reconstruction of Life from the Skeleton.* New York: Alan R. Liss, Inc., pp. 109-127.

Ubelaker DH (1989) *Human Skeletal Remains.* Second Edition. Washington: Taraxacum.

Weinmann JP, and Sicher H (1955) *Bone and Bones.* Second Edition. St. Louis: The C.V. Mosby Company.

Westwood JCN (1980) *The Hazard from Dangerous Exotic Diseases.* London: The MacMillan Press Ltd.

17

The 1918 Influenza Epidemic in the Central Canadian Subarctic

D. Ann Herring

Virgin soil epidemics of European origin figure prominently in most of the recent discussions of the histories of Aboriginal people in the Americas. The vital importance of understanding the socio-ecological context of such epidemics is illustrated by variations in mortality rates and the duration of the 1918 Spanish Flu epidemic in several Cree/Métis communities in the central Canadian subarctic. The results illustrate how Aboriginal communities directly along trade and transportation routes and in relatively close contact with the central source of infection suffered more extensively from Spanish Flu than those socially and geographically further removed from it. The findings also make it clear that caution should be exercised in generalizing the mortality rates from a single, or even a few communities, to wider geographical regions.

THE PROBLEM OF INFECTIOUS DISEASE

Diseases of European origin figure prominently in most of the recent discussions of the histories of Aboriginal people in the Americas (cf. Dobyns, 1983; Crosby, 1986; Thornton, 1987; Verano and Ubelaker, 1992; Merbs, 1992). From the 17th century onward, epidemics of smallpox, measles, influenza, dysentery, diphtheria, typhus, yellow fever, whooping cough, tuberculosis, syphilis, and various unidentifiable 'fevers' caused illness and death as they spread from person to person and from village to village in various regions of the continent.

Many of these outbreaks took the form of virgin soil epidemics. Virgin soil epidemics are distinctive because they produce unusually high death rates in all age groups and generally devastate the communities in which they occur. Their enhanced capacity to induce sickness and death results from the fact that the disease in question is either new to the affected community or has not been present in it for a long time, such that the population's immunity, and hence resistance to it, has been lost. Either way, the result is that there are few, if any, individuals with antibodies to the disease. This leaves a community immunologically susceptible to its effects (Mausner and Bahn, 1974:27). As T. Dale Stewart (1973) noted for the dreaded disease of smallpox:

> The rapidity with which this and probably other infectious diseases spread over America after 1492 had such a devastating effect on the native population that the diseases involved must presumably have been new to the Western Hemisphere. The American population lacked even a minimum level of immunity and people of all ages, not just the young, were struck down. (Stewart, 1973:38)

When almost everyone in a community falls ill during an epidemic, the toll from the disease is extremely high. This is not only because of the direct effects of the infection, but more importantly because there are few individuals who are healthy enough to tend the sick, care for children, stock the larders, bury the dead, and keep the community functioning even at minimal levels. In fact, the social disruption accompanying an epidemic has a greater influence on the population's ability to survive its ravages than does the lack of biological resistance to it in the form of antibodies (Neel, 1982). As McGrath (1991:418–419) emphasizes, *social* circumstances are instrumental in determining an epidemic's course and impact.

Lively debate continues to characterize discussions about the role virgin soil epidemics played in shaping the biology, demographic structure, and social fabric of Aboriginal communities after European contact. Some scholars contend that epidemic diseases introduced from Europe were the primary agents of destruction of Aboriginal societies (Borah, 1976; Dobyns, 1983, 1984; Cook, 1973; Cook and Borah, 1971). An eminent ethnohistorian, in fact, has used the epidemiological concept of virgin soil epidemic as a metaphor for the postcontact history of the Americas, characterizing the period as "the widowing of the 'virgin land'" (Dobyns, 1976).

Other scholars take the position that disease was not the most significant factor in the decimation of Aboriginal communities. Rather, social disruption in the form of warfare, changes in subsistence patterns, and political domination were instrumental in reshaping Aboriginal life and death after European contact (Kroeber, 1925, cited in Ramenofsky, 1987:9). Still others argue that epidemic diseases became significant agents of change and decline only after a pattern of sustained and intense contact had become established between Aboriginal and European groups (cf. Helm, 1980). In any event, there was a great deal of diversity in the experience of introduced epidemics in the Americas, expressing the particular social and ecological conditions in which they occurred (Merbs, 1992; Waldram et al., in press).

The vital importance of understanding the socio-ecological context of epidemic disease was brought home to me as I began to explore the impact of a 20th-century virgin soil epidemic, the 1918 influenza pandemic, in Aboriginal communities of the central Canadian subarctic (Figure 1). In this chapter I examine mortality in several Manitoba Métis/Cree communities from this epidemic that has been dubbed the "forgotten pandemic" (Crosby, 1989) yet paradoxically remains "the greatest disease holocaust of modern history" (American Journal of Public Health, 1968:2192).

Why the 1918 Flu?

The 1918 influenza pandemic was a unique outbreak in human history. Although influenza-like epidemics have struck human populations for at least 400 years (Stuart-Harris, Schild and Oxford, 1985:1), and possibly longer (Graves, 1969:14; Thacker, 1986:129), the 1918 pandemic was unusually lethal. Worldwide, more than 20 million people are estimated to have died from it during the short space of one year (Graves, 1969:13). No age group was spared, but children between 5 and 14 years old and adults between the ages of 20 and 40 were especially hard hit for reasons that are poorly understood (American Journal of Public Health, 1968:2193; Walters, 1978:855; Patterson, 1986:89).

Although the symptoms of headaches, spiking fever, and a hacking cough were severe and quickly debilitating, with good nursing care most people recovered within about a week. About 20% of the ailing developed pneumonia, sometimes within the short span of one day, and this deadly and untreatable complication eventually killed almost half of those who contracted it (Burnet and Clark, 1942:88).

And the cause of the epidemic was unknown because the elusive virus, later determined to be Influenza A, was not isolated until 1933 (Smith, Andrewes and Laidlaw, 1933). Influenza is acquired by inhaling aerosolized droplets containing virus that have been coughed, sneezed or otherwise launched from the respiratory tract of an infected individual. After a short incubation period of one-to-two days, the infection quickly leads to acute illness (Turk, Porter, Duerden & Reid, 1983:177).

Influenza A is a chameleonlike virus (Scholtissek, 1992). It has the ability to undergo sudden and radical changes in its surface antigens, *hemaglutinen* and *neuraminidase*. This process, known as *antigenic shift*, occurs when human Influenza A acquires genes from an animal influenza virus. This *genetic recombination* is facilitated because the RNA of influenza viruses is segmented into eight pieces, each of which defines a viral gene. During mixed infection with animal and human influenza strains, the sixteen gene segments now circulating in the individual can become reshuffled. This results in major changes in the surface antigens and new, virulent strains of virus (Scholtissek, 1992:4) to which few have antibodies and to which all age groups are potentially susceptible (Bannister, 1983:58). Although its origins are still debated, current evidence suggests that the 1918 strain of Influenza A was a new evolutionary product resulting from recombined RNA strands from human and swine viruses (Kaplan and Webster, 1977:102).

The eruption of epidemic influenza in the spring of 1918 was clearly rooted in war-time conditions in Europe, and closely connected to the arrival of American troops in France. Although it has been named the "Spanish Flu" because Spain was the first country to publicize its presence, one likely source of the epidemic seems to have been Fort Riley, Kansas in the United States of America. A new and lethal strain of influenza virus seems to have evolved there in March of 1918 (Kaplan and Webster, 1977:102), then boarded ship with American troops, travelling with them to the cities and trenches of Europe.

From there the virus moved explosively around the world in conjunction with troop and other population movements (Burnet and Clark, 1942:69; Graves, 1969:21; Beveridge, 1977:42–43; Kaplan and Webster, 1977:89). Since the surface proteins of this influenza virus were new, enormous numbers of people succumbed to it because they lacked antibodies that would have protected them against it. Indeed, the 1918 influenza pandemic is a classic example of a virgin soil epidemic.

Spanish Flu reached Canada in September 1918 with the first civilian outbreak occurring in Victoriaville, Quebec (Graves, 1969:19–20;

Pettigrew, 1983:8). The major source of infection was returning troops exposed to the virus in Europe while fighting for Britain during World War I. Soldiers freed from the appalling conditions of the trenches and troopships headed home by rail and road, carrying Spanish Flu across the country. The calamitous sickness swept west and north across the continent, afflicting an estimated 2 million Canadians and killing some 50,000 of them (MacDougall, 1985:2089).

Spanish Flu arrived in Winnipeg, the capital of the Province of Manitoba, on September 30, 1918 with a group of sick soldiers travelling westward on a troop train. Four days later, Winnipeg recorded its first civilian influenza death (Pettigrew, 1983:56–57). The virus diffused from this urban focus to rural and isolated parts of the province via an intricate network of railway lines, roads, and waterways. Lake Winnipeg was bustling with steamer traffic at the end of October, 1918, when the passenger steamer Wolverine made its last stop at Berens River before freeze-up closed the lake to traffic. Three days later, almost everyone at Berens River fell ill, overcome by influenza transported there by the sick crew of the Wolverine (Pettigrew, 1983:78–79).

Gathering Information on Historic Epidemics

In view of the devastation wrought by the 1918 Spanish Flu worldwide, I was surprised by the lack of published studies of the epidemic in Canada (cf. Pettigrew, 1983; MacDougall, 1985; Lux, 1992; Herring, 1993). This reinforces Alfred Crosby's (1989) view that the epidemic has been forgotten and supports his contention that "The average college graduate born since 1918 literally knows more about the Black Death of the fourteenth century than the World War I pandemic" (Crosby, 1989:313). A major part of the explanation for this apparent amnesia lies in the timing of the epidemic, which broke out immediately after World War I and was overshadowed by it. The epidemic arrived and disappeared quite quickly, failed to produce lingering disease or permanent and obvious scarring of the afflicted, and attracted little literary attention that would have immortalized its terror (see Crosby, 1989:311–315 for an excellent discussion).

This lacuna compounds the fundamental scarcity and dubious accuracy of information on disease, death, and virtually all other demographic parameters for Aboriginal communities in Canada before the 1960s (Piché and George, 1973). Even though historic epidemics were frequently described in detail in journals and reports, it is usually hard to gauge the extent of losses from epidemics in Aboriginal communities because the sources rarely provide detailed data on how many people died, how old they were, whether they were male or female, or even basic figures on the size of the community before and after the epidemic (Ray, 1974). This is quite true for the 1918 Flu, which coincides with a drastic reduction in the quantity and quality of information contained in the Department of Indian Affairs Sessional Papers published by the Government of Canada.

To find primary source data on the 1918 Flu, I had to scour a number of Archives in Toronto and Winnipeg to uncover bits of information that could then be pieced into a picture of the epidemic in the central Canadian subarctic. The material upon which this analysis is based was gleaned from a variety of primary sources, but relies heavily on Hudson's Bay Company [HBCA] Post Journals and Fur Trade Reports held at the Provincial Archives of Manitoba [PAM] (Winnipeg), and on parish records from the Anglican Church of Canada Archives [ACCA] (Toronto, Ontario) and the United Church of Canada Archives [UCCA] for Northwestern Ontario and Manitoba (Winnipeg, Manitoba).

SPANISH FLU IN THE CENTRAL CANADIAN SUBARCTIC

As Figure 1 shows, the Aboriginal communities under scrutiny were located either on the perimeter of Lake Winnipeg (Fisher River, Fort Alexander, Berens River, Norway House) or at interior sites in the Nelson and Hayes River trade route (Split Lake, God's Lake, Island Lake, Oxford House). All were Hudson's Bay Company posts and the people at each location were engaged to some extent in the fur trade or in fishing, though more southerly Fort Alexander and Fisher River were increasingly being drawn into a cash economy through local lumbering and mining activities (Moffat, 1992).

Figures 2 to 5 depict annual counts of burials listed in the parish registers for the communities. The marked mortality peaks for the sites around Lake Winnipeg (Fisher River, Berens River and Norway House) show very clearly the presence of unusual levels of mortality during the second wave of the epidemic that began in the fall of 1918 (Figures 2–4). Spanish influenza was mentioned specifically as a cause of death in the burial registers and it is likely that diagnosis was reasonably accurate, given the consistency of symptoms and the rapid onset of illness within two to three days following infection (Bannister, 1983:58).

In contrast, the burial sequences for Oxford House (Figure 5) and Split Lake (not shown) show no evidence of a mortality spike in 1918/19. Oxford House, in fact, experienced somewhat fewer burials than usual in and around the epidemic year. The obvious explanation for the absence of extraordinary mortality in these communities is under-reporting of deaths, a common occurrence when epidemics cause the breakdown of daily life. However, the 1918 Fur Trade Report for the Keewatin District notes that Oxford House was spared during the epidemic (HBCA A.74/48, fo.51), confirming the validity of the burial register data for that year. The situation for Split Lake is less equivocal, but the burial register indicates that there was a serious flu epidemic there several years later, in 1924. This is likely a late manifestation of the 1918 Flu, which continued to circulate in the north for a decade or so after its first attack.

The quality of the parish registers for God's Lake and Island Lake is poor and consequently are not analysed here. Nevertheless, entries in the Hudson's Bay Journal at Norway House (HBCA B154/a/87) and the 1918 Fur Trade Report for the Keewatin District (HBCA A.74/48, fo.51) indicate that Spanish Flu failed to reach either community.

Figure 1. Aboriginal Communities Studied in the Central Canadian Subarctic

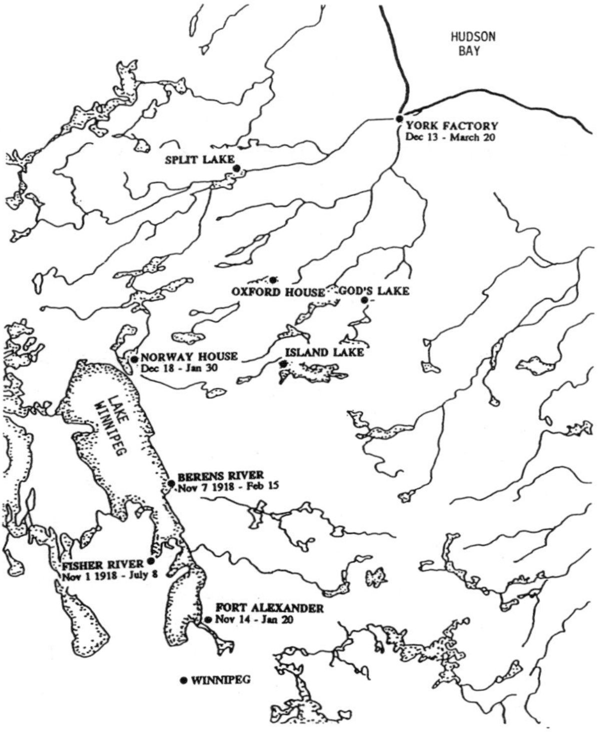

Figure 2. Methodist Burials at Fisher River, 1909 to 1929

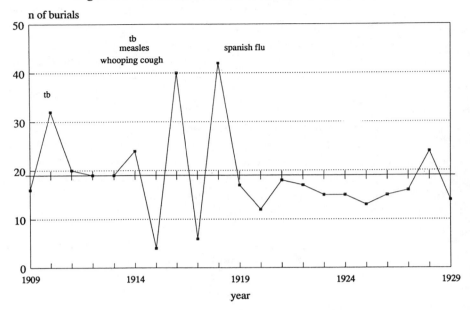

Figure 3. Methodist Burials at Berens River, 1909 to 1929

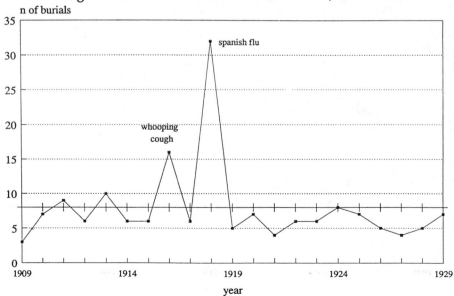

Figure 4. Anglican Burials at Norway house, 1909 to 1929

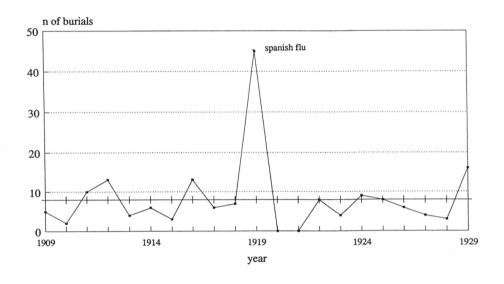

Figure 5. Methodist Burials at Oxford House, 1909 to 1929

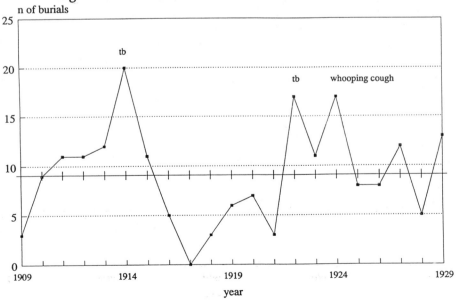

Figure 6. Estimated Spanish Flu Mortality Rates per 1000

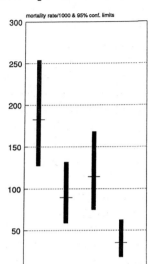

Mortality Rates

In any event, it is clear that there were wide disparities in the extent to which Aboriginal communities in the central Canadian subarctic were affected by the 1918 influenza epidemic. The magnitude of the difference is illustrated by the crude (overall) mortality rates per 1000 for each community (Figure 6). To derive this epidemiologic measure, I used information cited in the 1916 census report on the size and composition of the study communities (Government of Canada Sessional Papers, 1917). Since the Sessional Papers for 1916 also provide a breakdown of each community by religious group (Anglican, Methodist, Roman Catholic, etc.), it was a simple matter to divide the number of burials listed in the Anglican[1] and Methodist[2] parish registers by the population at risk for the appropriate denomination in the census, then multiply by one thousand.

To control for the effects of small sample size, I then calculated 95% confidence limits around the estimated crude mortality rates, according to the method described by Lilienfeld and Lilienfeld (1980:336-38). The confidence limits establish the upper and lower boundaries between which we can be 95% certain that the "true" mortality rate resides. Figure 6 displays the estimated rates and 95% confidence limits for the study communities. Where the confidence limits overlap, there is no statistically significant difference between mortality rates.

It is estimated that 3% of the total Canadian Indian population was lost to Spanish Flu (Graham-Cumming, 1967:149) and that the influenza mortality rate among Canadian Indians was 37.7 deaths per 1,000 (Titley, 1986, cited in Lux, 1992). The results for the central Canadian subarctic appear to have been much higher and certainly indicate that the toll from the epidemic varied greatly from place to place. Norway House experienced the highest death rate at about 188 deaths per 1000, compared to Fort Alexander where the mortality rate was less than one-quarter of this, at 35 per 1000.[3] Berens River and Fisher River fell between the two with death rates clustering around 100 deaths per 1000.[4]

Part of the explanation for the relatively high influenza mortality rates in the central subarctic lies in the subsistence economies of the communities. When Influenza A strikes, survival essentially depends on the ability to nurse the sick and keep them warm, and to maintain a steady food supply. All of the study communities had economies based on hunting and gathering and because the epidemic arrived in late fall and early winter, there were few provisions on hand beyond what was available at the Hudson's Bay Company store. As Dr. Stone noted in 1926:

> Their meat supply is often in the net in the river, or in the rabbit snare in the bush. Going about from house to house, one is at a loss to see where the food produced at meal times is kept between meals...When adversity comes they quickly come to want...The hardship of the sick and aged would be worse than it is if there did not obtain among them a very admirable community spirit. (HBCA A.95/53, p.4)

There must have been a complete breakdown of daily life when the flu erupted. Entire families would have been without an able-bodied member to feed them or keep the fires going in the cold subarctic winter. Many of the ill contracted deadly cases of pneumonia after going out to renew dwindling food and fuel supplies, dying shortly thereafter (PAM MG8 B47, page 8). Mr. Harry Everett, who was just 4 years old when the Spanish Flu broke out at Berens River Indian Reserve, recalls just such tragedies in his memoirs (1985):

> My first recollection is being on a hammock like swing and seeing beds all around the room and one woman reaching down inside her blouse in front and bringing out her small purse and giving it to my Dad. This was during the Spanish Flue (sic) Epidemic. My Dad was the only one that was not sick and was pretty well alone for a number of days making

the rounds to different houses to see that they had enough wood inside to keep the fires going and to take any bodies that were in the house. A few days later Old Jimmy McKay was able to help him in making the rounds. All the animals were turned loose from the stables and doors left open. They said if the sick that died had stayed in the house where it was warm (sic). They went out too soon and got cold and had a relapse. There was no such a thing as a doctor out there in those days. The only time the Indians saw a doctor was at Treaty time which was once a year, generally the end of June. Then he was there for only a day and half and was gone for another year.

During the summer of 1992, I had the opportunity to visit Norway House and interview people about their recollections of the Spanish Flu epidemic, assisted by two graduate students, Ms. Tina Moffat (McMaster U.) and Ms. Chris Egan (U. of Manitoba). Wherever possible, we taped and later transcribed our interviews. Even though the Spanish Flu may not have been immortalized in literary or historical accounts, the epidemic was remembered at Norway House. Mr. Tommy York, a man with an extraordinarily accurate memory for detail, recounted the entire history of the epidemic at Norway House in the space of about 20 minutes, confirming the deductions it had taken me 3 years to tease out of documentary sources! He described the difficulties of burying so many people who died suddenly, noting that they were brought to a cabin and stacked like wood until it was possible to bury them later. At many communities the dead were wrapped in sheets and placed on rooftops so the dogs could not eat them. These spectral white bundles remained there until spring, when they could be buried in the thawing ground (PAM MG8 B47, page 8). Mr. Nathaniel Queskekapow, born in 1920 after the epidemic, recalled stories he had heard about how people were walking about normally and then "dropped, just like a shot. Even the children...they just fell down and died. Like that."

The estimated mortality rate at Norway House was extremely high — about five times greater than the average for all Canadian Indians during the epidemic. There is probably no single explanation for this extraordinary experience. It is likely, however, that its strategic position in the trade and transportation network left it more vulnerable to imported diseases, as Ray (1976:156) has suggested for the mid-19th century (see also Decker, 1988). Clearly, the number of routes of viral spread to Norway House had increased by 1918 through the expansion of the railway and roads in the province. The Oxford House and God's Lake Post Journals indicate that Norway House was under quarantine during December and January of the epidemic (HBCA B.156/1/44, fo.8 and HBCA B.283/a/8/, fo.54). This probably helped to contain the spread of infection, but ironically and tragically may also have served to increase the Norway House mortality rates because of the concentration of virus and infectious individuals there (Herring, 1993). Elsewhere, it has been suggested that inadequate medical care and crowded houses in Aboriginal communities facilitated the spread of infection (Lux, 1992).

Figure 7. Burial Chronology at Berens River

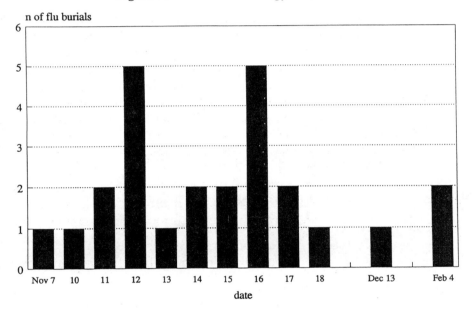

Duration of the Epidemic

Examination of the burial chronologies for Berens River (Figure 7) and Fisher River (Figure 8) show that the duration of the epidemic also varied. At Berens River, the first flu burial took place on November 7; within eleven days (Nov 18), twenty-two people had died from the epidemic. A subsequent burial on December 13 marks the end of the epidemic, for two individuals buried in February actually died the previous November. Clearly, the epidemic at Berens River was over quickly, within about 5 weeks. Like Berens River, most of the Fisher River flu burials occurred within the first two weeks. However, the epidemic was substantially more protracted, exacting a small but consistent flu death toll over a 6 month period until July 1919.

Figure 8. Burial Chronology at Fisher River

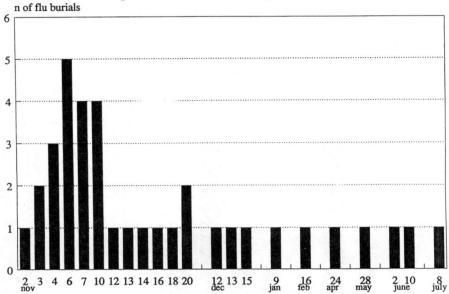

Communities Untouched By the Epidemic

Having discussed the communities hard-hit by the Spanish Flu, I would now like to consider some of the reasons why other communities apparently escaped it altogether. Several interdigitating factors appear to have buffered them from the epidemic.

The first and most obvious barrier to the spread of Spanish Flu was location. Split Lake, Oxford House, Island Lake, and God's Lake were relatively removed from the major transportation routes by which it is generally acknowledged the virus travelled. On the other hand, Fort Alexander, Berens River and Norway House were stops on the Lake Winnipeg steamer route. Indeed, it was the steamer Wolverine that brought the flu to Berens River on October 30, 1918 (Pettigrew, 1983). The Wolverine and other steamers may have disseminated the virus to stops along the fringe of Lake Winnipeg, although analysis of the Hudson's Bay Company post records suggests that the disease arrived at Norway House overland from the north (Herring, 1993). Fisher River was not a stop on the steamer route, but it was relatively close to Winnipeg, the central place from which the disease probably diffused, as well as to the CNR railway and to roads emanating from Winnipeg. Fort Alexander, on the other hand, appears to be the exception to the rule, showing the lowest mortality rate of the study communities, despite the fact that it is the closest location to Winnipeg. This looked quite suspicious, so I cross-checked the Anglican Church burial register (Mf 77-5, Reel #1) results with the influenza deaths mentioned in the daily HBC post journal (HBCA B.4/a/9) during the epidemic. The HBC entries produced a mortality rate of 79 deaths per 1000, which is about twice the rate derived from the Anglican mission burial register (35 deaths per 1000), but the 95% confidence intervals overlap, indicating the two rates were not significantly different. The Anglican burial register data still strike me as questionable and I will explore this issue further in future research.

Ray has argued that, historically, Hudson's Bay Company personnel were primarily responsible for the transmission of disease from one location to another in the central subarctic (1974:156-157), demonstrating the importance of trade routes as means by which diseases spread. Decker's (1988:18-24) study of smallpox in the early 19th century found, however, that individuals travelling overland or by river from their camps to trade or to obtain aid, brought the disease to York Factory and Cumberland House.

The velocity of the spread of influenza never exceeds the speed of human travel (Patterson, 1986: 86) and this helps to explain the decay of the epidemic as it moved toward the interior. Travel to the more isolated and northerly locations of Split Lake, Oxford House, Island Lake and God's lake was accomplished by the relatively slow means of canoes and dog teams (compared to steamer travel) well into the 1920s. During the spring, the journey from Norway House to Oxford House took about 3 days; another 8 days of travel was necessary to reach Island Lake. Fall journeys took longer, with 7 days needed to travel to Oxford House from Norway House and a further 10 days to arrive at Island Lake (Harris, 1987:63). Clearly, time and distance were also factors in the dimunition of the flu epidemic as it moved toward the more isolated interior locations.

The timing of the outbreak was fortuitous for the more isolated communities as well. The epidemic arrived in late October and early November, when most of the people had left for their winter camps and when communication with places like Norway House was curtailed until freeze-up made it safe to travel. Reduced inter-community contact, cou-

379

pled with fissioning into small family trapping groups, meant that the outbreak was subsiding by the time campers returned for more supplies in December. Still, many small family groups out on trap lines contracted the deadly flu and the bodies of many who died were brought back to the settlements around the HBC posts for burial.

It is important to recall, moreover, that an incredibly rich and constant flow of information and gossip traverses the north. News of the epidemic may have spread faster than the epidemic itself. The Oxford House Post Journal for January 1919 notes, for instance, that the Island Lake chief forbade dog teams to proceed to Norway House because of sickness there (HBCA B.156/1/44, fo.9-11). In fact, the "great sickness" itself may have come as no surprise to many northern communities since a powerful dream about it had circulated in the year preceding the outbreak (Gary Granzberg, personal communication).

In sum, the relatively low intensity of trade, distance from major transportation routes, isolation, the onset of the epidemic in the fall, group fissioning owing to the seasonal round of activities in a hunting and trapping economy, and the swift passage of information about the progress of the epidemic that encouraged people to keep away from areas where sickness abounded, all appear to have saved Oxford House, Split Lake, Island Lake, and God's Lake from this virgin soil epidemic.

CONCLUSIONS AND INFERENCES

Clearly, local socio-ecological conditions significantly influenced each community's experience of the 1918 Spanish Flu. Variation in socio-ecological conditions, moreover, underlie the extensive variation in the death toll from the epidemic in the central Canadian subarctic. This suggests that it is extremely dangerous to generalize epidemiological information from one, or even a small number of communities, to wider geographical areas. Total mortality rates, the duration of the epidemic, and undoubtedly, the extent of community disruption must have shown substantial diversity in other epidemics in the past, as in the case of the 1918 Flu. The hypothesis that virgin soil epidemics introduced by Europeans were universally cataclysmic in Aboriginal communities (cf. Dobyns, 1983) reflects the poverty of our information, not a lack of variation in response.

The 1918 Flu epidemic illustrates how Aboriginal communities directly along trade and transportation routes and in relatively close contact with the central source of infection suffered more extensively from epidemics than those socially and geographically further removed from it (see also Dobyns, 1992). Given that our ideas about the devastation wrought by early virgin soil epidemics of European origin essentially come from communities in close contact with Europeans, and hence from communities with inflated death rates precisely because of that contact, it then follows that we may have over-emphasized the role played by mortality from infectious diseases in the postcontact history of the Americas.

The challenge for physical anthropologists is to develop more local, detailed epidemiological sequences from the historic record. Analysis of parish records offers one fruitful source of new information on the transmission, duration, and impact of postcontact epidemics of infectious disease.

ACKNOWLEDGEMENTS

I am grateful to the Norway House Band Council for giving me permission to study their records. I greatly appreciate assistance from Mr. Leonard McKay, Mr. Tommy York, Mr. Nathaniel Queskekapow, Mr. Charlie Queskekapow, and Mr. Harry Everett who shared their time, hospitality, and recollections of the 1918 epidemic with me. I also wish to thank the staff of the Hudson's Bay Company Archives, the Anglican Church of Canada Archives, and the United Church of Canada Archives for their invaluable assistance. I am also grateful to Chris Egan, Tina Moffat, Andrew Mathiesson, and Henry Weilenmann for help in collecting the primary source data. The research was supported by Social Science & Humanities Research Council award #410-89-0638 and Arts Research Board of McMaster University award # 5-58631.

ENDNOTES

1   Fort Alexander (Anglican Church of Canada Archives [ACCA Mf. 77-5, #2), Norway House (ACCA Mf.77-5, #3), Split Lake (ACCA Mf.77-5, #3).

2   Fisher River (United Church of Canada Archives (UCCA, #78-27), Berens River (UCCA #87-4), Oxford House (UCCA #78-27), God's Lake (UCCA #81-32).

3   This is lower than the rate of 79/1000 gleaned from HBC post journal records but the 95% confidence intervals overlap, indicating the two rates were not significantly different.

4   The 95% confidence limits in Figure 7 overlap for Norway House, Berens River, and Fisher River indicating that there is no statistically significant difference in these estimated mortality rates.

REFERENCES

ACCA (Anglican Church of Canada Archives, General Synod Office, Toronto, Canada) (1902-1937) Mf. 77-75, Reel #3, Diocese of Keewatin Records, Norway House Burials.

American Journal of Public Health. 1968. Editorial. 58(2):2192-2194.

Bannister, BA (1983) *Infectious Diseases.* London: Balliere Tindall.

Beveridge, WIB (1977) *Influenza: The Last Great Plague.* New York: Prodist.

Borah, WW (1976) The historical demography of aboriginal and colonial America: An attempt at perspective. In: *The Native Population of the Americas in 1492,* p. 13-34. WH Deneven, ed. Madison: U. of Wisconsin Press.

Burnet, FM and Clark, E (1942) *Influenza.* London: Macmillan & Co.

Cook, SF (1973) The significance of disease in the extinction of the New England Indians. *Human Biology* 45:485-508.

Cook, SF and Borah, WW (1971) *Essays in Population History: Mexico and the Caribbean, vol. 1.* Berkeley: University of California Press.

Crosby, AW (1986) *Ecological Imperialism: The Biological Expansion of Europe, 900-1900.* Cambridge: Cambridge University Press.

Crosby, AW (1989) *America's Forgotten Pandemic: The Influenza of 1918.* Cambridge: Cambridge University Press.

Decker, JF (1988) Tracing historical diffusion patterns: The case of the 1780-82 smallpox epidemic among the Indians of Western Canada. *Native Studies Review* 4(1-2):1-24.

Dobyns, HF (1976) Scholarly transformation: Widowing the "virgin land". *Ethnohistory* 23:161-172.

Dobyns, HF (1983) *Their Numbers Become Thin.* Knoxville, Tenn: The University of Tennessee Press.

Dobyns, HF (1984) Native American population collapse and recovery. In: *Scholars and the Indian Experience,* p. 17-35. WR Swagerty, ed. Bloomington: Indiana University Press.

Dobyns, HF (1992) Native American trade centers as contagious disease foci. In: *Disease and Demography in the Americas,* p. 215-222, JW Verano and DH Ubelaker, eds. Washington, D.C.: Smithsonian Institution.

Everett, HN (1985) Untitled memoirs. Winnipeg, Manitoba.

Government of Canada (1917) *Sessional Paper No. 27,* George V (9-10):18-19.

Graham-Cumming, G (1967) Health of the original Canadians, 1867-1967. *Medical Services Journal Canada* 23:115-66.

Graves, C (1969) *Invasion By Virus.* London: Icon Books.

Harris, RC (1987) *Historical Atlas of Canada, Volume I.* Toronto: University of Toronto Press.

HBCA (Provincial Archives of Manitoba, Hudson's Bay Company Archives, Winnipeg, Manitoba).

HBCA (1916-1920) HBCA B.4/a/9, Fort Alexander Post Journal.

HBCA (1917-1922) HBCA B.239/a/190, York Factory Post Journal.

HBCA (1917-1924) HBCA B.283/a/8/, God's Lake Post Journal.

HBCA (1918) HBCA A.74/48, Annual Reports from District Officers - Outfit 1918, formerly HBCA D.FTR.9).

HBCA (1918-1923) HBCA B.154/a/87, Norway House Post Journal.

HBCA (1918-1922) HBCA B.156/1/44, Oxford House Post Journal.

HBCA (1926) A.95/53, pp. 6-33. Health and Disease at the Norway House Indian Agency. Stone, EL.

Helm, J (1980) Female infanticide, European diseases and population levels among McKenzie Dene. *American Ethnologist* 7:259-85.

Herring, DA (1993) "There were young people and old people and babies dying every week": The 1918-1919 influenza pandemic at Norway House. *Ethnohistory* 41(1):73-105.

Kaplan, MM and Webster, RG (1977) The epidemiology of influenza. *Scientific American* 237(6):88-106.

Lilienfeld, AM and Lilienfeld, DE (1980) *Foundations of Epidemiology*, 2nd ed. New York: Oxford University Press.

Lux, M (1992) Prairie Indians and the 1918 Influenza Epidemic. *Native Studies Review* 8 (1):23-33.

MacDougall, H (1985) *The Fatal Flu.* Horizon Canada 8(8):2089-2095.

Mausner, J and Bahn, A (1974) *Epidemiology.* Boston: Little Brown.

McGrath, J (1991) Biological impact of social disruption resulting from epidemic disease. *American Journal of Physical Anthropology* 84(4):407-20.

Merbs, CF (1992) A New World of infectious disease. *Yearbook of Physical Anthropology* 35:3-42.

Moffat, C (1992) Infant Mortality in an Aboriginal Community: An Historical and Biocultural Analysis. MA Thesis, Department of Anthropology, McMaster University, Hamilton, Canada.

Neel, JV (1982) Infectious disease among Amerindians. *Medical Anthropology* 6(1):47-55.

PAM (Provincial Archives of Manitoba, Winnipeg, Canada) (1902–1930) MG8 B47, O'Reilly, Anna M. Notes re. history of the past — Le pas, Northwest Territories — Later Manitoba (Reminiscences re: The LaRose Family and the Pas).

Patterson, KD (1986) *Pandemic Influenza 1700-1900.* Totowa, N.J.: Rowman & Littlefield.

Pettigrew, E (1983) *The Silent Enemy. Canada and the Deadly Flu of 1918.* Saskatoon: Western Producer Prairie Books.

Piché, V and George, MV (1973) Estimates of vital rates for the Canadian Indians, 1960-1970. *Demography* 10(3):367-382.

Ramenofsky, AF (1987) *Vectors of Death: The Archaeology of European Contact.* Albuquerque: University of New Mexico Press.

Ray, AJ (1974) *Indians in the Fur Trade.* Toronto: University of Toronto Press.

Ray, AJ (1976) Diffusion of diseases in the western interior of Canada, 1830-1950. *Geographical Review* 66(2):139-57.

Scholtissek, C (1992) Cultivating a killer virus. *Natural History* 1:3-6.

Smith, W, Andrewes, CH, and Laidlaw, PP (1933) A virus obtained from influenza patients. *Lancet* 2:66-68.

Stewart, TD (1973) *The People of America.* New York: Charles Scribner's Sons.

Stone, EL (1926) Health and disease at the Norway House Indian Agency. *PAM HBCA.* A/95/53, pp.6-33.

Stuart-Harris, Sir CH, Schild GS, and Oxford, JS (1985) *Influenza: The Viruses and the Disease*. 2nd ed. Baltimore, Maryland: Edward Arnold.

Thacker, SB (1986) The persistence of Influenza A in human populations. *Epidemiologic Reviews* 8:129-42.

Thornton, R (1987) *American Indian Holocaust and Survival. A Population History Since 1492*. Norman, Oklahoma: U. of Oklahoma Press.

Turk, DC, Porter, IA, Duerden, BI and Reid, TMS (1983) *Medical Microbiology*. Toronto: Hodder and Stoughton.

UCCA (United Church of Canada Archives, Conference of Manitoba and Northwestern Ontario, Winnipeg, Canada).

UCCA (1894-1926) 81-32 God's Lake Narrows Burial Register.

UCCA (1895-1908) 78-36 Fisher River Burial Register.

UCCA (1918-1951) 78-27 Fisher River Burial Register.

UCCA (1918-1951) 78-28 Oxford House Burial Register.

Verano, JW and Ubelaker, DH, eds. (1992) *Disease and Demography in the Americas*. Washington, D.C.: Smithsonian Institution.

Waldram, JB, Herring, DA, and Young, TK (in press) *Aboriginal Health in Canada: Historical, Cultural and Epidemiological Perspectives* Toronto: University of Toronto Press.

Walters, JH (1978) *Influenza 1918: The Contemporary Perspective*. New York: Academy of Medicine 54(9):855-864.

18

Burning Point
Canadian Case Studies of Intentionally Cremated Human Remains

Scott I. Fairgrieve and Eldon Molto

There are multiple contexts in which human remains are cremated. Those with forensic implications include instances of mass disasters (plane crashes and train derailments), structural fires (e.g., houses, factories), and remains intentionally cremated for the purposes of destroying evidence and concealing death. The latter scenario has occurred in two recent cases in Ontario, Canada. After a general discussion of cremation analysis in forensic anthropology we detail the contexts of these cases and comment on their unique circumstances. We discuss similarities and differences in the collection of evidence (in situ controls), analytical procedures, aspects of positive identification, and the overall problems of analysis of these cremated remains. In both cases dental evidence was critical in identifying the deceased.

FORENSIC ANTHROPOLOGY

Forensic anthropology is an applied field of biological anthropology. It is 'applied' because biological anthropologists trained in human osteology use their skills of skeletal analysis in legal situations (Reichs, 1986). This may include any instance in which human remains are initially discovered and rendered 'non-archaeological' in the sense that they date from the modern or recent era. Forensic anthropologists will generally be consulted when they can supply information about the identity and circumstances surrounding the death of someone represented only by bones and teeth.

This chapter discusses human remains that have been subject to fire sufficiently intense that only the bones and teeth of the deceased individual remain. The special methods employed by forensic anthropologists investigating such situations are discussed and illustrated with two recent case studies of burned human remains from northern Ontario. In each case the authors were requested by law enforcement officials to excavate at the crime scene and subsequently, to analyse intentionally cremated human remains.

Prior to discussing these cases we will briefly outline the responsibilities of the forensic anthropologist in relation to law enforcement agencies and individuals accused of committing the crime.

FORENSIC ANTHROPOLOGY

Snow (1982) notes that the protocol of questions addressed in most forensic anthropological analyses has not changed in more than 100 years. The forensic anthropologist asks the following sequence of questions (Snow 1982: 104):

(1) Are the remains human?
(2) Do they represent a single individual or the commingled remains of several?
(3) When did death occur?
(4) How old was the decedent?
(5) What was the decedent's sex?
(6) What was the decedent's race?
(7) What was the decedent's stature?
(8) Does the skeleton (or body) exhibit any significant anatomical anomalies, signs of old disease and injuries or other characteristics which singly or in combination are sufficiently unique to provide positive identification of the decedent?
(9) What was the cause of death? (e.g., gunshot wound, blunt force trauma, tuberculosis, unknown, etc.).
(10) What was the manner of death? (e.g., natural, accident, suicide, homicide, unknown).

The same questions are asked, regardless of the condition of the remains. However, the analyst's ability to answer these questions is often dependent upon the condition or quality of preservation of the remains.

Forensic anthropologists are called upon for their expertise in analysing bone (Stewart, 1979). Not all biological anthropologists are trained in osteology and hence, it is generally skeletal biologists who seek specialized training to become qualified for this role. Iscan (1988: 204) notes that, 'members of the criminal justice system as a whole do not really understand that all physical anthropologists do not have the proper background or credentials, and are thus not qualified to serve in a forensic capacity'. Post graduate training and population research in skeletal biology (including field work) are critical components in the pursuit of certification in the American Academy of Forensic Sciences (AAFS), the formal body that accredits forensic specialists (Iscan, 1988). Although it is basically an American organization, Canadian members are eligible to join the AAFS and are subject to the same standards of professional assessment (Bass, 1987a). Although the value of population field research to forensic anthropology is rarely stressed, studying large skeletal collections from different populations, which are often derived from prehistoric or historic contexts, provides a unique form of training that can be applied to forensic cases. Given the serious nature of forensic investigations, there should be great concern as to who is assisting law enforcement agencies.

LEGAL RESPONSIBILITIES

If the forensic anthropologist is called to a potential crime scene, he/she normally works with police specialists from the identification branch or forensic recovery unit. To preserve the context, standard archaeological techniques are utilized. The practice of applying archaeological methods to the gathering and excavation of forensic evidence has been dubbed 'forensic archaeology' (see Morse et al., 1976; Skinner and Lazenby, 1983; Krogman and Iscan, 1986).

A police officer is usually in charge of recovering the evidence and supervises the recording and numbering of everything gathered from the crime scene. He or she is the first link in the 'chain of evidence'. This 'chain' is a record of all individuals who have had custody of and/or have worked on any portion of the evidence. This ensures that tampering with the evidence does not take place. To further guard against tampering, the evidence is housed in a secure facility to which only authorized persons have access.

Forensic anthropologists must maintain objectivity and be neutral vis à vis the evidence. Police officers often wish to volunteer a great deal of information concerning the suspected identity of the deceased, but this must be discouraged because it may bias the forensic anthropologist's interpretations and conclusions (for more details, see Galloway et al., 1990). Generally, the responsibilities of forensic anthropologists in Canada are similar to those working in the United States of America, although subtle differences occur.

In order to appreciate the special difficulties encountered in analysing bodies that have been burned, it is important to review the cremation process and the changes it induces in bone tissue.

THE CREMATION PROCESS

The cases discussed in this chapter involve tissue burned beyond the clinically defined fourth degree where the skin and underlying tissues have been completely destroyed, soft tissue has been eliminated, and direct charring of the underlying bone has begun (for further information see Spitz, 1980). It is important to note that just because bones have been charred, this does not mean that the individual actually died as a direct result of the fire or from smoke inhalation. However, some evidence of the manner and cause of death may be present even in the most thoroughly charred remains.

There is wide variation in the colour of bones that have been burned (Heglar, 1984:148; Mayne, 1990). These may vary from 'yellow-light brown, black-blue-grey, to white' (Heglar, 1984: 148). Bone exposed to fire undergoes colour changes due to the dehydration process in which the organic constituents of bone are lost, resulting in bone that is lighter and more brittle. The colour of the bone is a clue to the temperature, time of exposure and location of burning, as well as to direct or indirect heating or burning (1984: 148). Shipman and colleagues (1984) tested this apparent link between bone colour and the conditions under which it was burned. They found that the colour of burned bone starts in the yellow range, proceeds through the reds and purples, then 'changes to diverse neutral hues above about 400°C' (1984: 312) and falls into five distinct stages (1984: 312-313):

> STAGE I (20–<285°C) — specimens are commonly neutral white, pale yellow and yellow.
> STAGE II (285–<525°C) — common colours are reddish brown, very dark grey-brown, neutral dark grey, and reddish-yellow.
> STAGE III (525–<645°C) — specimens are neutral black, with medium blue and some reddish-yellow appearing.
> STAGE IV (645–<940°C) — neutral white predominates with light blue-grey and light grey also present.

STAGE V (940+$^{\circ}$C) — neutral white with some medium grey
   and reddish-yellow.

They caution that colour alone is insufficient to identify the exact temperature to which a tooth or bone has been heated, but it can provide a reasonably accurate temperature range.

In addition, variations in colour make it possible to map a burn pattern onto bone diagrams, which can be useful for gauging the position of
the remains relative to the fire source. If the body was not disturbed during cremation, the skeletal elements will remain in the position they were
in when the person was alive. The action of the fire itself, however, will
cause bones to crack as a result of shrinkage (Heglar, 1984: 149). If the
remains are disturbed, however, individual bones may become commingled to such an extent that determining how many individuals are represented by the cremated bone fragments becomes problematic. This cannot be resolved until each bone has been identified as to its type and
anatomical position. If, for example, two right patellae (knee caps) were
found, then there would have to be at least two individuals represented
by the remains. The degree of difficulty in determining the minimum
number of individuals represented by the remains depends on the extent
to which they have been cremated.

Different regions of the body burn at different rates. The arms and
legs burn quickly and fall from the body, while the skull explodes due to
the expansion of fluids in and around the brain (Bass, 1984: 160).
Unfortunately, forensic anthropologists are not generally called to the
crime scene to conduct an archaeological recovery of the remains and this
may result in incomplete collection of all the bones, many of which are
quite tiny. In such cases, the torso is normally the only portion of the
body recovered (1984: 160) and the fragments most likely to facilitate positive identification of the deceased — the teeth, cranial bones and limbs —
remain at the scene of the crime.

In brief, there are many structural changes that occur to human
remains during the cremation process. The destruction of tissues, shrinkage and cracking of bone can severely hamper the analysis and hence
identification of the burned individual at all stages.

CASE STUDIES

The two instances of burned human remains from northern Ontario
presented below illustrate some of the special analytical problems such
cases present to the forensic anthropologist. In both cases, the authors

were requested by law enforcement officials to carry out controlled archaeological excavation at the crime scene and subsequently, to analyse the recovered remains.

We do not discuss the location of the crime scenes, the names of the victims, or the accused, to spare the victims' families and the accused further publicity. However, we do discusss the circumstances surrounding the discovery of the remains, the problems of establishing a positive identification for the deceased individuals, and determining the cause/manner of death for each. Both cases involve individuals who confessed to cremating the remains in question.

CASE #1

One of the authors (S.F.) was contacted by a Northern Ontario law enforcement agency to examine an area of charred material discovered in and around a stone block and concrete fire pit behind a suburban home (Fig. 1). The police had responded to enquiries by out-of-town relatives and co-workers as to the whereabouts of a 48-year-old man who had not been seen for several weeks. The missing man's duties as a travelling salesman explained why no enquiries had been made sooner.

**Figure 1. Photographs of Stone and Concrete Fire Pit
With Ash and Scattered Charred Bone**

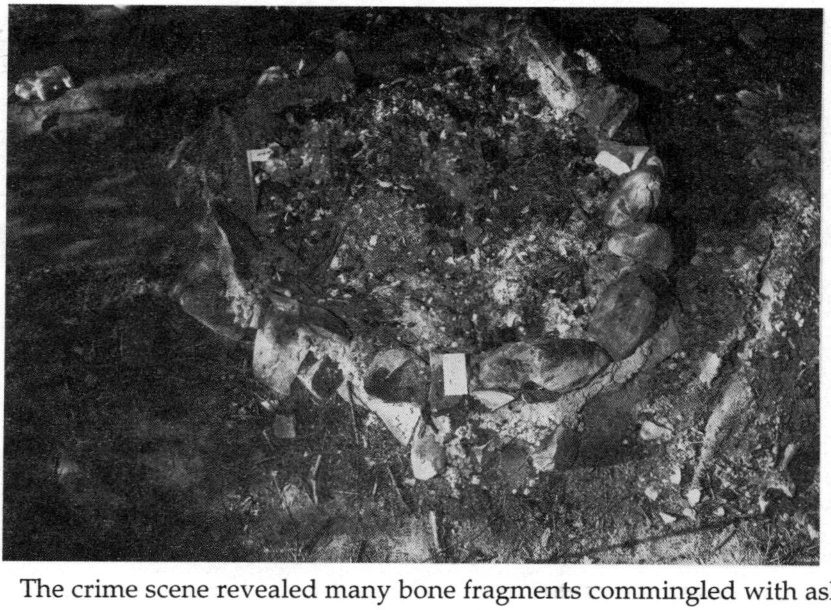

The crime scene revealed many bone fragments commingled with ash and charred wood (which included a charred creosoted railway tie). The bones showed heat induced fractures, evidence of purposeful crushing and scattering, and were widely dispersed across a 9 square metre area. The presence of the largest bone fragment, an almost complete and mature occipital bone (a large bone at the back of the head) immediately confirmed the presence of human remains. The police initiated an investigation of these remains and requested the assistance of S.F. in the collection of the remains and with the subsequent analysis.

Figure 1 depicts a portion of the area in which scattered charred bone fragments and other material were found. The complex nature of the crime scene necessitated establishing a large perimeter in which only authorized personnel could enter. In this particular case only police personnel were at the crime scene and, fortunately, they were careful not to disturb any of the charred bone. Some members of the law enforcement agency had received basic training in forensic anthropology through taking a course at a local university. This helped them to recognize that the help of a forensic anthropologist could benefit the investigation.

The most important aspect of any field recovery procedure is the recording of the context of the remains. The location and relative positions of all remains one to the other must be recorded. A record of the context of the crime scene can provide information on, for example, the position of the body. In this particular case, the bones were scattered extensively because the perpetrator tried to conceal evidence of the crime. In instances of widespread bone scatter, a grid must be established over the area and tied to a relatively permanent landmark, referred to as the datum. For this case the northeast corner of a garage foundation was used for the datum point. A line was then extended along magnetic north and a series of one metre squares was surveyed in place, marked by stakes at each corner.

Each one metre square must be examined and excavated individually. Because each corner of a square has locational co-ordinates that indicate its position relative to the datum point (corner of the garage) these, in turn, become reference points for measuring the position of each piece of evidence. For convenience, the coordinates for the northwest corner stake in each square also serve as the designation (or reference number) for that square. Once all the remains are recovered from each square, the task of identifying the type and position of each bone fragment can be undertaken.

The difficulties of analysing this case were compounded by the intentional scattering and crushing of the remains. Bone in the white calcinated stage (stages IV or V), which predominated in these remains, is very brittle. The further crushing to which the bone was subjected virtually destroyed any chance of positively identifying much of the recovered material. Because osteological analyses are often presented as evidence in court, the identifications of the type and position of bones must be accurate. If you identify a bone fragment to be a portion of the right femur (or thigh bone) you must be able to justify that conclusion with a high degree of probability; mere speculation is inadequate.

All recovered bone is catalogued according to evidence number and identified by type and position. This process includes marking the number directly onto the fragment itself. The fragmentary and fragile nature of cremated bone makes a count of all fragments an unrealistic exercise. Instead, all bone and tooth remains were weighed when catalogued. This was done for two reasons; first, should the bone break during handling, at least the weight of the remains will be preserved; second, the total mass of the remains can be compared to cremation weight standards for adult males (Sonek, 1992). In some cases, bone fragments could be mended with other fragments, providing information on the fracture pattern of the bone. This can be helpful for determining whether a fracture occurred as a result of the cremation process or from traumatic impact.

The same general process was followed for cataloguing tooth fragments. Teeth subjected to intense heat dehydrate in a similar fashion to bone. However, the enamel crown dehydrates at a different rate than the cementum and dentine tissues of the root. The enamel is normally fractured and separated from the other dental tissues. Another by-product of cremation in this case was the melting away of all dental restorations, such as fillings, from the teeth. This meant that dental filling patterns could not be compared to dental records. However, it was possible to identify the type and position in the jaw of some of the victim's teeth recovered from the site.

It became evident from the inventory of the bones that the remains of only one individual were present at the crime scene because there was no duplication of skeletal elements. Other criteria, such as age and bone size and rugosity, presented a consistent picture of an adult male. None of the recovered bones showed evidence of juvenile features. The characteristic surfaces of actively growing bones, such as the presence of the detached ends of growing bone (epiphyses) were not evident and the size and form of the bones were what one would expect for an adult frame. The occipital bone and the brow ridges of the frontal bone recovered from the site were more robust and heavily muscle marked than is usual for females. The total weight of the bone and tooth fragments (2083.0 grams) when compared to the range of cremated adult male bone compiled by Sonek (1992) further supported the conclusion that this individual had been an adult male. Obviously the weight of the fragments is only provisional support of sex and age identification. However, it is important to consider all available data.

Determining the 'race' (a cultural concept not accurately based in biology) of an individual also depends on the familiarity of the analyst with skeletal remains. In this instance the only factor to suggest the possible 'race' of the deceased is the presence of a bone ledge at the lower margin of the nasal opening (aperture). According to Bass (1987a,b) this feature is distinctly Caucasoid, or 'European'. It should be noted that only the widest possible categories can be used in determining 'race' or genetic heritage. Other skeletal and dental traits help refine this process further, but these areas were largely destroyed in the individual in question during the cremation process (see Sauer, 1992 for a discussion of 'race' identification in skeletal remains).

Although age, sex and 'race' are certainly important in the personal identification process, they can only provide clues for narrowing down the range of possible identities of the deceased. In homicides, personal identification also often serve to establish leads on potential suspects. The key to positive identification in this case was the dental evidence, which would not have been gathered without the systematic method of recovery associated with forensic archaeology. The missing 48-year-old male mentioned earlier had excellent medical and dental records. These records also included a plethora of radiographs (X-ray films) from various regions of the body including dental records.

Two teeth in the collection provided striking evidence for positive identification. The upper right first incisor was the only tooth found with the crown still attached to the root (Fig. 2). The crown was manufactured by a local dentist and attached to a metal post installed in the root and was so distinctive that when the dentist was contacted to inspect the tooth, he claimed to recognize it as belonging to the missing person. Furthermore, the type and position of this tooth were identical to the dentist's records for this individual. In spite of the dentist's recognition of the tooth, it was felt that more evidence was required for a positive identification.

One other tooth was found that matched the dental X-rays perfectly. The lower right first molar lost all the enamel of its crown in the fire, but the tissue directly beneath the enamel was perfectly preserved. This underlying dentine had four projections that in profile appeared as two (Fig. 3a). These two projections matched the two dentine projections directly beneath a filling in the missing salesman's dental records and showed clearly on the X-ray (Fig. 3b). Taken together, these two dental features served as a positive identification for that individual.

Figure 2. Photograph of the Upper Right First Incisor with an Artificial Crown Attached to a Metal Post Within the Root

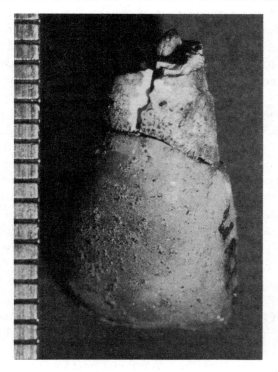

A further study of the teeth was conducted using a scanning electron microscope (SEM) to investigate dental drill striations on the enamel in which the filling had melted away during the cremation (Fairgrieve, 1994). A dental drill leaves parallel striations in the surface of the tissue drilled (in this case enamel or dentine) confirming the type and position of the dental filling. This information can then be compared to the dental record. This technique, developed for this case, confirmed that three more teeth were consistent with the salesman's dental record for type and position of fillings on identified teeth.

**Figure 3a. Photograph of the Lower Right First Molar
with Exposed Dentine Peaks (Arrows)**

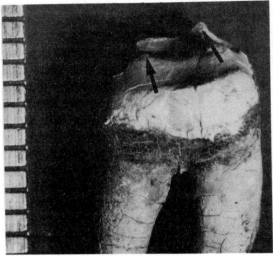

**Figure 3b. Bite-wing Radiograph of the Lower Molar Dentition
Showing the Dentine Peaks (Arrows) on the Lower Right First Molar**

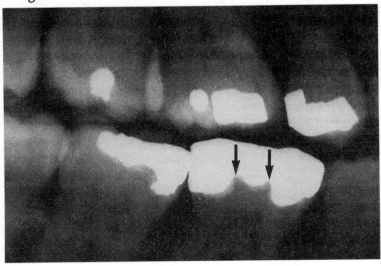

Unfortunately no cause or manner of death could be ascertained from the analysis. Several perimortem (around time of death) fractures were noted, but could not be ascribed to the death of the individual. Other evidence in this case did lead to a charge of second degree murder.

CASE #2

The second case of intentionally cremated remains discussed here parallels many of the circumstances found in case #1. However, in this case, the police were initially notified of the possibility of burned human remains by the suspect, who was seeking 'leniency' for providing information pertaining to a missing person. He stressed that he had found the remains and burned them, not to destroy evidence, but to protect the loved ones by sparing them the grim circumstances of the person's death. The deceased was a child who had been missing for a number of years and was presumed dead. The suspect led police to the burial site, which was located in a remote bush area.

**Figure 4. Drawing of the Excavated Context of
Cremated Remains in Case #2**

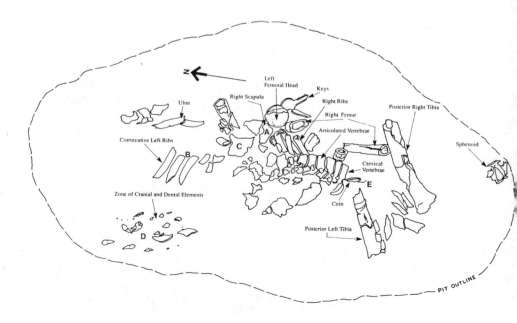

The police immediately partitioned off the area and began clearing the brush in the immediate vicinity of the crematory pit. Only authorized personnel were allowed in the area. Although a datum was not established, a one metre grid system was superimposed over the crime scene. A floorless tent was placed over the immediate burial area, as the spring weather was cold and damp. The excavation proceeded first by recovering and mapping scattered evidence near the surface, then slowly excavating the crematory pit in 5 cm layers. The identification officers quickly realized the problems inherent in the identification of burned remains and requested forensic archaeological assistance. Two professional archaeologists, one from the local university and the other from the Ontario government, joined the excavation. They modified the approach to the burial pit, working from the periphery toward the core area so the extent of the cremation area could be established and the context of the remains better documented. A datum was established.

The archaeologists requested the assistance of the authors in the excavation and identification of the remains. Throughout the excavation, slides and prints (both black and white, and colour) were taken, and most of the excavation was recorded on video. The 'in situ' analysis included the identification of key skeletal elements, particularly articulations and evidence of skeletal damage. The remains from each section of the site were placed in individual containers labelled with the site unit and any identifications of bones we were able to make on the spot (e.g., proximal left femoral fragment). As the excavation proceeded it was clear that we were dealing with the primary cremation (burned in the flesh) of an immature individual and that the remains had not been disturbed after the crematory event. The fact that the remains were only approximately 10 cm below the surface and were not disturbed by animals was noteworthy and indicated that there was likely very little, if any, soft tissue remaining once the fire had been extinguished. The excavation took six days. The non-skeletal elements, such as insect remains, clothing and other personal effects were sent to the Centre of Forensic Sciences in Toronto for analysis.

After completing the excavation, the remains, which were contained in 214 units were brought to the University laboratory. To satisfy the 'continuity of evidence' requirement, a daily log of the use of the lab was kept by the University security. Each unit was studied separately and those skeletal elements large enough were labelled with the site unit. Skeletal reconstruction was done per unit followed by attempts at broader

Figure 5. Skeletal Inventory of Elements
Recovered and Identified in Case # 2

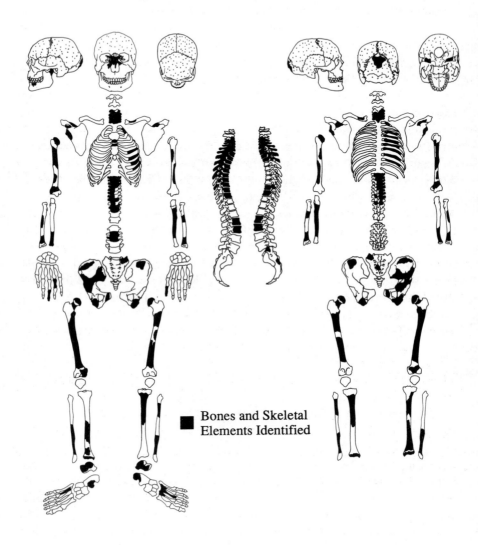

Bones and Skeletal
Elements Identified

reconstruction. These were cross referenced to the slides and photographs taken in the field, a procedure that helped document the burial circumstances, including the amount of disturbance. Figure 5, drawn directly from a slide, depicts the final burial position including the pit outline. Note the articulated spine and the position of the lower limb. From this and other identifications we were able to deduce that the individual was oriented in a southwest direction in a tightly flexed position on the right side. The intense heat had caused the skull to explode, displacing it to the northwest sector of the pit, but leaving a part of the skull base (the sphenoid bone), near the original skull position, uncharred, since this bone in life is immersed in the fluid of the internal cranium. Perimortem disturbance of many bones such as; (A) the glenoid region of the right shoulder bone (scapula) next to and under the left hip (femoral head and part of the right ilium) (C). Several consecutive left ribs were located inferior to the hip region adjacent to the zone of dental and cranial remains. These obviously are not correct anatomically! This figure was used in court in conjunction with a labelled diagram of the human skeleton to illustrate to the jury the disturbance of the remains. The cremator later admitted to disturbing the body, which contrasted with his initial statement to the police.

Figure 6 shows two dimensional reconstructions of the skeletal inventory and burn pattern respectively. We estimated that 70 to 80 percent of the bone was recovered and that 20 to 30 percent of the skeleton was reconstructed. This included several teeth that, like case #1, had separated into their various tissue elements (e.g., enamel crowns were separated from the dentin) because of the intense heat.

A report was made to the crown and defence prior to the court appearance. The suspect, like all individuals unfamiliar with cremation analysis, was apparently surprised to learn of the amount of preservation of the deceased individual. The burn pattern was typical of an open hearth and primary cremation, with the limbs and head showing more severe burning (white burn) than the torso, which has less relative surface area and more soft tissue mass. The diaphyses (shafts) of the long bones were 'white charred' right through, as were the hips and cranium. As noted above, it is difficult to determine the length of time and temperature used in burning the remains because so many variables are involved. From experimental data on colour and fracture patterns produced by Mayne (1990) we estimated a minimum time of 2 hours with temperatures possibly reaching 700 degrees celcius. The latter was based on the fact that measurable shrinkage and warpage of skeletal elements (which were absent even on the white coloured bones on this skeleton), begin around this temperature. The cremator, whose initial statement indicated that he burned the remains for one-half hour, changed his response in court after hearing this evidence. His revised time-frame was from three to four hours.

Figure 6. Burn Pattern Mapped Onto Skeletal Drawing in Case # 2. The Varying Degrees of Burn are Represented in this Figure.

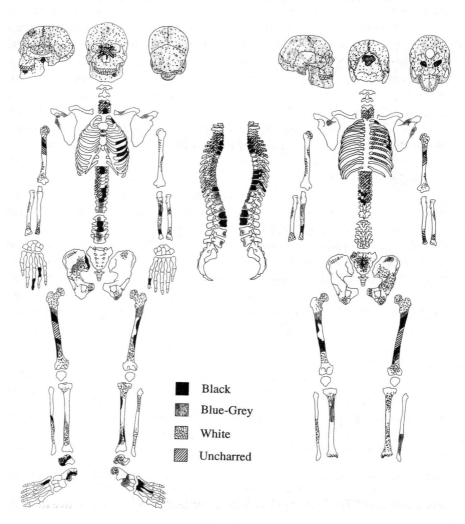

Black
Blue-Grey
White
Uncharred

Personal identification was not an issue in the case, as it was in case #1. Nevertheless, we used dental evidence to estimate the age of this Caucasian child. Sex could not be estimated from the immature remains. To assist with estimating the child's age, a scanning electron micrograph (SEM) of the molar root tips was used to determine if the apices (root canal openings) were 'heat bevelled' or represented biological growth. Finding the latter, and using a dental standard for Caucasians, the estimated dental age of this person is 11.01 to 15.28 years. His known chronological age was 13 years 3 months. None of his tooth crowns (12 complete in total) had any evidence of dental work, consistent with the fact that he had never visited a dentist. These data, plus the cremator's statements and the 'in situ' recovery of housekeys, left no doubt as to the identity of this unfortunate person.

As in the first case, there was no unequivocal evidence of antemortem trauma, though heat induced and perimortem traumatic fractures were extensive. The coroner thus left cause of death unknown in his final report. The remains were returned to the police for proper burial and a week long court case was held 9 months later.

SUMMATION

Both of these cremations were carried out with the intent of concealing evidence. Nevertheless, positive identification of the victim in each case was achieved, albeit utilizing different methods.

It is important for law enforcement officials to note that the analysis of cremated human remains are most likely to yield important information when an experienced forensic anthropologist is included in the collection/excavation process in the field. A lack of familiarity with this type of situation can result in vital pieces of evidence being overlooked.

REFERENCES

Bass WM (1984) Is it possible to consume a body completely in a fire? In TA Rathbun, and JE Buikstra (eds.): *Human Identification: Case Studies in Forensic Anthropology.* Springfield: Charles C Thomas, pp. 159-167.

Bass WM (1987a) Forensic anthropology: The American experience. In A Boddington, AN Garland, and RC Janaway (eds.): *Death, Decay and Reconstruction: Approaches to Archaeology and Forensic Science.* Manchester: Manchester University Press, pp. 224-239.

Bass WM (1987b) *Human Osteology: A Laboratory and Field Manual.* Third Edition. Columbia MO.: Missouri Archaeological Society.

Fairgrieve SI (1994) SEM analysis of incinerated teeth as an aid to positive identification. *Journal of Forensic Sciences*. 39 (2):557-565.

Galloway A, Birkby WH, Kahana T, and Fulginiti L (1990) Physical anthropology and the law: Legal responsibilities of forensic anthropologists. *Yearbook of Physical Anthropology*. 33: 39-57.

Heglar R (1984) Burned remains. In TA Rathbun, and JE Buikstra (eds.): *Human Identification: Case Studies in Forensic Anthropology*. Springfield: Charles C Thomas, pp. 148-158.

Iscan MY (1988) Rise of physical anthropology. *Yearbook of Physical Anthropology*. 31: 203-230.

Krogman WM, and Iscan MY (1986) *The Human Skeleton in Forensic Medicine*, Second Edition. Springfield: Charles C Thomas.

Mayne PM (1990) The identification of precremation trauma in cremated bone. M.A. Thesis, Dept. of Anthropology, University of Alberta, Edmonton.

Morse D, Crusoe D, and Smith HG (1976) Forensic archaeology. *Journal of Forensic Sciences*. 21(2): 323-332.

Reichs KJ (1986) Introduction. In KJ Reichs (ed.): *Forensic Osteology: Advances in the Identification of Human Remains*. Springfield: Charles C Thomas, pp. xv-xxxi.

Sauer NJ (1992) Forensic anthropology and the concept of race: If races don't exist why are forensic anthropologists so good at identifying them? *Social Science in Medicine*. 34(2): 107-111.

Shipman P, Foster G, and Schoeninger M (1984) Burnt bones and teeth: An experimental study of colour, morphology, crystal structure and shrinkage. *Journal of Archaeological Science*. 11: 307-325.

Skinner M, and Lazenby RA (1983) *Found! Human Remains: A Field Manual for the Recovery of the Recent Human Skeleton*. Burnaby: Archaeology Press, Simon Fraser Univesity.

Snow CC (1982) Forensic anthropology. *Annual Review of Anthropology*. 11: 97-131.

Sonek A (1992) The weights of cremated remains. Paper presented at the 44th Annual Meeting of the American Academy of Forensic Sciences, New Orleans. February 17-22, 1992.

Spitz WU (1980) Thermal injuries. In WU Spitz, and RS Fisher (eds.): *Medicolegal Investigations of Death*. Springfield: Charles C Thomas, pp. 295-319.

Stewart TD (1979) *Essentials of Forensic Anthropology*. Springfield: Charles C Thomas.

19

Applying Anthropometry in the Classroom

Hermann Helmuth

Measurements of the human body provide essential data on which to base design and engineering in the context of modern technology. For more than 200 years, scientists have applied a large variety of measures of human beings in order to design the products of technology for improved convenience, efficiency and safety. Our knowledge of human variation over geographical range and historical time and with regard to age, sex, clinical syndromes and user groups offers us important criteria to engineer for a better world. The classroom with its seats and desks is an ideal example which should be fitted to the dimensions of today's students.

THE SCIENCE OF APPLIED ANTHROPOMETRY

In the Greek saga of Theseus, the giant Procrustes (the Stretcher), living beside the road to Athens, had two beds in his house, one small, the other large. He offered night lodging to travellers and would lay the short people into a long bed and stretch them to death to make them fit in; whereas he put the tall ones in a short bed and cut off what was left at the upper and lower end of the bed, thus also "fitting" them to death. He was finally overcome and killed by the hero Theseus...(Graves, 1955).

This story describes vividly what the science of applied anthropometry tries to prevent. In this context, we, the human beings, are the measure of all things, and the "bed" must be made to fit us rather than us suffering in it.

The contemporary environment in which we live from crib to coffin, from foot to head and from morning to evening, is to a very large extent human-made and engineered; as a logical consequence, the Science of Applied Anthropometry evolved to facilitate this task. As understood here, it is defined as the "organized, scientific gathering of human data and their application in design". Other authors use somewhat different words to describe the same objective:

> "Engineering Anthropometry" ... is the application of scientific physical measurement method to human subjects for the development of engineering design standards..." (Roebuck et al., 1975:6) or, as a part of Ergonomics, it is part of the "technology of work design." (Singleton, 1972:9)

The latter author divides Ergonomics into three major areas, Anatomy, Physiology and Psychology with Anthropometry falling under Anatomy and being the science of the "dimensions of the (human) body". However, this leaves out important physiological data of the human being that are "body"less in a strict physical sense, such as strength, endurance, mobility, thermal factors, timing of events and other such processes (Kroemer et al., 1990). In a broader sense, then, we are not only interested in gathering data on the dimensions of the human body, but also on its functions. Other, similar, terms that are used in our context of the technological world of design are: Human Factors, Human Factors Engineering, Engineering Anthropometry and Industrieanthropologie (Jürgens, 1978). Though not all terms are strictly referring to the same process, they at least overlap in describing a major portion of each other and they can well be used more or less interchangeably for our term: Applied Anthropometry.

As is well known to the student of Anthropology, "anthropos" (Greek) means the human being; "metry" refers to measuring.

HISTORY

In the context of the Western European scientific tradition, the first systematic application of human data in design was conducted by the Dutchman Pieter Camper who published "An investigation about the best kinds of shoes" in 1781. Here he points out the value of anatomical and anthropometric design criteria over fashion concerns in the production of shoes — as is still all too often the case even 200 years later. In 1870, the Belgian statistician Quetelet first coined the word "Anthropometry" and

404

applied human measures for the science of growth and development. France, which was in the forefront of (Physical) Anthropology at the middle of the last century, also led in applied anthropometry; in 1882, P. Bertillon proposed the introduction of a battery of eleven easily measured body and facial dimensions for the identification of criminals — a system that was soon abandoned due to inaccurate measuring, to two (or more) individuals having nearly identical measures and to the fact that fingerprint patterns were superior in personal identification (Moenssens, 1971). Wars on both sides of the Atlantic proved how widely applicable is the study of human dimensions. In Germany, Braune and Fischer (1889) published their study on the "Centre of Gravity of the human body as related to the equipment of the German infantryman." Here, the value of anthropometry and biomechanics for the modern army in warfare was recognized for the first time. In the U.S.A., large-scale anthropological studies were conducted during the Civil War (Gould, 1869) as well as later (Baxter, 1875; Davenport and Love, 1921), with many other applications to come, particularly during and after the Second World War (Damon and Randall, 1944; Damon et al., 1966).

The first application of human growth data to the classroom occurred at the meeting of the "Institute Internationale d' Anthropologie" in Liège (1921) at which a resolution asking for the development of mobile chairs and desks with special considerations of infant growth was adopted.

On this continent, E.A. Hooton (1945) conducted an important "Survey in seating" of railway car seats. Though not the first application of human data for the improvement of equipment (see Asa, 1942), its large scale and scientific import made this study a milestone in Human Factors Engineering. Much more military work was conducted during and after WW II. In Canada, both the Defence and Civil Institute of Environmental Medicine and the Department of National Health and Welfare conducted important studies of Army personnel and civilians (Pett, 1955; Pett and Ogilvie, 1956; Nutrition Canada, 1975; Nutrition Canada Anthropometry Report 1980; MacDonald et al., 1978). Considering the diverse origins of modern Canadians, relatively little is known about the normal height, weight and other dimensions of Native Indians, Inuit, Québécois and other Canadians (Auger, 1966; Benoist and Auger, 1965; Hall, 1972; Hall and MacNair, 1972; Helmuth, 1983a).

METHODS AND TECHNIQUES OF APPLIED ANTHROPOMETRY
In the context of Physical Anthropology, it is customary to measure

the nude human body, or, since this is often not possible for cultural and ethical reasons, to measure lightly clothed subjects. This, however, results in an accumulation of data that are useful only for limited or special purposes such as working in warm or hot environments. In praxis, design in the real world often requires the measuring of a dressed person, and his/her data with different kinds of garments are needed. The clothing may be general summer or winter clothing; however, very specialized garments, such as for firefighters, or for workers in cold rooms, may be included. For simplicity's sake, and not always from the practical viewpoint, all measures of the human being (not only the human body!) may be summarized into static, functional, dynamic and temporal measures.

For static measures, three dimensions and the X, Y, and Z-axis (see Fig. 1) must be considered. Their combinations: X-Y axes for measures in the "frontal" or "coronal" plane, X-Z for measures in the "horizontal" or "transverse" plane, and Y-Z for measures in the "sagittal" plane are applied for measuring heights, lengths, depths and widths (or breadths). Height is defined as a measure of the whole body, length is a measure of a segment, depth is a measure in the Z-axis and a breadth or width is a measure in the X-axis of the body in the anatomical position.

Figure 1. Body Coordinate System (After Roebuck et al., 1975)

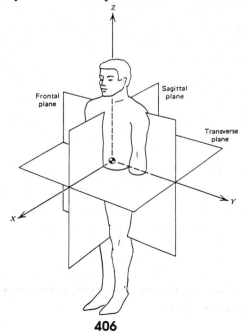

Other simple, static measurements are curvatures, circumferences, prominences and sizes. The human body must not always be in the anatomical position since many other postures such as sitting, kneeling, lying, crawling, squatting etc. may well be more appropriate for the task in question (see Lohman et al. 1991; Roebuck et al., 1975 for more information).

The variety of measurements in applied anthropometry requires many different types of measuring equipment. They range from the simple anthropometer and callipers to photogrammetry, and from stopwatches to complex, sophisticated machines such as force plates, accelerometers, torque wrenches and tanks for underwater weight measuring.

In nearly all applications, the data collection will be followed by various statistical analyses with regard to the range, the statistical mean and its standard deviation, correlations, and many more sophisticated procedures.

DIVERSITY AND VARIATION IN HOMO SAPIENS

Naturally, the object of our studies is the human being (*Homo sapiens*). In this species, we find an unusual degree of variation combined from age, sex, geographical, chronological, social and medical sources. The concept of variation is central to the problem of design for humans and is intricately interwoven in all considerations (Chapanis, 1975).

As a species, we are numerically large, geographically widespread and therefore subject to very different environments, ranging from tropical heat to the extreme cold of the Arctic and Siberia. We are also historically subject to everchanging conditions of environments that shape us (Partington and Roberts, 1969; Pfeiffer and Dibblee, 1982; Rode and Shephard, 1973) as evidenced by the poverty of early industrialization in Western Europe in the last century. These alone would be good reason to suspect a large degree of variation in all sorts of traits, but others add to these and cause even greater variability. As such, we can, foremost, list age and sex variation as most noticeable and important. The latter, called sexual dimorphism, is also subject to ethnic-populational influences; greater height differences were found among American Natives than among Europeans who show greater differences than Africans (Eveleth, 1975).

One aspect of this natural (=biological) variation in our species *Homo sapiens* is reflected in the measure of stature or body height and the difference between males and females (see Table 1; Demirjian, 1980; Martin and Saller, 1959; Pheasant, 1986).

Table 1. Body Height in Some Selected Adult Human Populations
(50th Percentile, in cm)

Population	Males	Females	Differ.	% M/F
British	174.5	161.5	13.0	108.0
U.S.Adults	175.5	162.5	13.0	108.0
French	171.5	160.0	11.5	107.2
German	174.5	163.5	11.0	106.7
Swedish	174.0	164.0	10.0	106.1
Swiss	169.0	159.0	10.0	106.3
Polish	169.5	157.5	12.0	107.6
Japanese	165.5	153.0	12.5	108.2
Hong Kong Chinese	168.0	155.5	12.5	108.0
Indian	164.0	151.5	12.5	108.2
Canadian (national)	174.7	160.3	14.4	109.0
Canadian Native Indian	170.2	156.8	13.4	108.6
Canadian Inuit	166.9	152.5	14.4	109.4
Negrito, Asia	146.3	137.8	8.5	106.2
Mawambi-Pygmies, *	140.8	135.6	5.2	103.8
Kung-Bushman, *	156.4	148.2	8.2	105.5
Dinka, Africa *	177.3	165.7	11.6	107.0

*   statistical average instead of 50th percentile.

It should be pointed out that the distinction of two sexes may well be insufficient for design in various fields, and that the anatomy and body of intersexes poses additional problems for the study of variation. The increased body height in XYY males (Hook & Kim, 1971) or the decreased height in XO "Turner syndrome" females would tend to increase the height dimorphism, usually amounting to approximately 12 to 13 cm in the tallest age group of 20–24-year-old males and females (Flügel et al., 1986:75; Kroemer et al., 1990:19). Also, the proportional increase of elderly persons among Western industrial populations is well documented and again requires special design considerations (Kelly and Kroemer, 1990). For reasons of isolation, health and ethics, the process of collecting data on the elderly is particularly difficult. Due to vertebral osteoporosis, an erect body posture may not be attainable by older individuals, prohibiting height comparisons with younger ages. As well, data collected on the

408

elderly in nursing homes may not be representative of the elderly population in general.

The other end of the spectrum is presented in the collection of data and design for infants. They are especially prone to accidents and to the effects of prolonged habituation to situations that may not acutely affect them, but that may cause long-term adverse effects to their health and wellness, such as scoliosis of the vertebral column.

The migration of people from geographically diverse locations is well documented for countries such as Canada and greatly adds to the degree of biological variation. In addition, from about the middle of the last century on, changes in our biology occurred such as an increased height and weight growth and an advanced and accelerated maturation, which are summarized under the term "Secular Trend" or "Secular Growth Changes" (Van Wieringen, 1978). This trend affects other height- and weight-correlated dimensions and proportions of our human body, such as the relative weight per centimeter or foot length (Demirjian et al., 1972; Helmuth, 1973, 1974, 1983a,b). The question, whether or not this secular trend is still affecting us, is as yet unanswered (Bakwin, 1964).

Special social groups, often also classified as ranks or classes (white collar, blue collar workers, etc.) and special user groups of certain products, such as truck drivers, air force pilots, and many more, must be considered as having special dimensions and proportions (Hopkins, 1947; Stennett and Cramp, 1969; Welch et al., 1971).

The number of factors contributing to human diversity already be enormous, but we still have to add the large variety of genetico-medical syndromes and various disabilities that play an important role in the field of medical design, i.e., artificial limbs, protheses and equipment.

By extending the concept of variation even further, differences between left and right sides exist and vary even between individuals and between the sexes. Though handedness cannot be determined with absolute certainty, the frequency of left handedness decreases slightly with increasing age among both sexes, but left-handed males are consistently about twice as common as females (Flügel et al., 1986:255).

Does an "average man" or "average woman" exist? Certainly not; this must be relegated to the realm of imagination. Statistically, if we take the "middle" one-third of all people centring around one dimension, A, then the chance of finding the middle one-third centring around the average of a second dimension, B, is equal to $1/3*1/3 = 1/9$ and for a third dimension, C, it is $1/3*1/3*1/3 = 1/27$. Logically, it is nearly impossible to find people who would centre around the middle third for more than a few dimensions. It is therefore not surprising that the application of anthropometric data has developed into a specialized field, related, but distinct from the other areas of Physical Anthropology and Human Biology.

Let me give two examples for these theoretical points. The body height (= stature) and weight of Canadians is better documented than any other dimension. These are used to demonstrate the magnitude and diversity of the variation found in this country.

The Nutrition Canada Survey (Demirjian, 1980) lists the heights and weights of social groups as defined by income: A = lowest, C = highest. In the "A" income group, age 20–29 years, males weigh an average of 70.21 kg, females weigh 55.59 kg, whereas the equivalent "C" group shows averages of 73.75 (males) and 60.06 kg (females). Accordingly, the female/male ratio among the "A" group averages 79.18 percent versus 81.44 among the "C" group, or, the difference between the two sexes is larger among the lower income than among the higher income people. But, if height is also considered, the "C" groups of that age show a higher centimeter-weight than the "A" males and females. Also, some dimorphism in the centimeter-weight ratios is maintained, with the "C" group showing one percent less difference between the two sexes than the "A" group.

Historically, the growth pattern of males and females has changed. Summarized under the term "secular trend in growth", the changing environment of roughly the last one hundred years has caused physical changes in our bodies. The data presented in Table 2 illustrate how self-induced environmental changes, most probably nutritional changes, affected our growth and development.

One of the first comprehensive surveys on the height and weight of Canadian schoolchildren was reported on in 1892. The following observations are based on these and newer data collected in 1939, 1952, 1970–72 and 1974–76 (Demirjian, 1980; Farkas and Wood, 1982; Helmuth, 1982a, 1983b; Meredith and Meredith, 1944). Only the ages 10, 12 and 14, most affected by an earlier onset and an acceleration of their adolescent growth spurt, will be presented (see Table 2).

Table 2.   The Body Height (in cm) and Its Percent Ratio of Some
Selected Age Groups of Canadian Boys and Girls.

		1892	1939	Year 1952	1970/72	1974
Age 10						
Males	X	128.7	136.1	135.9	136.6	139.9
Females	X	127.5	135.5	135.4	137.5	140.9
% M/F		100.9	100.4	100.3	99.3	99.2
Age 12						
Males	X	137.6	145.6	145.8	148.3	151.0
Females	X	138.8	148.0	147.8	147.3	153.0
% M/F		99.1	98.4	98.6	100.7	98.7
Age 14						
Males	X	147.6	156.3	158.0	159.1	162.8
Females	X	150.7	156.2	155.7	156.7	159.5
% M/F		97.9	100.0	101.5	102.5	102.1

Over the years from 1892 to 1974, the body height of boys, 10 years old, increased by 11 cm, that of girls by more than 13 cm. The increase was considerably steeper among the 14-year-old adolescents, amounting to nearly 15 cm in the male, but only 9 cm in the female sex.

Accordingly, the pattern of sexual dimorphism also changed. In 1892, the ten-year-old boys were nearly 1% taller than the same-age girls; in the same year, the 12-year-old boys were nearly 1% shorter since the adolescent growth spurt had already started among the females, but not so among the boys. This spurt is clearly evident among the 14-year-old girls since they are now more than 2% taller than the other sex. In 1939 and also in 1952 with little change during the years of WW II, the adolescent growth and the sexual dimorphism during this period of development have already changed slightly. At a young age of 10, as is usual, the boys are slightly taller than the girls, though the degree of difference seems to decrease. At 12 years of age, the girls increase their height difference over the boys. But at 14 years of age, the boys of 1939 equal the female height and in 1952, they overtake the girls and are now 1.5% taller. This means that the adolescent growth spurt accelerated to an earlier age among the boys who are now some 2.3 cm taller than the same-age girls.

Another interesting change had taken place at age 12, since the girls started their growth spurt resulting in a larger difference in height than 40 or 60 years earlier. A similar picture emerges from the 1970/72 data, except that on the national level, the girls overtake the boys at age 10, but soon after, at age 12, the boys start to exceed the girls in their height. In earlier years, (1892, 1939, 1952) this process had occurred two years later. However, this national trend is not evidenced by the two sexes in the two cities of Toronto and Montreal as measured by Farkas and Wood (1982). Here, the boys were about two percent shorter than their female counterparts. It is doubtful that the data gained from the smaller sample are as reliable as those from the national survey. The trend then becomes clear at age 14, when the males exceed the girls by about 1 to 2% at a consistent rate, showing that their growth spurt has set in.

These data demonstrate how profoundly this secular trend in growth, in combination with sexual dimorphism in height, changed the proportions of adolescent Canadians over a period of time of less than one hundred years!

APPLICATIONS OF HUMAN DATA

Western-industrialized people such as Canadians live all their lives in a human-made and -engineered environment. In all aspects of our daily life, we are constantly surrounded by and continuously using products of industry. From shoes to hats and from birth to death we have shaped our own environment in significant ways. Human data are needed for the design of everything that is human-made to improve the effectiveness and usefulness of our products, to ensure their safety vis-à-vis occupational health over short and long periods of time, to improve the comfort and convenience of products and, last, but not least, to make them aesthetically appealing (National Design Council, 1975). Also, the producer is interested in selling the product. Since the time of the Industrial Revolution, if not long before, these products are increasingly mass-produced rather than individually made. They are often completely new designs rather than invented, tried out and slowly improved over many centuries, and now they are often designed for export to other countries and to people with different dimensions and physical characteristics. All these factors combine to ensure the products a greater significance in our lives than 100 or 1000 years ago. Several areas of applications for human data can be highlighted; however, there exists considerable overlap between them.

(1) *The house and home environment.* So many details of our house and housing are designed for our efficiency, safety and convenience that it is impossible to mention more than a few. A bed needs not only the right dimensions of length, width, height (think of the elderly, or disabled humans!), but also the right firmness, surface characteristics, temperature, weight and texture. The Canadian Mortgage and Housing Corporation has edited at least two books with useful suggestions and guidelines (*The Use and Design of Space in the Home*, 1977; *Housing the Elderly*, 1981; Anon., 1986). Elderly people are of particular relevance to our topic because of their numerical increase over the last decade and in the years to come.

(2) *Transportation and vehicular design.* Clearly, the one design product that comes to mind, is the car. Huge amounts of money and scientific work are applied to this single, most important means of modern transportation. Over the years, changes to its interior design have been manifest in all sorts of features to improve their efficiency, convenience and safety. Another machine designed for personal transport, the bicycle, has also seen significant changes. Special attention for improved safety, comfort and efficiency has been given to the three areas of human-machine interaction by introducing clipless pedals, a shock-absorbing seat and an aerodynamic handlebar.

(3) *Garments and clothing.* It seems that numerous changes are necessitated in everyday clothing when one considers the effects of Secular Trends that have caused a height increase of some 10 cm or more over the last one hundred years (Tanner, 1990). With height and weight, other bodily dimensions also change and the question of proportional or disproportional changes at certain periods of individual growth and development are still poorly explored (Helmuth, 1974). The use of soft, pliable textile materials usually lessens the importance of detailed human bodily data .

Naturally, more specialized clothing such as safety vests or firefighter's suits, requires sophisticated research into often contradictory requirements, such as lightness, sturdiness, temperature control, impact protection and others.

(4) *Military equipment and personnel.* This very diverse field of

Human Factors Engineering will not be discussed in any detail since it is too large. From tank to aircraft and to helmet design, the Army has probably the greatest need for precise and widespread human data. It should be emphasized that the inclusion of females into a modern army introduced a vast field of research since variability and the extremes of strengths, endurance, centres of gravity, etc. widened over the previous male-only army.

(5) *Medicine and health.* This vast area needs not only data to distinguish between the "normal" and the "abnormal", or the healthy and the sick, in the distinction of medical syndromes (Farkas et al., 1985a; Feingold and Bossert 1974; Kolar et al., 1985), but also in rehabilitation, equipment design, designing new, artificial body parts, evaluation of proper growth and development of infants, and also in plastic surgery. In the latter field, L. Farkas and his team (1981; 1985 b,c,d) have done outstanding work in Canada. Among other congenital syndromes, they studied the familiar facial disproportions of individuals with Down's syndrome (Farkas et al., 1985a), in order to give plastic surgeons essential advice for how and when to plan surgical corrections.

(6) *Work and work design.* Again, a wide field of anthropometric application can be envisaged to work in industry, forestry, agriculture, at home, and for the design of all sorts of tools for work, for sports, recreation and pleasure. The school and other academic institutions pose a variety of special problems. One of the areas, the unit of chair and desk, will be investigated in greater detail in this article.

Our contemporary life style is to a larger extent than ever formed by learning and the processing of "information". In the environment most often encountered, the human being is sitting on a chair and behind a table or desk from kindergarten on through (often) thirteen years of school, three, four or more years of post secondary education and then behind the office desk. We may well spend more time sitting than walking or even sleeping and lying down. The forces acting on the upper body, the thigh and particularly on the spine and the vertebral column, have been explored and documented (Corless and Baldwin, 1985; Hirschfeld, 1982; Lindh, 1980; Morris, 1973; Nachemson and Morris, 1964; 1966; Singleton, 1972). Inordinate amounts of time spent sitting may well be one of the factors why Canadians, among others, suffer more from back injuries than from any other single source of injury. In 1984, across the country, 28% of all Workers' Compensation claims were for back injuries (Murray, 1988).

In one survey (Grandjean und Hunting, 1980), out of 246 individuals with a sitting type of occupation, 14% felt discomfort in the head, 24% in the neck and shoulders, 57% in the back, 16% in the buttocks and 29% in the knees and feet (the percentages do not add up to 100% due to multiple answers). Generally, the disadvantages of sitting are impaired functioning of internal organs (intestines, lungs), strain on the support area (upper leg, buttocks), muscle fatigue and consequently spinal distortions (Grandjean, 1973).

Ultimately, this part of our body has flaws that may well have their origins in the evolution of an upright posture, but here, we have to investigate the intricate interaction between the designed product and our body from a proximate viewpoint (Grandjean and Hunting, 1980; Helmuth, 1982b).

Though a simple arrangement such as a chair, a desk and a human being do not fulfil the definition of a human-machine system, they still resemble such an interactive system in several details. The human being in a classroom varies between a young child, an adolescent, an adult, an elderly person, a disabled person, a male, or a female (Evans et al., 1988; Holden et al., 1988). Young children encounter special life-styles hazards that can be detrimental to their health; because of their soft, cartilaginous bones and because of their weak muscles, children cannot maintain one body position for long. Bad postures and sitting habits can be "ossified" into life-long health problems. A child's knowledge of what is medically good or bad is still underdeveloped; children are unable to defend themselves adequately against badly designed products and are more prone to follow fashionable trends.

Many children and adolescents, therefore, already suffer from problems of the spinal column, such as scoliosis and back ache, and costly programs have been developed to cure "after the fact" what could more easily have been achieved by a preventive measure. The application of body height as a general measure of relevance to the seat and seat design are shown in Table 3.

Table 3. Body Height (in cm) Among Young Canadians

	Males				Females		
Age	1953	1970/72	1981	Age	1953	1970/72	1981
17	169.4	174	174.2	17	158.8	162	162.2
18	172.7	173	174.1	18	159	159	158.9
19	172.7	176	178.2	19	159	162	164.7
20	172.5	177	178.2	20	159.5	162	164.7
21	172.5	177	176.1	21	159.5	162	160.9

Even over the short time of approximately 30 years, body height increased by 4–5 cm in the male, and by about 3–4 cm in the female sex. Another obvious difference evident from Table 3 is that a greater height is reached at an earlier age (see also Table 2).

Overall, the height-age relationship has changed over a relatively short time frame. These changes in height, and logically also in other body dimensions, have implications for the design of chairs and desks, their proportions and their proportionate frequencies in a classroom, which all together constitute the children's and adolescents' work place (Berquet, no date). A chair has to fulfil different tasks and functions: it must be used for work, for relaxation and for both in combination. Usually, a class room chair is designed for work. Therefore, it should allow free and easy movement, access and egress of the subject sitting in it. The problem of fitting people and chairs can be approached in two ways: one can ask people to adjust a chair until they find it most comfortable as to height, width, angles, etc., or one can measure the user population to find the right dimensions for a scientifically designed chair. With children and adolescents, the first approach is more difficult because they do not know enough about the critical features causing either comfort or discomfort and are easily distracted by unimportant features such as colour or style. Consequently, the second approach is more sensitive to the task at hand and it is therefore recommended. In the school and other institutions of learning, the task is usually limited to asking students to try out and, if needed, to change the chair according to individual requirements. This does not necessarily lead to the purchase of new chairs (and desks), but it may lead to a rearrangement in the frequency of different sized furniture up and down the age and height groups. In order to achieve the desired effects of students who feel comfortable and who are seated properly and healthily, a number of criteria must be pointed out to the teacher and to the student as well. These are demonstrated in Fig. 2. The student can be instructed to take care of his/her own needs at the beginning of a school year so that the efficiency of working in the class-room is properly addressed at least over an academic year. The teacher can contribute to eliminate hazards to learning and to help alleviate posture problems that may well become costly and disabling diseases later in life.

Figure 2. Chair and Desk Criteria To Fit the Person

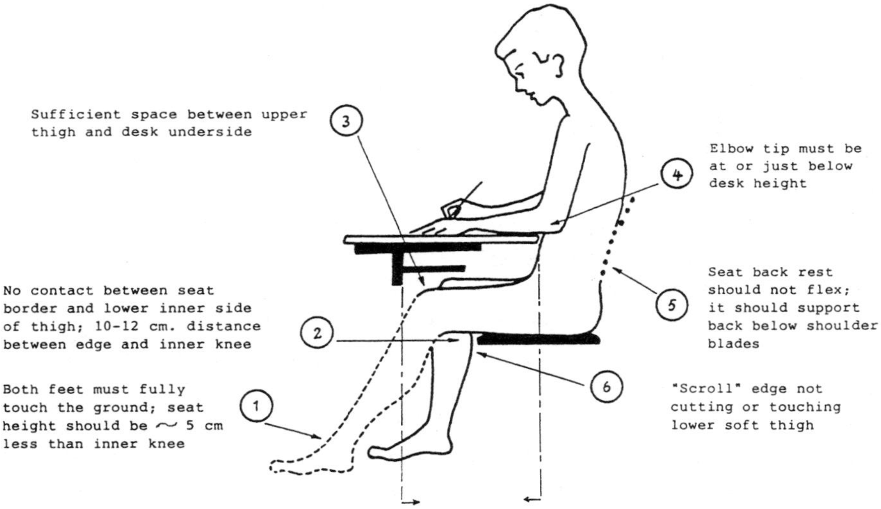

Sufficient space between upper thigh and desk underside ③

④ Elbow tip must be at or just below desk height

No contact between seat border and lower inner side of thigh; 10-12 cm. distance between edge and inner knee ②

⑤ Seat back rest should not flex; it should support back below shoulder blades

Both feet must fully touch the ground; seat height should be ~ 5 cm less than inner knee ①

⑥ "Scroll" edge not cutting or touching lower soft thigh

To achieve the best results, any teacher should have a knowledge of applied anatomy, human variation, human auxology, and also be able to consider financial requirements and limits. A knowledge of the physical human being is useful and desirable not only for the teacher of biology and physical education, but also for the teacher in other disciplines. The argument here is that with greater awareness, some discomfort stemming from many years of sitting and working in a classroom and from a young age on, can be prevented and some of the ailments of later life such as scoliosis and chronic back pain can be minimized or even eliminated. On a more positive note, the application of anthropometry in the school/university situation can help to improve the comfort, efficiency, safety and long-time health of the student.

To aid the student in this task, the following questionnaire was developed:

**Survey questions: simply answer with yes/no
or answer using a +1, 0, or -1 system:**

Can you rest your foot fully on the floor?
If so, is your lower leg reasonably vertical?
Is the front edge of your seat rounded or scrolled?
Is there sufficient space between this edge and your inner knee?
Is there sufficient space between the upper thigh and table edge?
Is there sufficient space between kneecap and table?
Is your elbow tip at about the height of the desk - upper surface?
Is there comfortable space between the backrest and your shoulderblade - lower tip?
Is your seat wide enough for your buttock width?
Is there sufficient room for easy ingress to and egress from the seat?
Are contours and surface characteristics of your seat comfortable?
Can you rest your back against the backrest without sliding forward and slouching?
Can you move freely between a forward-working, an upright and a reclining position?
If there is an armrest, can you rest your lower arm comfortably on it with the upper arm hanging down vertically and the lower arm at about 90 degrees?
Is the length (depth) of the armrest comfortable?

In conclusion, measurements of the human body provide essential data on which to base design and engineering in the context of contemporary technology. For more than 200 years, scientists have applied a large variety of measures of human beings in order to design the products of technology for improved convenience, efficiency and safety. Our knowledge of human variation over geographical range and historical time and with regard to age, sex, clinical syndromes and user groups offers us important criteria to engineer for a better world. Contemporary classrooms should be fitted to the dimensions of today's students!

REFERENCES

Anonymous (1986) The most important room is the kitchen. In: *The Toronto Star* March 13, 1986.

Auger F (1966) La correlation comme statistique descriptive recherche sur les Canadiens-Français. *Societe de biometrie humaine*, 1: 147-164.

Asa ML (1942) A study of workplace layout. Master's thesis. Dept. of Ind. Eng. Univ. of Iowa.

Bakwin H (1964) Secular increase in height. Is the end in sight? *The Lancet* 2: 1195-1196.

Baxter JH (1875) *Statistics, Medical and Anthropological of the Provost-Marshall-general's Bureau.* Washington, D.C.: Govt. Ptg. Office.

Benoist J and Auger F (1965) Note sur l'anthropometrie des Canadiens-Français. *Anthropologica* 7: 5-11.

Berquet, K.-H. (?) *Sitzschaden - Haltungsschaden. Anleitung zur richtigen Anpassung und Auswahl der Schulmöbel.* 2nd ed. Düren.

Braune W und Fischer O (1889) *Über den Schwerpunkt des menschlichen Körpers im Hinblick auf die Ausrüstung des deutschen Infanteristen.* Leipzig.

Camper P (1781) Untersuchung über die beste Art von Schuhen. Cit. from: Geschichte der Anthropologie. In *Anthropologie. Handbuch der vergleichenden Biologie des Menschen.* Hrsg. von R. Knussmann, Stuttgart: G. Fischer Verlag.

Canadian Mortgage and Housing Corporation (1977) *The Use and Design of Space in the Home.* Ottawa: CMHC.

Canadian Mortgage and Housing Corporation (1981) *Housing the Elderly.* Ottawa: CMHC.

Chapanis A (1975) (ed.) *Ethnic Variables in Human Factors Engineering.* Baltimore: J. Hopkins University Press.

Corless D and Baldwin J (1985) Gracovetsky and Farfan on the human spine. *Industrial Accident Prevention Association Newsletter* 32: 3.

Damon A, Stoudt HW and McFarland RA (1966) *The Human Body in Equipment Design.* Cambridge: Harvard University Press.

Damon A and Randall FE (1944) Physical anthropology in the Army Air Forces. *Am. J. Phys. Anthropol.* 2: 293-316.

Davenport CB and Love AG (1921) *Army Anthropometry.* Washington D.C.: Govt. Ptg. Office.

Demirjian A, Jenicek M and Dubuc MB (1972) Les normes staturo-ponderales de l'enfant urbain Canadien français d'age scolaire. *Can. J. Public Health* 63: 14-30.

Demirjian A (1980) Nutrition Canada Anthropometry Report. *Height, Weight and*

Body Dimensions. Ottawa: Ministry of National Health and Welfare Health Promotion Directorate.

Evans WA, Courtney AJ and Fok KF (1988) The design of school furniture for Hong Kong schoolchildren. *Applied Ergonomics* 19: 122-134.

Eveleth P (1975) Differences between ethnic groups in sex dimorphism of adult height. *Annals Hum. Biol.* 2: 35-39.

Farkas LG (1981) *Anthropometry of the Head and Face in Medicine.* New York: Elsevier North-Holland.

Farkas LG. and Wood MM (1982) Height and weight in caucasian school children in Central Canada. *Can. J. Publ. Health* 73: 328-334.

Farkas LG. et al. (1985a) Abnormal measurements and disproportions in the face of Down's Syndrome patients: Preliminary report of an anthropometric Study. *Plast. Reconstr. Surg.* 75: 159-167.

Farkas LG et al. (1985b) Vertical and horizontal proportions of the face in young adult North American Caucasians: Revision of neoclassical canons. *Plast. Reconstr. Surg.* 75: 328-337.

Farkas LG. et al. (1985c) Inclinations of the facial profile: Art versus reality. *Plast. Reconstr. Surg.* 75: 509-520.

Farkas LG, Kolar JM and Munro IR (1985d) Craniofacial disproportions in Apert's Syndrome: An anthropometric study. *The Cleft Palate J.* 22: 253-265.

Feingold M and Bossert WH (1974) Normal values for selected physical parameters: An aid to syndrome delineation. *Birth Defects: Original Article Series X, no. 13.* White Plains, N.Y.: The National March of Dimes.

Flügel B, Greil H and Sommer K (1986) *Anthropologischer Atlas.* Grundlagen und Daten Deutsche Demokratische Republik. Verlag Tribuene Berlin.

Gould B (1869) *Investigations in the Military and Anthropological Statistics of American Soldiers.* U.S. Sanitary Commission, N.Y.

Grandjean E (1973) *Ergonomics of the Home.* London: Taylor & Francis.

Grandjean E und Hunting W (1980) *Sitzen Sie richtig? Sitzhaltung und Sitzgestaltung am Arbeitsplatz.* Munchen: Bayer. Staatsministerium fur Arbeit und Sozialordnung.

Graves R (1955) *Greek Myths.* Cassell & Co. London.

Hall R (1972) Secular changes in anthropometric measurements of indigenous populations of British Columbia. *Am. J. Phys. Anthropol.*: 37: 439 (Abstract).

Hall R. and MacNair PL (1972) Multivariate analysis of anthropometric data and classification of British Columbia natives. *Am. J. Phys. Anthropol.* 37: 401-409.

Helmuth H (1973) Anthropometry of university students - Trent University, Peterborough, Ontario. *Z. Morph. Anthrop.* 65: 174-185.

Helmuth H (1974) Body height, foot size and the secular trend in growth. *Z. Morph. Anthrop.* 66: 31-42.

Helmuth H (1982a) Anthropometrie und akzeleration in Kanada. *Humanbiol. Budapest.* 12/4: 157-177.

Helmuth H (1982b) Seats, desks, and students. *Orbit 61,* 13: 25-27.

Helmuth H (1983a) An anthropometric survey of Tyendinaga Mohawk children: Secular trends. *Canadian J. of Anthrop.* 3: 131-142.

Helmuth H (1983b) Anthropometry and the secular trend in growth of Canadians. *Z. Morph. Anthrop.* 74: 75-90.

Hirschfeld F (1982) Human spine — Biomechanics. *Mechanical Engineering* 1982: 24-30.

Hook EB and Kim DS (1971) Height and antisocial behavior in XY and XYY boys. *Science* 172: 139-150.

Holden JM, Fernie G and Lunau K (1988) Chairs for the elderly. *Applied Ergonomics* 19: 281-288.

Hooton EA (1945) *A Survey in Seating.* Gardner, Mass.: H. Wakefield.

Hopkins JW (1947) Height and weight of Ottawa elementary school children of two socio-economic strata. *Hum. Biol.* 19: 68-82.

Jurgens HW (1978) Aufgaben und methoden der industrieanthropologie. *Anthrop. Anz.* 36: 169-176.

Kelly PL and Kroemer KHE (1990) Anthropometry of the elderly: Status and recommendations. *Human Factors*: 32(5): 571-595.

Kolar JM, Farkas LG and Munro IR (1985) Surface morphology in Treacher Collins Syndrome: An anthropometric study. *The Cleft Palate J.* 22: 266-274.

Kroemer KHE, Kroemer HJ and Kroemer-Elbert KE (1990) *Engineering Physiology. Bases of Human Factors/Ergonomics.* 2nd ed. New York: Van Nostrand Reinhold.

Lindh M (1980) Biomechanics of the lumbar spine. In VH Frankel and M Nordin (eds.) *Basic Biomechanics of the Skeletal System.* Philadelphia: Lea and Febiger.

Lohman TG, Roche AF and Martorell R (1991) *Anthropometric Standardization Reference Manual.* Abr. ed. Champaign, Ill.: Human Kinetics Books.

MacDonald GAH, Sharrard KA and Taylor MC (1978) Preliminary anthropometric survey of Canadian Forces Women. *DCIEM Technical Report No. 78X20.* Ottawa: Department of National Defence.

Martin R and Saller K (1959) *Lehrbuch der Anthropologie in systematischer Darstellung.* Bd. 2. Stuttgart: G. Fischer Verlag.

Meredith HV and Meredith EM (1944) The stature of Toronto children half a century ago and today. *Hum. Biol.* 16: 126-131.

Moenssens AA (1971) *Fingerprint Techniques.* Philadelphia: Chilton Book Co.

Morris JM. (1973) Biomechanics of the spine. *Arch. Surg.* 107: 418-423.

Murray L (1988) *Workshop on Workplace Back Injuries.* Can. Centre for Occ. Health and Safety. CCOHS no. P88-6E, Hamilton, p. 23.

Nachemson A (1966) The load on lumbar disks in different positions of the body. *Clin Orthop.* 45: 107-122.

Nachemson A and Morris JM (1964) In vivo measurements of intradiscal pressure. *J. Bone and Joint Surg.* 46: 1077-1092.

National Design Council of Canada (1975) *Design For People.* Ottawa: Information Canada.

Partington MW and Roberts N (1969) The heights and weights of Indian and Eskimo school children on James Bay and Hudson Bay. *Can. Medical Assoc. Journal* 100: 502-509.

Pett LB (1955) A Canadian table of average weights for height, age, and sex. *Amer.*

J. Public Health 45: 862-868.

Pett LB and Ogilvie GF (1956) The Canadian weight-height survey. *Hum. Biol.* 28: 171-188.

Pheasant S (1986) *Bodyspace. Anthropometry, Ergonomics and Design.* London: Taylor & Francis.

Pfeiffer S and Dibblee L (1982) The effect of urbanization on the growth of Canadian native children. *Can. J. Anthrop.* 2: 217-224.

Rode A and Shephard R (1973) Growth, development and fitness of the Canadian Eskimo. *Medical Sci. in Sports* 5: 161-169.

Roebuck JA Jr., Kroemer KHE and Thomson WG (1975) *Engineering Anthropometry Methods.* New York: John Wiley & Sons.

Singleton WT (1972) *Introduction to Ergonomics.* World Health Organization, Geneva.

Stennett G and Cramp DM (1969) Cross-sectional, percentile height and weight for a representative sample of urban, school-aged, Ontario children. *Can. J. Public Health* 60: 465-470.

Tanner, JM (1990) *Fetus into Man: Physical Growth from Conception to Maturity.* Cambridge, Massachusetts: Harvard University Press.

Van Wieringen JC (1978) Secular growth changes. In F. Falkner and JM Tanner (eds): *Human Growth.* Vol. II; *Postnatal Growth.* New York: Plenum House.

Welch JP, Windsor EJ and Mackintosh SM (1971) The distribution of height and weight, and the influence of socio-economic factors, in a sample of Eastern Canadian urban school children. *Can. J. Public Health* 62: 373-380.

20

Prehistoric Anemia and Contemporary Public Health Policy

Patty Stuart-Macadam

The roots of skeletal biology stem from comparative anatomy, which originated in the 17th century, and the human fascination with other peoples and cultures, dating from the 15th century. As a result, in the past skeletal biologists have been very much concerned with descriptive rather than analytical studies, and in exploring biological differences and similarities among various human populations. However, in recent years there has been a trend towards a more analytical, processural, and problem-oriented approach to research in skeletal biology. This has taken skeletal biology out of the realm of academia and into the real world.

This is particularly true with respect to the growing fields of paleopathology and paleonutrition. The following chapter illustrates how exploring signs of anemia in prehistoric populations have relevance to modern patterns of health and disease, and implications not only for the individual, but also for general medical practice, public health issues, and government policies.

WHAT IS ANEMIA?

Anemia, or below normal concentration of hemoglobin or red blood cells, is a condition that has intrigued people for over 3000 years. As early as 1500 B.C. an Egyptian manual of therapeutics, the *Papyrus Ebers*, describes a disease characterized by pallor, dyspnea (shortness of breath), and edema (accumulation of fluid) that was probably anemia (Stuart-Macadam, 1989). In the 16th century anemia was called "chlorosis" or "green sickness", with reference to the extreme pallor and greenish tinge to the complexion that characterized some cases. "Green sickness" was considered to be the result of unrequited passion, and afflicted many Shakespearian characters (Farley and Foland, 1990). However, until the 19th century there was little concensus on either the terminology or symp-tomatology of anemia. Only with the advent of modern laboratory meth-ods has it become possible to identify the various types of anemia (genetic or acquired) and determine the prevalence and severity of the condition.

One of the most common types of anemia is iron-deficiency anemia; it develops when there is insufficient iron for the hemoglobin in the newly forming red blood cells of the bone marrow. As a result, the cells become pale in colour (hypochromic) and small in size (microcytic). Today scien-tists attribute iron-deficiency anemia not to unrequited passion, but to a number of factors including blood loss (hemorrhage, parasitic infestation), deficiency in the diet during periods of accelerated demand for iron, inad-equate absorption (diarrhea), and nutritional deficiencies. The symptoma-tology of iron-deficiency anemia can be vague and nonspecific, but the more frequently reported symptoms include fatigue, weakness, light-headedness, headaches, dyspnea (difficult breathing), and palpitations. When the condition becomes severe and chronic then changes such as koilonychia (spoon-shaped nails), angular stomatitis (cracks at the corner of the mouth), glossitis (sore tongue), stomach inflammation with atrophy of mucous membranes, and bone changes in children may occur (Hoffbrand and Lewis, 1981).

HOW DID ANEMIA AFFECT PREHISTORIC POPULATIONS?

Today, iron-deficiency anemia is considered to be one of the most common conditions afflicting humankind, affecting millions of the world's peoples, especially women and children (Arthur and Isbister, 1987). What was the pattern in the past? It was not until 1929 that skele-tal biologists first made the connection between a palaeopathology seen on the skulls of prehistoric individuals and anemia. This palaeopathology is characterized by pitting of the compact bone of the skull and is usually associated with an increase in the thickness of the diploë or middle table of bone. The lesions or pits can range in size from less than 1 mm in diameter to large, coalescing holes, and are found on the orbital roof and skull vault, particularly the frontal, parietal, and occipital bones (Figures 1 and 2). Although in the past a number of terms have been used to describe these lesions, at present the most commonly accepted term is porotic hyperostosis (after Angel, 1966).

Figure 1.

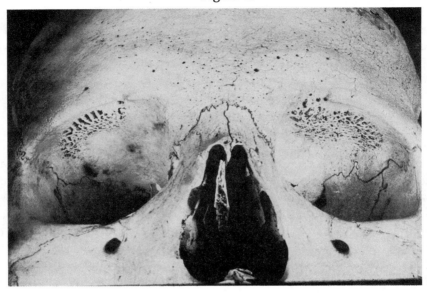

Figure 2.

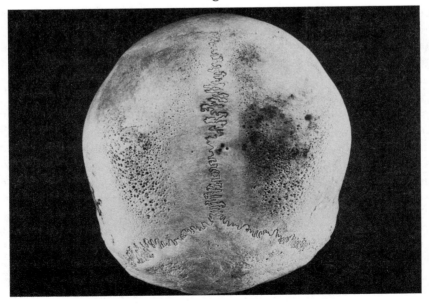

The palaeopathology had been observed by anatomists and anthropologists for over 100 years but no one knew what caused it. When X-rays came into use as a diagnostic technique in medicine several anthropologists (Moore, 1929; Williams, 1929; Hooton, 1930) noticed that X-rays of skulls with porotic hyperostosis looked very similar to X-rays of clinical patients with anemia. There was still a great deal of debate over the etiology of the lesions, but gradually the idea that anemia might be the main factor began to be accepted. I undertook a study to test the hypothesis that anemia was responsible for porotic hyperostosis by comparing X-rays of clinical cases of anemia with X-rays of a number of historic and prehistoric skulls with and without porotic hyperostosis (Stuart-Macadam, 1982). I developed a number of criteria based upon the bone changes that occur with anemia that were useful for comparative studies of ancient skulls. These included the presence of "hair-on-end" trabeculation, thickening of the diploë, thinning of the outer table of compact bone, and thickening of the orbital roof (Stuart-Macadam, 1982; 1987). As a result of my studies I became convinced that it was anemia, and in most cases probably iron-deficiency anemia, that caused the bone changes of porotic hyperostosis in these ancient skulls.

Researchers have examined porotic hyperostosis in prehistoric skeletal collections from around the world and found that it occurs in populations from almost every time period and geographic locale. In a survey of my own work and the published literature on porotic hyperostosis I found some interesting patterns. I was able to detect three major trends: temporal, geographic, and ecological (Stuart-Macadam, 1992a,b). Porotic hyperostosis is rare in populations older than the Neolithic period, and then it starts to increase in prevalence with the development of agriculture in the Neolithic. Generally it decreases in frequency towards the twentieth century. The nearer the country of origin is to the equator the greater is the prevalence of porotic hyperostosis. Ecologically, porotic hyperostosis occurs more frequently in lowland or coastal sites than in highland sites. This is a broad picture, and of course within these general trends there are many variations among sites and through time. It is the overall pattern of occurrence of porotic hyperostosis, however, that provides clues to the factors that are responsible for the development of anemia in prehistoric populations.

WHAT CAUSED IRON DEFICIENCY ANEMIA IN PREHISTORIC POPULATIONS?

For a long time, anthropologists felt that a diet low in iron was the major factor responsible for the development of anemia in prehistoric populations (Moseley, 1961; Hengen, 1971; Carlson et al., 1974; El-Najjar, 1976, El-Najjar et al., 1976; Lallo et al., 1977). This appeared to be supported by the fact that porotic hyperostosis began to occur more frequently with the development of agriculture. Cereal grains in general are known to be an inferior source of iron, particularly in comparison with meat. Studies by El-Najjar (1976) and El-Najjar et al. (1976) on differences in porotic hyperostosis among Southwest Indian populations also seemed to confirm this belief. El-Najjar et al. found that those groups who lived in canyon bottom sites where, presumably, meat was not readily available and there was a greater consumption of maize, had a higher prevalence of porotic hyperostosis than those who lived in sage plain sites. However, a closer look at the data revealed that the story was not so simple, and that there could be other factors that are even more important in the development of anemia.

Using data on pollen and coprolite (dried feces) studies from the same Southwest Indian populations, Reinhard (1992) showed that both canyon bottom and sage plain groups consumed about the same amounts of maize and meat, indicating that diet was probably not a major factor accounting for differences in anemia between the two groups. The collective data actually show that prehistoric groups with a heavy reliance on agriculture have varying prevalences of porotic hyperostosis, some low and some high, as do groups that are known to rely more heavily on animal protein food sources. For example, Ubelaker (1984) found little porotic hyperostosis in an Ecuadorian highland site where there was intensive agriculture. Conversely, Walker (1986) found that a prehistoric group from the Santa Barbara Channel Islands showed a high frequency of porotic hyperostosis in spite of an iron-rich diet from marine sources.

If diet is not the major factor in the development of porotic hyperostosis, then what is? The trends that I observed through time and space indicated to me that there may be a more compelling explanation for the occurrence of anemia in prehistory. It seemed to me that the thread that ran through the pattern of occurrence of porotic hyperostosis was the total pathogen load of a population, that is, the combined levels of parasites, viruses, bacteria, fungii, and other disease-causing micro-organisms. Pathogen load seemed to fit well with the three trends of porotic hyperostosis in time, space, and ecology. For example, with the advent of agriculture, populations and population density increased, and diseases that are population dependent for their transmission became more prevalent. With the development of larger communities people began living in close proximity; that and poor hygiene would have increased exposure to disease organisms. In many areas of the world, the clearing of agricultural land would have encouraged the spread of mosquitos, paving the way for a great increase in malaria. The decrease of porotic hyperostosis towards the twentieth century could be explained by the enormous improvements in hygiene and sanitation in many areas of the world. Differences in prevalence of anemia between temperate and tropical and lowland and highland sites could be explained by the more favourable conditions for micro-organisms in the warmer, more humid sites.

This pathogen load hypothesis is one that I have recently introduced into the anthropological literature (Stuart-Macadam, 1992a,b). Since it is a new idea it is controversial, but it has made researchers question the dietary hypothesis and realize that there may be other, equally valid, explanations for the development of iron deficiency anemia in prehistoric populations.

Various researchers are now testing the hypothesis and it will be interesting to see whether the hypothesis is supported or rejected.

THE RELATIONSHIP BETWEEN PATHOGEN LOAD AND ANEMIA

What is the relationship between pathogen load and anemia? This is a story that is just beginning to be told and accepted by the scientific and medical community. One of the more obvious connections is with parasites and micro-organisms that cause blood loss in humans. Good examples are the parasites causing malaria and hookworm. The malarial parasite invades the red blood cell and causes its premature destruction, resulting in iron-deficiency anemia. The hookworm parasite (*Ancylostoma duodenale* or *Necator americanus*) attaches directly onto the small intestine and causes chronic blood loss, ultimately leading to iron-deficiency anemia. A less obvious connection between pathogen load and anemia relates to our immune system and the elaborate and amazing ways in which humans have evolved with and adapted to our environment throughout millions of years of evolutionary history. This is the relationship between micro-organisms such as bacteria, fungi and parasites and iron stores in the human body. This relationship is one that has only been recognized and discussed by the medical profession since the 1970s (Bullen and Griffiths, 1987; Crosa, 1987; Griffiths and Bullen, 1987; Kluger and Bullen, 1987; Martinez et al., 1990; Payne, 1988; Strauss, 1978; Weinberg, 1974, 1977, 1978, 1984, 1992). Even now this relationship is considered by some to be controversial.

Many micro-organisms require iron for their own growth and development, but lack their own stores. However, they have the capability of manufacturing their own iron-binding substances, called siderophores, which can "capture" circulating iron in the tissues of hosts that they have invaded. Since iron is an essential element for almost all living creatures there is a dilemma for the host organism; it must have enough iron to maintain vital metabolic processes, but at the same time it must somehow restrict the iron available to invading disease-causing micro-organisms. The human body has several strategies for achieving this balance: reducing the absorption of dietary iron by the intestinal mucosa, decreasing the readily available iron in the blood serum by binding it to the transport protein, transferrin, or sending iron into storage in the reticuloendothelial system. This reduction of iron in the blood serum is known as "iron-withholding" or "hypoferremia"; it is now known to be an important aspect of the human immune system. There are in vivo, in vitro, and population studies that support the concept that being temporarily iron-deficient, or hypoferremic, is an advantage during exposure to a number of disease organisms. Weinberg (1992) refers to the fact that several hundred studies on animals and a number of studies on humans have shown that hosts with too much iron in their systems are at an increased risk of infection.

A number of conditions in humans that are characterized by high concentrations of plasma iron and increased transferrin saturation (indicative of high iron levels) are associated with increased susceptibility to bacterial, fungal and protozoal infections (Strauss, 1978; Bullen and Griffiths, 1987). Studies have shown that a functioning iron withholding system results in a decreased risk of infection. It appears then, that iron with-holding is an adaptive response to invading micro-organisms and is a condition that can occur with either acute or chronic diseases. In the case of many acute diseases, the body becomes temporarily hypoferremic as part of its defence system. With chronic diseases there is often an associated anemia, again probably related to attempts on the part of the body to defend itself against pathogens. Anemia of chronic disease is one of the most common forms of anemia, and is associated with a number of diseases such as tuberculosis and osteomyelitis (bone infection) that would have affected past human populations.

Going back now to the data on anemia obtained from studies of prehistoric populations, the parts of the puzzle start to fit together. It is not an iron-poor diet that is responsible for the observed pattern of anemia in prehistory (although this may contribute in a minor way since there is seldom one cause for a condition), but the pathogen load of the population. The greater the pathogen load, the more likely the group will suffer from iron-deficiency anemia, either directly, as a result of parasites such as hookworm that cause blood loss or indirectly, as a result of hypoferremia associated with acute or chronic diseases. The greater the pathogen load the more likely it will be that the body will be unable to maintain a balance between temporary hypoferremia as a defence against micro-organisms and outright iron-deficiency anemia. When this happens, porotic hyperostosis, the bone condition associated with anemia in prehistoric populations, will develop.

WHAT IS THE RELEVANCE OF DATA ON PREHISTORIC PATTERNS OF ANEMIA TO CONTEMPORARY PUBLIC HEALTH POLICY?

As previously mentioned, the concept that iron deficiency is actually beneficial in terms of exposure to disease organisms has only been written about since the 1970s, and even now is not universally accepted. Until very recently iron deficiency was considered to be a condition that was deleterious and needed to be corrected. As well, many researchers believed that an iron-poor diet was the most common predisposing factor for iron-deficiency anemia. Because public health policy is influenced by scientific research, these beliefs have had a direct effect on government policy and medical practice.

In actual fact, even though iron is a critical nutrient in human metabolism, it is a trace element required only in very small quantities. For example, the Recommended Dietary Allowance (RDA) of the United States Food and Nutrition Board is 18 mg per day for pre-menopausal women and 10 mg per day for men and older women (Eaton et al., 1988). Most of the iron needed by the body is recycled; it is liberated by the destruction of red blood cells after their normal life span of 120 days. Absorption of iron by the intestine is a very dynamic process and in circumstances when more iron is needed (after blood loss, or in premenopausal women and growing children), the intestine will increase its absorption of iron. For example, the average western diet provides 15–20 mg of iron daily, of which 5–10% is absorbed in the healthy adult. The level of absorption will increase to 25% in a situation of iron deficiency (Arthur and Isbister, 1987). Iron loss is similarly dependent on iron status. Iron losses in males with normal iron stores are about 0.9 mg per day, whereas iron-deficient males lose only about 0.5 mg per day, and those with iron overload lose about 2.0 mg per day (Finch, 1989). Even so these losses are very small and there is no physiological mechanism for the excretion of excess iron. This means that any increase in iron intake eventually produces an increase in iron stores in the body unless there is a pathological increase in iron losses (Halliday and Powell, 1992). The flexibility of the absorption of iron, and the difficulty of removing excess iron from the body mean that, except for cases where there is outright mal- or under-nutrition, iron-deficiency anemia is much more likely to be caused by factors other than an iron-poor diet. I must stress however, that this is my opinion, based on my interpretation of the data, and not an opinion that is universally subscribed to.

The facts, that diet plays a minor role in the development of iron-deficiency anemia in most cases, and that hypoferremia is part of the body's defence system, have not been appreciated by many researchers. As a result, it is my belief that governments and the medical profession have endorsed health and nutrition policies that may in some cases actually be detrimental. These policies have traditionally encouraged the consumption of more iron without recognizing the dangers of too much iron. For example, since 1940 the Food and Nutrition Board of the United States National Academy of Sciences has endorsed the fortification of wheat flour with iron, in addition to other nutrients. This endorsement became a mandate during World War II. Eventually most flour and commercially prepared foods were fortified with iron and other nutrients, even those prepared foods that naturally contain some iron. It is now standard practice to supplement with iron a broad range of foods including many of the items available on the shelves of supermarkets around the world. These foods range from candy bars and microwave popcorn to peanut butter, frozen vegetables, and fish. For example, an inventory of a large supermarket showed that of the 39 different brands and flavours of powdered drinks (e.g., Kool-aid), all contained added iron. Of the 77 different chips of various types, more than half were enriched with iron (Kent et al., 1990). Iron prophylactics are routinely administered to pregnant women by the medical profession, and mass programs to administer iron prophylactics to infants and children have been implemented in many areas of the world. Nutritionists who work with feeding programs for starving peoples in third world countries provide iron supplements as part of the program. On the agenda of the first International Conference on Nutrition is a proposal for adding iron to sugar in Guatemala and to salt in India (Falini, 1993).

The negative aspects of too little iron have always been emphasized, to the neglect of the negative aspects of too much iron. Because of the North American belief that "more is better" we are exposed to excessive amounts of iron in our daily lives. In the U.S. for example, an estimated 25% of dietary iron comes from the deliberate incorporation of inorganic forms of the element into processed foods. One serving of many fortified cereals provides 100% of the daily requirement of iron (18 mg) and if an individual eats anything else during the day, including milk with the cereal, the daily iron requirement will be exceeded (Kent et al., 1990). Many people have no choice but to ingest large amounts of iron; the Virginia WIC (Women, Infants and Children) Program for underpriviledged single mothers states that only infant formulas fortified with iron can be purchased and that "low iron formula" may not be purchased under any circumstances (Kent et al., 1990). Individuals are also encouraged by the medical profession and the media to ingest daily vitamin pills, which contain varying amounts of iron. This may not be a problem for groups at risk of iron- deficiency anemia, such as pre-menopausal women and growing children, but men and post-menopausal women will ingest far more iron than is required. Studies are beginning to show that too much iron, especially for men and postmenopausal women, may be detrimental in ways never before imagined (Boelaert et al., 1987; Caroline et al., 1969; Gordeuk et al., 1986; Lauffer, 1991, 1992; Rosenberg et al., 1985; Selby and Friedman, 1988; Stevens et al., 1988; Sullivan, 1981, 1989).

The data on anemia from prehistory shows that iron-deficiency anemia is related to the levels of micro-organisms in the environment of a population, not the diet. This supports the concept of hypoferremia as an adaptive response to pathogens and provides important information that can be applied to the present. It indicates that, since iron is involved in the immune system, we should be careful about ingesting too much. Recent research on contemporary populations supports this contention and identifies populations for whom too much iron can be detrimental, such as infants and pregnant women, people with a genetic disorder called hemochromatosis, those with some diseases, such as cancer and heart disease, and residents of third world countries where the disease load is high.

INFANTS AND PREGNANT WOMEN

During infancy and pregnancy iron levels are often low and iron deficiency may be considered to be present. The medical profession has traditionally encouraged iron supplementation at these times. However, women actually decrease their absorption of iron from the diet in the first trimester of pregnancy (Stuart-Macadam, 1988), so there may well be a physiological reason why it is important not to have too much iron. This early stage of pregnancy is the most vulnerable time for the embryo because of rapid growth and development. If the iron status of a pregnant woman is lowered, increasing resistance to disease, then this would be advantageous to the developing baby. In this case, a reduction in iron status during pregnancy could be seen as beneficial, rather than a condition needing correction.

It has long been recognized that children from six to eighteen months of age are prone to iron-deficiency anemia. It is so common that it has been called a "physiological iron lack", although this has not stopped the medical profession from wanting to correct it. Once again, there may be a physiological reason for this condition. This "physiological iron lack" also occurs in animals at comparable stages of life and perhaps should be considered normal. It is possible that it occurs to maximize the body's defence system for its fight against pathogens. At this period of life, the passive immunity conferred by the mother through breastfeeding is being lost, and there is a period of immunological vulnerability as the immature immune system is being developed. In this situation, infants who are iron deficient would have an increased resistance to many diseases. Confirmation of this comes from the fact that human milk is quite low in iron compared to that of other mammals and contains an iron-binding protein called lactoferrin. It is widely recognized that breast-fed infants are healthier than bottle fed infants, who receive formula richer in iron and lacking lactoferrin.

HEMOCHROMATOSIS

Hemochromatosis is a disorder that results from an inherited intestinal absorption defect that leads to increased assimilation of iron from a normal diet. It is an autosomal (involving a non-sex chromosome) recessive condition, with the responsible gene being located on the short arm of chromosome 6. Although the full manifestation of the disease occurs only in affected homozygotes (those who inherit the gene from both parents), a small proportion of heterozygotes (those who inherit the gene

433

from one parent) have been found to exhibit minor abnormalities. The incidence of hemochromatosis in a presumably healthy population of 11,065 Euroamericans was 5 per 1000, which is a homozygote frequency of 1 in 300 (Edwards et al., 1988). Studies conducted in Scotland and France yielded a lower, although still substantial, number of affected individuals, ranging from 2 per 1000 to 2.5 per 1000. This makes the condition one of the most common genetic disorders in Western countries (Halliday and Powell, 1992). Iron stores sufficient to produce clinically overt disease are acquired slowly, and the disorder is ordinarily not recognized until the age of 40 to 60 years. Males are affected about ten times more often than females. The clinical picture is characterized by skin pigmentation, liver dysfunction, diabetes mellitus, and cardiac involvement. The outlook is variable, but in untreated patients the average life expectancy appears to be less than five years. Because increased body iron stores can result from the ingestion of dietary iron these individuals are at risk from the extensive iron fortification of food dictated by government policy.

CANCER

Cancer is a multifactorial disease, but high iron levels have been implicated in an increased risk of developing cancer and in increased overall death rates. Some data suggest that high body iron stores increase the risk of some types of cancer, and that men are being affected more than women because of their greater iron stores (Stevens et al., 1988; Selby and Friedman, 1988). Men have a significantly higher risk of cancer of the colon, bladder, esophagus, and lung. It appears that women who are post-menopausal or have greater iron stores than normal are also more prone to cancer. Apparently neoplastic (cancer) cells require more iron than normal cells, so excess iron may increase the chances that cancer cells will survive and flourish. Iron is also involved in the production of substances called oxygen radicals, which are thought to be carcinogenic (Stevens, 1992).

HEART DISEASE

The risk of myocardial infarction (heart attack) appears to be correlated with greater iron stores (Sullivan, 1992). In 1981 the hypothesis was proposed that iron depletion protects against ischemic heart disease (Sullivan, 1981). Men, with higher iron levels than pre-menopausal women, have more heart disease than women, and post-menopausal women, who have higher iron levels than pre-menopausal women, have a higher risk of heart disease than younger women. Women taking oral contraceptives, which reduce the amount of menstrual bleeding, are also more prone to heart disease, as are women who undergo hysterectomies, which result in early menopause. Supportive evidence that iron levels are involved in heart disease comes from epidemiological data; in general, iron deficiency is most severe and prevalent in regions of the world with the lowest prevalence of ischemic heart disease (Sullivan, 1992). A recent international study (Lauffer, 1991) shows a correlation between high iron stores and mortality from coronary artery disease.

THIRD WORLD POPULATIONSI

In third world countries, where easy access to medical intervention is not always available, hypoferremia as a defence against disease may be an important aspect of the immune system. This defence system can be compromised if indiscriminate iron supplementation is given without appreciation of the consequences. As early as 1868 it was noticed that iron supplementation reactivated quiescent pulmonary tuberculosis (Keusch and Farthing, 1986). Contemporary studies show similar results; the health of individuals from third world countries can actually deteriorate after the administration of what is thought to be beneficial iron supplements to correct anemia. For example, malaria infections in people from Niger were reactivated by refeeding programs that included iron supplements (Murray et al., 1976). A study of 110 Africans revealed that those with iron deficiency had fewer malarial attacks than those with higher iron levels. The iron-deficient patients developed malaria only after iron therapy was initiated (Masawe et al., 1974). Refeeding programs in Somalia resulted in the return of a number of different infections, including parasitic and bacillary dysentery, acute infectious hepatitis, brucellosis, tuberculosis, and other bacterial infections (Murray and Murray 1977; Murray et al. 1976). In Polynesia, where infants were given intramuscular iron dextran to prevent iron-deficiency anemia, the incidence of *Escherichia coli sepsis* significantly increased (Barry and Reeve, 1973). After iron administration was stopped, the incidence of this disease in the infants dropped from 17 per 1,000 to 2.7 per 1,000. Infants in New Guinea with respiratory infections who were given iron dextran had a longer hospital stay and were sicker than those not given iron supplements (Oppenheimer et al., 1986).

CONCLUSIONS

As a result of government policy and medical practice, we cannot escape ingesting high levels of iron. It begins in infancy, as most infant formulas, cereals, and baby foods are heavily fortified with iron, and continues throughout our lifetime. Women are bombarded with media and medical pressure to "take our daily iron pill", mothers are encouraged to give iron and other supplements to their children, we eat iron-fortified breakfast cereal and any number of other foods, and governments are contemplating mass fortification of sugar and salt supplies. All this without critical assessment of the negative affects of too *much* iron! Although iron supplementation is necessary in some situations and for some people, it is important to realize that the indiscriminate administration of iron to everyone can be potentially harmful. Certainly in the case of infants, pregnant or post-menopausal women, men, individuals with hemochromatosis, or those exposed to high pathogen loads, too much iron can result in disease. Rather than alleviating a perceived problem, iron-deficiency anemia, it actually causes problems.

How did I come to these conclusions? It all started with research on an obscure condition affecting some prehistoric individuals known as porotic hyperostosis. I never imagined that it would take me into the realm of disease, medicine, contemporary public health and government policy. My work on palaeopathology has enabled me to draw knowledge from the past that is useful in the present. I believe that data on anemia from prehistory illustrate that disease and pathogen load, not diet, are the critical factors in the development of iron-deficiency anemia. This knowledge highlights the importance of the role of iron-withholding in the body's defence system and emphasizes the need to critically assess our current attitude that "more iron is better". It encourages us to question the indiscriminate adulteration of our food with iron and to develop an awareness of groups at risk in terms of too much iron.

Yes, we can learn from the past!

REFERENCES

Angel, JL (1966) Porotic hyperostosis, anemias, malarias, and the marshes in prehistoric Eastern Mediterranean. *Science* 153:760-763.

Arthur CK, and Isbister JP (1987) Iron deficiency: Misunderstood, misdiagnosed and mistreated. *Drugs* 33:171-182.

Barry DM and Reeve AW (1973) Iron injections and serious gram-negative infections in Polynesian newborns. *New Zealand Med. J.* 78:376.

Boelaert J, Van Landuyt H, Valcke Y, Cantinieaux B, Lornoy W, Vanherweghem JL, Moreillon P, and Vandepitte J (1987) The role of iron overload in *Yersinia enterocolitica* and *Yersinia pseudotuberculosis* bacteremia in hemogialysis patients. *J. Inf. Dis.* 156:384-387.

Bullen JJ, and Griffiths E (1987) *Iron and Infection.* Great Britain: John Wiley and Sons.

Caroline L, Rosner F, and Kozinn PJ (1969) Elevated serum iron, low unbound transferrin and candidiasis in acute leukemia. *Blood* 34:441-451.

Carlson D, Armelagos G, and Van Gerven D (1974) Factors influencing the etiology of cribra orbitalia in prehistoric Nubia. *Journal of Human Evolution* 3:405-410.

Crosa JH (1987) Bacterial iron metabolism, plasmids and other virulence factors. In JJ Bullen and E Griffiths (eds.): *Iron and Infection.* Great Britain: John Wiley and Sons, pp. 139-170.

Eaton S, Shostak B, and Konner M (1988) *The Paleolithic Prescription.* New York: Harper and Row.

Edwards CQ, Griffin LM, Goldgar D, Drummond C, Skolnick MH, and Kushner JP (1988) Prevalence of hemochromatosis among 11,065 presumably healthy blood donors. *N. Engl. J. Med.* 318:1355-1357.

El-Najjar MY (1976) Maize, malaria and the anemias in the pre-Columbin New World. *Yearbook of Physical Anthropology* 20:329-337.

El-Najjar MY, Ryan DJ, Turner CG II, and Lozoff B (1976) The etiology of porotic hyperostosis among the prehistoric and historic Anasazi Indians of the Southwestern U.S. *Am. J. Phys. Anthropol.* 44:447-488.

Falini B (1993) Diet, demography, and diseases. *Lancet* 341:545-546.

Farley P and Foland J (1990) Iron deficiency anemia: How to diagnose and correct. *Postgrad. Med.* 87:89-101.

Finch CA (1989) Introduction: Knights of the oval table. *J. Int. Med.* 226:345-348.

Gordeuk V, Brittenham G, McLaren G, and Spagnuolo P (1986) Hyperferremia in immunosuppressed patients with acute nonlymphocytic leukemia and the risk of infection. *J. Lab. Clin. Med.* 108:446-472.

Griffiths E, and Bullen JJ (1987) Iron-binding proteins and host defence. In JJ Bullen and E Griffiths (eds): *Iron and Infection.* Great Britain: John Wiley and Sons, pp. 171-209.

Halliday JW and Powell LW (1992) Hemochromatosis and other diseases associated with iron overload. In Lauffer RB (ed.): *Iron and Human Disease.* Florida: CRC Press, pp. 131-160.

Hengen OP (1971) Cribra orbitalia: Pathogenesis and probable etiology. *Homo* 22:57-75.

Hoffbrand AV and Lewis SM (1981) *Postgraduate Haematology.* New York: Appleton-Century-Crofts.

Hooton EA (1930) *Indians of Pecos Pueblo.* New Haven: Yale University Press.

Keusch G, and Farthing M (1986) Nutrition and Infection. *Ann. Rev. Nutr.* 6:131-154.

Kent S, Weinberg E, and Stuart-Macadam P (1990) Dietary and medical prophylactic iron supplements: Helpful or harmful? *Human Nature* 1:53-79.

Kluger MJ, and Bullen JJ (1987) Clinical and physiological aspects. In JJ Bullen and E Griffiths (eds.): *Iron and Infection.* Great Britain: John Wiley and Sons pp. 243-282.

Lallo J, Armelagos, GJ and Mensforth RP (1977) The role of diet, disease and physiology in the origin of porotic hyperostosis. *Human Biology* 49(3):471-483.

Lauffer RB (1992) *Iron and Human Diseases*. Florida: CRC Press.

Lauffer RB (1991) Iron stores and the international variation in mortality from coronary artery disease. *Med. Hypotheses* 35:103.

Martinez JL, Delgado-Irabarren A, and Baquero F (1990) Mechanisms of iron acquisition and bacterial virulence. *FEMS Microbiol. Rev.* 75:45-56.

Masawe AE, Muindi JM, and Swai GB (1974) Infections in iron deficiency and other types of anaemia in the tropics. *Lancet* 2:314-317.

Moore S (1929) Bone changes in sickle cell anemia with note on similar changes observed in skulls of ancient Mayan Indians. *J. Missouri State Med. Assoc.* 26:561-564.

Moseley, JE (1961) Skull changes in chronic iron deficiency enemia. *AJR.* 85(4):649-652.

Murray MJ and Murray A (1977) Starvation suppression and refeeding activation of infection: An ecological necessity? *Lancet* 1:123-125.

Murray MJ, Murray A, Murray N, and Murray M (1976) Somali food shelters in the Ogaden famine and their impact on health. *Lancet* 1:1283-1285.

Oppenheimer SJ, Gibson FD, MacFarlane SB, Moody JG, Harrison JC, Spencer A, and Bunari O (1986) Effect of iron prophylaxis on morbidity due to infectious disease: Report on clinical studies in Papua New Guinea. *Trans. Royal Soc. Trop. Med. Hyg.* 80:596-602.

Payne S (1988) Iron and virulence in the family Entero-bacteriacease. *Crit. Rev. Microbiol.* 16:81.

Reinhard KJ (1992) Patterns of diet, parasitism, and anemia in prehistoric West North America. In PL Stuart-Macadam and S Kent (eds.): *Diet, Demography and Anemia: Changing Perspectives on Anemia*. New York: Aldine de Gruyter Press, pp. 219-260.

Rosenberg SA, Seipp CA, White DE, and Wesley R (1985) Perioperative blood transfusions are associated with increased rates of recurrence and decreased survival in patients with high-grade soft-tissue sarcomas of the extremities. *J. Clin. Onc.* 3:698-709.

Selby J, and Friedman G (1988) Epidemiologic evidence of an association between body iron stores and risk of cancer. *Int. J. Cancer* 41:677-682.

Stevens RG, Jones DY, Micozzi MS and Taylor RP (1988) Body iron stores and the risk of cancer. *New Eng. J. Med.* 319:1047-1052.

Stevens RG (1992) Iron and cancer. In RB Lauffer (ed.): *Iron and Human Diseases*. Florida: CRC Press, pp. 333-348.

Strauss R (1978) Iron deficiency, infections, and immune function: A reassessment. *Am. J. Clin. Nutr.* 31:660-666.

Stuart-Macadam PL (1982) A correlative study of a palaeopathology of the skull. Ph.D. thesis, University of Cambridge.

Stuart-Macadam PL (1987) A radiographic study of porotic hyperostosis. *Am. J. Phys. Anthropol.* 74:511-520.

Stuart-Macadam PL (1988) Nutrition and anemia in past human populations. In BY Kennedy and GM LeMoine (eds.): *Diet and Subsistence: Current*

Archaeological Perspectives. Calgary: Chacmool, pp. 284-287.

Stuart-Macadam PL (1989) Nutritional deficiency diseases: A survey of scurvy, rickets, and iron-deficiency anemia. In MY Iscan and KAR Kennedy (eds.): *Reconstruction of Life from the Skeleton*. New York: Alan R. Liss, Inc, pp. 201-222.

Stuart-Macadam PL (1992a) Porotic hyperostosis: A new perspective. *Am. J. Phys. Anthropol.* 87(1):39-47.

Stuart-Macadam PL (1992b) Anemia in past human populations. In PL Stuart-Macadam and JS Kent (eds.): *Diet, Demography and Disease: Changing Perspectives on Anemia*. New York: Aldine de Gruyter Press, pp. 151-172.

Sullivan JL (1981) Iron and the sex difference in heart disease risk. *Lancet* 1:1293-1294.

Sullivan JL (1989) The iron paradigm of ischemic heart disease. *Amer. Heart J.* 117:1177-1188.

Sullivan JL (1992) Stored iron as a risk factor for ischemic heart disease. In RB Lauffer (ed.): *Iron and Human Diseases*. Florida: CRC Press, pp. 295-312.

Ubelaker D (1984) Prehistoric human biology of Ecuador: Possible temporal trends and cultural correlations. In MN Cohen and GJ Armelagos (eds.): *Paleopathology at the Origins of Agriculture*. New York: Academic Press, pp. 491-513.

Walker PL (1986) Porotic hyperostosis in a marine-dependent California Indian population. *Am. J. Phys. Anthropol.* 69:345-354.

Weinberg E (1974) Iron and susceptibility to infectious disease. *Science* 184:952-956.

Weinberg E (1977) Infection and iron metabolism. *Am. J. Clin. Nutr.* 30:1485-1490.

Weinberg E (1978) Iron and infection. *Microbiol. Rev.* 42:45-66.

Weinberg E (1984) Iron withholding: A defense against infection and neoplasia. *Physiol. Rev.* 64:65-102.

Weinberg E (1992) Iron withholding in prevention of disease. In PL Stuart-Macadam and S Kent (eds.): *Diet, Demography and Disease: Changing Perspectives on Anemia*. New York: Aldine de Gruyter Press, pp. 105-150.

Williams H (1929) Human paleopathology. *Arch. Anthropol.* 7:839-902.

21

Migration, Ethnicity and Health
Anthropological Approaches to Epidemiology

Joseph So

Research into population movements is a key in the understanding of human evolutionary history and the diversity of contemporary populations. The migrant model as a research design is useful in elucidating the factors that influence disease incidence and prevalence. Migration and urbanization in general impact upon human fertility, growth, and the prevalence of such conditions as hypertension, coronary heart disease, non-insulin dependent diabetes mellitus, and overall mental health, through complex interactions of genetic, environmental, as well as socio-cultural variables. The case study of the Ontario Health Survey demonstrates significant differences in migrant health status compared to the nonmigrant populations, taking into account inherent methodological limitations of the survey method. A combination of the quantitative approach used in epidemiology with the more qualitative nature of anthropological fieldwork provides the most complete picture of the health and disease of contemporary peoples.

INTRODUCTION

It is safe to say that migration is as old as human history itself. The paleoanthropological record demonstrates an early spread of hominids from Africa during the time of *Australopithecus*. By the emergence of *Homo erectus*, examples of these early humans could be found in many parts of the Old World. Indeed, the genus *Homo* is the most geographically diverse among members of the Order Primates. Through the process of adaptation, humans have successfully adjusted to living in extreme conditions of tropical heat, arctic cold, hypoxic conditions of high altitude, and in our recent history, crowded urban environments. Such adaptation may take the form of biological changes as well as through behavioural, cultural, and technological means, but the end result is an increase in reproductive success. If, in simple Darwinian terms, such reproductive success is a measure of population fitness, human population growth and geographic diversity are a testament to the success of the human species. Arguably a more precise measure of the fitness of a population is its health status, based on the assumption that disease is as potent a selective force as physical pressures such as environmental heat and cold experienced in the course of evolution. The mortality rate and disease prevalence of human populations are good indicators of their stability. A stable mortality rate reflects a balance between population growth and environmental pressures, while disease patterns can tell us a great deal about the biological, physical and social factors that impact on a population. This chapter deals with the inter-relationships between migration of human groups and their health status.

TYPES OF MIGRATION STUDIES

Because migration is such an integral part of human history, biological anthropologists have long been interested in studying population movements in prehistory. The goal of this approach is to better understand the course of human evolution. Early studies focussed primarily on morphology, looking at bones and teeth as indicators of population affinity. In recent years, the research has become increasingly interdisciplinary, involving genetics, epidemiology, demography, medicine as well as anthropology. For example, the studies of mitochondrial DNA and the Eve Hypothesis use population movements as a key for interpreting human evolution in the Pleistocene (Vigilant, 1991). In other studies, migration in the past is often cited as an important factor in explaining human diversity today, such as the comparisons of genetic markers in order to explain population affinities, as in the studies on Siberians and indigenous Northern Americans. Most researchers are interested in population affinities per se while some of them look specifically at those gene markers having to do with susceptibility to certain diseases (Szathmary, 1983).

A second approach involves looking at contemporary population movements and comparing the biology of migrants and non-migrants in order to measure the relative impacts of genes versus the environment on health. This type of research frequently involves comparing the health status of migrants versus that of "sedentes", or versus those of the "donor population". This approach is also known as the *migrant model* and compares migrants, non-migrants from the country of origin, and natives of the country of adoption. If the disease experience of the migrants is different from that of people in the migrants' country of origin, but similar to that of the people in the country of adoption, it can be said that environmental factors are primary influences on these diseases. Conversely, if the disease profile of the migrant group continues to be the same as the donor population and similar to what it was prior to migration, genetic factors are said to be more important.

While the migrant model is theoretically simple and attractive, the researcher needs to control for confounding variables such as pre-migration environment, time and age at migration, and "migrant selection", a phenomenon in which only healthier, physically-fit persons migrate, making them un-representative of the people from the "old country" (Lilienfeld and Lilienfeld, 1980). Despite its limitations, this model is useful for epidemiological research, especially in case-control studies and longitudinal studies where the researcher follows the health of a cohort of individuals over time. The migrant model can also be used in descriptive epidemiology to explain similarities and differences observed in comparisons of mortality, incidence and prevalence of disease among populations. This paper focusses on contemporary populations and how migration affects their health.

WHAT IS ETHNICITY?

Physical anthropologists have used the concept of *race* in the past to denote biological populations, but this term has been misused for social and political ends in the course of human history. Since it is now recognized that traditional racial typologies have little biological meaning, the concept of *cline* has replaced race to explain human diversity in physical anthropology. However, until very recently, race continued to be considered a valid concept in biomedical research, without recognizing the myriad of social and cultural factors that are equally strong determinants of health and disease. Now, *ethnicity* is generally accepted as a means of identifying culturally and biologically distinct populations. Ethnicity can be defined as "those behavioural and ideational characteristics of

individuals or groups that identify them as belonging to a distinct, culturally recognized category in terms of presumed shared cultural heritage
and/or presently active cultural characteristics" (Hogle et al., 1982). In
other words, ethnicity refers to populations defined by their culture as
well as their biology, and it takes into account the importance of behavioural factors as determinants of health. Ethnicity impacts on health in
several ways: 1) ethnic groups often have distinctive disease rates; 2) they
often have health maintenance and home treatment modalities unique to
their culture; 3) they have different disease concepts; 4) there is often variation in illness behaviour; 5) ethnic groups frequently show different patterns of health service utilization; and 6) variation in their interactions
with care-givers and health care organizations (Harwood, 1981). In an
increasingly pluralistic world, research in ethnic variations in health and
disease has an important role to play in the understanding of the interactions of culture and biology, and the knowledge gained will be useful in
the formulation of public health policies to ensure effective health care
delivery, treatment and prevention.

URBANIZATION AND HEALTH
Among events in human history and their impact on health, an
important consideration is the issue of urbanization. The past two centuries have seen large scale population movements from predominantly
rural environments to urban areas, and the trend is expected to continue.
For example, Canada, once an agricultural society, is now primarily urban
in nature. It is thought that urbanization and over-population in general
often have a negative impact on health due to crowding and unsanitary
conditions, as seen in the London slums of the industrial age. Infectious
diseases with person-to-person mode of transmission rose dramatically
with urbanization in the last Century. It was only in the early part of the
twentieth century that, with advancement in medical knowledge, public
health measures and the subsequent improved sanitation that these diseases could be more effectively treated. Today, migration from rural areas
to urban centres continues to be common in developing nations, and in
many instances, conditions that led to diseases are still common. Among
infectious diseases, schistosomiasis, malaria, tuberculosis and leprosy are
far from eradicated, and with westernization, a host of heretofore uncommon conditions such as obesity, hypertension, coronary heart disease,
hiatus hernias, circulatory diseases, cancer of the digestive tract, and
non-insulin dependent diabetes mellitus (NIDDM) have become more

prevalent (Trowell and Burkitt, 1981). A number of studies focussed on the effects of rural-urban migration on health. Nadim et al. (1978) found a higher prevalence of hypertension among Iranian migrants to Teheran compared to sedentes. Walker (1981) reported higher blood pressure among descendants of South Asians living in South Africa compared to those in India. Blacks who have migrated from rural to urban areas in South Africa show a similar increase in blood pressure. The causes have been attributed to many factors, including a change in diet and lifestyle, as well as an increase in psychosocial stress.

MIGRATION ON FERTILITY AND GROWTH

It has long been observed that the offspring of migrants are taller and heavier than sedentes. None other than Franz Boas (1912), considered by many to be the father of American anthropology, noted that children of immigrants to America were taller and had different body proportions compared to their parents. This phenomenon was attributed to heterosis[1] by others while Boas maintained that it was due to adaptation during the period of child growth. Various studies since then have come up with somewhat contradictory results. Some found urban migrant children to be taller and heavier (Shapiro, 1939; Tanner & Eveleth, 1976; Johnston et al., 1985) while others found rural populations taller (Steegmann, 1985). This discrepancy may be explained by selective migration, where the taller and physically more able individuals are the ones who migrated. Also, one must not underestimate the power of factors such as socioeconomic status in determining growth and development after migration. It is safe to say the effects of migration on growth are multifactorial, and dependent on the complex interactions of genetic, environmental, nutritional, and psychosocial conditions.

Fertility rates of most urban populations are lower than rural areas while a few studies found the opposite. On the surface, this seems to contradict the notion that better health care and living conditions in urban areas, at least in the developed world, would result in higher fertility rates. However, higher socioeconomic status, increased education, lower infant mortality, availability of contraceptives, changing attitudes towards family size, and a desire to have a higher standard of living all contribute to the desire of urban dwellers to have smaller families. This illustrates the complex nature of the interactions of a host of biological and sociocultural forces in determining fertility levels (Bogin, 1988).

MIGRATION AND DISEASE

Migrants are exposed to both the pre-migrational and post-migrational environments, both of which impact on health status. In the case of communicable diseases, migrants exposed to infectious agents before migration may become carriers of disease transmission in the country of adoption. This is increasingly a concern as a result of greater population mobility in the Twentieth Century, and movements of refugees from war-torn countries where sanitary conditions and health care have deteriorated as a result of warfare. Conversely, migrants are exposed to "new" diseases after migration, diseases to which he/she has no natural immunity. In the case of non-communicable diseases, the longer incubation period in most cases results in less immediate and dramatic changes in disease rates. A great many studies have focussed on international comparisons of mortality and morbidity between immigrants and donor/recipient populations. Most are cross-sectional studies that look at disease rates at one moment in time, while a few are longitudinal studies tracing migrant groups over a longer period.[2] This latter approach, while more time consuming and expensive, offers a more realistic picture of migrant health. Among many cross-sectional studies of both descriptive and case-control[3] in nature are those dealing with coronary heart diseases among Chinese migrants in New York (Gerber & Madhavan, 1980); cancer among Chinese Canadians in Ontario (So, 1988); hypertension among South Asians living in South Africa (Walker, 1981); hypertension among migrants in the Philippines (Hackenberg et al., 1983); alcoholism among immigrants from Dominica (Gordon, 1978); and prescription drug use among Cuban women in Florida (Kirby, 1989). The best known longitudinal studies of migrant populations include studies on blood pressure and other biomedical parameters among migrants and sedentes of the Tokelau Island population in Polynesia (Prior and Tasman-Jones, 1981); the effects of urbanization on the health of Samoans (Baker and Crews, 1987); and the health of Andean migrants of highland and coastal Peru (Little & Baker, 1988).

With varying research designs, the above studies focus on the effects of migration, urbanization, and modernization on physical and mental health. Gerber and Madhavan (1980) compared the PMR (proportional mortality rate) of Chinese in Hawaii and New York City and found that Chinese Hawaiians have greater PMR from coronary heart disease than those in New York. Among the New York Chinese, the American-born have a greater PMR from CHD. In a study of Chinese in Ontario, based on data from the cancer registry from 1964 to 1977, Chinese Ontarians have a different mortality profile than the general population, with lower rates of cancers of the breast, ovaries, prostate, and intestine, but higher rates for liver and nasopharynx (So, 1988). These differences are likely a result of diet, lifestyle, environment, as well as cultural factors. In a study on blood pressure levels in four Philippine communities with contrasting environments, Hackenberg et al. (1983) found higher blood pressure for city dwellers as well as migrants, and this difference is true after having adjusted for age and sex. The authors also found hypertension prevalence rates higher in urbanites and migrants. In another study, Weitz (1982) also found higher blood pressure among Tibetan villages who have migrated to the city of Katmandu. The higher values persist when altitude and body composition are taken into account, and are attributed to diet, lifestyle, and physical activity. The Samoan Migrant Study examined several groups of contrasting history and environments, including sedentes in traditional villages in remote areas; in less remote islands; in the Western Pago Pago harbour; those who have migrated to rural areas outside Honolulu, the city of Honolulu itself; and finally to urban California. Prevalence of obesity, elevated blood pressure and susceptibility to cardiovascular diseases are found to be higher with increased modernization, and to a lesser extent, with migration, although the Samoan rates of CHD are still below that of U.S. Whites (Baker & Hanna, 1987).

Another well known study, which began thirty years ago, focusses on Japanese migrants. It compares three groups of Japanese: sedentes in Japan, migrants in Honolulu, and migrants in San Francisco. Myocardial infarctions are found to be lowest among sedentes, intermediate among the Japanese Hawaiians, while the Bay Area Japanese have the highest rates. It was suggested that changes in diet since migration were a primary etiological factor (Glober and Stemmermann, 1981; Schull, 1993).

A great deal of research has focussed on metabolic disorders, the most prominent being non-insulin dependent diabetes mellitus (NIDDM). Various authors have attributed the rise of NIDDM in several populations to westernization, migration, and changes in diet and lifestyle. Weiss, Ferrell and Hanis (1984) proposed the theory that high prevalence of diabetes and other metabolic disorders among native North Americans, excluding the Inuit is the consequence of a once-beneficial genotype that is no longer adaptive as a result of the change from hunting and gathering subsistence to an increasingly western diet. Their hypothesis is an elaboration of the "thrifty genotype" idea first proposed by Neel (1962). More recently, researchers (Ritenbaugh and Goodby, 1989; Szathmary, 1990) have proposed an alternate explanation, the "northern hunting adaptation" model. An up-to-date review of the debate on the causes of high prevalence of NIDDM among native North Americans can be found in Young (1993).

While most studies concentrate on the impact of migration and urbanization on physical health, a few studies focus on the mental health of migrants. The psychosocial stress faced by most migrants often results in various psychiatric symptoms. This is particularly true in refugees or other displaced persons who are forcibly uprooted due to conflict. Westermeyer (1984) studied Laotian refugees resettled in Minnesota. He finds evidence of difficulties in adjustment, which shows up in higher prevalence of anxiety, depression, somatization, phobia, and paranoia. A study on Cuban women in South Florida finds the uprooting and forced migration, and the accompanying separation anxiety, post-migration insecurities and under-employment have resulted in a high level of prescription drug use (Kirby, 1989). Other researchers on refugee resettlement have documented cases of post-traumatic stress disorders due to warfare and atrocities faced by these migrants in their home country (Beiser et al., 1989).

CASE STUDY: THE ONTARIO HEALTH SURVEY (OHS)

The government of Ontario carried out a large-scale general health survey of its residents in 1990. Since Ontario is an ethnically diverse province, an examination of the migrant data can tell us a great deal about their health status in Canada. The goal of the OHS was to provide baseline statistical data on the health of the population with meaningful information at the local (public health unit) level. The data collected are useful for research into biological, social, and behavioural determinants of health. It allows for accurate assessment of health needs of the population, for planning and targeting programmes, and for monitoring changes in the health of Ontarians over time (Ministry of Health, 1992). Because data on place of birth and ethnicity were collected, it allows for separate, secondary analysis of the health of migrants, who make up a substantial portion of the Ontario population. In the OHS, of the 61,239 respondents, 21% were born outside Canada. Because immigrants primarily live in urban areas, and the OHS participants are selected evenly across the province by public health units, as a result migrants are under-represented in the sample. In 1991, I was given permission by the Ministry of

Health to study the physical and mental health status of Chinese Ontarians contained in the OHS.

THE IMMIGRANT SAMPLES

A sample of individuals of Chinese ethnicity (N=615) was extracted, based on place of birth, self-declared ethnic and cultural identity, and language spoken at home. A second sample of a randomly selected 1,000 "European" immigrants was created. This sample includes immigrants from Italy, Portugal, Poland, Germany, Holland, Greece, Hungary, and Yugoslavia. A small third sample of off-reserve Aboriginal people (N=193) was selected. While they are obviously not immigrants in a contemporary sense of the word, off-reserve Aboriginal people are faced with living as ethnic minorities in a predominantly Eurocanadian society. Because the OHS excluded reserve Aboriginal people from the survey, this sample offers a limited glimpse into the health of the Aboriginal population in Ontario. As a comparison group, a randomly selected sample of 1,000 Canadian-born subjects was selected (So, 1992, 1993). The respondents, selected based on enumeration records, were visited by interviewers at home. The survey was administered to the head of household, who answered questions about all household members. A self-completed questionnaire was left behind for each household member 12 years and older, to be completed and picked up later by the interviewer.

THE OHS QUESTIONNAIRE

The interviewer questionnaire has a total of over one hundred questions, covering a possible total of over twelve hundred variables. Among the variables are data dealing with health service utilization, two week disability, use of medication, accidents and injuries, vision, hearing, mobility, cognition, activity restrictions, pain, chronic health problems, and basic socio-demographic data. The self-completed questionnaire goes into greater detail on the respondents' physical and psychological health, prescription drug use, alcohol consumption, smoking, family wellbeing, occupational health, "lifestyle" variables such as smoking, drinking, driving behaviour and sexual behaviour. In the case of female respondents, women's health questions were administered (Table 1).

RESULT

Analysis of the data reveals some interesting differences between the migrants and the general population (Table 2). In terms of socio-demographic variables, migrants' age distribution is typically bimodal, with the

Table 1. Major Variables in the Ontario Health Survey 1990

A. Socio-demographic Variables
age, sex, marital status, household size, type of dwelling, place of birth, ethnicity/immigration history, language spoken at home, education, employment, income.

B. Health Service Utilization
- frequency of consulting health care professionals
- frequency of consulting a psychologist/social worker
- frequency of emergency room/ hospital visits

C. Physical Disability
- two-week disability
- motor vehicle accidents and injuries
- vision, hearing, mobility, cognition
- activity restriction
- pain and discomfort
- chronic health problems

D. Health Status
- self-perceived health
- number and nature of health problems
- prescription drug use
- alcohol consumption
- smoking behaviour
- occupational health
- women's health
- sexual health

E. Physical Activity and Nutritional Variables
- food consumption
- sports and recreational activity participation
- body composition

F. Derived Variables
- psychological well-being
- family functioning
- social support

Table 2. Summary Findings of Chinese immigrant health of the
OHS compared to the general Ontario population

- Bimodal age distribution
- Overwhelmingly urban
- Higher proportion are married
- Much lower divorce rate
- Larger household size
- Higher percentage with post-secondary education
- No difference in frequency of consulting a physician
- Much less likely to consult psychologist/social worker
- Tendency to under-utilize health service in general
- Fewer bed days or cut-down days
- Larger proportion reporting no health problems
- Low prevalence of obesity
- Higher than average self-reported stress level
- Lower alcohol consumption and possible alcoholism
- Lower prevalence of smoking
- Lower participation in sports and recreational activity
- Well-being and Family Functioning similar to general population
- Lower prevalence of high-risk sexual behaviour

greatest number of individuals in their thirties, and a second peak of older individuals at retirement age, due to the peculiarities of the selection process and changes in immigration policies over the years. Migrants tend to be urban-dwellers, with less than 1% living in rural areas. A greater proportion of Chinese migrants are married compared to the general population, and their divorce rate is one-seventh of the Canadians.

The marital profile of European migrants, however, is not significantly different from that of the general population. The household size of migrants is larger than the Canadian average; furthermore, a much higher percentage of them have post-secondary eduction, again a result of the immigration selection process.

In terms of health service utilization, there is no significant difference in the frequency with which they consulted a general practitioner. This can be explained in light of the universal access to health care in Ontario. However, the Canadian-born are five times more likely to consult the services of a psychologist or social worker than Chinese migrants and two and a half times more likely than migrants from Europe. The lower service utilization may be due to the language barrier as a result of a lack of "ethno-specific services", or to cultural differences where migrants are less likely to seek help on psychological or family problems from the outside, preferring to resolve the difficulties at home. When all health care providers are considered, Chinese migrants tend to underutilize service, with a slightly greater number of "no visits". European rates are similar to the general population, while off-reserve Aboriginal people have a higher frequency of consulting physicians, and a significantly higher number of consultations with psychologists and social workers in 1990, the year the survey was done. Fewer Chinese migrants experience "bed days or cut-down days", adjusted for age, meaning they show less work absenteeism. However, such data must be interpreted with caution since lower service utilization does not necessarily mean better health, as language and cultural barriers may be responsible. Lower absenteeism may simply mean those migrants working part time or doing piecework at factories, for example, are reluctant to take days off because of illness since they may not get paid "sick days" as full-time employees do.

A detailed probe into the number of health problems based on International Classification of Diseases (9th revision) indicates that over half of the Chinese migrants report no health problems. For those who do, fewer report multiple health problems compared to both the European and the Canadian-born. One interesting finding is the higher proportion of health problems classified as "signs, symptoms and ill-defined conditions" among migrants. This may signify a language barrier between the interviewer and the subject, which will affect the accuracy of the data. European migrants report a higher proportion of circulatory, urogenital, musculoskeletal diseases or complaints. This is in part due to the older age distribution of European migrants. Data on body mass index indicate the Chinese are less likely to be overweight than the other groups. Aboriginal people report a higher proportion of endocrine and metabolic disorders, primarily diabetes mellitus, as well as respiratory disorders such as influenza, pneumonia, bronchitis, and asthma.

A major component of the survey involves questions dealing with assessment of mental health. From data on individuals and households, several derived variables were constructed to measure such variables as individual psychological well being, as well as family functioning, and degree of social support. In the individual well being index, European migrants report the highest self-perceived stress level. Chinese migrants report a higher than average stress level as well, while the off-reserve Aboriginal people report the lowest. In "family functioning" and "well being", off-reserve Aboriginal people have a greater percentage of individuals in the "dysfunctional" and "low well being" self-ratings. Compared to Canadian-born residents, Chinese and European migrants report lower prevalence of behaviour putting the individual at risk to HIV infection, while the prevalence among Aboriginal people is higher. Alcohol screening indicates Chinese migrants have the lowest number of individuals in the "possible alcohol problem" categories. European migrants are similar to the host population, while Aboriginal people report a higher proportion. In smoking behaviour, Chinese migrants smoke the least, while a greater number of natives smoke than the other three groups.

METHODOLOGICAL LIMITATIONS

While the OHS data reveal some fascinating findings, one must interpret the results with caution. The OHS is a general survey based on interviews and self-reporting by participants. No clinical examinations were given. It brings into focus the larger question of the relative utility of health surveys in minority health research. Several methodological problems come to mind, namely the issue of targeting of the ethnic population, representativeness of the sample, validity of the questionnaire, the problem of low response and high attrition rates, and the reliability and validity of the responses (McGraw et al., 1992). In the case of the OHS, the questionnaire was translated into several languages to minimize nonresponse. Still, the response rates of Asian and Southern European migrants are considerably lower than Canadian-born residents, suggesting cultural and language barriers coming into play. Migrants tend to live in urban areas, and in a geographically stratified sampling like the

OHS where urban and rural residents are equally sampled, migrants are therefore proportionately under-represented. The use of enumeration records for sample selection omits those with no fixed address, namely the homeless, as well as the institutionalized and the incarcerated. The use of proxy responses where the head of household answers for other members, may result in inaccuracies in the data.

Despite these limitations, general health surveys are useful in ethnic and migrant health research if efforts are made to accurately target the sample population, to ensure high response rates, low loss to follow-up, and more importantly, that the instrument is culturally sensitive and appropriate. This is where the approach of medical anthropology in studying health and disease is of benefit. Medical anthropologists are well aware of the importance of contextualizing health. Health is more than just the absence of disease, nor does it exist in a vacuum. Rather it is an all-encompassing condition where the individual is in a state of complete physical, psychological, social, political, and economic well being. Despite the ingenuity of health survey designs, some of the above information is best left to qualitative data-collecting, such as anthropological fieldwork. It is obviously impossible to undertake fieldwork on the same scale as health surveys. Therefore one needs to achieve the proper balance between the larger scope of survey research and the sensitivity and attention to detail of the more qualitative approaches.

At the time of writing, Statistics Canada is about to undertake the first large scale National Population Health Survey, to begin in May, 1994. A sample of 22,000 households will be studied, with one member in each household followed for up to twenty years, with data collected every two years. There are indications that this upcoming survey has learned from the deficiencies of the OHS. For example, proxy information is held to a minimum; data on visits to health care providers include non-traditional ones outside the biomedical sphere; and more emphasis is placed on psychosocial determinants of health, including stress, self-esteem, and social support. For the first time, a subset of items will be used in the survey of institutionalized individuals, but the homeless are once again left out. Still, this represents an improvement over the OHS. Given the caveat above, well designed health surveys, can be useful as a first step in assessing the health profiles among minority groups for further in-depth study.

CONCLUSIONS

The reasons for doing research into migrants and ethnic minorities are many. Quite apart from satisfying a certain intellectual curiosity, especially in regard to questions on human origins and migration, which was enough reason to do the research in the past, it has a number of practical benefits today. In an increasingly pluralistic world, where population mobility is greater and swifter than ever, governments and health policy makers are scrambling to understand the impact of population movements on the health of citizens. As international boundaries break down, the need to control the spread of communicable diseases, from "old" diseases such as leprosy and plague to new ones that are looming ever so large at the end of the millennium such as AIDS, becomes all the more urgent. The spread of infectious diseases is more than just a function of two individuals coming into physical contact. It is often their culture and behaviour that determine the likelihood of transmission, such as their lifestyle, social and physical activities, customs, mores, and belief systems. As many biological anthropologists have training in epidemiology and public health as well as the social sciences, they are in a position to make a genuine contribution in helping to elucidate the process of disease transmission; the promotion of effective treatment and prevention methods that are appropriate and culturally sensitive; and to act as a liaison between the clinicians and the patient on matters pertaining to cultural practices. Some work in government agencies or academic institutions as members of a health research team (Hubert, 1990), while others work along side front-line health care providers in the delivery of service, particularly in the developing countries as well as in ethnically-diverse urban areas in the developed nations.

A current debate in critical medical anthropology is the notion that physical anthropologists, by applying their knowledge to promote more effective health care delivery, based on the western biomedical model, put anthropology at the service of clinicians, and in the worst case scenario, serve to undermine the significance of alternative, or traditional health care practices and beliefs (Browner et al., 1988; Scheper-Hughes, 1990). The contrary view is the belief that if the ultimate goal is to apply biomedical knowledge to improve the health of those in need, as measured by a reduced infant mortality and a drop in general incidence and prevalence rates, it does not matter what method is used to achieve this, as long as it works.

The two divergent views are based on a fundamental philosophical difference, which in my opinion, need not exist. A middle ground is possible, one where medical anthropologists are not just doing work dictated by medical scientists, but as full members of a team, as equal partners participating in the decision-making process, whether on the design of the research protocol or on the appropriateness of care given within the context of the culture of the recipient.

It is clear that western bioscience is more effective in the treatment of acute, communicable diseases, while traditional medicines are often efficacious in chronic diseases and psychological disorders, and particularly in effecting a behavioural change in the patient. These medical systems need not be mutually exclusive, as long as the application is culturally sensitive and appropriate. As the most humanistic of the social sciences, anthropology has had a long tradition of cross disciplinary research, and physical anthropologists, with one foot in biology and the other in our mother discipline, are well placed to play an active role in the continuation of this tradition.

ENDNOTES

1   Heterosis refers to an increase in body size and vigour as a result of increased heterogeneity.
2   A cross-sectional study looks at a population at a particular moment in time, as in a snapshot. A good example is the Canada Census. On the other hand, a longitudinal study follows a population over a period of time, sometimes as long as twenty years or more, as in the proposed Canada National Health Survey 1994.
3   In epidemiology, case-control studies compare a group of individuals (cases) with characteristics of interest, such as the presence of a disease, with a reference group (controls) where in this case the disease is absent. Any meaningful differences identified in the comparison may be associated with the said disease.

REFERENCES

Baker PT, and Crews DE (1986) Mortality patterns and some biological predictors. In PT Baker, JM Hanna and TS Baker (eds.): *The Changing Samoans: Behavior and Health in Transition.*New York: Oxford University Press, pp. 93-122.
Baker PT, Hanna JM, and TS Baker (eds.) (1986) *The Changing Samoans: Behavior and Health in Transition.* New York: Oxford University Press.
Beiser M, Turner RJ, and Ganesan S (1989) Catastrophic stress and factors affecting its consequences among Southeast Asian refugees. *Soc. Sci. Med.* 28:183-195.

Boas F (1912) Changes in the bodily form of descendants of immigrants. *Am. Anthropol.*14:530-563.

Bogin B (1988) Rural to urban migration. In CGN Mascie-Taylor and GW Lasker (eds.): *Biological Aspects of Human Migration.* New York:Cambridge University Press, pp. 90-129.

Browner CH, Ortiz del Montellano BR, and Rubel AJ (1988) A methodology for cross-cultural ethnomedical research. *Current Anthropol.* 29:681-702.

Glober G, and Stemmermann G (1981) Hawaii ethnic groups. In HC Trowell and DR Burkitt (eds.): *Western Diseases: Their Emergence and Prevention.* Cambridge, Mass.:Harvard University Press, pp. 319-333.

Gerber LM, and Madhavan S (1980) Epidemiology of coronary heart disease in migrant Chinese populations. *Med. Anthropol.* 4:307-320.

Gordon AJ (1978) Hispanic drinking after migration: The case of Dominicans. *Med. Anthropol.*, 2:61-84.

Hackenberg RA, Hackenberg BH, Magalit HF, Cabral EI, and Guzman SV (1983) Migration, modernization and hypertension: Blood pressure levels in four Philippine communities. *Med. Anthropol.* 7:45-71.

Harwood A (1981) *Ethnicity and Medical Care.* Cambridge, Mass.: Harvard University Press.

Hogle J, Pelto PJ, and Schensul S (1982) Ethnicity and health: Puerto Ricans and blacks in Hartford, Connecticut. *Med. Anthropol.* 6:127-146.

Hubert A (1990) Applying anthropology to the epidemiology of cancer. *Anthropol. Today* 6:16-18.

Johnston FE, Low SM, Baesa Y de, and MacVean RB (1985) Growth status of disadvantaged urban Guatemalan children of a resettled community. *Am. J. Phys. Anthropol.* 68:215-224.

Kirby DG (1989) Immigration, stress and prescription drug use among Cuban women in south Florida. *Med. Anthropol.* 10:287-195.

Lilienfeld AM, and Lilienfeld DE (1980) *Foundations of Epidemiology* New York: Oxford University Press.

Little MA, and Baker PT (1988) Migration and adaptation. In CGN Mascie-Taylor and GW Lasker (eds.): *Biological Aspects of Human Migration.* New York: Cambridge University Press, pp.167-215.

McGraw SA, McKinlay JB, Crawford SA, Costa LA, and Cohen DL (1992) Health survey methods with minority populations: Some lessons from recent experience. *Ethnicity and Disease,* 2:273-287.

Ministry of Health (1992) *Ontario Health Survey 1990: Volume 1: Documentation.* Toronto, Ontario: Ministry of Health.

Nadim A, Amini H, and Malek-Afzali H (1978) Blood pressure and rural-urban migration in Iran. *Internat. J. Epidemiol.* 7:131-138.

Neel JV (1962) Diabetes Mellitus: A "thrifty" genotype rendered detrimental by "progress". *Am. J. Hum. Genet.* 14:353-362.

Prior I, Tasman-Jones C (1981) New Zealand Maori and Pacific Polynesians. In HC Trowell and DR Burkitt (eds.): *Western Diseases: Their Emergence and Prevention.* Cambridge, Mass.: Harvard University Press, pp.227-267.

Ritenbaugh C, and Goodby C (1989) Beyond the thrifty gene: Metabolic implications of prehistoric migration into the new world. *Med. Anthropol.* 11:227-236.

Scheper-Hughes N (1990) Three propositions for a critically applied medical anthropology. *Soc. Sci. Med.* 30:189-197.

Schull WJ (1993) The Raymond Pearl Memorial Lecture 1992: Ethnicity and disease — more than familiarity. *Am J. Human Biol.* 5:373-385.

Shapiro HL (1939) *Migration and Environment: A Study of the Physical Characteristics of the Japanese Immigrants to Hawaii.* Oxford: Oxford University Press.

So JK (1988) Cancer mortality of Chinese Canadians in Ontario 1964-77: A study in descriptive epidemiology. *Can. Rev. Phys. Anthropol.*6:22-30.

So JK (1992) Migration, ethnicity and health: Physical and mental health status of Chinese in Ontario. *Internat. J. Psychol.* 27:230 (Abstract).

So JK (1993) Migration, ethnicity and health: An epidemiologic analysis of immigrant health of the Ontario Health Survey, 1990. *Am. J. Phys. Anthropol.,* Supplement 16:185. (Abstract)

Steegmann AT (1985) 18th century British military stature: Growth cessation, selective recruiting, secular trends, nutrition at birth, cold and occupation. *Hum. Biol.* 57:77-95.

Szathmary EJE, Ferrell RE, and Gershowitz H (1983) Genetic differentiation in Dogrib Indians: Serum protein and erythrocyte enzyme variation. *Am. J. Phys. Anthropol.* 62:249-254.

Szathmary EJE (1990) Diabetes in Amerindian populations: The Dogrib studies. In AC Swedlund and GJ Armelagos (eds.): *Disease in Populations in Transition: Anthropological and Epidemiological Perspectives.* New York: Bergin and Garvey, pp.75-103.

Tanner JM, and Eveleth PB (1976) Urbanization and growth. In GA Harrison and JB Gibson (eds.): *Man in Urban Environments.* Oxford: Oxford University Press, pp.144-166.

Trowell HC, and Burkitt DR (1981) *Western Diseases: Their Emergence and Prevention.* London: Edward Arnold (Publishers) Limited.

Vigilant L (1991) African populations and the evolution of human mitochondrial DNA. *Science* 253:1503-1507.

Walker A (1981) South African black, Indian and coloured populations. In HC Trowell, and DR Burkitt (eds.):*Western Diseases: Their Emergence and Prevention.* Cambridge, Mass.: Harvard University Press, pp.285-318.

Weiss KM, Ferrell RE, and Hanis CL (1984) A New World Syndrome of metabolic diseases with a genetic and evolutionary basis. *Yearbook of Physical Anthropology,* 27:153-178.

Weitz CA (1982) Blood pressure at rest and during exercise among Sherpas and Tibetan migrants in Nepal. *Soc. Sci. Med.* 16:223-231.

Westermeyer J, Bouafuely M, and Vang TF (1984) Hmong refugees in Minnesota: sex roles and mental health. *Med. Anthropol.* 8:229-245.

Young TK (1993) Diabetes Mellitus among native Americans in Canada and the US: An epidemiological review. *Am. J. Hum. Biol.* 5:399-413.